CHICAGO

The Big City Food Biography Series
as part of the Rowman & Littlefield Studies in Food and Gastronomy

General Editor:
Ken Albala, Professor of History, University of the Pacific (kalbala@pacific.edu)
Rowman & Littlefield Executive Editor:
Suzanne Staszak-Silva (sstaszak-silva@rowman.com)

Food helps define the cultural identity of cities in much the same way as the distinctive architecture and famous personalities. Great cities have one-of-a-kind food cultures, offering the essence of the multitudes who have immigrated there and shaped foodways through time. **The Big City Food Biographies series** focuses on those metropolises celebrated as culinary destinations, with their iconic dishes, ethnic neighborhoods, markets, restaurants, and chefs. Guidebooks to cities abound, but these are real biographies that will satisfy readers' desire to know the full food culture of a city. Each narrative volume, devoted to a different city, explains the history, the natural resources, and the people that make that city's food culture unique. Each biography also looks at the markets, historic restaurants, signature dishes, and great cookbooks that are part of the city's gastronomic makeup.

Titles in the Series

08/2016

CHICAGO

A Food Biography

Daniel R. Block and Howard Rosing

ROWMAN & LITTLEFIELD
Lanham • Boulder • New York • London

Published by Rowman & Littlefield
A wholly owned subsidiary of The Rowman & Littlefield Publishing Group, Inc.
4501 Forbes Boulevard, Suite 200, Lanham, Maryland 20706
www.rowman.com

Unit A, Whitacre Mews, 26-34 Stannary Street, London SE11 4AB

British Library Cataloguing in Publication Information Available

Library of Congress Cataloging-in-Publication Data

Block, Daniel R., 1967–
Chicago : a food biography / Daniel R. Block and Howard Rosing.
pages cm. — (Big city food biographies series)
Includes bibliographical references and index.
ISBN 978-1-4422-2726-2 (cloth : alk. paper) — ISBN 978-1-4422-2727-9 (electronic) 1. Food—
Illinois—Chicago—History. 2. Food industry and trade—Illinois—Chicago—History. 3. Grocers—
Illinois—Chicago—History. 4. Restaurants—Illinois—Chicago—History. 5. Cooking, American—
Midwestern style—History. 6. Chicago (Ill.)—History. I. Rosing, Howard, 1965– II. Title.
TX360.U63C45 2015
641.59773'11—dc23
                        2015011759

Printed in the United States of America

CONTENTS

ACKNOWLEDGMENTS

This book could not have been written without the support of the authors' colleagues and family and a wonderful group of librarians and archivists throughout Chicago. In particular, the authors would like to thank the librarians and archivists at the Chicago History Museum, the Harold Washington Library Special Collections and Preservation Center, and the Newberry Library. We also had assistance from individuals and organizations throughout the city. Raeanne Sarazen greatly assisted with cookbook research. Jill Niewohner assisted with recipe testing. Richard Block, John Owens, Amandilo Cuzan, Centers for New Horizons, and the Bronzeville Alliance Neighborhood Garden all assisted with images. Thank you to all. We also thank our editors and assistants at Rowman & Littlefield, including Suzanne Staszak-Silva, Wendi Schnaufer, Kathryn Knigge, and Joe Miller, and series editor Ken Abala.

In addition, Daniel Block would like to thank his colleagues and staff at Chicago State University for their support and assistance. Particular thanks go to Celia Francies, Mike Siola, Gebeyehu Mulugeta, Janet Halpin, Tekleab Gala, and Arthur Redman. Howard Rosing would like to thank all his colleagues at DePaul University for their support and encouragement, including the wonderful staff at the Steans Center, faculty in the Department of Geography, Department of Environmental Science and Studies, and Community Psychology Program, Caryn Chaden and the Office of the Provost, Euan Hague, Patrick McHaffie, Nila Ginger Hofman, Jacqueline Lazú, Barbara Willard, and Susan Reed.

Most importantly, we thank our families for supporting us through the writing period. Daniel Block thanks his wife, Marta, his daughter, Madeline, and his son, Joey. Howard Rosing thanks his wife, Lisa Joy, and sons Joah, Levi, and Asher.

INTRODUCTION

In 1909, the Plan of Chicago, also called the Burnham Plan, was released to great fanfare. The plan, sponsored by the Commercial Club of Chicago, beautifully detailed a vision for a more livable and efficient Chicago, full of grand boulevards and plazas, as well as reconfigured and more efficient train stations, an improved harbor, and a series of forest preserves surrounding the city. A line of recreational islands was to be built along the Lake Michigan shoreline. While only some of these plans came to fruition, the Burnham Plan, and the 1893 World's Columbian Exhibition that inspired it, is famous in Chicago and elsewhere not merely for being innovative, but in its goals and size. The electrically lit White City of the Fair was meant to showcase Chicago's rebirth from the ashes of the 1871 fire that destroyed much of the city, and to announce itself as a world-class city on the order of New York and London. The Burnham Plan itself went further, predicting that Chicago would soon surpass New York as the largest city in the United States, and perhaps even become the largest city in the world.[1]

Chicago never would become the largest city in the United States, much less the world. This was already clear to the writers of the city's second comprehensive plan, led by Daniel Burnham's son, in the late 1930s.[2] Chicago is now the third largest city in the country, having dropped below Los Angeles in the 1990 census. After gaining population in the 1990s for the first time since the 1940s, the city lost two hundred thousand people during the 2000s. Chicago also suffered a perceived insult when its bid for the 2016 Olympics was not just defeated but eliminated on the first vote. Currently, it seems to be in the news mainly for a rash of youth violence that has done nothing to dissuade potential visitors from its hard-to-shake reputation as a violent city built on Prohibition-era gangsters such as Al Capone.

Despite the recent rash of bad news, Chicago is a world-class city, propelled at least somewhat by big thinkers like Daniel Burnham. It is not just the central city of the Midwest or an industrial center, but a global financial and cultural hub, recently ranked by urbanist Richard Florida as the world's sixth most economically powerful city in the world. Chicago aims to not just rival but surpass New York and Los Angeles in many fields.[3] Much of its financial power is built on the Chicago Board of Trade, the world's largest derivatives market, which grew based on speculation on the future prices of Midwestern agricultural products. But Chicago is more than just a financial powerhouse. It is also a center of culture. Along with live theater, improvisational comedy, blues music, and architecture, Chicago is currently a center of innovation in fine dining, including the molecular gastronomy of Grant Achatz's Alinea, as well as a number of James Beard award winners and "star chefs," including, among others, Rick Bayless, Graham Elliot, Carrie Nahabedian, Jean Joho, Stephanie Izard, and Mindy Segal. People come to Chicago to eat. While Chicago does house restaurants that focus on traditional cuisines, such as Jean Joho's Alsatian Everest and Rick Bayless's Mexican Topolobampo and Frontera Grill, Chicago fine dining often involves pushing limits and combining tastes as well as capitalizing on the agricultural bounty of the Midwest, which particularly in the winter may involve root vegetables and game. The latter, as we shall see, allows for an ironic reemergence of a seemingly nouveau "local" cuisine that, unknowingly to most diners, has origins in the pre-European food landscapes of the surrounding Great Lakes region.

While the work of Chicago's chefs is an important part of the city's foodie identity, most Chicagoans would not first think of Alinea when asked about Chicago food. Instead, Chicago hot dogs, topped with a garden of vegetables, as well as the Italian beef sandwich, just called a "beef"—slow-roasted beef served on a hard roll dipped in gravy and topped with either sweet or hot peppers—would probably top the list. Hot dog and beef stands, usually with bright yellow and red signs, pepper the city. Also on the list would be deep-dish pizza, a dish so unlike traditional Italian pizza that when an author of a recent traditionalist pizza book was interviewed on Chicago public radio and asked about it, he claimed that he had not included it since it was not pizza at all. Chicago is one of the birthplaces of soul food, and particular South Side specialties such as rib tips are also characteristic of the city, as are Polish pierogies, Mexican taquerias, and pad Thai. Perhaps most characteristic of the city are hundreds of storefront restaurants that showcase the food of one or more particular ethnicity, sometimes designed to serve people of that ethnic group and other times designed for a larger audience.

The diversity of cuisines available in Chicago neighborhoods highlights the diversity of the populations that have made Chicago their home. Chicago was (and still is, for some groups, particularly Mexicans and Polish and other Eastern Europeans) a gateway city, both to immigrants from overseas and groups from elsewhere in the country, in particular to African Americans who came up the Illinois Central and other railroads from the Mississippi Delta and elsewhere in the South. Wealthy Northeasterners of Western European descent also came, such as Chicago's first mayor, William B. Ogden, who came to the city to invest and decided to stay. While the city's food history and cuisine is a combination of the influences from these many groups, the reality they faced was very different. Moneyed Easterners could step right into Chicago high society, if they so desired. A long-time Chicago white tablecloth restaurant, Henrici's, begun by a member of a Viennese family of restaurateurs, was open from 1864 until 1962 and catered to this population. In contrast, African Americans were confined to live in small areas, in particular a strip of the South Side, until after World War II. The "Black Belt," was the home of a vibrant business section, including restaurants and groceries.

With the fall of legally supported segregation (segregation occurred in Chicago beginning in the 1920s through restrictive real estate covenants that disallowed the selling of homes to particular races), African Americans moved into many other parts of the city, but segregation remains, as do vast differences in the retail food resources available in predominately black and white communities. While there are a growing number of African American–owned sit-down restaurants in a few neighborhoods on the South Side, many Chicago African American neighborhoods currently have few supermarkets or sit-down restaurants. Inequalities in our society often can be seen most clearly though the food system.

Despite its high level of segregation, from Chicago's beginning different races and ethnicities came together in eating places and in food itself. Even well before European contact, archaeologists and historians tell of the diversity of indigenous groups moving through Chicago, mixing with each other and bringing with them prior mixtures. Early Chicago foodways, centered on hunting local game and growing maize, beans, and squash, reflect the region's incredibly diverse ecological landscape, its politics, and its native cultural richness, of which sadly few Chicagoans remain aware. Chicago's location along the banks of the Chicago River, at the site of one of the easiest portages between the Great Lakes and Mississippi River watersheds, promoted the mixing of races, first among native groups and later between French and British Canadian traders, Native Americans, and other groups, leading to a Métis, a racially and ethnically mixed culture. Trader Jean-Baptiste du Sable, for example, was the first permanent non–Native American resident of Chicago. Most sources point to du Sable as being at least partially of African descent, most probably from the island of Hispaniola (present-day Haiti and Dominican Republic). He brought with him his Native American wife. Understanding Chicago's foodways, as for most cities, is dependent on understanding the city as a place of mixing and exchange, both of products, cultures, and ideas.

Chicago's history as a U.S. city began as a frontier town on the edge of a white settlement, then grew into a place of speculation with the planned building of the Illinois and Michigan Canal. It became a boomtown in which the bounty of the West merged into a mature city of immigrants from overseas and migrants from elsewhere in the United States and their descendants. In this environment, cultures mixed, first at the taverns around Wolf Point, where the forks of the Chicago River join, and later at the jazz and other clubs along the "Stroll" in the Black Belt, and in the storefront ethnic restaurants of today. In addition, as detailed by William Cronon and many others, Chicago was the place where the transcontinental railroads from the West ended and the "trunk" roads, such as the New York Central and Baltimore and Ohio to the east, met.[4] Many downtown restaurants catered specifically to passengers transferring from train to train between one of the five major downtown railroad stations. Lou Mitchell's, a West Loop diner and one of the oldest restaurants in the city, is a legacy of this and still performs this role for Amtrak customers transferring between trains from the East and West. Near the entryway there is often a pile of suitcases belonging to patrons eating omelettes and the lunch special. This also led to "destination" restaurants, such as The Pump Room, where Hollywood stars and those who gawked at them would dine during overnight layovers between trains. This transfer point was an ideal place for industry, in particular industries such as meatpacking, which processed Western animals and sent meat to the East Coast and elsewhere. Similarly, Chicago became the candy capital of the United States because the ingredients, in particular corn syrup derived from Midwestern corn, could be easily shipped to the city, and the candy itself could be shipped across the country to consumers. Finally, this city in the center of the country also became a leading city for national conventions, as many participants wanted to eat one of the outcomes of the meatpacking plants, a steak.

Beyond hosting conventions and commerce, Chicagoans also simply needed to eat—safely and relatively cheaply. Chicago grew amazingly fast, from about one hundred in 1830 before the city was founded to 112,172 in 1860, becoming the second largest city in the United States in 1890. Chicago topped three million people in 1930. To provide provisions for such a quickly growing city was not easy, and to protect these provisions was even harder. Chicago is not unusual in this sense. Quickly growing cities and countries struggle with provisioning their populations throughout the world. However, Chicago, growing precisely during the time of the formation of the germ theory of disease and the subsequent revolution in public health, served as a test case for many regulations and policies. Chicago itself and its immediate surrounding area was the site of agriculture, both producing food for the city and for shipment elsewhere. Within the city, industrial food manufacturers prospered, highlighted by the meat processors at the Chicago stockyards, but it also included candy makers such as Brach's and Curtiss and companies such as Kraft Foods. At the same time, large markets for local consumption emerged. While the population of the city itself has stagnated and declined since 1940, the population of the region continues to grow, although not as quickly. The food biography of Chicago is a story of not just culture, economics, and innovation, but also a history of regulation and regulators, as they protected Chicago's food supply, particularly during its time of fast growth, and built Chicago into a city where people not only come to eat but where the locals can rely on the availability of safe food and water.

I

THE MATERIAL RESOURCES
Land, Water, and Air

Chicago was founded and developed not because of the particular characteristics of its site, a generally swampy lowland, but because of its situation—its location in relationship to other places. Chicago is a place of connection. Before becoming a town, Chicago was a portage, the shortest connection between the Mississippi and Great Lakes watersheds. The Chicago Portage ran between the West Fork of the South Branch of the Chicago River and marshy Mud Lake, from which a creek flowed into the Des Plaines River, which connects to the Illinois and then the Mississippi. At high water times, the divide between the Chicago and Des Plaines rivers flooded, and one could paddle all the way from the Des Plaines to Lake Michigan. At low water times, the portage was a seven-mile-long slog through muddy and leach-infested Mud Lake, or, more often, a bypass around it. At truly low water times, when the Des Plaines and Chicago rivers dried up, the portage could be even longer, up to fifty miles.[1]

Despite the swampiness and the irregularity of the flow of the Chicago and Des Plaines rivers, the route of the portage was tantalizing to those who dreamed of a canal to facilitate easy passage between the two watersheds due to the lowness of the divide (around thirteen feet above average lake level) and the short distance between the Des Plaines and Chicago rivers. In 1673, the French explorers Jacques Marquette and Louis Jolliet and their party became the first people of European descent to cross the portage. After traveling from Green Bay to the Mississippi using the Fox and Wisconsin rivers and a portage near Portage, Wisconsin, the Native Americans of the region told them of a more direct route home. They traversed the portage in September 1673. On a subsequent trip south, Marquette and companions then overwintered in 1674 near the future site of Chicago. Jolliet, always a promoter, immediately began to envision a short canal to eliminate the need for the portage that he claimed needed only to be about half a league, or two miles, in length.[2] Following Jolliet's lead, early visitors and settlers were entranced by the portage and its possibilities. Samuel Storrow, an 1817 visitor, remarked:

> The source of these two rivers (Mud Lake) illustrates the geographical phenomenon of a reservoir on the very summit of a dividing ridge. In the autumn, they are both without any apparent fountain, but are formed within a mile and a half of each other by some imperceptible undulations of the prairie, which drain it and lead to different directions. But in the spring, the space between the two is a single sheet of water, the common reservoir of both, in the center of which there is no current towards either of the opposite streams. The circumstance creates the singular fact of the insulation of all the United States excepting Louisiana, making the circumnavigation of them practicable, from the Gulf of St. Lawrence to that of Mexico, with the single hindrance of the Falls of Niagara.[3]

Such enthusiasm led the federal government to request the mouth of the Chicago River be ceded by Native Americans to the federal government in the 1795 Treaty of Greenville and the strip of land ten miles on either side of the river be ceded in an 1816 treaty with the Native American tribes that sided with the British in the War of 1812. The portage was also the reason for the establishment of the ill-fated Fort Dearborn near the mouth of the river in 1803, and why Jean Baptiste Point de Sable built a cabin for his family near the mouth of the river in the 1780s.[4] Soon after Illinois was founded in 1818, the state government began to push for a grant of this federal land to the state to support canal building. The canal itself, and particularly the funding for it, turned out to be a somewhat more difficult project than originally envisioned, mainly due to state financing issues and the fact that, at least at first, the potential traffic for the canal was based on projections, rather than current, levels of future Western settlement. When it opened in 1848, the short canal that

Jolliet envisioned had lengthened to ninety-six miles and cost about $6.5 million (the equivalent of about $170 million today). It not only involved cutting through the shallow divide between Lake Michigan and the Des Plaines River but also building locks downstream to the Illinois to allow boats to descend a drop of 141 feet along a canal running parallel to the Des Plaines.[5] The canal was almost an immediate success, immediately boosting Chicago's trade in maize and wheat, as well as southern products such as sugar, molasses, and cotton.[6]

The Chicago Portage and the generally flat landscape of the city and its surroundings are the result of glaciation. Some fourteen thousand years ago, as the most recent glacial episode, called the Wisconsin, retreated toward the north, a lake, much higher than the present Lake Michigan, formed. Called Lake Chicago, this lake was centered in the current Lake Michigan basin, but it covered most of present-day Chicago as well as surrounding areas all the way up to the edges of the Valparaiso Moraine, a crescent of hills made of up glacial material that had been deposited as the glacier receded. This moraine runs through Valparaiso, Indiana, and then around the south end of the lake through Chicago's southwest, west, and northwest suburbs. At the time, the north end of Lake Michigan was blocked by ice. Lake Chicago emptied through the current Des Plaines River and Cal-Sag channel "outlets" (collectively called the "Chicago outlet") into a proto-Illinois River and further downstream into the Mississippi. These outlets were large and wide, and when the lake was highest, a bay extended toward them. In the past fourteen thousand years, there have been numerous lake levels, both higher and lower than today, some with the lake continuing to flow out through the Chicago outlet, and some toward the St. Lawrence. During this period, the general landscape of the city was formed, mainly a flat former lake bottom with linear beach ridges marking various levels of the lake as well as a few former islands of hillier glacial moraine. It was only in the very recent geologic past, just 1,700 years ago, that current lake levels were established.[7]

"NATURE'S METROPOLIS"

Despite its proximity to the future Corn Belt, Chicago's geography initially led more to shipping and processing of foodstuffs rather than growing crops. As historian William Cronon describes in has masterful book *Nature's Metropolis*, the relatively flat landscape not only of Chicago but also of the area that surrounds it made it an ideal place to center a system of railroads that connected the city to what would become one of the chief farming areas in the world. Chicago's lake harbor (via the Erie Canal), as well as the system of "trunk line" railroads going toward the East, connected the city to eastern ports as well as Europe. Chicago processed, shipped, and priced much of the bounty of the West for the rest of the world. Chicago's situation, in the center of the country, at the focus of rail transport and at the site of the Illinois and Michigan Canal connecting the Great Lakes and Mississippi River drainages, helped shaped its food history. Chicago was (and still is) a place where materials were offloaded, often transformed through manufacturing, and then transferred, to trunk train lines to the east, or ships bound for Europe or the East Coast. It is the role of Chicago as a transfer site for raw materials and a potential shipment site for finished goods that gave the city a competitive advantage in the development of food-based manufacturers such as the great meatpacking plants of Armour and Swift, as well as Kraft, Quaker Oats, and numerous candy companies (Chicago at one time called itself the "candy capital of the world"). Chicago's situation as a transportation hub for outgoing retail shipments and incoming parts and product shipments also assisted agricultural implement companies such as International Harvester, and the Sears and Montgomery Ward catalog companies. Merchandise also flowed to Chicago from the East, and Chicago became a western shopping outpost for East Coast and European goods. In addition, the pricing of shipments of grain that originally were sold along the south bank of the Chicago River led the city to be the hub of the pricing and much of the financing of the American agricultural system through the Chicago Board of Trade and other mechanisms.[8]

A major issue with the development of this city based on the transferring and processing of the bounty of the West was its port. While Chicago may not be thought of today as a significant port city, the success of the Illinois and Michigan Canal depended upon a port that allowed easy access to the lake as well as a way to transfer between the canal and lake boats. The port grew even before the canal opened. Cheap lake transportation to the East Coast, when compared to the connections available in cities such as Cincinnati and St. Louis, made grain prices to farmers higher in Chicago than in competing cities. Its first railroad, the Chicago and Galena Union opened in 1848, was built not to connect the city to the East Coast but instead led from northwest Illinois to a location along the Chicago River. To proceed further east, freight continued by boat. Freight coming up the canal itself included sugar and molasses from New Orleans, as well as wheat and corn from Midwestern farms. Transported out from Chicago were lumber, salt, and manufactured goods. By 1854, only six years after both the canal and the Chicago and Galena Union railroad opened, the *Cleveland Herald* declared that Chicago was the busiest port on the Great Lakes.[9] By 1871, the Port of Chicago was the largest grain and lumber port in the world. International shipments were primarily imports and particularly exports to Canada, but also included shipping flour, grain, and even lard to Europe.[10]

An initial barrier to the success of the port was a sandbar. While the Chicago River was naturally wide in the two miles before its mouth, the mouth itself was almost entirely blocked by a large sandbar caused by the north-to-south current along Lake Michigan's western shore that pushes sand southward. In addition, the sandbar led to the development of a curve just before the river's mouth. Even if boats made it across the bar in their journey from the lake into the river, they would have to do a right-angle curve just past the bar. At first, most boats anchored in the lake and then ferried their cargo onto the shore. As early as the 1820s, soldiers at Fort Dearborn made a cut through the bar in order to ease the delivery of supplies. In 1830, piers were proposed to protect a larger cut through the sandbar. Over the next forty years, successively longer piers on the north side of the cut were made, which, along with constant dredging, kept the port open. The issue was finally solved (at least for the most part) when breakwaters were added to create an "outer harbor." North of the piers, an increasing amount of sand accumulated, resulting in an addition of sandy land east of what is now Michigan Avenue, the area known as Streeterville. This area was a sort of no-man's land, since it did not exist on Chicago's original plat maps, and nobody knew who owned it. In the late 1800s, it was known as an area of sin, and it became known as Streeterville after George Washington Streeter, who ran his boat aground in the area in 1886, claimed he owned some 168 acres. He was not evicted until World War I.[11]

WATER, SOILS, AND DRAINAGE

In its first century, the population of Chicago grew at an incredible rate.
Such quick population growth created a large number of issues, particularly with sanitation and the need to provide fresh water. Sanitation was a
particular issue. The flatness of the lake plain upon which the city was
built meant that sewage had nowhere to drain. To deal with the issue, in
1855 the city brought in Ellis Chesbrough, the engineer of the city of
Boston, to develop a sanitation system. He proposed a system of sewers
leading to the Chicago River, based somewhat on a system in London.
The system, when put in place, improved the situation on the streets but
quickly fouled the river and the lake along with the drinking water.
Drinking water for the city was and is collected through offshore cribs in
the lake and transported via pipes into the city. As the water near the
mouth of the Chicago River became increasingly foul smelling as well as
dangerous, the cribs needed to be moved further and further from the
shore. Successive outbreaks of cholera also followed periods of rain or
thaws. These issues led to the transformation of the Illinois and Michigan

Figure 1.1.   An imaginary view of Chicago circa 1779 illustrating the Chicago Riv-
er bend, the sandy shore, and du Sable's house and farm. From A. T. Andreas,
History of Chicago, vol. I (Chicago: A. T. Andreas, 1884). Chicago Public Library,
Special Collections and Preservation Division, GP-Smith 194.

Canal into a sewer, delivering waste (diluted somewhat with lake water) toward the south and the Mississippi River rather than into the lake.[12]

In addition to water and sanitation, such a quickly growing city also needed to feed itself, and for this the city's site was not as well equipped. From today's vantage point, one would think otherwise. In addition to the relatively flat terrain, glaciers also helped create the landscape that became the Corn Belt that spreads out from the city toward the south and west. While generally not quite as flat as Chicago itself, the Corn Belt was made by the glaciers that bulldozed their way southward, carrying a mixture of rocks, often ground into a glacial flour, or "loess." This contains, among other things, ground limestone, which, when combined with sand and clay, served as an almost perfect substrate for prairie grasses, which replaced forests in Illinois during a period of dry and relatively hot weather about 8,500 years ago. Even as the climate grew wetter over the past thousand years, and thus more conducive to forest, the prairie was maintained by fire, started both by lightning and by Native Americans, who coveted the large animals, such as elk and bison, that ate the prairie grasses. In general, the ecology of the region included prairies, oak prairie savanna (prairies interspersed with fire-resistant trees, mainly oaks), and oak-maple forests, which mainly occurred along rivers and streams. The prairie grasses die off every year, adding layers of organic matter to the soil, and they create thick, organic-rich, black topsoil, called by soil scientists a "mollic epipedon." Among other things, the organic material in this topsoil, as well as the generally basic pH the decomposing grasses create, results in conditions in which nutrients are held in the soil itself, creating, all in all, one of the most productive soils in the world.

Despite the fertile soil, early commentators were mixed on the productivity of the area. Marquette mentions being given (with an expected return gift) corn, blueberries, dried meat, pumpkins, and beaver skins by Native Americans, and that they lived "only 18 leagues from here, in a fine place for hunting cattle, deer, and turkeys."[13] Henry Schoolcraft stated that the soil along the Chicago River consisted of "a black . . . fertile soil," which produced abundant wild garlic, onions, and leeks (wild leeks are also called ramps by current-day foodies).[14] William H. Keating, another early visitor, was generally unimpressed by the prairie landscape around Chicago and pointed out that despite spending much of their time on agricultural pursuits, provisions for Fort Dearborn were mainly shipped from Mackinac Island, although historian Bessie Louise

Pierce remarks that the garrison was better equipped than most due to the game, cranberries, and maple sugar available in the surrounding wilderness.[15] Sarah Margaret Fuller, a daughter of a wealthy Massachusetts politician, toured Chicago in 1843 and was overwhelmed by the beauty of the blooming prairie flowers and the vastness of the landscape. Speculator Charles Butler, writing about the 1830s from 1881, spoke of Chicago as being at the edge of virgin prairie, "a vast flower garden—beautiful to look at in its virgin state and ready for the plough of the Farmer."[16] Butler was a Chicago booster, but his view was probably typical. Following and just preceeding incorporation as a town in 1833, the main focus of those who invested or moved to the city was not on the productivity of the land upon which Chicago stood but on its situation at the edge of the "Great West," and particularly along the to-be-built Illinois and Michigan Canal.

A major issue with large-scale cultivation of the future Corn Belt was lack of drainage. The flattened landscape left few "natural" drainages, especially away from the larger rivers, so artificial drainage was a must before large-scale farming could begin. The land that currently makes up Chicago, as well as much of Illinois, was swampy. In order to be planted, the prairie needed to be drained. The drainage issue was also huge for the city itself, which raised the street level downtown and in many other areas of the city. Before he began the Pullman Palace Car Company, George Pullman helped lead a heroic effort to raise a block of buildings along Lake Street, then the city's commercial center, four feet eight inches to match the raised streets. In many older Chicago neighborhoods, yards are still up to ten feet below street level, and house entryways cross over bridges into second floors. Charles Cleaver, an early industrialist specializing in soap making from tallow who came to Chicago in 1833, later reminisced, "I built (a factory), in the fall of '36, at the corner of Washington and Jefferson (now on the near West Side), and many a time had to wade ankle-deep in water to get there before I cut a ditch to the river to drain it."[17] Farms in the Chicago area and throughout Illinois also had to deal with poor drainage. Much of the "lake plain" directly surrounding Chicago was extremely wet, as Cleaver remembered what became Chicago's West Side: "for ten miles out the water lay in places two feet deep, and in wet weather the whole surface was covered with water, with the exception of two ridges between the city and the Des Plaines River."[18] Drainage was often a speculative pursuit, as land investors would invest in swampy land, drain it, and then attempt to resell it at a higher price.

Such piecemeal draining caused large issues. The 1868 digging of a long ditch to drain Mud Lake and its surroundings, where former Chicago mayors William B. Ogden and John Wentworth owned land, resulted in the Des Plaines forcing water into the South Fork of the Chicago River during flood periods. This filled the Illinois and Michigan Canal with silt, negating the efforts of a state-sponsored dredging of the canal a year before that was focused on reversing the flow of the Chicago River to flush waste down the canal.[19]

In 1879 the state-sanctioned drainage districts, allowing groups of farmers or other citizens or municipalities to come together to fund mutual drainage projects, often involved the use of heavy machinery in the creation of drainage ditches and underground pipe. In 1889 the Sanitary District of Chicago was organized and began planning the Chicago Ship and Sanitary Canal, which opened at the very beginning of the twentieth century, on January 2, 1900. It linked the South Fork of the Chicago River to the lower Des Plaines, south of Joliet, turning around the flow of the Chicago so it flows out from Lake Michigan into the Mississippi River system, pushing the city's waste downstream as well as providing a channel for much larger boats than the earlier Illinois and Michigan Canal.[20] Today, an additional system of "deep tunnels" runs beneath the metropolitan area to provide drainage in extreme rainfall events.[21]

Despite the importance of the portage and canal, what truly built Chicago in its early days was land speculation, spurred by the future opening of the canal and the role of the city as a potential, rather than actual, marketplace. The original township plat map of the area, completed in 1822, divided the land into sections, and indicated the head of navigation on the South Branch of the Chicago River, the point from which the Illinois and Michigan Canal would begin. Eight years later, in 1830, the first plat map of Chicago itself was completed, including many of the streets that now make up downtown Chicago, and separating the city into neat, generally square blocks, divided into parcels to be sold to the public. Soon, the real estate boom commenced. The plats and Chicago street grid, with streets every eighth of a mile (or in some places every sixteenth of a mile) and alleys in between, speculatively rolled out over the prairie. Land inflation was incredible. A plot of land at Clark Street and South Water (now Wacker Drive) that was valued at $100 in 1832 sold for $3,400 in 1834. Charles Butler, the speculator quoted above, bought a tract of land for $100,000 in 1835, five times what it had sold for in 1834.

Butler subdivided the land and paid off his investment from sales of just one-third of the lots. A few years later, in 1837, the nationwide Panic of 1837 caused real estate values in Chicago and elsewhere to plunge.[22] More importantly, for Chicago, the state of Illinois nearly went bankrupt and could not fund continuing construction of the canal. Furthermore, the Illinois state bank, along with many others, became insolvent. Most of the currency in the city was close to worthless. After 1841, the city and country began to rebound. Following a four-year stagnation between 1837 and 1841 at about four thousand, the city resumed its growth in population, reaching almost thirty thousand by 1850, sparked by the canal and the first railroad serving the city opening in 1848. Chicago became a chief Great Lakes port and industrial site.[23] Overall, speculation built much of the early city, but it was trade and manufacturing that sustained it. Chicago, from its start, was not a farm town, or simply a marketplace for the surrounding areas. Even before incorporation, its dreams were far larger, to be the city that connected the Great American West to the world.

RAILROADS AND AGRICULTURE IN CHICAGO AND ITS SURROUNDINGS

Since its founding as a city in 1837, Chicago's motto has been *Urbs in Horto* or "City in a Garden." Even so, if you talk to many current urban agriculture and community gardening enthusiasts, one might think that farming in the city is something new. Instead, in-city farming dates back to its founding. Early Chicago maps focused on real estate development, and rarely showed existing farms. The 1857 Palmatary View of the city depicts the urban city extending out into the surrounding land. Open areas on the periphery appear generally empty, ready to be developed.[24] The marshy lake plain was crossed only by occasionally higher beach ridges. However, food has been grown in Chicago and its immediate surrounding area both commercially and noncommercially since its beginnings as a small town, and prior to that by settlers and Native Americans. Agriculture in the region did get off to a relatively slow start. The focus of the early city was on land for speculation, not for agriculture. During the 1830s, Chicago was notable in that its provisions came primarily from the outside, causing very high prices. Just setting up a farm in the Chicago

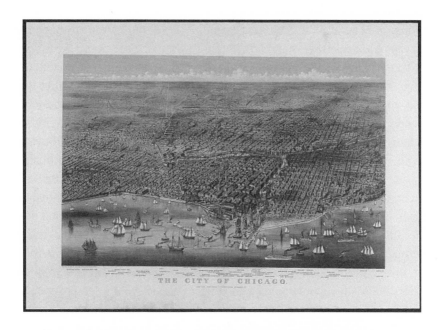

Figure 1.2. An 1892 Courier & Ives view of Chicago, showing downtown, the busy harbor along which the South Water Market flourished, and the grid system of streets running off into surrounding farmland. Library of Congress.

region was extremely difficult, as indicated in the diaries of Charles Bartlett, a New Hampshire farmer who moved to what became Lake County, Illinois, in 1834, moving his possessions, including furniture, by railroad, steamboat, and lake schooner to Chicago and then by oxen and wagon the rest of the way. Going to Chicago, which he did frequently both to buy supplies and to sell produce, butter, and animals, involved an overnight trip each way on unimproved roads, just to go approximately thirty miles.[25] Other farmers came to the city from much further afield than Bartlett. Peaking in the early 1840s, farmers came up the Vincennes Road from southwestern Indiana, as local farms could not provide enough food for even the relatively small population at the time.[26]

The difficulty of land-based travel was extreme. Charles Cleaver recalled traveling by wagon to a farm just a mile and a half away across the prairie: "It was with the greatest difficulty that two good horses could pull the empty wagon through two feet of mud and water across the prairie we had to pass."[27] The situation bettered with the building of improved "plank" roads, such as what became Ogden Avenue, in the area just surrounding the city. This increased farmer settlement in northeastern Illinois in general, and even more with the development of railroads and increasingly organized markets within the city.

The primary key to Chicago's growth was its position as the center of the U.S. rail system. By 1855, just seven years after Chicago's first railroad opened, seventeen railroad lines served the city. In 1856, the Rock Island Bridge Company built a rail bridge across the Mississippi River, leading to the formation of the Chicago, Rock Island and Pacific Railroad that in 1869 connected to the Union Pacific, which led to California. Among other things, these lines brought massive amounts of corn and wheat into the city, as well as massive amounts of merchandise out of the city to its hinterland.[28] In 1855 over 4.5 million bushels of wheat and over 3.7 million bushels of corn arrived on the Chicago and Galena Union railroad alone.[29] Importantly for Chicago's food history, the rail lines also crisscrossed the countryside surrounding the city, so most farmers in the region were now conveniently located to the city. As this happened, farms began to specialize. Market farms for the city opened nearby, while dairy farms developed somewhat further away, mainly to the north and west. In its first century and later, once the land was drained and cleared, a ring of vegetable farms that intermingled with urbanized areas surrounded the city. The township of Lake View, just north of the city boundaries until it was annexed in 1889, was once a center of celery production.[30] Further north, the Bowmanville area was a national producer of cucumbers for pickles, and it also produced many other vegetables. Chicago's connections to national markets also allowed areas both north and south of the city to become producers of cut flowers, giving the current South Side Roseland neighborhood its name.[31] The farming area on what is now Chicago's South Side is beautifully presented early in Edna Ferber's Pulitzer Prize–winning novel *So Big*. The protagonist and his mother drive a cart full of produce to Chicago's South Water Market through what was to become Chicago's South Side. Along the way they passed miles of vegetable plots: "So they jolted up the long Halsted road through the late October sunset. The prairie land just outside Chicago had not then been made a terrifying and epic thing of slag-heaps. . . . Mile after mile of cabbage fields, jade-green against the Earth."[32] The year was 1885, and Ferber spoke from 1924, describing what by the 1920s had become Chicago's South Side but earlier were vegetable farms surrounding the city. The plot they were driving from was in a Dutch community located further south called Hope, likely meant to be Roseland, now a predominately African American community on what is now Chicago's far South Side, or south suburban South Holland. Further south, in the southern suburb of Lansing, the De Jong Brothers Farms still exists, producing primarily spinach. It is now surrounded by houses.

It is not only south of the city that remnants of Chicago region's agricultural past remain. Just north of the city, near Evanston's southern border, is Clesen Wholesale, a large set of greenhouses, now producing for the wholesale ornamental and garden plant market, taking up about three acres of prime real estate. Anton's, a similar greenhouse open to the public, stands on a west Evanston residential block, and Urhausen, another greenhouse, is on a residential corner in nearby Lincolnwood. These are what are left of a large area of greenhouses that produced year-round flowers and vegetables for Chicago. The greenhouse zone extended into the city itself until after World War II, when most of them were torn down to be replaced by raised ranch homes.

The Chicago area actually had three major vegetable-producing areas just outside the city borders as late as 1947: the South Holland district in the southern suburbs where De Jong Brothers still exists; the Worth district southwest of the city; and, the largest, the Maine District, centered on Maine township just north of present-day O'Hare Airport but stretching from the west Evanston greenhouses through the city's far Northwest Side to what are now the northwest suburban areas of Palatine and Schaumburg. Farms in these areas included both market garden farms, averaging thirty acres and focused on the regional vegetable market, and larger truck farms (some exceeding five hundred acres) focused both on specialized vegetable production for the regional market and also production for canning, including a large amount of contract farming to large canning companies such as Campbell's and Libby's. The larger truck farms were relatively industrial and hired Latino migrant laborers. While all these regions included market gardens, they also specialized. The South Holland area was particularly focused on the production of onion sets, used for planting, of which it was the national center. The Maine district focused, among other things, on horseradish. [33]

These regions, particularly the Maine district, were constantly affected by urbanization. As a 1947 thesis reports, many of the Maine-district farmers previously had farms in Niles and Norwood Park townships, some within the Chicago city limits. Some had just recently moved to the further-out areas of Schaumburg and Palatine.[34] In a history of Norridge and Harwood Heights, two suburban "islands" on Chicago's Northwest Side, Thomas McGowen describes the history of the first half of the twentieth century as a period in which agriculture mixed with residential districts. Like Ferber's earlier South Side farmers, the area farmers still "would load their trucks with produce and drive in to the markets on South Water Street or Randolph Street."[35] Meanwhile, schools were being built, often backing up to farmland. Many of these truck farms were fairly large operations. At least one post–World War II Norridge-area farmer hired migrant Jamaican workers, whose families attended the neighborhood school.[36] As late as 1952, an aerial photo shows new subdivisions next to small agricultural plots.[37]

Beyond just mapping the historical sites of agricultural production, this history is important because it both points out that fairly late in its history, areas within and close to the city limits were producing both vegetables for Chicago's consumption and for export to outside regions. Compared to such cities as New York and San Francisco, Chicago had a relatively compact "foodshed." Secondly, while increased urbanization did eventually force most of these farms to move further and further from the city limits until market gardening itself became more difficult and was outcompeted by vegetables from California and other areas of the country, this change did not happen all at once. In Chicago in 1925 there were 277 farms covering more than four thousand acres, over six square miles.[38] While most of these farms were on the outskirts of the city, decades existed during which communities such as Norwood Park, Roseland (both within the city limits), and South Holland had urbanized areas next door to farms. In South Holland, this pattern persists to a small extent. This was particularly true between the 1920s and the late 1940s, when residential development basically stopped during the Great Depression. In addition, the development of residential zones along train lines meant that areas between train lines stayed agricultural far later. Even so, the value of the agricultural land, the richness of much of the soil in the Chicago region, and the nearness of the Chicago market meant that some farmers kept producing long after their communities were generally built up.

One agricultural product stands out in Chicago's nineteenth- and early twentieth-century history, milk. Milk production in the city during its first century is a particularly interesting story of the decline and regulation of both industrial and small-scale agriculture in the city. The development of a separate agricultural sector focused on the production of fluid milk for urban consumption was considered part of the development of the modern city in the mid- to late 1800s. Previously, dairy districts had devoted themselves mainly to the production of butter and cheese. Fluid milk was primarily consumed by young children, and it was often provided by a cow in a neighbor's, or one's own, backyard. In the mid-1800s an intensive system of milk production appeared, first in New York, but later in Chicago, called "swill milk." Swill milk "farms" were attached to distilleries; cows were fed the "swill" or leftovers from the distilling process. This caused outrage both due to the metaphoric tie of "pure" milk drunk primarily by children linked to alcohol production and the often horrible conditions in which the cows were kept. These farms were within the city, with the cows being kept either in basements below the distillery or in an adjacent open field. While swill milk dairies were outlawed in New York State in 1862, they continued in Chicago for over a decade after this. An 1870 Chicago newspaper complained about them: "There is a general understanding that no one fountain is able to send forth sweet and bitter water, but from the wonderful distillery proceed both gin and milk."[39]

In addition to the swill dairies, there were still many small herds, but by 1903, 97 percent of milk consumed in the city came from outside the city by rail.[40] The number of cows within the city limits continued to decline in the early 1900s, from 5,901 in 1900 to 1,061 in 1920, the last agricultural census that reported the data. These 1,061 cows were on 866 enclosures, so the average number of cows per herd was only a bit more than one.[41] The demise of the city cow was considered a natural outcome of urban development. "Cows properly belong in the country," stated the Milwaukee health commissioner in 1887.[42] Beyond the antialcohol morality, the anti–swill milk campaign was about the relegation of cows to distinctly crowded, urban conditions. Later, U.S. Marine Hospital Service officer and Harvard Medical School professor Milton Rosenau stated: "It is practically impossible to keep a cow in a healthy condition for any length of time in a city."[43]

The issue was that if milk was not being produced in the city, the connections between the producer and consumer generally lessened, as did the ability for the city to regulate on-farm production practices. As Rosenau put it: "When the producer and the consumer were near neighbors and closely acquainted with each other, the one had a personal interest in the product he furnished the other."[44] Urbanization, and the movement of dairy production away from the city, usually paralleled the development of laws surrounding the milk sold in the city. A middleman, milk dealers, arose, who collected the milk from farmers or picked it up at train depots, and bottled and delivered it. The question about how to protect urban milk was fiercely debated between proponents of pasteurization, which protected milk, whether of high or low quality, and certification, which required farmers to agree to a long list of production practices. Then, as now, promoters of "raw" certified milk complained about the beneficial characteristics of milk that were lost through the "cooking" that occurred in pasteurization. It was much cheaper to clean milk than to require the production practices of certification. In addition, certification would not protect against certain diseases, such as bovine tuberculosis, passing from cow to human. In 1909, Chicago became the first city in the world to require pasteurization, for all milk except from cows with a negative tuberculin test.[45]

The story of milk in Chicago's (and other cities') urban history focuses the separation of production from the city and subsequent attempts to control that production from afar, primarily by the Chicago Department of Health. As urbanization proceeded and refrigeration improved, milk came from farther and farther afield, and the difficulty of control multiplied. Further regulatory barriers developed, but the main technology protecting milk continues to be pasteurization, a process that specifically separates the consumer from conditions on the farm. The city also relied on human barriers. Until the 1970s the City of Chicago employed a team of dairy inspectors, based primarily in Wisconsin, which approved farms to sell milk into the city.[46] This was eventually deemed unconstitutional (a city cannot regulate interstate trade), but the point is that urbanization and food protection laws had caused an abstraction of urban consumers from their food sources, most obviously with milk and perhaps meat, but also with vegetables.

The current urban agriculture and local food movements in Chicago and elsewhere are rooted in, among other things, a reaction to this increased food abstraction. Although it greatly varies among Chicago's communities, the use of local food providers at restaurants has become almost commonplace, and many local producers, even from inside the city, are selling at local farmer's markets. For example, North Side eatery

Figure 1.3. Cattle pasture in 1922 near 50th and Dorchester, in the upscale South Side Kenwood neighborhood. Agriculture and residential land uses mixed in Chicago communities, often long after development. Chicago History Museum, Daily News Collection, DN-0075190.

Uncommon Ground has a rooftop garden. "From one side of the garden, it's fifty steps to the kitchen," their farm director states.[47] Community gardens are blooming all over the city, as are urban agriculture projects. Social service organizations throughout the city, such as Bronzeville's Centers for New Horizons, now host community gardens. SEEDS, in the Roseland community, has built an urban farm in a large schoolyard. On the North Side, Peterson Garden Project has developed a network of community gardens based on the "victory garden" concept of the World War I and II eras. Nonprofit organization Growing Home operates its urban farm in the Englewood neighborhood as a job-training site, along with a farm in Marseilles, Illinois. It has a farm stand and a community supported agriculture (CSA) program. The Chicago office of Growing Power operates the Iron Street Farm along the South Fork of the South Branch of the Chicago River, or what used to be called "Bubbly Creek," as well as gardens in the far South Side Altgeld Gardens district and elsewhere.[48] Both Growing Power and Growing Home also sell at Green City Market, the premier farmer's market in the city. The Chicago Honey Co-Op, also a job-training program, produces "urban honey" on Chicago's West Side and sells at the Green City and Logan Square Farmers Markets, as well as a number of stores. The Plant, a vertical farm using aquaponics and a green business incubation center in the old stockyards district, is a model for businesses throughout the country. Chicago State, Loyola, and DePaul Universities, as well as the City Colleges of Chicago, offer urban agriculture within their curricula and host model gardens and aquaponics sites.

Outside the city, farms throughout Chicago's extended "foodshed," including the traditional market garden area, neighboring areas of Wisconsin and Illinois, and the Michigan fruit belt, sell to many Chicago restaurants and at many farmer's markets. Perhaps the largest of these is Nichols Farms, located in Marengo, Illinois, just outside of the traditional northwest suburban produce production ring, which sells at twelve farmer's markets in the city and suburbs, has a CSA, and sells to a large number of Chicago restaurants at a variety of price points. Beyond vegetables, the Chicago foodshed also has a number of local meat providers selling grass-fed beef, pork, and chicken to local consumers and restaurants, such as Slagel Family Farm and Wettstein Organic Farm, both in central Illinois, who are restarting the flow of meat from Chicago's Midwestern hinterlands to the city that once provided not only Chicago but also much of the country with its meat.

SEPARATION AND CONNECTION

The embracing and incorporation of the bounty of the West into its economy, while at the same time the creation of the separation between nature and the city, helped structure Chicago's food system for its first century and beyond. In the case of milk, this involved laws that pushed cows out of the city plus pasteurization and regulations that physically separated the farmer from the consumer. In the case of water, the city was naturally blessed with a large freshwater lake, but it took successive steps to separate urban effluent from the site of its drinking water by physically moving the water cribs out from the shore, and then by turning around the direction of flow of the river. In its beginning, Chicago was as much real estate investment as a city, with plots for sale laid out far beyond the city limits with little regard for nature. Yet its location on the edge of the prairie as well as at one end of the Chicago portage and the canal that followed it

Figure 1.4.   Community garden in the Bronzeville neighborhood sponsored by the Centers for New Horizons and the Bronzeville Alliance. It is one of many community gardens and urban agriculture sites that have opened in Chicago over the last fifteen years. Courtesy of John Owens, Centers for New Horizons.

were the reasons this speculation existed at all. The flatness of its site was one of the main things that allowed for the quickness of development, but in order to settle the city on a large scale, that flatness needed to be, at least somewhat, altered, with the building up of the grade level of city streets and the draining of areas that would soon become neighborhoods and farms. The Chicago River itself now runs through an artificial canyon downtown. In another example, the commodities trading, meatpacking plants, and industrial and agricultural equipment, and even the candy factories that helped build the new city, were all rooted in the processing, creating, and pricing of the agricultural products of the Midwest and the greater region which sent Chicago raw materials, but these created their own troublesome environmental and financial "nature," which the city struggled to control.

Perhaps a typical case is the Chicago Fire of 1871. Chicago was built using the lumber of the north woods that could be shipped easily down the lake. The cheapness and plentiful nature of this wood during the mid-nineteenth century was one of the things that allowed the city to physically grow so quickly, but it also made the city into a tinderbox. After the fire, the city put into place new fireproof building standards. Most new buildings following this time were made of brick, which was more expensive, but buildings were still primarily built using local clays, creating the typical Chicago yellow brick buildings. The fire shows the kinds of ways that Chicagoans negotiated with the nature around them—using and controlling it, but also pushing its limits—sometimes too far.

Chicago has also been both an edge city and a central city, built originally due its location at the edge of the nineteenth-century West but then flourishing as the central city of the Midwest and the nation. It also was founded because of its position between two watersheds, and it grew due to the canal connecting them. The food of Chicago follows these same themes, building on the bounty of the Midwest but also being a place of connection between cuisines and the introduction of new cuisines to the center of the county. Chicago is a place of creativity, where the idea that changing the direction of the river, or creating a luxury restaurant that changes cuisines every six months, is thinkable and, more importantly, accomplished. The new incorporation of food production back into the city also contains many stories of creativity and innovation, while also maintaining the mainstream American "steak and potatoes" cuisine that conventioneers and other visitors often seek out. Before venturing further into the origins of such creative and traditional cuisines, there is an earlier story to tell. That story begins well before Europeans set their eyes on the mouth of the Chicago River and envisioned a great metropolis on its swampy banks.

2

INDIGENOUS FOODWAYS
OF CHICAGO

Chicago's food history begins well before Europeans set eyes on the mouth of the Chicago River and imagined a robust commercial center and gateway to the Great West. To understand how Chicago became a hub of the global food economy, a center of food aggregation, debulking, and distribution, a place known for its diverse cuisines from across the planet, we need to look back to a time when commodification of food was ancillary to subsistence living. Indigenous foodways, transformed over thousands of years, had little resemblance to the foods that became dominant in the Chicago of the nineteenth and twentieth centuries. Foreshadowing the region's future foodways, pre-European diets reflected the city as a crossroads, a transit center, where people from diverse places and with diverse languages and customs engaged with one another, settled and resettled, and created cuisine and adapted and readapted to local social, political, and environmental realities.

The riparian systems that made up the Chicago Portage served various peoples at different moments in time and would eventually become a central freeway to the Mississippi. These peoples established ways of life and moved on, only to leave the land and for new groups to arrive, introducing new food-producing technologies and new forms of food distribution and consumption. For most of time, pre-European Chicago was not a place marked by long-term human settlement. Indigenous Chicagoans converted the offerings of rivers, prairies, forests, and marshlands into dietary ways that in some cases lasted hundreds and thousands of years and in others for only a handful of years. Chicago's indigenous foodways were a prototype for what the city would become—a dynamic place of mixing, substituting, and blending diets from culturally diverse origins. With an ecologically diverse terrain situated midcontinent at the base of the Great Lakes, Chicago was ripe to become an economic and cultural hub for the commodification of nature's bounty.

Prior to the arrival of Europeans, indigenous peoples did not likely envision Chicago as a place to build a metropolis, such as the ancient urban settlement of Cahokia in Southwestern Illinois across the river from present-day St. Louis. Such ideas came from the imagination of those orchestrating European colonial expansion and mercantilism. Visions of an urban gateway to the West required a French, British, and later U.S. mercantilist cultural framework that valued capital accumulation over subsistence living. Throughout the seventeenth, eighteenth, and nineteenth centuries, visions of transforming nature into wealth pushed Europeans into western North America, developing colonies and deploying merchants as a means to accumulate fur, metals, and other goods through the exploitation and commodification of natural resources.

Pre-European Chicago did not have gold or much of anything to exploit other than its location. The region's pre-European history is marked by the development of its transportation infrastructure, a system of waterways and upland indigenous trailways that over time connected peoples throughout the Midwest and beyond. Indigenous processes of transforming local flora and fauna into food and other resources such as clothing and housing depended on this transportation infrastructure for cross-fertilization of knowledge (e.g., the introduction of corn production). As we shall see in later chapters, this transit system would become the basis for Chicago emerging as a dynamic economic center, a place where the movement of food into and out of the city was not only central to regional development but also critical to the growth of the young U.S. nation and its eventual dominance in the global food system. The city's prototypical transportation infrastructure, and its inextricable links to food, is a gift to present-day residents from indigenous peoples.

To understand how Chicago became such an important national and global food hub, we need to look back to the period prior to European contact. What is known about early Chicago and its associated foodways is limited by the region's geographical and geological location as part of the ancient lake plain of Lake Chicago. For most of human history, habitation was not possible in the place we now call Chicago. Habitation, according to archaeologists, was a nonlinear process of starts and stops leaving an incomplete archaeological record filled with gaps and making it difficult to piece together the region's pre-European history. Understanding the foodways through such a record is thus difficult. It is largely an interpretive exercise based on what artifacts have been identified in proximity to the present-day city and what types of flora and fauna were known to exist prior to European contact. Archaeological literature, combined with later writings of early European and Euro-American visitors and residents, provides a glimpse of the region's pre-European foodways. Most importantly, it requires that readers be careful to not build Chicago for most of history into something more than it was: a place of seasonal and temporary settlement, a trading place, a transportation corridor, and at times a refuge.

As Tanner notes, "The vicinity of modern Chicago has never been a favored site for Indian habitation. The sand dunes and swamps, with restricted timber and agricultural land did not attract large numbers of Indian people."[1] On one hand, the region's hot, swampy summers and inhospitable winters with lake-effect winds and snow resulted in low population density. This also suggests possibly why the area was periodically a place of refuge for people fleeing conflict and intergroup hostility. On the other hand, the great ecological diversity of the lower Great Lakes and present-day northeastern Illinois provided for a vast array of flora and fauna from which human habitation could flourish. The postglacial population of birds, mammals, turtles, and fish throughout the Great Lakes Basin had been a source of sustenance and protection from the climate for indigenous groups since the emergence of the first prehistoric peoples.[2]

The first peoples likely to pass through or near present-day Chicago are referred to by archaeologists as Paleo-Indians. They are believed to have migrated to the Great Lakes region more than ten thousand years ago as glacial ice receded from central Illinois.[3] The level of the lake rose many times over what is now the area's vast urban terrain, flooding it and then drying for periods of time, suggesting to archaeologists why so little remains can be found of the earliest inhabitants of the region. Researchers know that Paleo-Indians definitely inhabited the Chicago area, however, through the discovery of what is called *fluted projectile points* used as spear points for hunting. As hunters and gatherers, these peoples are believed to have been fairly mobile, living off wildlife and whatever could be foraged around Lake Michigan, smaller lakes, in the prairies and marshlands, and along rivers and streams. Fluted points discovered near Chicago have been found mostly on the elevated moraines that surround the ancient glacial Lake Chicago.[4]

Fluted points found west of present-day Chicago and in other parts of Northern Illinois suggest a type of subsistence pattern that primarily involved foraging and the hunting of a variety of small-, medium-, and large-size animals. Faunal remains suggest that Paleo-Indians of the Western Great Lakes were taking advantage of a wide variety of mammals. Turtles, birds, fish, and freshwater mussels were also available to Paleo-Indians, who lived in small, mobile populations adjacent to rivers and lakes.[5] Little is known about the food customs of these first occupants, but various types of animal remains found near fluted points tell pieces of the food biography. The artifacts suggest a transition over time to greater consumption of white-tailed deer, a species that would become virtually extinct in the Chicago area by the late nineteeth century only to be reintroduced during the 1950s. Hunted year-round by Paleo-Indians, white-tailed deer was likely an important staple food of the region's first peoples.[6]

In general, Paleo-Indians of the Chicago region practiced seasonal hunting, ensuring food availability during harsh winter months. Fishing and hunting patterns aligned with the seasons: the spawning of fish in spring, the migration of waterfowl in spring and fall, hunting of larger mammals in fall and early winter, and the summer gathering of turtles and freshwater mussels.[7] Though little remains in terms of archaeological evidence, it can be presumed that these peoples also benefited from the diverse vegetation of the region, including various forest nuts and oil-rich seeds such as those from sunflowers, amaranth, or sumpweed. In Northwestern Illinois, archaeologists found stone tools that suggest grinding and pounding of seeds or nuts among the late Paleo-Indian populations.[8] These nutrient-dense foods, grounded and mashed into butters, seasonings, and nutmeats, would become a staple food of indigenous populations throughout the Americas. Recipes for indigenous nut-based foods can still be found published in cookbooks.[9]

There is strong evidence that approximately eight thousand to ten thousand years ago increasing floral communities emerged throughout the Western Great Lakes that provided indigenous groups with greater access to plant-based foods. Clear evidence of a shift away from Paleo-

Indian foodways in Illinois occurred during the Archaic period spanning some seven thousand years between three thousand and ten thousand years ago. The warming climate led to increased diversity of vegetation and the growth of nut-producing deciduous trees, such as oak and hickory. Human population density grew as groups built and expanded upon earlier hunting and fishing techniques by foraging and eventually cultivating a vast array of plant foods. Though hunting remained important during this period and up to and beyond European contact, the single most important shift during the Archaic period was further increase in the consumption of foraged nuts.[10]

One does not generally think of wild nuts, though still prevalent in the Chicago area, as a source of food, but Archaic peoples of northern Illinois collected, processed, and heavily consumed a variety; two of the most prevalent came from oak (acorns) and shagbark hickory trees, but others include black walnut and hazelnut. Evidence of burnt nutshell fragments and increasingly complex stone and bark tools during the Middle to Late Archaic (four thousand to five thousand years ago) era in central and southern Illinois illustrate that complex processing systems emerged to create nutmeats and other nut by-products that were transported from upland areas to lower-lying settlements along rivers and streams.[11] One site is located west of Chicago's O'Hare Airport in the area around Salt Creek, and nut trees are still found around present-day Chicago. This is reflected in names of suburbs such as Oak Park, Oak Lawn, and Hickory Hills.[12]

Though few contemporary Chicagoans view wild nuts as a source of food, Northern Illinois tree nuts were an extremely important and sustainable source of calories for Archaic peoples, who would store them for the long winter. In central Illinois, nut extraction appears to have been implemented as a method to produce large quantities of nutmeat and oil that were stored and processed at strategically planned base camps. Difficulty in predicting the location and timing of high-yield trees limited the exploitation of nuts from a single location. As a result, temporary extractive camps were established where bulk processing was followed by transport to the base camp. More complex manufacturing and storage of nuts not only improved sustenance but also brought significant changes in foodways, settlement patterns, and social structures for early Chicago residents. Women, for example, became more central to food procurement, and nut-processing methods by necessity led to longer-term settlements and likely a need for more communal planning. [13]

In addition to hunting and nut foraging, Archaic peoples of Illinois ate a number of wild fruits known by the archaeological record through the identification of carbonized seeds. [14] Consumption of fruits, bulbs, and tubers from a variety of foraged plants stretches back into the Paleo-Indian period for the Midwest. The most interesting of these foods is squash, as it appears to be the first food cultivated in Illinois. Archaeological sites of the Illinois River Valley in west-central Illinois illustrate squash production as early as the Middle Archaic period. The varieties grown, *cucurbita pepo*, are related to those grown throughout Chicago community gardens today and represent some of the earliest evidence of cultivated plant foods in the Midwest. [15] It is likely that squash seeds were transported to the region and propagated, perhaps initially for the oily seeds themselves. Squash production would represent an important shift in regional foodways by the Late Archaic period, three thousand to six thousand years ago.

Late Archaic groups in forested areas of Southern Illinois sustained themselves for millennia on the rich faunal and floral resources combining fishing, hunting, and nut and seed collection and processing. Late Archaic sites in southeastern Illinois, for example, illustrate some of the area's earliest evidence of plant domestication, including crops such as goosefoot, marshelder, and sunflower. [16] Although evidence of such plant domestication includes archaeological sites in Northern Illinois, [17] Late Archaic sites in and around present-day Chicago do not show strong evidence of plant domestication. Findings at these Chicago area sites suggest, nonetheless, longer-term settlements and advances in tool making and the increasing trade of goods during the Late Archaic. Primarily located on higher ground along marshlands and in forested areas along shorelines, these settlements remained highly dependent upon hunting and foraging, rather than plant domestication, for food consumption. [18]

Nut foraging, plant propagation, technological advances in hunting tools, and food processing and storage contributed to increased population during what archaeologists refer to as the Woodland period. Some one thousand to three thousand years in the past, native peoples of the Chicago region continued to focus heavily on hunting and gathering, but with greater sophistication and through complementary horticultural practices. The Woodland peoples of the area built elaborate effigy mounds, especially west of the present-day city, leaving remains that illustrate interregional trading systems that included subsistence goods. One such site in Chicago is in Bowmanville, near the present-day Lincoln Square neighborhood on the city's north side. The elaborate ceramics found at such mounds are considered part of the Havana Hopewell tradition that spread throughout Iowa, Missouri, and Illinois. One of the more interesting interpretations of these ceramics is their form, which suggests the use for cooking, perhaps boiling, starchy seeds into gruel. Such gruel could be used for infant weaning and/or easily stored for the winter months, hence contributing to greater sustenance. [19]

New forms of plant propagation would begin to change the landscape of the region toward the end of the Woodlands period, approximately 1,250 to 1,800 years ago, foreshadowing northern Illinois's future as an agricultural hub of the global food economy. Late Woodlands groups continued to live off prairies, marshes, and forests, developing increasingly complex ways to domesticate plants. In addition to squash production, cultivars included marshelder, sunflower, goosefoot, erect knotweed, maygrass, and little barley. [20] Viewed today as weeds or as an experimental food for urban foragers, Late Woodland peoples of the Hopewellian tradition mass-produced marshelder and goosefoot (lamb's quarter) as field crops and predecessors to maize (corn). [21] Marshelder, containing 32 percent protein and 45 percent oil, appears to have been of particular dietary importance. The food crop's disappearance, or more likely replacement by corn, may be partly because its pollen causes hayfever. [22]

Maize (*zea mays*) was cultivated in the Mississippi River Valley near East St. Louis, Illinois, as early as 170 BCE. [23] Though differing considerably from the corn Illinoisans know today, the ancient prototype would slowly become one of the food staples of the Late Woodlands residents of central and southern Illinois. Initially added to production among a variety of indigenous crops, maize would also gradually become a staple food in Northern Illinois and the Chicago area during the Mississippian period (approximately 550 to 1,100 years ago). [24] A major distinction from this period was extravagantly designed shell-tempered pottery strengthened by ground shells from freshwater mussels. Known as part of the Oneonta cultural complex that spread across the upper Midwest, the pottery's importance is in its durability for cooking maize and other starchy foods.

Indeed, maize would eventually outperform earlier seed crops through its capacity to feed growing and more sedentary populations.

Production and consumption of maize in Northern Illinois occurred at least since the end of the first millennium. Chicago-area populations first appeared to have integrated maize as a winter storage food rather than a year-round staple.[25] Evidence from what is referred to as Upper Mississippian sites suggests that groups maintained a highly diversified diet, integrating maize as part of their overall subsistence strategy. This strategy included hunting deer, bison, small mammals, turkey, and waterfowl as well as fishing and collecting wild plants and nuts and fruits, and eating turtles and mussels. Maize appears first as one of several foods; its earliest evidence near Chicago was found at the Cooke Site in northwest Cook County, established before the year 1100. The grain was found among the remains of a variety of mammals, including deer, elk, muskrat, raccoon, and beaver, with the most abundant being white-tailed deer. At a site in south suburban Oak Forest, inhabited approximately from the mid-fifteenth century through the early 1600s, maize was found with beans and squash and remnants of knotweed, goosefoot, and little barley, suggesting the continued cultivation of premaize starchy seed crops that had disappeared among Southern Mississippian peoples.[26]

The diversity of foods identified at the Oak Forest site represents one picture drawn from several Upper Mississippian archaeological sites clustered around riverways at the southwestern edge of Lake Michigan. The Des Plaines, Chicago, and Calumet rivers, waterways that today face significant ecological challenges, once teemed with aquatic life. Over the last two centuries, human impact on the rivers produced elevated levels of fecal matter, metals, various contaminants, and sedimentation, making them unsuitable as a food source. Little remains of the distinct foodways dependent upon these natural environments for millennia preceding European contact. In the centuries prior to the arrival of Europeans, Upper Mississippian peoples continued to take advantage of the region's diverse ecologies as a rich source of wildlife and plant foods. Depending on location-specific soil conditions, agricultural practices generated surplus production that, in theory, supported subsistence during winter months. Chicago-area sites were used during both summer and winter months, and discovery of food storage pits suggests sedentary habitation that may have been yearlong.[27]

Investigated by archaeologists during the 1950s, the Huber and Hoxie farm sites in south suburban Chicago are two Upper Mississippian sites clustered near the Calumet River. Residents of these sites, who may have been of the Miami tribe described later by European visitors, thrived off a rich, riverine environment. They likely engaged in Midewiwin ceremonial traditions, a religious practice shared by peoples of the Great Lakes region, that included medicinal practices to thwart off diseases and periodic starvation that was undoubtedly a part of living in Chicago's unpredictable climate. While harsh winters surely pushed some populations to migrate seasonally, nonutilitarian items, numerous storage pits, and evidence of large, permanent structures point to the possibility that such sites were permanently inhabited.[28] These settlements were complemented by smaller sites that served particular functions (e.g., ceremonial, burial, hunting, plant collecting). Regardless of the type of settlement, it is clear that residents at Huber, Hoxie Farm, and Oak Forest depended upon the diversity of natural resources and on key staples including deer, maize, starchy cultivated seeds, and beans.

When archaeologists excavated the Oak Forest site, they determined that it likely served as a seasonal farming settlement largely focused on the production of knotweed, goosefoot, and little barley. Evidence of maize, nuts, squash, and a vast array of seeds also materialized with a small quantity of the domesticated common bean (*phaseolus vulgaris*). Common beans from the Upper Mississippian period were also identified at the Knoll Spring site in the nearby suburb of Palos Hills.[29] The importance of the common bean as a staple crop for indigenous populations cannot be overstated. Along with corn and squash, these protein-rich beans completed the triad referred to by indigenous peoples as "three sisters." When cultivated and consumed together, the plants mutually benefit one another. Bean vines find support by climbing the corn stalk, while the former provides nitrogen to the soil needed by the latter. The bean plant thus supports the cornstalks during stormy weather, while the squash plant grows above the soil surface, spreading large leaves as cover to maintain ground moisture. When consumed together, the three foods offered a nutritionally rich diet of carbohydrates, proteins, and vitamin A.

Chicago's pre-European food history does not easily reduce to textbook images of seminomadic tribes roaming the landscape producing corn, beans, and squash and hunting deer. The reality is that some groups were clearly more nomadic than others and diets were much more complex and changing, never really conforming to stereotypes. The common bean that completed the "three sisters" trio didn't appear in the Chicago area until late in the Mississippian period. One theory is that an increase in corn production and storage was driven not by winter storage needs, but by demand for portable food during bison-hunting excursions.[30] Hunting of bison, or what Europeans referred to as buffalo, a name ascribed to American bison because of similarities in appearance to African and Asia buffalo, required travel to the west, southwest, or southeast of present-day Chicago. Dried meat and skins were more than likely transported to Chicago, explaining why archaeologists have found very little evidence of bison butchering in the Chicago area.

Bison hunting may have functioned as a military exercise and as a means to promote group solidarity, while infusing authority and discipline and the formation of larger and more cohesive villages with distinct tribal affiliations.[31] Communal hunting, advanced horticultural practices, and rich aquatic resources supported larger villages clustered along Chicago-area rivers and tributaries. Agriculture flourished, and durable longhouses constructed of wood poles and covered with woven mats, hides, and bark protected villagers from Chicago's unpredictable weather. Hunting territories, doubled as buffer zones between hostile groups, separated settlements. Increase in food production served the demands of growing villagers that through kinship, intermarriage, and linguistic affiliations amalgamated into tribal groups. Language and ceremonial feasts celebrating harvests and successful hunts fortified group identities. Trade of ceramics, tools, and ceremonial goods led to larger intertribal affiliations in the face of broader threats from warring parties. As Europeans began arriving in the Great Lakes region during the late seventeenth century to engage in commerce, such threats from unfriendly groups became inevitable.

CONTACT WITH EUROPEANS

Europeans brought with them new faith orientations and mercantilism with its inherent rivalries between nations seeking profit from New World resources. When French Catholic priest Jacques Marquette and his companion Louis Jolliet led the first documented group of white explorers through present-day Chicago in 1673, the area's inhabitants were already significantly transformed by the presence of Europeans in the Americas. Groups throughout the region were enmeshed in a conflict stretching from the Atlantic coast to the Mississippi and beyond. As noted earlier, Marquette and Jolliet were guided by the indigenous population to return to Green Bay by way of the Illinois and Des Plaines rivers, the Chicago Portage, the Chicago River, and into Lake Michigan. The explorers inadvertently came to understand the connection between southern Lake Michigan and the Mississippi River—today via the Chicago Sanitary and Ship Canal—that would make European control of Chicago geopolitically and commercially important. At the time, however, the Chicago area was at the crossroads of a conflict stretching all the way to New England.

Driven by the insatiable demand for pelts to send across the Atlantic to serve fashion trends in Europe, fur had far-reaching impact on peoples of the Americas well before white explorers, trappers, and settlers arrived in Northeastern Illinois. Competition between Dutch, French, and ultimately British fur traders during the mid-seventeenth century led to tension over trading territories and entangling indigenous groups throughout the Midwest into conflict that lasted for more than half a century. Primarily rooted in rivalry between the French and British, the Iroquois Wars, as the conflict came to be known, originated with trade between tribal members of the Iroquois Confederacy and the Dutch and later the English, who came to dominate the New York colony. As beaver pelts dried up in the New York region during the mid-seventeenth century, tension emerged between the Iroquois and the Huron, the latter being the primary trade partner of the French. Between 1641 and 1701, the conflict spread throughout the Great Lakes region into present-day Ohio, Michigan, Indiana, Wisconsin, and Illinois.[32]

There is very little knowledge of consistent settlements in Chicago during the time of European exploration of the area. When Marquette visited Northeastern Illinois in 1673 and again in 1674, the fur trade had already caused sweeping demographic shifts in the region. Thus, it is hard to draw direct connections between historic tribes of the region and the peoples of the Late Mississippian sites noted previously. French trading posts in the upper Great Lakes had also encouraged population shifts to the north toward Green Bay. The introduction of European goods had begun to replace indigenous stone tools and pottery even before white explorers and settlers arrived.[33] Evidence suggests that Chicago was not well populated during the latter half of the seventeenth century, as trade and conflict disrupted long-term settlement patterns.

The primary populations in northeastern Illinois at the time of Marquette's visit were Central Algonquian–speaking tribes: the Illinois Confederacy (the "Illiniwek" or "Illini"), the Potawatomi, and the Miami. They had developed trade relations with the French during the seventeenth century and experienced significant dislocation as a result of the Iroquois Wars. Other tribes that settled in the Chicago area included the Mascouten, who had had strong connections to the Potawatomi, and the Wea, with historical ties to the Miami. Although evidence suggests that the Illini once inhabited present-day Northeastern Illinois, European accounts depict them as having been pushed by the Iroquois attacks to the southwest and west of Chicago up to and at times beyond the Mississippi River.[34] Facing similar pressures, the Potawatomi, historically inhabiting the eastern shores of Lake Michigan up into northern Michigan, were pressured into northeastern and central Wisconsin and along the western shores of Lake Michigan down into present-day Illinois. The Miami, whose historical homeland was the southern end of Lake Michigan in northern Indiana, southwestern Michigan, and northern Ohio, were refugees in scattered settlements throughout Illinois and Wisconsin.[35]

The first settlements documented by Europeans in Chicago were those of the Miami (possibly the Wea tribe), who settled along the Chicago River during the 1690s. It is possible they had lived along the Chicago and Des Plaines rivers as early as the 1650s.[36] In 1696, the French established the Mission of the Guardian Angel somewhere along the Chicago River within the vicinity of present-day Chicago.[37] An account of that mission, which only lasted a few years, describes a nearby Miami village of 150 houses and a second one up the river of similar size. Description of the resident's way of life was limited, but portrayals of the Miami living as refugees in Illinois and Wisconsin are sprinkled throughout the writings of seventeenth-century French missionaries, traders, and explorers. The Miami were hunters and horticulturalists, and corn was their primary food crop for which they were well known for producing a high-quality, soft, white variety harvested in July and August.[38] While traveling through Chicago, Marquette noted an abundance of wildlife from which it is possible to discern something about the types of animals hunted by the Miami and other early residents: "During our stay at the mouth of the river, Pierre and Jacques killed three buffalo and four deer, one of which ran quite a distance with his heart cut in two. They contented themselves with killing three or four turkeys of the many which were around our cabin."[39]

In addition to corn, the Miami cultivated beans and squash, and the three "sisters" together were seen as essential to daily meals. Seventeenth-century trader Nicolas Perrot commented that if the Miami were without these foods, "they think that they are fasting, no matter what abundance of meat or fish they may have in their stores, the Indian corn to them is what bread is to Frenchmen."[40] Corn, which was largely sowed, cultivated, and harvested by women, was stored in bark-lined pits similar to those described at the Late Mississippian archaeological sites in the Chicago area.[41]

The Miami also cultivated melons and gourds and procured a wide variety of wild plants for food and medicinal purposes. In some areas, they were well known as communal bison hunters, a practice fostered by the European introduction of the horse. In Chicago proper, one can suspect that their primary hunting target was the white-tailed deer. Preservation was essential to survival and, in particular, meats, corn, and squash were dried to preserve them for winter, for traveling or fleeing attacks, and/or for general times of scarcity. The semisedentary nature of the Miami—shifting between more permanent, large summer villages along riverways to winter camps, meant corn stocks had to be in more mobile form, and corn meal, referred to by the French as "farine froide," was processed for travel.[42]

Sagamité, a common meal prepared by the Miami and other indigenous groups across the Midwest and Northeast, refers to a type of porridge or soup prepared with hulled corn, animal fat, and a variety of other possible ingredients.[43] French priest and explorer Charlevoix described sagamité as prepared "by roasting the corn, bruising it, and making it into a sort of pap, to which meat or fruit was added to give it relish."[44] European missionaries, explorers, and traders learned from indigenous populations that sagamité was a survival method since it could be easily prepared in a single pot outdoors, on an open fire with whatever ingredients were available. Dried corn stocks allowed for year-round sagamité and a variety of culinary creations depending on seasonal availability of local game, fruits and vegetables, and in some areas, wild rice. Such meals were conducive to building and strengthening community, as large pots were prepared for feasts and ceremonies.

Cultural differences in diet among pre-European groups in the Chicago area are impossible to ascertain given European colonial influence and the mixing of groups. The movement of people throughout the region at the time of contact intensified cultural hybridity between groups, and particular accounts of foodways recorded by European travelers have to be viewed as highly contextual and through a specific historical lens. Food practices documented by French travelers may have been more a product of social, economic, and political crises of the late seventeenth century than an accurate picture of longstanding foodways. Living in Chicago as refugees, the Miami were likely provisionally settled as they sought to return to their traditional homeland to the east. Because of Chicago's unique environment and history as a crossroads well before European contact, it is therefore difficult to map food practices described for the Miami in Wisconsin, Indiana, or other parts of the region onto the landscape of the present-day city.

The late seventeenth-century Miami in Chicago were part of an important trajectory of indigenous peoples in the area that would provide the basis for grievances with Europeans and eventually Americans who saw a different future for the place called Chicago (*sikaakwa*) in the Miami-Illinois language.[45] For the first half of the eighteenth century, Chicago laid at the center of continued conflict among native peoples and the French and British in the region. The Chicago River (and Portage) became a primary highway for the French in their establishment of the colony of New France. Led initially by the French explorer La Salle, the French colony expanded south of Chicago by way of the Kankakee, Chicago (Portage), Des Plaines, and Illinois rivers and ultimately the Mississippi River down to the Gulf of Mexico. Illinois was essential for expansion of the French fur trade and colony, and the British were in direct competition. As conflict ensued between the French and the Iroquois, additional tensions emerged at the onset of the eighteenth century between the French and the Mesquakie (Fox), who went to war with the French-allied Illini peoples.[46] Until the French succeeded in defeating the Mesquakie, waterways—including the Chicago route—to the Mississippi were unsafe for commerce. The Mesquakie peoples inhabited Chicago at various times during the first half of the eighteenth century, but all were temporary. Perhaps their greatest impact was the decimation of the Illini peoples (for whom Illinois is named after), who would never again sustain a significant population in Illinois.[47]

The French eventually succeeded in suppressing the Mesquakie, but the era of French domination of Illinois and Wisconsin would come to an end by midcentury. The Treaty of Paris in 1763 formally ended the Seven Years' War between Great Britain, France, and Spain (also known as the French and Indian War), the results of which were that the entire Great Lakes region up to the Mississippi River came under British control. As the Miami left the Chicago region, the Potawatomi migrated south from Wisconsin and northern Illinois into the area. By the 1760s, the Potawatomi, united with the Ottawa and Ojibwe peoples, would become the most influential tribe in Chicago. They would inhabit well-established villages at the mouth of the Chicago River and in other parts of Northeastern Illinois.[48] As a French ally, the Potawatomi resisted British control of the Chicago region as part of a conflict known as the Pontiac Wars; although mixed with several others, the tribe would be the primary population to engage European and Euro-American settlers arriving in Chicago during the early nineteenth century.[49]

Among the indigenous groups that settled in Chicago, the Potawatomi would also become the best documented. They migrated to the area from forests and lakes of northern Wisconsin and Michigan and brought with them expertise in procuring maple syrup and foraging for a variety of berries, roots, nuts, bulbs, milkweed, leafy greens, and other plant by-products. One can still find many of the wild foods consumed by the Potawatomi throughout Chicago, such as lamb's quarters, jerusalem artichoke, dandelion, wild garlic and leak, and cattail. Like their predecessors, the Potawatomi consumed red oak acorns for their starchy content as a means to enrich breads, to make soup or a porridge or gruel referred to as samp, or to accompany meat. Groundnut, a type of "wild potato" found in springs and bogs and either eaten raw, boiled, or roasted, provided another source of carbohydrates.[50] The Potawatomi also harvested wild rice in Southwestern Michigan and at Grass Lake in Lake County, Illinois, north of present-day Chicago. They likely transported and consumed the grain in Chicago during the late eighteenth century.[51]

The technological and geographic expertise of the Potawatomi allowed them to attain control over major waterways throughout the Western and Upper Great Lakes.[52] They brought to Chicago skills at constructing bark canoes that were used for fishing but that served them well as traders and guides. French traders depended upon Potawatomi canoes and geographical knowledge to expand business interests into the region. The

French relied heavily on the Potawatomi, who themselves became increasingly dependent upon trade in fur, food, and other goods; the Chicago Portage was a critical regional transit point for such trading activity.

Chicago's birth as a trading center is typically attributed to Jean Baptiste Point du Sable, who arrived in the 1770s. A man of reportedly African and possibly Haitian descent, though his actual origins remain the topic of debate, du Sable established a trading post at the mouth of the Chicago River and is known by many today as the "Founder of Chicago." He married a Potawatomi woman, establishing a pattern in the region of Potawatomi women intermarrying with nonindigenous settlers. These women would support the tribe's integration into the regional trading system, and by the end of the century, a number of families of mixed European and Potawatomi heritage established trading posts in Chicago.[53] The success of these businesses can be directly attributed to the indigenous women who, along with their kinship networks, brought expertise in native horticultural and artisanal practices.[54]

The Chicago area was only nominally under British control after 1763 until the close of the American Revolutionary War during the mid-1780s. Trade flourished among the Potawatomi, French, and the growing mixed-race (Métis) settlers. Following victory by the American colonists, the U.S. Congress passed the Northwest Ordinance establishing the Northwest Territory and U.S. control of the Great Lakes region. The new nation's intent to create new states and settle the territories led to direct conflict with indigenous populations. The Miami, Shawnee, and Potawatomi, along with several other tribes, formed a confederacy and fought under the leadership of Miami chief Little Turtle to prevent U.S. expansion west of the Ohio River. Despite having attained several decisive victories, the confederacy was defeated in 1794, and in the Treaty of Greenville in 1795 they ceded considerable territory, including present-day Ohio. As noted in the previous chapter, the treaty included an additional cession of "One piece of Land Six Miles square at the Mouth of Chickago River emptying into the Southwest end of Lake Michigan where a fort formerly stood." Thus began the next stage by which the future city of Chicago would develop. In the meantime, the site of present-day Chicago was no longer viewed by the Potawatomi as a trading post for fur and foodstuffs from the region, but as a symbol of U.S. colonialism. The U.S. government solidified this perception by building Fort Dearborn at the mouth of the Chicago River in 1803. That same year, the government purchased the Louisiana territory from France, including the Port of New Orleans.

Perhaps the most difficult outcome of the Treaty of Greenville for the Potawatomi and Miami was that the treaty would not curtail U.S. expansionism into the Northwest Territory. The colonial mentality fomented in the minds of the new nation now led by President Thomas Jefferson and his Secretary of State James Madison. Nonnative settlers and immigrants sought new land and opportunities with a heroic and spirited passion, while indigenous populations were gradually pressured to make concessions. Increasingly subjugated, the indigenous peoples were either viewed by white settlers with contempt or romanticized through simplistic characterizations of their culture and peoples that illustrated them as primitive and historical rather contemporary peoples. The latter made it all the more possible for policies that established settlement boundaries, such as the Treaty of Greenville, to be disregarded and viewed as a hindrance to Enlightenment-informed ideas about liberty, private property, and individualism. The indigenous populations with their more communal patterns of living, hunting, and farming contrasted with the colonial vision of individual farmers living on farmsteads.

Chicago lay at the heart of the U.S. strategy to expand west. It's strategic geographic position allowed for the control of commerce from the Great Lakes to the Gulf of Mexico. Within a century, the small trading outpost would be transformed into an epicenter of agricultural commerce for the country with its meatpacking industry, grain storage, and railroads. In less than two centuries, trade in agricultural commodities (corn arguably the most important) would make Chicago a financial center of the global food system. The Treaty of Greenville and the establishment of Fort Dearborn was the first stage in this process. Following the treaty, cessions were negotiated for much of south-central Illinois and then for most of northern and western Illinois, thus quickly enclosing the Potawatomi into Northeastern Illinois.[55] In 1805, a U.S. Indian Agency office was established outside Fort Dearborn to manage relations with the tribes in the region, the largest being the Potawatomi. That same year the government built a trading house or government store to provide discounted goods to the Potawatomi and began dispensing annuities and gifts to them. None of these measures seemed to change the Potawatomi's negative perception of the fort and the growing number of land concessions.[56]

By the time Fort Dearborn was built, du Sable had left Chicago, having sold his property in 1800 to John Kinzie, whose name survives on a side street running parallel to the Chicago River near the original mouth at Michigan Avenue. Kinzie and his wife moved to Chicago a few years later and lived among the Métis community. He and his partner built a successful private trading business that was deeply embedded in trade with the Potawatomi. A controversial character, Kinzie, who was born in Canada but of Scottish ancestry, had strong ties to Great Britain and the indigenous peoples but also maintained connections to U.S. officials at Fort Dearborn.[57] As relations between the settlers and indigenous peoples deteriorated, the fort became a target of attack from a growing pan-Indian movement resisting U.S. hegemony. In August of 1812, following the U.S. declaration of war against the British earlier that year, the garrison along with women and children sought to evacuate Fort Dearborn and retreat to Fort Wayne. Potawatomi warriors, in what came to be known as the Battle of Fort Dearborn, attacked them, the fort was destroyed, and Chicago was reduced to a place scarcely populated until 1816, when the U.S. government returned to rebuild. Potawatomi leaders spared the lives of Kinzie and his family, who were escorted out of Chicago.

Historical figures like Kinzie are important for understanding how Chicago's early foodways were enmeshed in the social upheaval resulting from conflict between indigenous peoples and European and U.S. colonial powers. Competition to control trade routes and good hunting territories combined with increasing dependency on imported trade goods significantly altered indigenous patterns of subsistence. Metal pots, utensils, and bowls replaced pottery making and woodworking, and corn production increasingly served the consumption needs of white settlers.[58] Potawatomi and other groups struggled to maintain a way of life and identity in the face of unyielding colonization. Whether European, American, or Métis, traders like Kinzie provided the economic machinery for these transformations, connecting the lifeways of indigenous peoples to financial networks spanning eastern North America to Europe and Asia. The power of these networks worked against indigenous ways of life. The rise of Chicago as a food marketplace in the mid-nineteenth century had much to do with the specific history of attempts at eradicating indigenous peoples from the region.

The first third of the nineteenth century was characterized by a series of battles, wars, and treaties that ultimately resulted in the removal of all

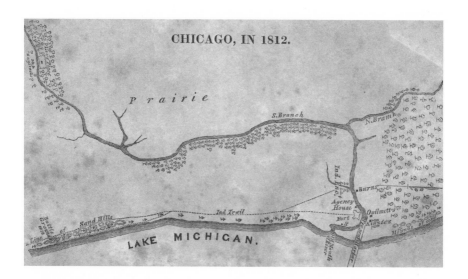

Figure 2.1. Juliette Kinzie, daughter of John Kinzie, included this map in her 1844 narrative of the 1812 Battle of Fort Dearborn. Newberry Library, Case Ruggles 209.

substantial indigenous groups to areas west of the Mississippi. They did not leave quietly, however. The Battle of Fort Dearborn, also called the Fort Dearborn Massacre, is usually remembered for its violence against whites (twenty-six army regulars, twelve militia, two women, and twelve children were killed, with the remaining regulars, women, and children taken prisoner), but it also was a victory for the indigenous peoples as part of a decades-long struggle. Even before the reestablishment of the fort in 1816, settlers continued to move back into the region. By 1832, as a result of numerous treaties and continued white settlement, many indigenous groups had been pushed out of the region. In April of that year, defying a treaty that banished them to west of the Mississippi, the Sac and Fox, led by Black Hawk, crossed back into Illinois, precipitating the Black Hawk War, which included an initial victory by Black Hawk's band as well as numerous raids on area forts. When the Potawatomi, Menominee, and Dakota to the west failed to support the insurgency, however, most of Black Hawk's band returned across the river or were killed or captured by U.S. troops or enemy indigenous groups.

The Black Hawk War was short-lived, and the closest battles to Chicago were about a hundred miles to the west. Yet the effect of the conflict

Figure 2.2. The village of Chicago in 1832 was centered around the taverns at Wolf's Point at the confluence of the north and south branches of the Chicago River. It remained a place of ethnic mixing. In this image, Elijah Wentworth's tavern is on the left, and the Miller Brothers' tavern is on the right. Chicago Public Library Special Collections and Preservation Division, GP-Smith 200.

on Chicago and U.S. Indian policy was significant. Chicago was used as a refuge for settlers in the region afraid of Black Hawk's band, many of whom fled even from those indigenous peoples opposed to Black Hawk. The city's population temporarily surged, and food shortages followed. Early meatpacker Archibald Clybourne, among others, made a name for himself by providing meat to those gathered in the fort.[59] Health problems became even more acute and outstripped the danger from the war itself. Numerous soldiers sent to Illinois from Buffalo for the war developed cholera both on the ships that took them to Fort Dearborn and once they arrived. They brought "a peril before which the menace of the hostile Indians paled into insignificance."[60] Combating the cholera epidemic of 1832 can be thought of as the settlement's first public health effort, and it involved residents both at the fort and its surroundings.

As a consequence of the conflict, the United States changed its Indian policy to one that specifically focused on the removal of indigenous peoples from areas of settlement, particularly of northern Illinois, rather than negotiating for the sale of particular pieces of land. The Sac and Fox, as well as the Ho-Chunk (Winnebago), who sympathized with them, were expelled by the treaty to Iowa (in the Sac and Fox's case) and Wisconsin (in the Ho-Chunk's case). The Potawatomi and their allies who had not allied with Black Hawk and even assisted in the battle against his band were brought to Chicago in September 1833, a month after the new town was incorporated. Known as the Treaty of Chicago, a council met, made up of thousands of people from multiple tribes as well as white speculators intent on profiting from land deals. After delaying for a while, the Potawatomi agreed to take five million acres of land west of the Mississippi and payments of close to a million dollars in exchange for approximately five million acres in northeastern Illinois and southwestern Michigan. About half of the payments were paid as an annuity to tribal members, given as development projects, paid in goods supplied by traders, or by gifts of land from the U.S. government to specific people. Many (but not all) of the recipients were traders in the area, some of whom were Métis, others of whom had indigenous wives or relations. Not coincidently, those granted these direct payments were almost exclusively also signatories to the treaty.

Northern Illinois was in September 1833 basically "cleared" of indigenous peoples. While the exact date the Potawatomi had to leave was three years later, they now seldom appeared in the new town. White farmers had actually been moving into northern Illinois for about ten years, but now the region was truly open for settlement. At the same time, payments and gifts of land had been made to many of the local business people, and the building of the Illinois and Michigan Canal was soon to commence. Speculators began to pour in, and the town went from an estimated population of 150 in 1832 to 350 in 1833. By 1834, the population had risen to 1,800, and then to 3,265 the next year.[61] Within two months following the treaty, the number of "regular stores" carrying foodstuffs rose from approximately five to twenty. An 1837 census showed twenty-seven groceries along with nineteen grocery and provision stores.[62] In one week in 1834, seven new buildings were added.[63] The foodscape of Chicago no longer resembled its indigenous past. It is often the case that indigenous foodways are romanticized as aligned with nature, and the people themselves are perceived as part of the "natural" landscape, rather than seen as innovators and experts in living on the land sustainably for millennia. Though in time indigenous peoples would return to Chicago and create a vibrant and sustained urban community, at least for the time being they and their foodways were forcibly removed from the landscape.

3

MIGRATION AND THE MAKING
OF CHICAGO FOODWAYS

Chicago, a bubbling melting pot of practically all the principal races in the world, offers splendid opportunities for gastronomical gallivantings in foreign fields. On the north side you will find the large German area, with its many eating houses, and the Swedish district; northwest, along Milwaukee Avenue, lie the Polish and Russian quarters; on the west side exists most of the foreign quarters—Greek, Mexican, Italian, Jewish, Roumanian, and Bohemian; the Chinese, Arab, and Japanese neighborhoods are found on the near south side; in the Loop are an English chop house and a corned beef and cabbage restaurant favored by the Irish; and just north of the Loop are two Filipino restaurants, as well as a number of French eating places.

—John Drury, *Dining in Chicago*, 1931

The influence of migrants on Chicago's foodways began from its very beginning. The 1830s was a turbulent decade in Chicago's early history. The removal of the indigenous population and departure of the Metís and their replacement by white settlers forever changed the sociocultural landscape of the region. Some of the Metís families acquired land as part of the Treaty of Chicago, but for the most part the area was open to new settlers. This process had been underway for some time, and even before the Treaty of Chicago, in 1831, the Illinois General Assembly created Cook County, making Chicago, with only one hundred and some residents, the county seat. Growth from a sleepy fur trading post to a bustling town under development, however, would not have happened if not for the government-funded military road between Detroit and Fort Dearborn. Following the route of the native Sauk Trail, the road facilitated the transport of people and cargo to and from downtown Detroit. Detroit's importance was in its proximity to Lake Erie and thus to the Erie Canal (completed in 1825) and ultimately the entire Eastern Seaboard. Construction of the "Chicago Road," as it would become known, started in Detroit in the 1820s and would be completed in Chicago by 1835 in the heat of the town's boom. Migration to Chicago in stagecoaches from the East rapidly increased the town's population during the 1830s and 1840s. By 1835, the population had risen to 3,265.[1] By midcentury the population would reach almost thirty thousand. In 1850, half of Cook County residents were born outside the United States, with most from Ireland, Germany, England, and Scotland. British and Scottish immigrants and their descendants had a particularly strong influence on Chicago's early days. Settler John Kinzie was himself of Scottish descent.

The Treaty of Chicago opened lands in Northern Illinois to more East Coast speculators who benefited from U.S. expansionism. They were partly driven by Chicago's infamous boosters, who promoted the town as a future metropolis, a "central city" and "great marketplace" guaranteed by the nature that surrounded it.[2] In the nineteenth century, the railroad would connect Chicago to natural resources across the continent, positioning the city at the center of the U.S. food system. The labor to make this happen would come from migration, the largest groups—but by no means the only—being the Irish, Germans, Polish, and later African Americans. Each group contributed distinct culinary practices, but their overall contributions were much larger than producing a city of diverse "ethnic foods." The masses that migrated to Chicago from vastly diverse parts of the world labored in Chicago food factories, restaurants, and streets to bring food to the city, region, and beyond. When they returned home to their neighborhoods, usually ethnic enclaves, they would make and eat food that would make the city one of the most gastronomically diverse on the planet. Chicago became and remains a city of neighborhoods often characterized by cultural traits of particular groups. Like all U.S. cities, the story of Chicago's foodways is a story primarily of migration, but what makes the city unique is its geography as a juncture, a meeting place where transportation by water, train, roads, and eventually airplanes would make it the food capital of the Midwest.

English, Welsh, and Scottish settlers and their descendants would become members of the property-owning class that would help build early Chicago by raising capital for large engineering works. Other migrants from Great Britain were skilled laborers, merchants, and professionals, and in 1850 they made up 16 percent of the city's population. Along with New Englanders and other English-speaking American-born transplants, merchants from the British Isles invested in the downtown area along Lake Street, turning it into a commercial center for shopping and services. By the 1840s, English, Welsh, and Scottish businessmen organized ethnic associations, the first being developed by the Scots. Established in 1846 and still in operation in the 2000s, the St. Andrew Society is the oldest charitable nonprofit in Illinois. A year earlier, the Scottish national dish, haggis, a pudding traditionally prepared with the heart, liver, and other sheep organs mixed with onions and oats and boiled in a sheep's stomach, was likely on the menu at the first St. Andrew's Day celebration in November 1845, held at the upscale Lake House Hotel and featuring oysters. Migrants from New England brought enough desire for oysters that they made them practically a staple food by the 1850s, and Chicago hosted oyster depots and saloons throughout the city. The serving of oysters as pub food continues in Chicago drinking establishments, a practice that partly has origins in the oyster craze of the mid-nineteenth century. Likewise, the St. Andrew Society still holds their "Feast of Haggis" annually at one of Chicago's downtown luxury hotels.[3]

On the city's North Side, the Duke of Perth, a Scottish pub opened in 1989, boasts haggis wings that are "the city's largest." And although a version of haggis was popularized in recent years by the late Chicago chef Charlie Trotter, traditional haggis consumption is significantly curtailed by federal policy that, since 1971, bans a key ingredient, sheep lung, which the government does not consider to be food. Nonetheless, Scottish and Scottish American influences on the city are scattered throughout the area, etched in the names of streets and suburbs and numerous restaurants and pubs. Perhaps the largest Scottish American imprint on Chicago's food history, however, lies in the city's influential early residents. This included Cyrus McCormick, whose mechanical reaper arguably contributed to transforming grain agriculture and the entire Midwestern region into a breadbasket. Also included is Philip Armour, whose meatpacking business would help establish Chicago as the meatpacking capital of the United States. Yet in time, Scottish immigrants increasingly became a minority in the growing city as massive demand for human labor ensued in order to complete large-scale infrastructural projects. A sizable body of laborers became essential for building Chicago, more importantly for constructing its transportation system made up of canals and railroads.[4]

THE IRISH

The Northwest Ordinance forbade slavery in the Northwest Territory in 1787, though it persisted in various forms in Illinois. Even after Illinois was admitted to the Union as a free state in 1818, free blacks experienced oppression through laws that made it difficult for them to live in the state. Even though Chicago became a seat in the abolitionist movement and Illinois constitutionally banned slavery, entrance of blacks into the state remained difficult under Illinois Black Laws that severely limited their settlement.[5] The masses of indigenous peoples, even if they could have been prospects for a labor pool, had been removed from the landscape. Hence, to resolve Chicago's labor shortage, town's boosters recruited immigrants from Europe. Recruiters, largely Eastern capitalist from New York, marketed a vision of Chicago as a future great Western frontier metropolis. Among them was William Ogden, a businessman who moved to Chicago from New York in 1836 to make money from soaring land prices. Along with fellow New York investors, Ogden raised money for the Illinois and Michigan Canal that would connect Lake Michigan via the Chicago River and Portage to the Mississippi and Gulf of Mexico. The project, which required a large pool of mobile labor, commenced in 1836 and was completed in 1848. Laborers were from a variety of racial and ethnic backgrounds, but the majority were Irish Catholic immigrants. By midcentury the Irish were fleeing the potato famine in Ireland, and they would become Chicago's largest immigrant group.

In the summer of 1836, Ogden advertised for laborers, and Irish immigrants responded en masse, eventually settling in Canalport (later Bridgeport). The village and emerging city neighborhood would become the epicenter of Chicago's Irish community. That same year Ogden helped write the charter making Chicago officially a city for which he was elected the first mayor. Ironically, the South Side neighborhood that Ogden helped produce would itself produce five Irish American mayors. By

1850, the pull of work on the canal, among other factors, made the 6,096 Irish immigrants 20 percent of Chicago's population and 40 percent of the foreign born. Twenty years later their numbers reached forty thousand, and by the turn of the century the number of first- and second-generation Irish Chicagoans was 237,478. Needless to say, the cultural, economic, and eventually political imprint of the Irish on early Chicago cannot be overstated. Chicago elected its first Irish Catholic mayor in 1893 when the majority of Irish households continued to subsist on manual labor—building canals and railroads and working in meatpacking plants, shipyards, and steel mills. In time, the Irish produced generations of Chicago politicians, police officers, fireman, priests, teachers, and nurses educated through Catholic schools. During the twentieth century, many second- and third-generation Irish immigrants attended Catholic universities such as Notre Dame, DePaul, and Loyola University Chicago, and they entered white-collar professions and moved into the middle class. Although their geographic presence became increasingly dispersed throughout the city and suburbs, cohesiveness as Irish Chicagoans persisted. Many derived their identity through the Catholic Church and communities built through parishes. A strong sense of nationalism prevailed, as did a historical memory of poverty and anti-Irish and Catholic discrimination both in Ireland and during their early days as a community in Chicago.

The cultural impact of Irish immigrants on Chicago foodways remains obvious to most Chicagoans. The seemingly ubiquitous Irish pubs and eateries are a reminder of the city's deep Irish past and persisting present. Chicago held its first St. Patrick's Day parade in 1843, and since the 1960s the famed event is known internationally for dyeing the Chicago River green and for a festive pub scene. The Irish pub was and remains one of the centers of the community's social and political life, what the former president of Chicago's Irish American Heritage Center stated as "a place to connect with family members and other immigrants, a place to find a job, a place to play some music, or just somewhere to provide a small sense of home."[6] Food was a central component of that sense of home. Irish corned beef and cabbage, a pub staple and tradition on St. Patrick's Day, can mistakenly be oversimplified and act as a caricature of Irish cuisine in Chicago and elsewhere. A common belief is that Irish immigrants in places such as Chicago, Boston, and New York popularized corned beef as Irish food. In fact, recent Irish food scholars have argued that corned beef has long been an aristocratic food in Ireland and that its popularity among Irish immigrants was due to availability at an affordable price.[7] It is not surprising then that Chicago's late nineteenth-century South Side Irish saloons—in the heart of Midwestern meatpacking capital—served corned beef and cabbage and that some offered free lunch to poorly paid workers who would remain loyal to their local drinking spot. As a second home, the pub was a place to relish in comfort foods but also to organize as workers, who often produced the very same meats they consumed. Consequently, many Irish Chicagoans still maintain loyalty to the pubs patronized by their parents and grandparents who found solidarity and a sense of cultural cohesiveness there.

IMMIGRANTS FROM GERMANY

The impact of Irish immigration on Chicago was far-reaching. In 1898, German immigrant Herman Berghoff opened Berghoff's Pub, which remains a downtown Chicago establishment on Adams Street. The bar and restaurant claims that it got its start "serving free corned beef sandwiches with the purchase of a stein."[8] Before they built their own pubs, the Irish patronized German-owned establishments.[9] Nineteenth-century German migration to Chicago paralleled and at one point outweighed that of the Irish, and immigrants from both countries interacted within industries and city neighborhoods. Before the end of the century, Germans would surpass the Irish in number and would become the city's largest immigrant group. After the Napoleonic Wars ended in 1815, the struggling German economy and various periods of political unrest spurred German immigration to the United States. During the 1830s, men left Germany to avoid conscription in the army; German migration to Chicago spiked as farmers, artisans, entrepreneurs, and laborers were lured to the Midwest from eastern states by access to land and work opportunities, often through direct recruitment by investors and governments. Wisconsin, Minnesota, and Michigan financially supported German resettlement. German farmers settled in Central and Northern Illinois as Chicago emerged as a distribution hub following the completion of the Illinois and Michigan Canal that, alongside the Irish, German laborers helped construct. By 1850, 32 percent of Chicago's immigrant population of 15,682 was originally from Germany. A decade later, Germans would surpass the Irish

Figure 3.1. Saloon run by P. H. Keegan in 1901 at 1957 W. Madison, now 3938 W. Madison. Chicago Public Library, Special Collections and Preservation Division, WGP 2.4.

with 41 percent of the immigrant population that totaled more than fifty-four thousand. By the time Berghoff's opened in 1898, one of every four Chicagoans was either born in Germany or was first-generation German American.

German impact on the city's early foodways far exceeded the introduction of weissbier. It is almost hard to fully grasp the group's influence on Chicago's foodways because of their omnipresence at all levels of the city's nineteenth-century food economy. Germans were factory laborers and owners, skilled craftsman, machinists, sausage makers, butchers, bakers, beer brewers, and wholesale grocers. They were millionaires and worker's movement organizers, capitalists, and socialists. Diversity of religions and regional origins also made the German community culturally diverse and politically animated. By the 1860s, German social organizations opened, including the German Aid Society and the Germania Club; public schools were offering German language programs; and the city hosted several German-language newspapers. With roots in the failed revolutions of 1848 ("the March Revolution") that fought repressive political structures emerging from the fall of Holy Roman Empire, working-class German immigrants engaged in the development of Chicago's union organizations—especially in the meatpacking plants—through much of the late nineteenth and early twentieth centuries.

German enclaves were scattered across Chicago near industry, with the largest enclaves in Lincoln Park and Lakeview as well as in parts of the South Side. Railroads, agricultural trade and distribution, and meatpacking fueled the economies of such neighborhoods. Food commodities, whether for livestock or human consumption, were at the core of Chicago's nineteenth-century economy, and German immigrants touched every end of the process from production to consumption. At McCormick's Reaper Works, German workers participated in producing machinery that became almost a necessity for newly settled farmers—many of whom were German—which revolutioned grain production.[10] German laborers and skilled workers were vital to railroad construction but also to farming wheat and corn and packing the meat that made Chicago a primary node in an increasingly integrated U.S. food system.

In 1848, the same year as the Illinois and Michigan Canal was completed, Ogden orchestrated the construction of the Galena and Chicago Union Railroad and, as with the canal, it was built largely by Irish and German workers. The railroads would spur the further development and centralization of Chicago's infamous meatpacking industry. Chicago's Union Stock Yard opened in 1865 and was a major draw for another wave of immigrant workers, initially from Europe. Residents of Packingtown lived in the adjacent "Back of the Yards" neighborhood to the south and west of the stockyards, an area settled by Irish and German immigrants who found work in butchering and packing hogs and cattle. By 1880, 36 percent of Chicago's butchers were German, and of the 32 percent of butchers that were American born it is likely that most were of German and Irish ancestry. Given the working conditions at the Stock Yards, famously illuminated in Upton Sinclair's novel *The Jungle*, and the history of German labor organizing in Europe, it is not surprising that German laborers played a central position in organizing meatpacking workers. German meatpackers would play a key role in the struggle for an eight-hour workday that in 1886 led to the violent clash between police and protesters known as the Haymarket Affair. The Affair, which for many symbolizes the birth of the modern labor movement and which gave rise to the American Federation of Labor, occurred in the heart of the city's wholesale food market district just blocks from branch offices of meatpacking moguls Philip Armour, Gustavus Swift, and Nelson Morris.

Chicago's first Jewish residents were also almost all from Germany, and though they would be considered by many as "German Jews" they created a distinct Jewish community and set of social structures. Jews began settling in Chicago during the 1840s as peddlers and merchants of clothing, shoes, and food, among other goods around the intersection of Lake and Clark streets. Chicago's first Jewish synagogue, Kehilath Anshe Maariv, would construct its first building at the corner of Clark and Quincy.[11] The community of German-speaking Jews would continue to grow during the mid-nineteenth century along with the German immigrant population. By the time of the Great Fire in 1871, there was an estimated four thousand Jews in Chicago with ten synagogues. An 1870 directory lists "dry goods" as the number-one Jewish occupation, and Jews were known to have been heavily involved in retail and wholesale markets, including those involving food. After the fire, the community began rebuilding in South Side neighborhoods and to a lesser degree on the North Side, building synagogues such as Anshe Emet in the largely German-speaking neighborhood around Division and Wells. The South Side Jewish community would eventually center around the Kenwood–Hyde Park neighborhood, while the North Side Jews would move up the lakefront into Lakeview and Edgewater.

One of those German Jewish immigrants was Nelson Morris, who in 1848 came to the United States as Moritz Beissinger, a ten-year-old from a small town in southern Germany. His name was changed to Nelson Morris, and as a young man he traveled from the East Coast up the Erie Canal to Chicago where he worked in a stockyard at 30th and Cottage Grove. At the start of the Civil War, Morris was successful enough to be awarded a contract with the government to supply meat to the war zone, and he went on to purchase his own slaughterhouse at 31st Street near the Lake. Nelson Morris and Company would become one of those original stockyards that relocated to the Union Stock Yards in 1865, and by the 1880s the company would have plants throughout the Midwest. Employing over 3,700 people, the company owned their own refrigerated freight cars, ranches, and processing plants across the United States. Morris's son, Edward, married the daughter of Gustavus Swift, and after Edward's death he would eventually sell the company to Armour and Company in 1922.[12] Another German Jewish immigrant, Isaac Osherovitz, started a matzo and wine company in Cincinnati in 1886 and then moved the company to Chicago in 1925. He and his sons opened up Best's Kosher Sausage Company near the Stock Yards and built the company into a kosher hot dog empire. Eventually supplying hot dogs for all of the major sporting events across the city, the company was bought by Sara Lee in 1993 and closed in 2008. "The End of a Chicago Tradition: Is Absolutely Nothing Sacred?" was the title of an article published in the *Chicago Tribune* by Osherovitz's great granddaughter in 2009.[13]

Many German immigrants, both Jewish and non-Jewish, were skilled sausage makers, a talent inherited from generations of culinary craftsmanship in Germany dating at least from the Middle Ages. The Chicago sausage factories of the late nineteenth century were not only infamous for their lack of hygiene but also for cost cutting through mechanization. German sausage craftsman struggled against the elimination of their jobs, and perhaps nowhere else did the age-old art of sausage making clash with industrialization than in Chicago. The city's meatpacking industry gave rise to the national—eventually international—distribution of sausages grounded partly in German ingenuity and its integration into modern industrialism and mechanized assembly-line production. German-speaking immigrants owned some of the most prominent sausage companies in Chicago. Chicago Jewish butcher David Berg is listed in the 1866 city directory as in business with his brother Adolph's meat market, and David Berg & Company, now owned by Vienna, holds the USDA Inspection Approval #1.[14]

The popular Oscar Mayer brand of products also got started during the 1880s. German immigrant Oscar Mayer came to Chicago in the 1870s, and after gleaning knowledge from working in Chicago's stockyards, he and his brother—trained as a sausage maker in Germany—opened a meat market in 1883. Located on Chicago's North Side, they began selling sausages to the predominantly German community.[15] Eventually, the company would distribute citywide, nationally, and internationally. By the mid-twentieth century, Oscar Mayer hot dogs (the infamous "Oscar Mayer weiner"), bacon, bologna, and other products became a household name in the United States by running some of the most successful advertising campaigns in the history of marketing. Oscar Mayer jingles still ring through the minds of Americans born in the 1950s and 1960s (e.g., "my bologna has a first name, it's O-S-C-A-R"; and "Oh, I'd love to be an Oscar Mayer wiener"). Oscar Mayer bologna became standard sandwich filler for school lunches nationwide during the mid-twentieth century, as did Butternut brand bread slices that surrounded it. The inventor of Butternut Bread, Paul Schulze, was a German immigrant who built Schulze Baking Company in Chicago's South Side Washington Park neighborhood. Schulze eventually sold the bakery to Interstate Bakeries Corporation, which would become the largest wholesale bread distributor in the United States. Oscar Mayer Company would be sold to Kraft Foods, which started in Chicago at the beginning of the twentieth century by a Canadian of German ancestry.

In a similar manner to Oscar Mayer, the company Vienna Beef started in Chicago as the Vienna Sausage Manufacturer by German-speaking Austrian Jewish immigrants who, along with other sausage vendors, sold all-beef hot dogs at the 1893 World's Columbian Exposition. The company did so well serving sausages at the Exposition that they bought a permanent location at 417 South Halsted, in the Maxwell Street neighborhood, and eventually moved to a plant on Damen and Fullerton on the North Side.[16] Although clearly not invented in Chicago (New York's Coney Island claims that right), the hot dog owes a great deal to German-speaking immigrants in Chicago who understood the profit-making power of a tube of processed meat by-products on a bun. The original German "frankfurter," a fully cooked sausage, changed to "hot dog" during World War I to de-emphasize its German origin, somehow became a quintessential Chicago food. After World War II, "hot dog stands" advertising "Vienna Beef" became ubiquitous in Chicago. For many residents, the iconic Chicago-style hot dog is only authentic with a Vienna Beef hot dog prepared on a S. Rosen's poppy seed bun. S. Rosen's got its start in 1909 on Chicago's North Side by a Polish Jewish immigrant (reflecting a second wave of European Jewish immigrants) who, according to the company's website, trained as an apprentice baker in Germany before immigrating to the United States.

Thanks to Chicago's German-speaking immigrants, Chicago has partly built its food image around the hot dog. Along with a pint at Berghoff's, tourists consider the Chicago-style hot dog a "bucket list" experience. Beer, Chicago-style hot dogs, and baseball underdogs (Cubs or White Sox) are characteristically Chicago. The underlying cultural and

Figure 3.2.   Jos. Kohler's Lake View Exchange, 1083 N. Halsted, now 2350 N. Halsted, ca. 1883. Chicago History Museum, Joseph T. Ryerson Collection of Chicago Storefronts and Residences, i35949.

historical foundation of this popular characterization lies partly in the hands of German-speaking sausage makers and craft beer brewers who brought their ingenuity to the city along with a sensibility that appreciated building and celebrating community around good food and drink. Alongside sausage makers and bakers, German beer brewers were once scattered throughout Chicago's North Side. German immigrants William Haas and Konrad Sulzer opened the city's first brewery in 1833, and Chicago's first mayor William Ogden was part owner. Eventually the brewery was owned by French immigrant Michael Diversey, whose name remains on a major North Side street, and William Lill. The Lill and Diversey Brewery or "the Chicago Brewery" was one of nineteen breweries destroyed by the Chicago fire in 1871.[17] Another of these breweries was started by John A. Huck, a German immigrant, who, in 1847, opened a North Side brewery producing a highly desired lager beer. Beer historian Bob Skilnik noted that "Huck's product was the precursor of the type of beer most Chicagoans enjoy today."[18] The brewery was situated in a square block bounded by Chicago Avenue, Rush Street, Superior Street, and Cass (now Wabash), and by 1871 it became the largest brewer in the West. According to Chicago's German-language newspaper, *Illinois Staats-Zeitung*, "much of the vacant part of the plot was used as a picnic ground where many of the German clubs and societies of that day gathered for their annual outings."[19] By the end of the century, German beer brewers and wholesalers dominated the industry, and a quarter of the city's revenues came from alcohol production.[20]

German breweries of the late nineteenth century served what seemed to be an unquenchable demand by Chicago's growing working-class immigrant communities. Barrels were delivered by horse and carriage throughout the city and suburbs, requiring the breeding of more horses and harvesting more ice to keep the lager beer cold. As a reflection of this success, in 1872 German immigrant John Siebel opened a school for brewing sciences, the Siebel Institute of Technology, that remains in existence today. A year earlier, however, the Great Chicago Fire hit brewers hard, and the industry, facing deep competition from German brewers in Milwaukee, would never fully recover. Nevertheless, the first wave of what today would be considered a craft beer industry occurred in Chicago that by 1900 would host sixty breweries, most of which were German owned. The German community would itself revel in their local brews consumed in numerous taverns and beer gardens throughout the city. This sensibility would clash with the city's Anglo-centric, American-born followers of the temperance movement. As early as 1855, Chicago mayor Levi Boone, the great nephew of Daniel Boone, attempted to enforce a law forbidding taverns from opening on Sundays. The largely German and Irish population of the city wouldn't have it, leading to what became known as the Lager Beer Riots. Countering Boone's efforts, German breweries and beer gardens passionately expanded in number during subsequent decades, forever changing the food and drink landscape of Chicago.

The seemingly ubiquitous presence of German cuisine in early Chicago, creating the city's first "ethnic" food, was inextricably linked to breweries that often owned or leased the businesses.[21] On the South Side this phenomenon was anchored in Old Vienna, a German-style beer garden opened in 1894 following the World's Columbian Exposition that hosted both German and Austrian villages. The site would eventually become the popular San Souci amusement park (named after the palace of Prussian king Frederick the Great) and later Midway Gardens designed by Frank Lloyd Wright. Opened in 1914 and encompassing a city block, Midway Gardens was sold two years after and became the German-owned Schoenhofen Brewing Company, maker of the once popular Edelweiss beer, during a time when Germans faced unpopularity as a result of World War I. Renamed Edelweiss Gardens, the business would face additional difficulties as a result of Prohibition before being sold again and demolished in 1929. Overcoming the war years, Chicagoans' interest in German cuisine and beer would continue to flourish, and in 1934 the German Eitel brothers opened the Old Heidelberg Inn on Randolph Street. The restaurant, located a handful of blocks from the Eitels' luxurious Bismarck Hotel (opened in 1894), would become a landmark for decades among Chicago's downtown restaurants. Designed to resemble a traditional German village, including a depiction of King Gambrinus, the purported inventor of beer, the now-closed restaurant's façade withstood the development of skyscapers and eventually became the face of Argo Tea Cafe.

German beer and food were nowhere more present than in immigrant enclaves established in the North Side neighborhoods of Old Town, Lincoln Park, and Lakeview. German food–oriented establishments were heavily concentrated along North Avenue in Lincoln Park, once deemed the "German Broadway," as well as along north-south corridors such as Southport Avenue, Halsted Street, and most prominently Lincoln Avenue. Beer gardens where community members relaxed on Sunday afternoons developed into restaurants and entertainment centers. Much to the disgust of the followers of the temperance movement, the German beer garden was almost considered a Chicago institution. In 1900, Royal L. Melendy wrote on Chicago saloons in the *American Journal of Sociology*:

> To the German the word "beer-garden" carries with it no moral idea whatever; indeed, among them it is a highly creditable feature of their social life. To the temperance enthusiast it stands for all that is base and low—an equally erroneous conviction. [22]

Melendy noted that the typical German beer garden accommodated 4,700. Perhaps the most famous of these gardens, Bismarck Gardens, opened in 1894. Where during the 2000s stands an International House of Pancakes at the corner of Halsted and Grace in the Lakeview neighborhood was once the Midwest's most popular beer garden and summer entertainment venue. Partly undercut by unpopularity of German-owned establishments during World War I and partly a victim of Prohibition, the establishment changed its name to the less German-sounding Marigold Gardens, and it was eventually sold in 1923 and subsequently closed. Most of the site was sold to a church in 1963. [23]

The legacy of Bismarck Gardens lives on—albeit at a lesser scale—in the numerous beer gardens that still dot the North Side of Chicago. Alongside beer gardens, German restaurants and bakeries still serve Chicago's North Side residents. The highly popular Dinkel's Bakery, opened in 1922 on Lincoln Avenue in Lakeview, is a reminder of the once heavily German neighborhood. Just up the street is Paulina Market, an old-style butcher shop that boasts a dozen or so varieties of bratwurst. Farther north on Lincoln Avenue, one can follow the Chicago German community's historical migration into the Lincoln Square neighborhood. On Lincoln Avenue just south of Lawrence (a stretch of Lincoln that is now a pedestrian-friendly one-way street) is what might today be considered the epicenter of Chicago German culture with beer gardens, restaurants, and cafes. The nearby DANK Haus German American Cultural Center opened in 1959. The Center hosts an exhibit "Lost German Chicago," which contains artifacts from the Delicatessen Meyer that served Lincoln Square from the mid-1950s until it closed in 2006. The German-owned deli was famous throughout Chicago for Leberkäse, a Bavarian-baked loaf made from a mixture of ground meats and onion. At the site of Delicatessen Meyer today is the Polish-owned Gene's Sausage Shop & Delicatessen, reflecting both a continued demand for locally made sausages in the now relatively affluent North Side neighborhood and the story of the ethnic transformation of Chicago.

POLES

There is no longer a German immigrant enclave in Chicago, and North Side neighborhoods once inhabited by the community have gone through significant ethnic transformation and more recently gentrification. Reaching the ranks of the middle class, Germans dispersed into the suburbs, a process prompted as much by their success in business, the arts, and education as by challenges faced as an ethnic enclave during and following both World Wars. The transformation of German neighborhoods began as early as the late nineteenth century as Polish immigrants began to settle alongside German and Bohemian residents in large numbers. Pushed by economic challenges, Poles left their country en masse; referred to as *Za Chlebem* (for bread), they were pulled by Chicago's late nineteenth-century demand for labor.[24] By 1892, when Poles still constituted a small percentage of the city's foreign-born residents relative to the Germans and Irish, there were already six Polish-language publications in Chicago. By 1910, Poles made up 16 percent of Chicago's immigrant population, and by 1920 that number would rise to 17 percent, surpassing Germans as the largest immigrant group in the city. That status would be maintained throughout much of the century through two additional waves of Polish immigration until Mexicans surpassed Poles as the largest immigrant group during the 1980s. In the 1930 census, having almost doubled in number over twenty years, Poles made up 12 percent of the total Chicago population. Chicago became the largest Polish city outside of Warsaw, with major enclaves on the South, Southeast, Southwest, and Northwest sides. The Northwest Side neighborhood of West Town became the community's cultural and commercial center, referred to as the Polish downtown ("Polonia"), but Polish commercial areas could be found adjacent to most major industrial complexes. Back of the Yards became predominantly Polish as Poles, recruited to Chicago during the 1880s as strikebreakers, increasingly took on work at the Union Stock Yards; South Chicago, near the Illinois-Indiana border, had a strong Polish community supported by jobs in the steel mills along the southern coast of Lake Michigan.

Steel mills may not seem like an obvious pillar of the food industry, but the Chicago mills got their start producing rails for the railroads that were booming from the city's grain and eventually meatpacking industries. North Chicago Rolling Mills produced the first steel rails in Chicago in 1865 along the north branch of the Chicago River, and by the 1880s the company's South Works plant in South Chicago was teaming with workers producing rails. Without railroads and the steel used to build them, Chicago would not have become the "stacker of wheat" and "hog butcher of the world." Carl Sandburg's famous poem "Chicago," published in 1914, opens with "Hog Butcher for the World, Tool Maker, Stacker of Wheat, Player with Railroads and the Nation's Freight Handler, Stormy, husky, brawling, City of the Big Shoulders," illustrating the brutal, laborious nature of the industrious city under development during the early twentieth century. Sandburg, who had recently served as secretary to the country's first socialist mayor in Milwaukee, is said to have written a love letter to the city but also an ode to the workers that built it. By 1914, a good percentage of those Chicago workers were Polish who, like their German counterparts, were skilled workers and active in labor organizing. Poles played, and still play, a central role in the Chicago-based labor movement originally developing out of the stockyard, steel mills, and most industries across the city. A strike by steelworkers in 1919 was largely led by Polish workers in Chicago, who continued throughout the century to produce union leaders that pushed for national policy reforms eventually under the United Steelworkers of America.

Following the Chicago fire, a city ordinance banning wood-frame buildings downtown helped lead to the first steel-framed skyscrapers constructed during the early decades of the twentieth century. Skyscrapers symbolized the city ("of broad shoulders") at the center of U.S. industrial capitalism, and housing the financial core of the Chicago economy was the new steel-framed Chicago's Board of Trade building. Completed in 1930, it was the tallest building in the city until 1965. Among many immigrant groups, Poles played a major role in producing the steel that "built" such Chicago icons. The city's economy, having largely developed out of trade in food commodities, and principally grains and meats, was at the heart of an emerging financial capitalism centered at the Board of Trade. Meanwhile, the mostly immigrant populations who originally "stacked the wheat" and packed the meat struggled in poorly constructed housing in neighborhoods with poor infrastructure that lacked basic city services. Polish immigrants, drawing on their peasant farmer experience in Poland, were particularly successful in re-creating a communal structure that provided resilience under dire urban conditions. During a packinghouse strike in 1921, strongly backed by the Polish community and its clergy, Polish women threw pepper and paprika in the eyes of charging police.[25] Such community activism prevailed into the 1930s and 1940s, when Poles, Irish, and other immigrant groups in South Chicago and Back of the Yards organized neighborhood associations to organize for improvements. The models they established with assistance from community organizer Saul Alinsky would become some of the foundational tools for community organizing in the United States.

The center of Polish community building in Chicago was at one time located around the intersection of Milwaukee, Ashland, and Division on Chicago's Northwest Side. The neighborhood was Chicago's first Polish settlement, and the "Polish Downtown" is still known as the Polish (Polonia) Triangle. Nearby is Pulaski Park, completed in 1914 and named after a Polish immigrant who became an American Revolutionary War hero following his death at the Battle of Savannah. Polonia spanned northwest and west in the early 1930s. Crawford Avenue was changed to Pulaski Road, with some level of controversy that instigated claims of anti-Polish sentiment. Pulaski Road still changes to Crawford Avenue as you leave Chicago toward the north and south. The strength in numbers of the Polish community in many ways made Polonia the capital of U.S. Polish political, economic, and social life. National Polish organizations got started in the neighborhood and, in a similar manner to the Irish, the core of community life were Polish Catholic parishes such as Holy Trinity and St. Stanislaus Kostka (built in 1867). Eventually, dozens of Polish Catholic churches dotted Chicago's landscape, and out of these neighborhood enclaves came the introduction of Polish cuisine into Chicago foodways.

Like many of their European neighbors, Poles owned saloons that provided cheap or free lunch in proximity to major industrial sectors. In part two of Melendy's two-article series on the saloons in Chicago, he puts forth that "it is the free-lunch counter that has made the Chicago saloon notorious."

> In the saloon or in the cheap restaurants the 30,000 of the floating population get their meals. But nowhere in the city, aside from the saloons, can one fully satisfy his hunger for 5 cents. [26]

By the end of the nineteenth century, Poles owned numerous saloons, and it was through the saloon that the community entered Chicago politics. As the temperance movement was heating up, saloon owners joined city politics as alderman. The first Polish alderman elected in the 1880s was a saloonkeeper who organized the Polish Saloonkeepers Association. [27] Forty-five saloons and twenty-four food stores lined Commercial Avenue in the South Chicago neighborhood in 1891, and in 1897 the Polish-owned White Eagle Brewery opened on the Southwest Side. [28] Polish saloonkeepers did so well serving free lunches that five of them created a corporation and bought the brewery that, according to the *Polish*

Daily News (*Dziennik Związkowy*) in 1917, was the largest Polish brewery in Chicago, located near the Union Stock Yards.[29]

Along with saloons that served Polish beer, early twentieth-century Polish neighborhoods teamed with restaurants, delicatessens, butchers, and bakeries, and in some ways they continue to do so to the present. The second and third waves of Polish migration during the twentieth century would further increase the enclaves on the Northwest and Southwest sides of the city, and by the 1970s multiple waves of Polish immigrants made Chicago a national epicenter of Polish American culture. A central feature of the community is the Polish Museum of America, opened in 1935 down the street from the Polonia Triangle. Another central feature of the Chicago Polish enclave is the sausage business. According to a study in 1928, one thousand Poles worked in the sausage industry.[30] One of those businesses was Slotkowski Sausage Company, started by Joseph P. Slotkowski in 1918 out of a delicatessen in the South Chicago neighborhood. Slotkowski expanded into a nationally known brand at his sausage plant on 18th Street in Chicago's Southwest Side Pilsen neighborhood. His "Polish sausage" or kielbasa would become the core ingredient of the famous "Maxwell Street Polish," a Chicago iconic food (though not created by a Pole). Slotkowski Sausage persisted for seventy years until it was sold in 1992, and it is now owned by Chicago-based ATK Foods. Across town on Division Street, Chester Mikolajczyk opened a sausage shop the same year as Slotkowski. The business was eventually sold to another Polish immigrant, Andy Kolasa, and Andy's Deli still operates on North Milwaukee Avenue as an icon in the heart of Polish Chicago. By the end of the twentieth century, Chicago had produced other sausage landmarks such as Bobak on the southwest side and Bacik Deli on the Northwest Side. Originating in old Polish enclaves, Bobak and Bacik followed the Polish migration southwest and northwest up the diagonal Archer Road and Milwaukee Avenue, respectively (both originally Native American trails).

While Chicago is best known for its Polish sausage, available at the city's ubiquitous hot dog stands, one also finds an array of Polish foods in restaurants and grocers scattered throughout the Polish neighborhoods. From *paczki* (a type of doughnut) to *pierogis*, Polish food remains a fixture in Chicago. Poles and non-Poles flock to "smorgasbord" buffets on the Southwest and Northwest sides of the city for an array of favorites. Other than sausage, however, there is no Polish food more popular in

Chicago than pierogi. As Chicago historian Dominic Pacyga notes, "Everyone in Chicago knows what pierogi and kielbasa are, even if they could not find Poland on a map or tell you anything about Poland's history or the background of Chicago's Polonia."[31] The boiled and then baked or fried dough pockets filled with sauerkraut, meat, mushrooms, cheese, potatoes, or fruit are a central feature of Taste of Polonia held annually by the Copernicus Foundation since 1979. Pierogis, beer, and polka are celebrated by residents of the heavily Polish Jefferson Park neighborhood on the far Northwest Side along Milwaukee Avenue. Across town, residents of Whiting, Indiana, just over the border from South Chicago in proximity to the old steel mills, hold a popular annual Pierogi Fest. Most recently, the Polish community on the Southwest Side organized their own South Side Polish Fest in the suburb of Bridgeview that claims to be the largest Polish festival in the United States. Held at a soccer stadium, the event is complete with a pierogi-eating contest. Such celebrations reflect a long history of pierogi consumption in Chicago furthered by immigrants who conceptualized that their food had appeal well beyond the Polish community. At 2303 West Cermak in what became a predominantly Latino neighborhood once stood Pola Foods, one of the first companies to sell pierogi in Chicago supermarkets. Present-day pierogi manufacturers Kasia's and Alexandra Foods were started by third-wave Polish immigrants who saw the potential to mass-produce their beloved food throughout the city and beyond.

EASTERN EUROPEAN JEWS

Following a distinctly different path, Polish- and Russian-speaking Jews fleeing anti-Semitism settled in Chicago during the 1880s. European Jewish migration skyrocketed from some 10,000 during the 1880s to an estimated 225,000 by 1920. The largely Yiddish-, Polish-, and Russian-speaking immigrants first settled in poor neighborhoods in the area around Halsted and Maxwell streets on the Near West Side. They found jobs in the garment industry where they became active in the union, but they also gained income as street peddlers, pushcart vendors, storefront retailers, and as wholesalers. In time, a street market coalesced into what would become Chicago's famous Maxwell Street Market. Vendors from a variety of groups lined the neighborhood streets in the shadow of store-

Figure 3.3.   Pierogi makers at Pola Foods, 1988. Chicago History Museum,
Changing Chicago Project Photographs by Richard Younker, 165899.

front retailers, all of which served the burgeoning immigrant market des-
perate for inexpensive prices.

Jews on Maxwell Street, in what was known to others as "Jew Town,"
engaged with groups from across the city, including those in the nearby
Italian community and the rapidly growing Greek enclave on Halsted. It
was this confluence of immigrant groups that led to the creation of the
Chicago-style hot dog and the Chicago polish sausage sandwich. Culturally diverse European immigrant peddlers would eventually contribute to
the city's vibrant wholesale produce market when in 1925 South Water
Market was moved to the corner of South Racine Avenue and 14th
Place—just a few blocks west of the Maxwell Street Market. For decades
the relocated "South Water Market" (originally on the south bank of the
Chicago River) brought together, among others, Jews, Italians, Greeks,
and their offspring in the early morning hours to settle trades and fill
trucks with produce to be delivered to grocers and restaurants across the
city and suburbs.

Within a matter of decades, Eastern European Jews left the Near West
Side, moving into neighborhoods across the city, the largest of which

Figure 3.4.   Maxwell Street, c. 1939. Note "Vienna Red Hots" stand. Chicago Public Library, Special Collections and Preservation Division, WS 2.4, photographer unknown.

were on the South and West sides. Jewish neighborhoods grew rapidly with a new wave of Jewish refugees fleeing Nazi Germany during the 1930s. Historian Irving Cutler notes that "a large number of the 425 kosher butcher shops found in Chicago in 1940 were located in Lawndale."[32] The concentration of Jews in North Lawndale and the West Side was particularly high; other heavily Jewish neighborhoods included South Shore, Lakeview, Wicker Park, Albany Park, and Rogers Park. The entrepreneurial passions that emerged out of struggles against anti-Semitism in Europe produced a strong Jewish communal response to poverty, resulting in a strong ethos of education and thriving commercial, entertainment, social service, and religious institutions. Out of these Jewish enclaves came famed food establishments such as Eli's Steakhouse (and later Eli's Cheesecake), started as the Ogden Huddle Restaurant at Ogden and Kedzie on the West Side. From the South Side came Charles Lubin, the enterprising neighborhood baker whose daughter Sara Lee became the namesake for his business Kitchens of Sara Lee, the predecessor to the Sara Lee Corporation eventually headquartered in suburban Downers Grove.

Following World War II, Jews followed many white residents out of the West and South sides into the northern and southern suburbs, especially Skokie, Flossmoor, and Highland Park. In defining the next phase of their diasporic identity, Jews took a clearly different path from their non-Jewish European neighbors. While one still finds several Jewish delicatessens and bagel shops in Chicago and its suburbs, including the legendary Manny's at 1141 S. Jefferson located blocks from the old Maxwell Street, these are distinctly Jewish places that lack any broader nationalist orientation. Restaurants such as Max and Benny's, the Bagel, and Max's Deli in north suburban Chicago offer Jewish reminders of growing up in the old neighborhoods. Bagel bakeries such as Kaufman's and New York Bagels and Bialys in Skokie, which was once home to the highest concentration of Holocaust survivors outside of Jerusalem, are places that one thinks of as Jewish more than in relation to any other national identity. Tainted by centuries of anti-Semitic experiences in the old country, the second wave of European Jews largely assimilated as quickly as possible into the white American cultural landscape and focused on supporting a distinctly Jewish identity. De-emphasizing their Polish, Russian, Ukrainian, and other European languages (including Yiddish) was a necessary catharsis in the post-Holocaust survival process. Even so, in the heavily Jewish West Rogers Park neighborhood on the far North Side, home to the largest Hasidic and Orthodox Jewish communities in the region, one can still find Polish babka baked in a distinctly Jewish style.

THE GREEKS

Like Jews and Italians, by the 1920s, Greeks became especially important in the city's produce business and food industries, such as the once booming meat market west of downtown along Randolph Street. The city's original Greek community developed in the 1870s as immigrants arrived to work in construction following the Great Fire. They initially settled north of the river around Clark and Kinzie (the first Greektown), but later they moved into the area known as the "Delta" around Halsted and Harrison, where the community expanded rapidly after the turn of the century. Chicago's Greeks and Greek Americans became the largest Greek community in the United States until the mid-twentieth century. There they became deeply involved in food vending as street vendors, grocers, produce wholesalers, ice cream producers, and, most prominently, restaurant owners.

As the Greek community grew beyond Halsted Street, they built parishes in other parts of the city where they settled and opened restaurants that can still be found throughout the city and suburbs. Many Greeks and Greek Americans first migrated to suburbs such as Niles and Morton Grove, where they would eventually open independently owned supermarkets such as Produce World and Fresh Farms that successfully compete with corporate chain supermarkets. Restaurants such as Mykonos and Kappy's on Golf Road in Niles have been around for decades, the latter serving up "Greek House Specialties" such as Athenian chicken alongside a "lox plate" from the Kosher Korner menu. Especially crafty restaurateurs, Greek Chicagoans mastered the art of combining a variety of non-Greek entrees while maintaining a core Greek-influenced menu. This type of Greek-owned family restaurant is a Chicago staple, mixing foods from a variety of cultural influences that serves the taste of any customer. Meanwhile, Chicago's "Greektown" on Halsted west of downtown is in the middle of booming urban renewal and has become a vibrant restaurant district where locals and visitors search for genuine Greek cuisine. In suburban Glendale Heights is Kronos Foods, developed by Greek immigrant Chris Tomaras into one of the largest Greek foods distributors in the United States. Tomaras may be best known, however, for creating the broiler that cooks Chicago's native gyros sandwich (see chapter 7).

AFRICAN AMERICANS

As new European immigrant groups arrived in Chicago during the late nineteenth century, they encountered black migrants from the South whose migration experience to Chicago was distinctly different. From the time of du Sable, Chicago had been home to African Americans, but centuries of forced migration of Africans, southern slavery, and migration north would result in their complex integration into Chicago's increasingly diverse cultural landscape. Africans arrived by force in the American colonies in the early sixteenth century, the first arriving in the Virginia Colony in 1619 more than half a century before Europeans set eyes on Chicago. Nineteenth-century migration to Chicago of freed blacks and refugees from slavery was a decades-long process of redefining racial categories as they entered a city teeming with European immigrants competing for low-wage jobs driven by industrialization.

Chicago systems of racial privileging in jobs, education, and housing was to become particularly harsh, the product of which still makes the city one of the most racially segregated in the world. The origins of Chicago segregation are in meatpacking, wheat stacking, and steel making, among other early industries. Efforts by African Americans to enter the late nineteenth-century labor force were challenged by nineteenth-century definitions of whiteness that were shifting in Chicago, as elsewhere.[33] Anglo-centric elite did not initially perceive Irish and Polish among other immigrants as fully white, and the introduction of race as a tool to control labor was a particularly powerful force. According to the 1850 census, there were only 323 African Americans in Chicago, most of whom lived south of the Chicago River along the southern corridor between Lake Michigan and State Street. They initially lived dispersed among others, renting housing and rooms, but the drive for economic freedom led to home ownership and the establishment of black-owned businesses and religious institutions. Even with the Fugitive Slave Act of 1850 requiring free states to return escaped slaves to their owners, and the Illinois Black Laws (1819–1864) that greatly restricted the movement of African Americans into Illinois ("mulatto, bond, or free"), African Americans in Chicago found ways to survive and prosper.

Six years before the Emancipation Proclamation, in 1857, the first African American family built their own home on present-day Plymouth Court, and accounts suggest that there were black grocers and a saloon-keeper in Chicago.[34] In 1876, Chicagoan John W. E. Thomas became the first African American elected to serve as a representative in the Illinois General Assembly, and Chicago's first black newspaper was published in 1878 by attorney Ferdinand Barnett, who later sold the paper to his wife, Ida B. Wells.[35] Wells, who was a leader in the early civil rights movement, moved to Chicago in 1895 and would spend a good part of her life working to better conditions for African Americans on the South Side.

The first African American congregation built its church, Quinn Chapel
A.M.E., at the site of the present-day Monadnock Building on Jackson
Street in downtown Chicago. The church played a strong role in the
abolitionist movement and was a stop on the Underground Railroad, providing refugees from slavery access to food, housing, and assistance in
moving on to other free states and Canada.[36] Like much of Chicago, the
building was destroyed in the Chicago Fire, but the church was rebuilt in
1892 at 2401 South Wabash, where the congregation remains today. The
year after Quinn Chapel was rebuilt, Frederick Douglass spoke there on
the subject of Haiti, the world's first Black republic, where he had been
ambassador. By that time, the north-south corridor along South State
Street was referred to by the media as the "Black Belt" because it had
become home to a growing number of African Americans. The end of the
Civil War and repeal of the Illinois Black Laws resulted in the arrival of
more African Americans to work as laborers, and a small middle class
and upper class made up of merchants and professionals emerged.

By 1890, Chicago's African American population had risen to fifteen
thousand. Douglass's speech at Quinn Chapel in 1893 was given in the
context of protests that he and Wells orchestrated as a result of the exclusion of African Americans from the World's Columbian Exposition
(World's Fair). Fair attendees gazed at cultures from around the globe
and dined on their delicacies, but there was no representation of the
seven-and-a-half million African Americans in the United States in a way
that positively reflected advances since the Civil War. In the space of the
Haitian Pavilion—highlighting Haitian coffee—Douglas and Wells pro-
tested the relatively few African American employees at the Fair, which
hosted twenty-seven million people over six months. In the end, Fair
organizers agreed to "Colored Person's Day," which included a series of
speeches on the plight of African Americans. Elsewhere the Fair depicted
stereotypical images of black Americans, such as in the Louisiana Building that highlighted an "antebellum Creole kitchen" with black cooks and
waiters overseen by white supervisors. Former slave Nancy Green was
introduced as Aunt Jemima as part of a pancake-making exhibit that was
so successful that reportedly there had to be crowd control. R. T. Davis
Milling Company, the firm that hired Green, found the mammy stereo-
type to be such a hit at the Fair that they kept Green as the trademark for
the remainder of her life and eventually changed the company name to
Aunt Jemima Mills Company in 1914. In 1926, Chicago-based Quaker

Oats bought the company and introduced a new Aunt Jemima, who would again be exhibited at the Chicago World's Fair in 1933. The face of a black woman—albeit modernized—remains on Aunt Jemima syrup bottles owned by Quaker Oats, a subsidiary of PepsiCo.

Colored Person's Day would be marked by a belittling cartoon appearing in *Puck* magazine in August 1893 titled "Darkies Day at the Fair," presenting caricatures of black people wearing costumes lining up to eat watermelon. The cartoon affirmed the worst fears among local African Americans, many of whom had originally called for a boycott of the Fair. The paradoxical nature of the cartoon is that it was in stark contrast to the emerging realities among Chicago's African American residents living just blocks from the Fair. Not withstanding the fact that black residents of Chicago were generally excluded from public spaces patronized by whites, the city's relatively small African American community had made significant achievements. The Civil Rights Act of 1875 was an attempt to guarantee African Americans equal access to public accommodations such as restaurants, theaters, and trains, but the Supreme Court had ruled it unconstitutional in 1883. Within this context, notes historian Christopher Robert Reed, Chicago's Colored Men's Professional and Business Directory of 1885 lists "fifteen restaurants and twenty saloons" owned by black Chicagoans.[37] Reed further describes the existence of black-owned catering companies serving the elite (apparently white and black), an ice cream shop, and a coffee shop at Fifth Avenue (Wells Street) and the Chicago River. The *Puck* cartoon and the Fair organizers' relative dismissal and stereotyping of black Americans ignored a vibrant culture emerging out of slavery that included a unique cuisine mixing African, European, and indigenous foods.

By the end of the nineteenth century, Chicago dominated national markets for grain and livestock. The city's growing labor pool, regional geography, and railroad network positioned it at the economic and physical center of the largest food-producing region in the world. This was a position that produced obvious contradictions between labor and capital that would seek resolution in conflicts between workers and owners and in tension among workers of diverse racial and ethnic identities. While the small black middle class and upper class was the product of both an entrepreneurial spirit emerging from their unique struggle and the city's wealth more generally, masses of African Americans began to arrive in industrial Chicago directly from farms and villages of the Jim Crow

South. The introduction of African American cuisine into Chicago comes within the context of a growing black population increasingly marginalized to a section of the city where they settled and competed with European immigrants for low-wage jobs. Black migrants brought with them a sense of resiliency seasoned by years of struggle under slavery and sharecropping. The result was a diet that reflected African heritage and life under slave conditions where plantation owners fed slaves inexpensively using what was available or discarded and what slaves themselves could produce in gardens. The social and economic constraints of the post–Civil War South would carry over into northern cities like Chicago, where the majority of African Americans by the turn of the century were largely offered the lowest-paid jobs.

By 1900, labor opportunities doubled Chicago's African American population to 30,150 in a single decade. Most continued to live on the South Side to the northeast of the stockyards across a set of railroad tracks from the heavily Irish Bridgeport neighborhood. Running north-south along the tracks, Wentworth Avenue became a racial dividing line, and Chicago's stark racial segregation began to materialize. This was a place where packinghouses provided twenty-five thousand jobs in 1900. Though African Americans had been excluded from these jobs, over time owners learned to take advantage of their growing numbers, proximity to the packinghouses, and demand for income opportunities. In 1904, the Amalgamated Meat Cutters and Butcher Workmen of North America went on strike, and plant owners proceeded to hire African Americans as strikebreakers. This prompted thousands of union members to riot, resulting in attacks on African Americans and the elevation of racial tensions for decades to come. Such tensions would intensify as World War I closed down immigration from Europe, demand for Chicago meat products grew, and increasing numbers of black workers—including many women—took jobs in the stockyards. In 1919, racial tensions erupted on Chicago's South Side into a five-day deadly conflict known as the Chicago Race Riots, in which twenty-three black Chicagoans were killed and hundreds were injured. The riots became a central feature in what became known as the "Red Summer," in which racially charged conflicts occurred across U.S. cities. The conflicts took place in the context of World War I veterans, white and black, returning from Europe seeking jobs and housing and finding nonunion African Americans working in factories.

By 1920, there were thousands of African Americans employed in the Union Stock Yards, despite the earlier attacks. During this time, African Americans continued to migrate to northern industrial cities, bringing with them unique culinary skills that made a deep imprint on Chicago foodways. Food was and remains intricately connected to the concept of freedom by illustrating how even under brutal, inhumane conditions of slavery and Jim Crow, the origins of emancipation could be seen through access to and the preparation of good food.[38] Ironically, while probably at least one in ten African Americans in Chicago worked in a meatpacking plant in 1920, meat had been a tremendous delicacy for blacks in the South. Greater access in the North led to specific kinds of culinary styles that blended old and new ways. In 1920, the African American population in Chicago had more than tripled in twenty years to 109,894. The origins of a unique Chicago-style African American cuisine can be found during the 1920s when greater wealth within the black community offered opportunities to build businesses around food.

Along with packinghouses, the Pullman Corporation was a major employer of African American men, who were hired as porters, among other jobs, in support of a burgeoning passenger train business. Combined with women's wages from domestic work and manufacturing, a black working class and middle class emerged with discretionary income. Race restrictive covenants, supported by the Chicago Real Estate Board, were used to maintain white neighborhoods and to isolate black residents by restricting them from buying or leasing property in white neighborhoods of the city. In turn, the burgeoning African American community on the South Side built their own businesses, and their neighborhood flourished into a lively cultural and commercial center with a rich array of food, entertainment, and art venues. Restaurants such as Southern Home Cooking and Southern Lunch Room reflected the tastes of new migrants who were arriving daily in the neighborhood.[39] Chicago's Black Belt emerged into a jazz capital in places like the Royal Gardens or the Sunset Café, some of the city's first integrated nightclubs where stars such as Ella Fitzgerald, Benny Goodman, and Louis Armstrong performed.

The Depression years would take a toll on the neighborhood economy as jobs largely went to whites even in black neighborhoods. This compelled the *Chicago Whip* newspaper to run the "Don't Spend Your Money Where You Can't Work" campaign advocating for a boycott of white-owned stores in black communities. Drake and Cayton's groundbreaking

1945 sociological study *The Black Metropolis: A Study of Negro Life in a Northern City* would give voice to residents, highlighting their dilemma. In a section titled "Race Pride vs. Prices," the authors quote a woman who apologetically states "I buy at the A&P where I can get food cheapest. I try to patronize my race but I can't on my husband's salary." The woman highlights sentiments of residents who see black-owned stores as more expensive in what was now an area of the city that housed more than three hundred thousand people. Only 10 percent of Chicago's black residents lived outside of Bronzeville. The population of African Americans had grown to 337,000, second to New York, making black Chicagoans one of every ten residents of the city. The Black Metropolis they note is "a unique and distinct city within a city." "Understand Chicago's Black Belt and you will understand the Black Belts of a dozen large American cities."

At the time that *Black Metropolis* was published, the majority of the African Americans in Bronzeville lived under the race-restrictive covenants put in place during the 1920s. Covenants were ruled unconstitutional by the Supreme Court in 1948 after which less formal segregation practices such as "redlining" would continued to limit African American home ownership and renting in the city. Within this neighborhood context, a uniquely Chicago-style African American cuisine emerged, a key component of which was southern barbecue. The origins of southern barbecue can be partly traced to the Spanish, who introduced pigs to the Americas during their early explorations. Over the centuries, pork became an integral part of southern cuisine. Additionally, there are both indigenous American and African influences on the practice of smoking meat and slow cooking above wood flames. *Barbecue (barbacoa)* is derived from a word indigenous to the Caribbean basin.[40] Smoking sausage was also a German, Polish, and Czech practice these groups brought to the South. Saucing meat while cooking where meat is rubbed periodically and applying spicy sauce to meats over flames has clear African origins and strongly reflects West African Suya cooking. However complex its origins, saucing and smoking meat over wood-burning grills became a southern culinary art. African Americans played an important role in bringing this art to Chicago, a practice that had as much to do with the style of barbecue as the preparation of distinct sauces—a sweet and tangy type—that would become markers of barbecue establishments across the city. These establishments multiplied following the Great Depression when a new wave of African Americans began settling in the city seeking jobs spurred on by World War II production demands.

Southern-style barbecue was likely present in Chicago since the late nineteenth century, and its arrival can be attributed to both white and black residents. Russell's Barbeque was established in predominantly white suburban Elmwood Park in 1930, and it remains open, making it the oldest operating barbecue restaurant in the region. Yet out of Chicago's Black Metropolis emerged a unique Chicago-style barbecue restaurant combining southern meat-cooking traditions, street vending, and backyard barbeque pits (including reusing discarded metal drums) to eventually arrive at the "BBQ joint." Among the earliest known establishment was Leon's BBQ, started by Leon Finney Sr., who migrated from Mississippi and opened his first restaurant in 1940 on East Garfield in Bronzeville. Finney started his operation with $700 and the help of an aunt, and he eventually opened three restaurant locations on the South Side that he managed into his eighties.[41] Another South Side barbecue legend, Lem's Bar-B-Q, had two locations and one that remains open on 75th Street in the Greater Grand Crossing neighborhood. Two brothers opened the first restaurant during the early 1950s, and a third brother, James Lemons, a chef trained at a Greek restaurant on the North Side, joined them and managed the remaining Lem's after their death.[42]

Lem's and Leon's popularized the Delta-style barbecue, a style redeveloped in Chicago using an "aquarium pit" that roasts and smokes meat slowly over a wood-burning grill within a rectangular glass aquarium (see chapter 7). Along with ribs and sausages, black barbecue restaurateurs popularized rib tips, a truly Chicago invention (also see chapter 7). Chicago's meat wholesalers and butchers used to discard the tips, but Leon's and Lem's took what was considered waste and popularized it into what is now consider a delicacy. Most importantly, the bringing together of barbecue ribs, sausage ("hot links"), French fries, and white bread is truly an unrivaled Chicago invention.[43]

In typical Chicago fashion, competition remained largely internal as to who makes the best sauce, who invented the rib tip, or simply who had the best ribs. In 1982, Chicago's nationally syndicated newspaper columnist Mike Royko claimed he made the best ribs and hosted the first Mike Royko Ribfest on Chicago's downtown lakefront. Hundreds of contestants flocked to the event that spawned competitive barbecue and rib festivals drawing thousands to the city (including a massive one at Sol-

dier Field, home of the Chicago Bears). Judges claimed the winner to be
Charlie Robinson, originally from Mississippi, and Robinson proceeded
to take his fame and turn it into a restaurant and sauce business Robinson's #1 Ribs in suburban Oak Park. By that time, Chicago barbecue ribs
had become so ingrained in the city's cultural framework that even vegetarians were competing for the best faux ribs. From the beginning, Royko
got repeated complaints about excluding vegetarians, and in 1986 he
agreed to include them in the competition. Deploying his infamous sar-
casm, Royko referred to their entry as "gluten-on-a-stick barbecued ribs"
noting "the texture is very interesting" and "much like a soft, chewable
piece of rubber, a gum eraser or something like that. And you have to
concede that something with the texture of a gum eraser is very interesting." His article went as far as to include the vegetarian rib recipe, but he
ended it by expressing: "If you don't want to go to all that work, there is a
shortcut. Cover an eraser with sauce, chew and swallow."[44] By that time,
however, Chicago's African American community had perfected vegetarian barbecue in a style far from erasers. Just steps from Lem's barbecue
on 75th Street, the popular Soul Vegetarian Restaurant was opened in the
early 1980s by Chicago-born Black Hebrew Israelites. The restaurant
arguably mastered a very Chicago-style vegan soul food, including "barbecued twist" (with fries) and glutinous "protein tidbits."

ITALIANS

Barbecue restaurants were certainly not exclusive to the African
American community that by the 1960s had reached 813,000 (22 percent
of the city), most of whom lived on the South Side. After World War II
and the end of race-restrictive convenants, redlining, a process that de-
nied mortagage-lending services to certain areas, continued to inflict
harm on the predominantly black neighborhoods of the city. Refusal to
lend to African Americans or increasing their rates maintained segregated
neighborhoods, as did real estate agents steering buyers away from neighborhoods based on race. Highways such as the north-south Dan Ryan
Expressway (1962) on the South Side largely divided black from white
neighborhoods, such as Bridgeport. Though race and national or ethnic
identity divided Chicago neighborhoods, cuisines and flavors crossed
boundaries in ways that highlight the essence of Chicago's cultural and

culinary complexity. In 1955, the Glass Dome Hickory Pit was opened by Anthony Beninato, out of a tavern operated by Italian immigrants Graziano and Filippa Beninato in largely white Bridgeport just a mile or so west of Bronzeville. The restaurant, which stayed open into the 1990s, was a favorite for White Sox fans following the game at the old Comiskey Park. The establishment was known for its smoked barbecue ribs but also for its Italian staples such as "parmesans: veal, chicken and steak." Also on the menu at the Hickory Pit was reportedly "a neighborhood staple," the breaded steak sandwich.[45] By mid-twentieth century, Bridgeport's famous sandwich became a favorite among Chicagoans as a result of the migration of Italians into the once largely Irish enclave.

When Italians began arriving in Chicago during the 1850s from mainly southern Italy, they were themselves discriminated against by the largely Anglo-Saxon elite who stereotyped them as not entirely white and as criminals.[46] In 1881, when Chicago had only 1,357 foreign-born Italians, the first Italian Catholic parish, Assumption Church, opened, and its building was completed in 1886 at 323 West Illinois near the present-day Merchandise Mart building. By the end of the nineteenth century, the number of Italian-born residents quickly grew to sixteen thousand. Advertisements recruited Italians to work on Chicago's railroads, and the majority settled into the increasingly overcrowded near West Side neighborhood around Taylor Street not far from Maxwell Street Market. Italians found work in garment factories, where they played a strong role in labor organizing, and they opened restaurants, grocery stores, and bakeries and became produce wholesalers and street vendors around Maxwell Street. Jane Addams established Hull House, the first settlement house in the United States, in this diverse neighborhood in 1889, and the first generation of urban sociologists conducted studies that laid the groundwork for the Chicago School of Sociology. During the early 1960s, Little Italy would take a hard hit when the University of Illinois Chicago (UIC) campus was built in the area and residents were forced to leave.

As Taylor Street became "Little Italy," a second concentration of Italians from Sicily settled on the North Side during the turn of the century in what would become known as "Little Sicily." Sicilians began settling north of Chicago Avenue and south of North Avenue in an area referred to as "Little Hell" because of a "gas house" that produced large flames. In 1929, the crowded neighborhood became the subject of sociologist Harvey Warren Zorbaugh's study that provided a detailed depiction of the area's impoverished conditions. Tensions between the elite "Gold Coast" residents and nearby Sicilians, referred to as "the Dark People," were attributed to the latter's disorganization resulting from the failure of institutions—family, church, schools, and others—that resulted in criminality. Critique of the study by sociologist William Foote Whyte led to a new view in sociology that "distressed neighborhoods can have an effective social organization of their own."[47] Little Sicily would be completely demolished for the construction of Cabrini-Green public housing. By naming the latter after Mother Cabrini (Green is the last name of a former governor), the first North American saint, the hope by clergy was that the latter would be integrated and that the Italians would stay. Following World War II, however Italians left the neighborhood and moved to the Northwest Side and the suburbs.

It is safe to say that Italians and Italian Americans have had an enormous impact on Chicago foodways. Many of the best-known Chicago food businesses got started in the city's Italian enclaves, including Gonnella Bakery, Al's Italian Beef, Turano Bakery, and Dominick's Supermarkets. In 1886 Alessandro Gonnella opened his small storefront bakery on De Koven Street in Little Italy.[48] For example, the family-owned Gonnella Baking Company, headquartered in suburban Schaumburg, delivers bread across northeastern Illinois and to a good part of Wisconsin. Similarly, Al's Italian Beef got started as a Little Italy street stand in 1938, after which it moved to a storefront at 1079 West Taylor from which it eventually expanded to fifteen locations, including twelve in the Chicago area and the remainder in Nevada and California.[49] In 1962, Italian immigrant Mariano Turano opened his Compagna Bakery on the Northwest Side and later opened Compagna-Turano at 6441 West Roosevelt in Berwyn. Turano Bakery expanded to become a distributor to supermarkets and food businesses across the region.

In recent decades, Chicagoans have developed a deep nostalgia for the city's Italian eateries. A resurgence of interest and investment in Taylor Street during the 1990s led to the reemergence of a dynamic Italian restaurant district. Popular local chain restaurants such as Rosebud, which got their start on Taylor Street during the 1970s, began to expand to other neighborhoods by marketing a timeless Italian Chicago décor. Furthering this concept, in 1991, Chicago's Lettuce Entertain You Restaurants opened Maggiano's Little Italy on the corners of Clark Street and Grand Avenue in the affluent near North Side neighborhood and then opened a second site in 1994 at a shopping mall in suburban Skokie. Maggiano's, which prides itself on serving an overabundance of food family style, was later sold to Brinker International, the owner of the Chili's chain. Brinker proceeded to open Maggiano's across the country in more than twenty states.

On a smaller scale, the opening of trattorias, informal neighborhood restaurants marketed to regular customers and serving regional recipes, has increased the visibility of Italian food in many of Chicago's more affluent neighborhoods. Nonetheless, one can still find the remnants of lesser-known Italian neighborhoods that contain pockets of eateries and cafes; for example, along Oakley Street south of 24th in the largely Latino Lower West Side. Of course, Chicago-style pizza remains a key icon of the city's food culture (see chapter 7), and in Bridgeport, the breaded steak sandwich served on Gonnella bread is still served at Ricobene's, which was opened by Italian immigrants on 26th Street during the 1940s.[50]

CHINESE

Adjacent to Bridgeport in the South Side Armour Square neighborhood near Wentworth and Cermak is Chicago's Chinatown. Established during the second decade of the twentieth century, Chicago's Chinatown is actually its second location, the original having been located downtown near the intersection of Clark and Van Buren. Shortly after the transcontinental railroad was complete in 1869, Cantonese-speaking Chinese began arriving in Chicago from California. Included among them was Moy Dong Chow, who bought a building in the 1870s and opened a grocery store on Clark and Madison. He moved the popular Hip Lung during the 1880s to 323 South Clark Street, where it would become the community's largest grocer and cultural center.[51] As a result of the U.S. Chinese Exclusion Act of 1882 that limited Chinese immigration to the United States (until its repeal in 1943), the small Chinese community was mostly made up of men. The Act made it difficult for male laborers to bring over families and, besides a handful of states, antimiscegenation laws made it difficult for Chinese men to marry white women. Illinois repealed the laws in 1874, but many states upheld them until they were ruled unconstitutional in 1967. Consequently, the mostly male Chinese community of Chicago opened laundries, grocery stores, and restaurants with the intent of earning money to return to China. In 1883, when Chicago's Chinese population was less than 1,500, there were 190 Chinese-owned laundries, and that was a reduction from the previous decade.[52]

Besides laundries, food businesses, and particularly restaurants and grocery stores, became a foundation of the Chinese community's economy. Moy, his brothers, and his extended family not only turned Hip Lung into the largest Chinese grocer in the city but also into a transnational enterprise with branches in San Francisco and Hong Kong.[53] Using kinship networks, the Chinese provided loans for capital investments in stores and restaurants across the downtown neighborhood. The Chinese-American Museum of Chicago notes the presence of Chinese farms to raise "Chinese vegetables from imported seeds—turnips, pumpkins, summer squash, cabbage, foot-long string beans, snow peas, watermelons" for households, grocers, and restaurants.[54] Commenting on the Chinese New Year's celebration in 1890, the *Chicago Tribune* describes the menu including "Bird's Nest Soup, Shark's Fin Soup, Fried Flat Fish, Roast Chicken, Roast Pig, Roast Duck, Roast Pigeon, Rice Gin, 'Medicine' Wine, Oranges."[55] The food business, and especially Chinese restaurants, would become a major source of income for the small community. In 1906, when a devastating earthquake hit San Francisco, many Chinese refugees were hired as cooks in Chicago's growing number of chop suey restaurants.

By 1910, there was still less than two thousand Chinese in Chicago, and immigration restrictions meant the vast majority were still men. As rents increased downtown, businesses moved south to the area around Wentworth and Cermak, the present-day Chinatown, in what was largely a poor Italian, Greek, and Eastern European neighborhood. In addition to Hip Lung, which moved its operation to 2243 Wentworth in 1912, the popular white-tableclothed Guey Sam Restaurant first opened in 1901 and moved to South Wentworth during the 1920s.[56]

By the 1920s, the downtown Chinese enclave on Clark Street had few Chinese residents but continued to serve as a dining destination for a largely white clientele who enjoyed formal eateries with orchestras and dance floors.[57] Meanwhile, Chinese investors at Wentworth and Cermak created the foundation of a South Side restaurant and business district. The neighborhood also became a home to many Chinese as well as a destination for tourists and locals who sought both food and Chinese medicine and souvenirs. The Chinese-influenced architecture and design of many businesses represented both the pride of the community and the imaginations and desires of non-Chinese who visited regularly to spend their dollars in the neighborhood. A reflection of the community's early economic success was the On Leong Merchants Association Building completed in 1928 (now Pui Tak Center). The historical landmark remains at the center of Chinatown on the corner of Wentworth and Cermak, anchoring Chicago's Chinese to the neighborhood. Designed by a non-Chinese firm, it's considered to be an example of the Orientalism architectural movement with elements of both Chinese and Chicago design styles.

After World War II and the repeal of the Chinese Exclusion Act, Mandarin Chinese migrated to Chicago and settled across the metropolitan area. Though the population remained at only six thousand in 1950, another wave of immigration during the 1970s expanded the Chinese community, and Chinatown extended into the Bridgeport neighborhood. During the late 1980s, Chinese business owners bought property on Archer Avenue and built a two-story mall with restaurants, shops, offices, and townhouses. While the neighborhood is not comparable in size or population to the Chinatowns of San Francisco or New York, the Chinese community continues to sustain itself as a vibrant enclave where people live, work, and support grocers selling foods that are otherwise hard to find in the city. Chinatown remains the center of Chicago's Chinese food culture with restaurants, grocers, noodle factories, and even a handful of fortune cookie bakeries. Wholesale food companies service hundreds if not thousands of Chinese restaurants and caterers across the region.

Chinese businesses downtown on Clark Street existed until 1975 when the core of the neighborhood was demolished to build a federal building and the Metropolitan Correctional Center at Van Buren and Clark. Some businesses moved north to the Uptown neighborhood on Argyle Street east of Broadway, and during the mid-1970s, ethnic Chinese began arriving there as refugees from Vietnam. In time, the neighborhood would attract thousands of Vietnamese, Cambodians, and Laotian refugees and would be variably referred to as Little Saigon or New Chinatown. During the past few decades, the strong presence of Vietnamese resulted in their solid cultural footprint; Argyle and Broadway are lined with numerous pho (noodle) shops and Vietnamese grocery stores. A sign above the largest Asian grocer in the neighborhood, Broadway Supermarket at 4879

Broadway, is in Vietnamese, Chinese, and English. Pressures of urban redevelopment, however, loom large on the neighborhood, which is no longer an affordable resettlement site for most new immigrants.

MEXICANS

Similar gentrification patterns have occurred near Chinatown on the South Side, leading to drastic changes in the landscape. Over the past decade, the massive University Village housing development with sprawling townhouses and condominiums replaced public housing developments and demolished the old Maxwell Street neighborhood. Furthermore, racial segregation that once divided South Side neighborhoods between white and black residents shifted over the past half century as new immigrants from Mexico replaced white residents. Much of the surrounding Irish, Polish, and Italian neighborhoods have been settled by Mexicans and Mexican Americans, while the historic South Side African American community in Bronzeville expanded rapidly across much of the South and Far South sides. Following the end of legalized race-protective covenants, redlining efforts were challenged by real estate agents who persuaded white property owners on the South and West sides to sell houses below market value—spreading racist fears that black residents were going to move into their neighborhood, change the culture, and reduce housing values. During the late twentieth century, "white flight" opened vast sections of Chicago's South and West sides to housing ownership and rental by African Americans. Meanwhile, immigrants from Mexico and Central America increasingly settled in the older white (redlined) South and Southwest side neighborhoods, including Back of the Yards, Pilsen, and South Lawndale (Little Village).

Mexican migration to Chicago would profoundly change the demographics of the city. Among Spanish-speaking groups to settle in the city, Mexicans were the earliest. They arrived during the second decade of the twentieth century, responding to labor demands in Midwestern agriculture and Chicago spurred by World War I. Recruitment of Mexicans to work in the meatpacking plants, steel mills, and railroad companies resulted in Mexican settlements in South Chicago, Back of the Yards, and eventually the Near West Side. In 1910, there were less than 1,500 Mexicans in the city, but by 1930 that number was almost 20,000 (yet still less than 1 percent of the overall population). Tightened immigration policies during the 1920s didn't include Mexicans, and their numbers continued to grow. During the Depression, however, a Mexican repatriation policy led to thousands being forcibly repatriated and deported under both the Hoover and Roosevelt administrations. The population drastically declined to an estimated seven thousand by 1940.

The small early Mexican community of Chicago, historian Gabriela Arredondo notes, feared "de-Mexicanization" among the new generation, a concern that carried over into how they felt about their cuisine. "One Mexican restaurant famous for its food reportedly served tamales," she explained, "in waxed paper made of wheat flour with a 'pickle' in place of traditional pork." Outrage led a customer writing into the Mexican newspaper complaining that the restaurant had made a "basterdization [sic] of the tamale."⁵⁸ Like other immigrant communities, food establishments were the core of the community. Mexicans brought tacos, tamales, enchiladas, and mole to Chicago served in family-owned restaurants, many named after their hometowns, a phenomena that continues today. Early restaurants included Bella Jalisco (Beautiful Jalisco) on the Near West Side, El Azteca, and El Chapultepec, which Arredondo notes is "a South Chicago restaurant and pool hall whose name evoked the beautiful park in Mexico City."

Mexican restaurants served both community members and a wider public who visited eateries on South Halsted Street in what John Drury in 1931 described as "most of the foreign quarters." Drury described the once popular El Puerto de Vera Cruz at 811 South Halsted (now the UIC campus), a densely packed immigrant neighborhood, as serving "consul and consular attaches from Latin-American countries, Mexican caricature artists, Spanish tenors from the Civic Opera, residents of Hull-House, newspaperman, sightseeing students from the universities and gourmets—all these indulge their fondness for hot dishes in this little unpretentious Mexican restaurant directly across the street from Jane Addams's famed tenement community center, Hull House."⁵⁹

The early Mexican community of Chicago got a boost in population during World War II. Laborers were recruited to the United States as a result of a U.S-Mexican agreement seeking to bring workers into the country for the war effort. Though government deportation efforts returned again during the 1950s, by 1960 the city's Mexican population reached more than fifty-five thousand. Immigration reform in the 1960s further supported growth of Mexican neighborhoods. Like Irish, Poles, and Italians, Mexicans settled in scattered clusters, *colonias*, across the city in proximity to work sites and Catholic churches. At first they lived among white Chicagoans, but over time their steep number and the departure of whites to suburbs made them the majority in South Chicago and on the Near West Side. Discrimination in jobs, housing, and education would limit social mobility but would not stop the Mexican community from building a thriving and robust neighborhood economy.

During the 1960s, Mexicans and others were removed from the Near West Side, as the UIC campus would replace the historical neighborhood home to generations of Chicago immigrants. The city's Mexican immigrant population would dramatically surge from 38,771 in 1970 to 174,709 in 1990. Mexicans moved south down Halsted Street and Ashland Avenue into the Lower West Side Pilsen neighborhood, Chicago's old Bohemian community. They built business, local institutions, and organizations, and an active political structure. In time, the community expanded west into South Lawndale, a place renamed "Little Village" by earlier residents to distinguish it from North Lawndale. Little Village became "La Villita," and Mexicans began to buy and rent single-family homes and apartments that filled the historically working-class neighborhood.

By the 1980s, 18th Street in Pilsen became a thriving Mexican art, food, and entertainment district and included the National Museum of Mexican Art. In 1962, the Gutierrez family opened Nuevo Leon Restaurant at 1515 West 18th Street that became a fixture in Pilsen. Many other restaurants joined, as did tacquerias, panaderias, and coffee houses. Though the street continues to maintain a Mexican identity, the neighborhood was targeted for redevelopment in recent decades, causing tension between the community and developers. Community organizers have led a resistance against the continued displacement of the still largely immigrant community by predominantly white professionals buying newly developed condominiums that raise property taxes and rents. Since 1972, the community has organized Fiesta Del Sol, an annual reminder of Pilsen's Mexican identity, attracting thousands for a local food and entertainment event advertised as the "Largest Latino Festival in the Midwest."

By 1980, Mexicans surpassed Poles as the largest immigrant group in Chicago with 28 percent of the immigrant population; in 1990 that percentage would rise to 37 percent. A year later, a terra cotta gateway over 26th Street was erected reading "Bienvenidos a Little Village" (a gift from the Mexican government). In addition to the older South Chicago settlement, Mexicans also settled in Northwest Side neighborhoods and around Clark Street in far north Rogers Park. Pilsen and Little Village, however, remained a primary entry point for new immigrants, who largely entered service sector and construction jobs. In 2000, the number of Chicagoans of Mexican origin was estimated at 530,000, many still settling in neighborhoods throughout the Southwest Side. *La Veintiseis*, or 26th Street, west of Western Avenue in Little Village has become the Mexican commercial capital of the Midwest.

As a consequence of Mexican migration to the Southwest Side, the area is known as Chicago's epicenter for tortilla manufacturing. Little Village and Pilsen host numerous *tortillerias*, producing for restaurants and grocery stores throughout the region. These businesses began opening in the 1960s and have proliferated with the growth of interest in tortillas among the broader population. Local brands such as Sabinas, Atotonilco, El Popocatepetl, and El Milagro can be found across Chicago-area stores. The founder of El Milagro, Raul Lopez, got his start in Chicago as a freight handler making tortillas on the side. In 1950, he opened his business on Roosevelt Road in what is today the center of the UIC campus. The family would build the business into three factories, becoming one of the largest tortillas makers in Chicago.[60]

Today, people travel from all over the Midwest to shop and to eat among the dozens of Mexican restaurants on Chicago's Southwest Side. Reportedly, the 26th Street corridor, filled with shops, bakeries, butchers, restaurants, and grocery stores, is second only to the "Magnificent Mile" (Chicago's high-end shopping district on Michigan Avenue) in terms of generating retail tax revenue. In 1988, a *Tribune* reporter, commenting on the transitioning nature of the street, mused how the "generous amount of energy, the markets, street vendors, restaurants and bakeries contribute their tastes, fragrances and colors to the street's gastronomic mosaic."[61] By that time, Little Village already had a thriving street-peddling business, reminiscent of Maxwell Street, including itinerant vendors selling produce from the back of pickup trucks. Today, vendors remain as subsequent generations of migrants earn income from pushcarts selling tamales, *churros*, ice cream, and *paletas* (popsicles made from fresh fruit). Not only can they be seen in Little Village and Pilsen but also in neighborhoods across Chicago and increasingly in the suburbs. A particular streetside favorite for Chicagoans is *elotes* (a spicy corn on the cob—see chapter 7). Unlike the first wave of Mexicans in Chicago, de-Mexicanization is not as critical an issue among the community in Little Village. At the annual Festival de La Villita, the neighborhood's annual Mexican Independence Day celebration held on 26th Street since the late 1980s, hundreds of street vendors sell Mexican delicacies to thousands who attend the festivities and parade, openly expressing pride in Mexican heritage.

PUERTO RICANS

While community building, identity, and food remain central to daily life for residents of Little Village, across town in the Humboldt Park neighborhood, Puerto Ricans exhibit an equally passionate pride in their origins. Puerto Ricans began arriving in Chicago when a firm recruited them during the 1940s and 1950s to work in the steel industry and domestic service. They lived in a variety of neighborhoods, but by the 1960s they had built significant enclaves in what was then racially diverse Lincoln Park, West Town, and Humboldt Park. Pressures from urban redevelopment in Lincoln Park, now a predominantly white, affluent neighborhood, spurred community activism through the 1970s as residents resisted displacement resulting from increased rents and discrimination in education and employment. When police on Division Street shot a young Puerto Rican man in 1966, a major conflict ensued between community members and the police, an event labeled by media as the "Division Street Riots" (old-time residents remember it as a "rebellion"). The event was a defining moment for the community that proceeded to recharge and build numerous organizations, including the Pedro Albizu Campos High School, named for one of the founding leaders of the Puerto Rican independence movement.

Following limited success in Lincoln Park, a second wave of community organizing emerged in the once heavily Polish neighborhood of West Town. During the 1990s, developers sought once again to buy up properties for renovation or redevelopment geared to young, predominantly white professionals. As developers pushed west down Division Street (*la Division*) and North Avenue, the community strengthened its resolve, and in 1995 it erected two massive steel Puerto Rican flags over Division. One of the flags faces the corner of Division and Western, reminding those to the east that the community is no longer "for sale." The other flag is a mile or so west enclosing an area designated as Paseo Boricua (*Boricua* is the indigenous Taino word for a person from the island of Puerto Rico). Paseo Boricua is now a commercial strip that includes numerous Puerto Rican–owned businesses, community-run social service agencies, and a set of affordable housing developments with designs drawn from the architecture of Old San Juan on the island.

Puerto Ricans remain Chicago's second largest Latino population, with an estimated population of over one hundred thousand. Since the 1970s many have moved away from the North Side enclave to other neighborhoods and to the suburbs. In Humboldt Park there is a tension between the push and pull of intraurban migration resulting from intensive gentrification more broadly on the North and Northwest side. Part of the Puerto Rican community's development strategy is to build an economic base along Paseo Boricua that provides Puerto Ricans with affordable housing and with places to create businesses and employment opportunities. Murals along Division Street highlight important struggles in the community and historical figures in Puerto Rican history. They reflect a strong sentiment toward self-determination, as the status of the island and the politics of gentrification in Humboldt Park are intricately intertwined. Food is central to this politics.

Restaurants, grocery stores, and street vendors have become an important part of a campaign to claim a Puerto Rican space in Chicago.[62] Puerto Rican cuisine, with its mix of indigenous Taino, African, and European foods, can be found in restaurants throughout Humboldt Park and nearby neighborhoods, including a popular Borinquen Restaurant (the original location is now closed), inventor of Chicago's famous jibarito sandwich (see chapter 7). Several long-time restaurants such as Casa Central have held out in the old Puerto Rican West Town neighborhood, even though much of the community has moved. Long-time restaurants Sabor Latino and Latin American Restaurant & Lounge provide pillars on both sides of the massive park that divides the neighborhood and gives it its name. Residents and visitors are particularly fond of *pollo chon*, the famed rotisserie chicken at Papa's Cache Sabroso (along with a side of fried plantains). Other local favorites include *alcapurrias*, deep-fried dough made from plantains and bananas filled with meat; *mofongo*, made from mashed green plantains mixed with pork; and *pinchos*, a type of kabob served on a stick. Dishes such as roasted chicken, sautéed steak, and pork chops are typically served with fried plantains (green or ripe), and rice and beans or rice and pigeon peas (*gandules*). La Bruquena, across from the Puerto Rican Cultural Center on Division Street, serves as the unofficial headquarters for many community meetings.

Puerto Rican food and art intermix in the park that hosts the National Museum of Puerto Rican Arts & Culture, housed on Division Street near one of the steel flags in renovated early twentieth-century horse stables. Across from the museum, which hosts exhibits by Puerto Rican artists from across the world, are perhaps some of the most cherished culinary creations of Chicago's Puerto Rican community. Scattered throughout the park are numerous food trucks (*kioskos*) that have claimed space in the same parking spots since the 1970s. Serving up full Puerto Rican meals to a loyal clientele of residences and visitors, the truck owners are early pioneers of what is now a resurgence of interest in urban food trucks in the United States. The vendors become the center of attention annually in June when the community organizes Fiestas Puertorriqueñas, a lively celebration of Puerto Rican history and identity followed by a parade down Paseo Boricua.

MAKING CHICAGO'S CONTEMPORARY FOODWAYS

Chicago's Latino population includes many other groups—Cubans, Guatemalans, and Salvadorians—who, along with Mexicans and Puerto Ricans, made up almost 779,000 city residents in 2010 (almost 29 percent of the city's population). Though richly diverse in origins, Latinos have had a deep cultural impact on Chicago's foodways. The result has been a unique movement toward fusion of Latin American and other cuisines, including Latin-American-Indian and Korean–Puerto Rican restaurants. This movement emerges not only from innovative chefs but also from the mixing of groups that have continued to diversify the city in recent decades. Koreans began arriving in large numbers to the city in the late 1960s, eventually building enclaves on the Northwest Side packed with restaurants and supermarkets. Those same migrants expanded their enclave into the northwest suburbs, with Korean restaurants lining strip malls on Milwaukee Avenue in Glenview. The massive H Mart in suburban Niles is one of the largest Korean supermarkets in the Midwest. Chicago continues to develop a vibrant food culture driven by migration from across the world. The city attracted a large Thai population that built restaurants not in a neighborhood enclave but dispersed throughout the city and suburbs. In contrast, Indians and Pakistanis began replacing Jewish-owned shops on Devon Street in the West Rogers Park neighborhood during the 1970s and 1980s, creating what is now considered "Little India" and "Little Pakistan" along a several-mile strip teeming with restaurants and spice-packed grocers. Arabic-speaking groups, residing in the city since the early part of the twentieth century, have also maintained a strong food presence throughout Chicago. Middle Eastern eateries, bakeries, and falafel stands are scattered across the urban and suburban landscape. A cluster of restaurants and grocers surrounding the municipal train stop at Kedzie and Wilson on the North Side serves recent Arabic-speaking immigrants (including many Iraqi refugees) and others living in Albany Park, an immigrant neighborhood considered one of the most diverse in the city.

From its days as frontier town, Chicago's foodways were made by migration to the city, a process that produced hundreds of neighborhoods often defined by the identities of their inhabitants. This process also shaped one of the most racially segregated cities in the world, a phenomenon that all Chicagoans know well. Food in Chicago, however, has been one of the few bridges that has historically brought disparate and culturally diverse groups together, whether it be to challenge the status quo by eating in each other's restaurants and pubs, attending each other's neighborhood festivals, or by finding ways to work together in food companies that have made the city a food manufacturing giant. Most importantly, borrowing and mixing to create eclectic, distinctive, and complex Chicago foodways has always been a commonplace and acceptable practice in the city. The "Gym Shoe" (or "Jim Shoo"), one of the lesser-known but highly popular sandwiches originating in Chicago, mixes gyro meat, roast/Italian beef, and corned beef, partly reflecting Chicago's unique migration story. This is a story about groups meeting and crossing boundaries—sometimes contentiously—through producing, distributing, and eating food. To this end, the annual Taste of Chicago started in 1980 based on the concept of bringing together the flavors of Chicago's communities, allowing locals and visitors to celebrate the city's unique culinary products. The Irony of "The Taste," as it became known, is that it takes place just blocks from where Jean Baptiste Point du Sable, a man likely of mixed African descent who married a Potawatomi woman and erected his home and farm in the 1780s—including a dairy, bake house, smokehouse, and poultry house—started a process that would make Chicago a culturally diverse U.S. food capital.[63]

4

MARKETS AND RETAIL

While Carl Sandburg may have called Chicago the "Hogbutcher to the World," it has never been just a city of manufacturers and food processors. The city also grew because of Chicago merchants' ability to market provisions and equipment to the vast Western frontier the city bordered upon. Chicago in the late 1800s played a similar role in the United States that Bentonville, Arkansas, the home of Walmart, does today. In addition to being a center of food manufacturing, in 1900 Chicago was the home of Sears, Roebuck, and Company and Montgomery Ward, the giant catalog houses and the two largest merchandizing companies in the world. Chicago companies bought, marketed, and shipped massive amounts of goods throughout the vast interior of the United States.

The role of Chicago as a central place in the late nineteenth-century American West has been studied by William Cronon, among others.[1] Cronon did not, however, specifically discuss the wholesale or the door-to-door retail grocery business. Nor did he describe how and from where the city got its food. Chicago's motto, "City in a Garden," might seem to imply that the city and its surrounding area grew much of its own food, but the Chicago area never came anywhere close to providing its own food, even when it was a Native American and Métis trading place. Chicago has always relied heavily on imported food. A grocery and dry goods store was established outside of Fort Dearborn far before the city was founded. Later in the nineteenth century and into the twentieth century, the city attempted to establish central retail markets, such as occurred in Philadelphia, New York, and elsewhere. But relative to other nineteenth-century American cities, Chicago had a relatively low population density and was split by difficult-to-cross river channels, and the central markets were not as successful as in many other places. Small neighborhood groceries were numerous in business districts throughout the city, however, as well as peddlers and delivery services. In the early twentieth century, self-service "cash and carry" stores gradually replaced more full-service options, and supermarkets appeared, first not much larger than the previous grocers, but standardized and marketed as particularly pure and clean. These competed with the neighborhood markets, although smaller stores remain important in many neighborhoods today.

Chicago, like many other American cities, has seen a growth in farmer's markets over the past thirty years. These vary from the Green City Market, located in Lincoln Park but moving inside in the winter, which is used by many top chefs to source fresh local produce, to downtown markets catering to workers on their lunch breaks, to neighborhood markets in both the suburbs and city, which are both sources of fresh produce and social spaces, often providing music and crafts in addition to food. The Green City Market is representative of a set of new farmer's markets and groceries focusing on specialty items for generally upscale consumers, a trend that builds on a series of upscale specialty markets and grocers that trend back to Chicago's founding. At the same time, new larger ethnic markets, particularly in suburban areas, built on the model of the neighborhood grocery, focused on specialty items for particular ethnic groups. In Chicago, as elsewhere, groceries are markers of the ethnicity and class status of particular neighborhoods. Groceries, supermarkets, and farmer's markets perform a social role in communities, particularly for women. Where you shop may be an important part of your identity.

Given the important role groceries and supermarkets often play in a community, it is not surprising that the presence or lack of groceries and supermarkets in particular communities has also been an issue of importance to community and antipoverty activists. In recent years, Chicago has been a focus of research and activism around "food deserts," generally defined as areas with low access to full-service supermarkets.[2] In Chicago, as in many other U.S. cities, food deserts tend to be located in predominantly lower-income, African American communities. While the *food desert* term and its relationship to race, income, as well as health issues in lower-income minority neighborhoods is a topic of great debate nationwide, the power of the concept lies largely in its ability to convey differences in living conditions between areas with high and low resources. This is an issue that stretches back long before the food desert term was popularized in the early twenty-first century, back to mid- to late twentieth-century studies of the prices of groceries in poor and wealthy communities and early twentieth-century studies of the relationship between the efficiency of the grocery delivery system and prices from the Progressive and Depression eras. Food prices have almost always been a focus of activism.

This chapter covers the history of markets and retail from frontier Chicago to its role as a wholesale marketing center to the growth of supermarkets, both mainstream and specialty, in the twentieth and early twenty-first centuries. Throughout, it is clear that food provisioning has meant more to Chicago residents than just what stores were where. Food stores, whether retail or wholesale, have been an integral part of what defines particular neighborhoods, as well as one of the economic pillars upon which the city was built.

A GROCER ON THE FRONTIER

Following the treaty mandating the removal of indigenous populations from the area in September of 1833, speculators began to pour in, and Chicago went from an estimated population of 150 in 1832 to 350 in 1833 to 1,800 in 1834 and 3,265 the next year.[3] Within two months following the treaty, the number of "regular stores" rose from approximately five to twenty. An 1837 census showed twenty-seven groceries along with nineteen grocery and provision stores.[4] In one week in 1834, seven new buildings were added.[5] In this quickly growing town on the frontier, basic necessities, in particular food, became difficult to come by, particularly when lake navigation was closed during the winter. A local newspaper wrote that in June 1835 that flour was $12 a barrel, up from about $5.75 a barrel in 1833. Three weeks later, the price was above $20. Somewhat lower but similar price increases occurred for beef, salt, corn meal, and other commodities. Those coming to Chicago from further east were advised to buy provisions there.[6] By 1837, the high prices for produce and meats helped entice the development of local agriculture, which grew quickly enough that by 1839, these began to sell to the East Coast. Still, in the 1830s, a large part of Chicago's food supply was from afar, mainly from further east. By 1841 and 1842, local agriculture had grown enough to easily support the community, but this coincided with the stagnation of population growth and the crash in land prices that went along with the delay in the building of the Illinois and Michigan Canal.[7] This led to Chicago becoming even more of a net exporter of produce, particularly meats. Even before the opening of the canal and the railroad in 1848, Chicago was becoming part of the national food economy, both as a supplier and customer. While meat was being shipped to the East Coast, Chicagoans were working hard to open other trade routes. In 1842, the first refined sugar was shipped from St. Louis to Chicago via riverboat to Galena and then overland.[8]

How these changes influenced one business is seen in the business records of Charles L. Harmon, an early Chicago grocer. His papers show us both the kinds of products one early grocer sold as well as the difficulties owning such a frontier business had. Harmon opened a grocery, together with other family members, outside Fort Dearborn in 1832, immediately after the end of the Black Hawk War. Harmon was the son of Isaac Harmon, a doctor at Fort Dearborn and in private practice who was known for his success in treating a group of cholera-ridden soldiers. Harmon's brother was one of Chicago's first lawyers. Charles L. Harmon appears to have been the grocer of choice for Chicago's most established families.[9] His clients included Mark Beaubien, who owned the Sauganash Hotel and was the brother of Jean-Baptiste Beaubien, the former Chicago agent for the American Fur Company and one of Chicago's most long-established citizens, as well as James Kinzie, John Kinzie's son, who also owned a tavern, and Archibald Clybourne, the first constable of Chicago, and also the first butcher in the city, who supplied Fort Dearborn with meat and possessed the city's first mansion.[10]

Purchases listed from Harmon's store in these early years include a wide variety of shelf-stable foods, as well as alcoholic beverages and hardware. Among many other purchases, the July 1834 account books show that the United States Harbor purchased flour, salt, mustard, and dishes. A John Watkins purchased candy and molasses. One Truman Wright purchased over the course of the month coffee, molasses, shoes for his daughter, sugar, one-fourth of a bushel of dried apples, a box of hook and eyes, brandy, silk, paper, more silk, paper, and coffee, plates, two pitchers, a gallon of an illegible liquid (probably wine or liquor), and tablespoons. Others bought bolts, locks, playing cards, and a whole variety of shippable food and goods that would be typical of a city being quickly built. Spices, tobacco, tea, pepper, ginger, and coffee were purchased, along with nails.[11] While Harmon's well-connected store probably had few issues, the fact that groceries also sold alcohol caused them to be included in the town's first "Sunday law," passed on September 1, 1834, outlawing any "tippling shop" or grocery from being open on Sunday.[12] Complaints including loitering seem to have been similar to those about corner stores today.

Grocers such as Harmon seem to have specialized initially in relatively shelf-stable goods and did not generally sell meat. At first, much of what was sold in the new town was from the East, much of it passing through the Erie Canal and over the lakes. The Erie Canal itself helped build the new town, which was isolated from the Mississippi River, the main highway of the West, but the lack of easy connections to the river and south helped isolate Chicago. Produce and meats came in from the Wabash Valley, carried along the Vincennes Road by wagons driven by "Hoosier" farmers and from the small number of area farms, but it was not enough to feed the city. They brought in dried and fresh apples, butter, ham, bacon, and other goods and returned with coffee and salt.[13]

Running a grocery in early Chicago was not easy. Much of what was sold had to be procured from afar and was difficult to control. Charles L. Harmon by 1846 seems to have worked largely on a commission basis, taking a percentage of the sales of goods consigned to him. His letters indicate that this had many issues, although it allowed him to minimize investment in the stock he sold. Consigned items might not sell well, or the price might be lower than expected. Shipped items could be rejected by the customer. Both sales and procurement were often hampered by weather and bad roads. In a sense, Harmon almost had to have acted much like a current-day company like Amazon works as a middleman between producers and consumers, dealing with issues from both suppliers and customers. In one case, Harmon appears to have paid for a quantity of whiskey to resell, which was only partially delivered.[14] In December 1848, a shipment of corn was stuck in the ice on the new Illinois and Michigan Canal. Harmon explains to the seller who consigned the corn to him that the canal boat captain will look to sell the corn near where the boat was stuck for a much lower price than available in the city.[15] Quality control was also a problem. In an 1846 letter, Harmon apologizes to a client for the low quality of two boxes of fish that had been sent to them: "the (F)ish man . . . is very ready to replace them at his own expense."[16] In another case, he states that the butter sent him by a local supplier "is good, but not such an article as I want for table uses."[17] Harmon seems to have worked with a number of local producers of products such as vinegar, honey, and butter, although, as in this case, their products did not always meet quality standards or match demand. On the sales side, demand seems to vary greatly, both due to weather and transportation issues and extreme financial modulations. Harmon explains to a supplier in 1848 that the demand for whiskey is low and he has not been able to sell the quantity sent "at any reasonable rate . . . but I am endeavoring to sell it in small parcels to go into the country. The roads are now improving and I hope to work it off truly during the present month."[18] In a case from 1846 that highlights Chicago's continuing site on the frontier and the kinds of goods that were particularly abundant, Harmon appears to be dealing with a local who asks him to sell honey and deer skins: "Honey is unusually abundant in this market and I cannot get an offer for this lot which I think would be satisfactory. . . . I have some time since wrote you in regard to the Deer Skins . . . which (were) taken out of season & consequently nearly worthless. The only offer I had for them was 10¢ each . . . I called upon about every Fur dealer in the place. They are yet in store but if you wish to sell them for that price, I will do so. I will make further efforts to get a better price for the Honey."[19]

While Harmon dealt with goods of all types, his account books and letters also show the sales of luxury items, particularly oysters and lobsters. In 1846, as Chicago recovered from the speculation bust of the late 1830s and early 1840s, Harmon wrote a supplier that he has "no doubt a large trade" could be had in oysters and lobster.[20] In a December 1848 letter and attached account statement, Harmon states that "the new lots of oysters give good satisfaction and sale in consequence will be larger." He also states that he has been able to sell some oysters to "The Agent of the Baltimore Oysters" and also his customers. Harmon apparently had oysters available while others did not due to poor weather, so his sales were good despite the weather lowering demand. While he had not yet sold out, Harmon earned a $19.47 commission on a total of $243.34 sold of oysters, about an 8 percent commission. Minus expenses, Harmon returned $192 to the oyster provider.[21]

Harmon's grocery was located along South Water Street, Chicago's original wholesale marketplace, just south of the main branch of the Chicago River. Ship's chandlers, who specialized in supplying the ships in the busy harbor with supplies, were also located on South Water. In an 1858 account book for Harding and Hall, a ship's chandler lists the provisions sold to a lake schooner named *Racer*. Supplies included butter, eggs, potatoes, sugar, apples, hard bread, tea, mackerel, lard, turnips, vinegar, mustard, pickles, brown beans, and many other food and non-food items.[22] Unlike Harmon, ship's chandlers needed to procure items quickly, since a ship in port is not making money. Harding and Hall must have worked with grocers such as Harmon to do so.

CHICAGO AS THE WHOLESALE FOOD CENTER

In 1881, *The Grocer's Bulletin*, a short-lived Chicago weekly trade paper, explained its reason to exist in a statement that summarizes and hyperbolizes Chicago's strengths and central economic place in the United States, and it goes on to place Chicago as the retail giant of the hemisphere:

> Located at the terminus of a magnificent marine highway, in the heart of a region of boundless agricultural possibilities, destined to teem with a thriving population which would convert wilderness and plain into field freighted with stores of food to supply the globe . . . all pouring vast returns of wealth into the great central reservoir. . . . Our groceries, dry goods, drugs, and other merchandise are finding their way to the borders of Pennsylvania, to the very doors of St. Louis and southward, to the Pacific Coast and nearly all intermediate points, and throughout the more northern States and Territories. New York for a time contended desperately against the encroachments upon her territory of the young western Hercules, but finding longer opposition useless, she has finally endeavored to compromise by established branch houses at this point, but with, it would seem, very indifferent success.[23]

Boosterism was a way of life in the growing cities of the West, but *The Grocer's Bulletin* statement is triumphant. Chicago's longtime rival, St.

Louis, was depicted as a mere customer, and the new rival, New York, was aging and destined to be passed by soon.

As Charles L. Harmon's letters and the careers of John Kinzie and Jean Baptiste Point du Sable make clear, Chicago businesses provided food and other provisions to the surrounding region even before the opening of the Illinois and Michigan Canal and the Chicago and Galena Union train in 1848. While Chicago continued and built on this role, much of its true power came from its position as a wholesaler, a position that truly strengthened with the growth of Chicago as a railroad center. Much of this power centered on Chicago's situation as a transfer point between a system of railroads that reached from the city to every compass direction from the west, collecting unprocessed foods (such as wheat and cattle) at small and large towns throughout the middle of the continent to "trunk" lines that carried manufactured and processed goods to the east. Similarly, boats brought in lumber, iron ore, and other raw materials from the north, as well as sugar and cotton up the Illinois and Michigan Canal, and shipped out manufactured goods. This position, at a joining point between multiple transportation systems, was not just a good place to manufacture things, it also was a central place from which to ship things, and thus the ideal place to base a wholesale business. As William Cronon states: "Whether breaking up shipments from the East or assembling bulk shipments from the West, (Chicago) served as the entrepôt—the place in between—connecting eastern markets with vast western resource regions."[24]

The railroad changed small-town markets throughout the Midwest since it meant that they could now order goods directly from Chicago merchants, rather than either going to Chicago itself or buying from middlemen who connected the Chicago merchants to small towns. Direct retailers in Chicago actually initially suffered, since the zone from which people would travel to Chicago for basic supplies dropped. However, the city now was the center of a large network that provided much of the inventory for stores in smaller towns and cities. Chicago's wholesale grocery trade developed particularly quickly during the 1860s, mainly selling processed foods from afar to rural stores. In 1860 there were thirty-four wholesale grocery firms in the city, and in 1864 a Grocer's Exchange was established, where the prices at the New York grocery and gold markets arrived via telegraph and were posted and large lots of groceries were sold to out-of-town buyers.[25] Wholesalers also sold grains, produce, and meats, both to regional and local markets. A key tool in the development of this network was the innovation of shipping produce on ice from California and other warmer climates in 1869 by a wholesaler named Washington Porter, which began just a few weeks after the transcontinental railroad was completed.[26] An 1878 market report includes prices and conditions of, among other items, dried fruits, apples, cranberries, flour, corn, oats, and other grains, beeswax, maple sugar, dressed hogs, poultry, veal, onions, potatoes, cider, eggs, and a lengthy discussion of butter quality and the particular shapes it is sold in.[27]

In 1862, Steele-Wedeles, destined to become one of the largest grocery wholesalers in the country, opened as a retail and wholesale grocer on South Clark Street near 12th Street (now Roosevelt Road). The business grew steadily, soon buying out competitors. Their building luckily survived the Chicago fire and, while they claimed not to have raised prices afterward, the company thrived as the city was rebuilt. In 1879, the company moved to the heart of the South Water Market. While they maintained an operation in South Water Market, in 1907 Steele-Wedeles built a large warehouse just to the north of the Chicago River, over the Chicago and Northwestern train line, at the north end of the Dearborn Street bridge, highlighting the continued industrial role of the main branch of the Chicago River into the twentieth century.[28]

Steele-Wedeles was an "importing and jobbing grocer," a middleman packaging and distributing goods brought in from around the country and the world. The company marketed its own "Savoy" house brand products, becoming the second large-scale jobber to advertise in newspapers and trade magazines in 1918.[29] They considered themselves an essential component of the modernization of the grocery industry. In a December 1885 letter available in English and German accompanying a calendar sent to retail grocers in Chicago, the company included depictions of a "well arranged and flourishing Grocery, the owner in full dress suit" and a "neglected and unthrifty" store with a "discouraged and distressed" proprietor. While the company admits that the dress suit was an exaggeration, they emphasize that the clean grocery represents the grocers it sold to who "constitute the cream and the solidity of the Retail Grocery business in the Metropolis of the West."[30] While Chicago was its core market, Steele-Wedeles sent out sales personnel to stores, often small, throughout the country, and while Steele-Wedeles was vastly larger, it encountered some of the same issues that Charles L. Harmon did in the control of payments. A 1901 notice to sales staff asks them to not sell more than a certain amount of tobacco to smaller stores, due to the inability of many of these stores to pay. "Fruit stores, cigar and candy stores, as a rule . . . are of very light financial caliber, and it will be necessary to confine orders in these cases."[31]

SOUTH WATER MARKET AND THE HAYMARKET

The giant Steele-Wedeles warehouse was replaced by what is now the Westin River North Hotel in 1987. However, its longtime presence along the main branch of the Chicago River, in the heart of what is now Chicago's tourism and business district, shows that food distribution was at the very center of Chicago itself almost from its founding for a hundred years through the middle of the twentieth century. Across the street from the Steele-Wedeles warehouse, on the current site of Marina City, was a wholesale fresh fruit business.[32] Across the river to the south stretched Chicago's national wholesale market, the South Water Market. South Water Market, focused mainly on goods shipped in from afar, as well as Fulton Street, the nearby market for meats, and the Randolph Street Haymarket, where both hay and local produce were sold, together served as the hub for the wholesale food trade of both Chicago and the Midwest.

The vibrancy of the markets during the 1890s were highlighted in Edna Ferber's *So Big*. Protagonist Selina brings a wagon full of produce to the Haymarket in the week after her farmer husband dies. She parks the wagon east of the corner of Des Plaines and Randolph. Ferber describes the scene as she arrives, racing with a German farmer from north of the city to an open space in the double line of wagons that lined the street: "Fruits and vegetables—tons of it—acres of it—piled in the wagons that blocked the historic square. An unarmed army of food to feed a great city. Through this little section, and South Water Street that lay to the east, passed all the verdant growing things that fed Chicago's millions."[33] Along wide Randolph Street, the grocers and peddlers who purchased the local produce had easy access. The wagons would line up the evening before to get the best positions. The first peddlers arrived at about 4 a.m., followed by grocers and restaurant owners. The market closed at noon, and sellers were fined $5 if they remained after this time.[34]

Unfortunately, Selina had chosen a bad day, a Jewish holiday, to sell her wares, and after a slow morning headed east to South Water Market. There she found a different scene entirely. Here were the huge "commission" houses, the descendants of Charles L. Harmon (who was located on South Water himself) that sold goods from around the country to the high-end buyers in the city, as well the large national wholesalers, such as Steele-Wedeles, that brought together goods from around the country, repackaged them, and shipped them both to Chicago grocers and to buyers throughout the nation and even the world. Perry Duis in his book *Challenging Chicago* reports that just the wholesale firm run by Washington Porter handled eight thousand rail carloads a year. In addition to the California produce, Latin American produce came in from New Orleans along the Illinois Central. The presence of the market also allowed Chicago-area truck farmers to sell for nationwide distribution.[35] A local high-end candymaker, Charles Frederick Gunther, utilized Chicago's lo-

Figure 4.1.   The Haymarket, 1893. From *Chicago, Souvenir Album of Chicago and the Columbian Exposition* (S. L. Stein, 1893). Chicago Public Library, Special Collections and Preservation Division, CCW 15.8.

cation to help ship his popular caramels throughout the county and to Europe. Chicago was also a leader in the distribution of salt, particularly with the rise of the Morton Salt Company in the late 1800s.[36] Ferber describes the store of William Talcott, a fictional wholesaler that knew Salina's deceased husband: "The Great Lakes boats brought him choice Michigan peaches and grapes; refrigerator cars brought him the products of California's soil in a day when out-of-season food was a rare luxury." Talcott catered to the finest hotels and the grocers in the wealthy sections of town.[37] South Water Market was a tourist attraction, full of exotic tropical fruits, some of which, such as bananas, had to be shipped green and then stored in often fragrant cellars to ripen, described in 1897 by a *Chicago Tribune* reporter as "an underground passage, . . . some seven or eight feet in height, and lighted every four of five feet with gas jets . . . suspended on strings fastened to hooks in the ceiling are glistening rows of the yellow fruit."[38]

South Water Market's situation in the very middle of Chicago, along the Chicago River but not adjacent to Chicago's train lines, made traffic in the area a constant issue. The market originally developed before the railroads. Merchants would bring grain and produce in by wagon, which would then be resold either to Chicago merchants or to commission merchants who would arrange shipment, generally by boat, to larger cities.[39] Since South Water Street ran along the harbor (the main branch of the Chicago River), its location originally made sense, particularly for exporters. However, with the rise of the railroads and the increasing size of the city and its central business district, the location became more and more difficult. Still, the concentration of businesses in this central wholesale core continued to increase, particularly after the Great Fire of 1871, as rebuilding merchants chose to locate in the central market zone. Steele-Wedeles is a good example of this. They were originally located in what is now the South Loop and relocated in 1879 to LaSalle and South Water, in the heart of the produce market. With the increased concentration and the growth of the city came increased congestion. In order to reach the site, wagons often had to cross much of the increasingly congested Loop, which could take over an hour at the worst times. Farmers' wagons going to the markets also increased congestion themselves.[40] In addition, the location of South Water Market along the river led to a large amount of direct waste disposal from stores into the river itself, causing pollution issues.[41] When in 1909 Steele-Wedeles moved its warehouses across the

Chicago River, it boasted in a letter to merchants that "the congestion heretofore existing at our corner . . . has been removed and made most convenient for quick and unobstructed approach."[42]

The Burnham Plan of 1909 recommended that South Water Market be removed and replaced by a double-decker boulevard. In 1926 this part of the plan came to fruition as Wacker Drive. The plan recommended decentralizing produce sales, including allowing for the sale of produce in schoolyards and elsewhere, and building a municipally owned wholesale market away from the city's core. The congestion in South Water Market was seen as a major contributor to the cost of groceries in the city, an issue that grew as food prices rose precipitously during World War I. In 1925, a new South Water Market, keeping the original name, was built on the Near West Side, adjacent to the Chicago, Burlington, and Quincy and Chicago and North Western rail lines, between Racine and Morgan and 14th and 16th streets. This area, which had previously been a slum known as "The Valley" due to its location along a railroad embankment, became a modern, city-owned market space, with room for 166 tenants, with elevators and good access to both rail lines and the street and in a central location, but outside of the most congested area of the city.[43] While it was no longer along the river, the role of boats in shipping food had declined, and for the wholesale trade, the river was mainly now an obstacle for trucks to cross.

The new South Water Market was a success, but it quickly became congested itself. By 1940, the U.S. Department of Agriculture (USDA) completed a study of the congestion, blaming it mainly on the practice, continuing from the old South Water Market, of selling produce directly off trucks rather than unloading it and selling from the adjacent stores, as well as buyers parking their cars and trucks illegally (in the loading zone while not loading) along 15th Street, the main street of the market.[44] Interestingly, addresses remained the same as in the original South Water Market, and they did not comply with Chicago's newly regimented street address system. Wholesalers were located at, say, "24 South Water Market" rather than at "1100 W. 15th St." In 1949, it remained the second largest wholesale produce market in the country. At this time, more than fifty thousand carloads of fruits and vegetables were distributed to the Chicago metropolitan region per year. The market also was a supply point for smaller wholesale markets and a repackaging and shipping point for shipments to the East and South. This reshipping function accounted for about 40 to 45 percent of the produce entering the Chicago market during the mid-twentieth century. South Water Market, thus, continued to be a focal point not only for produce distribution in the Chicago market but also the national market.[45] The market continued to take incoming shipments from both local farmers, which mainly arrived on trucks, and from faraway farms, which mainly arrived by train, although the produce needed to be transferred into smaller trucks in order to access South Water Market. It also continued to be the site of a great amount of activity, as buyers and brokers raced to find the best or the cheapest produce.

Competing markets to South Water did exist. While the new market was built next to a freight train line, it did not have good facilities to receive and sort incoming produce. This allowed for the development of competing sites. The "Chicago Produce Terminal," a trainyard where incoming produce was sorted, was developed about two miles southwest of the market in the industrial district along the Chicago Sanitary and Shipping Canal. It included seasonal yards devoted to particular produce items, such as potatoes and watermelon. Once separated, produce would be either reshipped or put on trucks to sell at other markets such as South Water. A competing potato yard was built on the Chicago and Northwestern Railroad, a mile-and-a-half west of South Water Market. In addition, the old Randolph Street Haymarket as well as a market on South State Street persisted after the destruction of the original South Water Market, and they continued to act as wholesale markets for produce.[46] A few produce wholesalers still survive in the Randolph Street area today, as well as a larger number of meat wholesalers in neighboring Fulton Market, although the number of these is declining as land prices skyrocket in what is now the heart of Chicago's hip West Loop. In 2015, Fulton Market is the home of a group of Chicago's most popular new restaurants.[47]

Already in 1950, the issues that would eventually lead to the replacement of the second South Water Market were being seen. While the amount of shipments through the market continued to increase, the increase was not as much as the overall increase in production of most produce items during the 1940s. The main issues were that refrigeration technology for trucks was gradually improving, and that the Southeast was growing as an area for produce production. On the national scale, South Water Market's main advantage was the concentration of railroads leading into Chicago from the West, bringing in produce, mainly from

Figure 4.2.   The New South Water Market, 1941. Library of Congress, Prints & Photographs Division, FSA/OWI Collection, LC-USF34-063118-D.

California, for the Chicago and eastern markets. Produce from the southeastern United States might be shipped to Chicago to be sold in the city and the Midwest, but more direct paths were present for shipment to the East Coast. Furthermore, with the growth in the use of trucks for long-distance shipments, shipments to secondary markets did not have to go through a central market like Chicago but could be delivered directly to warehouses in cities such as Milwaukee and Indianapolis, rather than passing through Chicago. The rise of the interstate system made truck shipments of foodstuffs even more advantageous. Also, large supermarket chains have their own distribution system and do not rely on central "terminal" markets like South Water. Still, the second South Water Market survived until 2001, when it was replaced by the state-of-the-art Chicago International Produce Market, located only a mile southwest of the second South Water Market. This new market remains large—the largest in the Midwest—at 450,000 square feet. It is much more efficient than the previous market, being designed for today's larger trucks and also being on one story. Tenant Atom Banana has an innovative ripening room, the descendant of the nineteenth-century tunnel under South Water Street. It also continues to concentrate on both the local market and on reshipping and repackaging to regional vendors. This being said, the goals of the market have become less grandiose. The aim is no longer to be the central produce market of the United States and the world, but to provide a particular service to a particular group of vendors in a particular area of the country.

FROM PEDDLERS AND NEIGHBORHOOD STORES TO SUPERMARKETS AND BEYOND

The story of Chicago told through its groceries and supermarkets is in many ways much less remarkable than the history of its huge wholesale markets or its food processors. Chicago has generally not been the hometown of the largest supermarket chains in the United States. While some stores do have a strong following, Chicago is not marked by stores that engender the kind of following that stores like Wegmans in the Northeast does. In terms of its groceries, Chicago has perhaps played another of its stereotypical roles, the quintessential American city, typified at first by neighborhood grocery, largely replaced during the twentieth century by larger supermarkets that were increasingly controlled by just two chains. Chicago was, and is, quintessential in other, more negative ways. Chain groceries and later supermarkets were more prevalent in higher-income areas of the city almost from the beginning, and became more so after many stores closed during the Depression and other economic downturns. At the same time, chains were built out into the suburbs, often preceding housing development. More recently, Chicago has been the site for many of the "food desert" studies indicating the persistence of these patterns. Related to this, food shopping has been the focus of consumer activism in terms of building alternate buying systems, such as consumer cooperatives. As in many cities, farmer's markets have made a resurgence in Chicago, both high-end markets such as Lincoln Park's Green City Market, a browsing zone for Chicago's top chefs, to community markets in the Loop and in communities throughout the city and suburbs, although the most successful markets tend to be in relatively upscale or downtown locations.

One thing missing from early Chicago, as compared with many other cities of the time, was a successful central retail market. While South Water Street was both a commercial and retail market in the beginning, the closest Chicago came to a central marketplace was along State Street, where the "Hoosier" wagons of southern Indiana farmers would line up to sell their wares. In 1848, a two-story central market building was erected in the middle of State Street. The building was Chicago's first municipal building. The second floor was used for civic meetings, including the city council and city hall. Elaborate regulations were given for the food sold, including against selling rotten meat. In 1850, markets were added both north of the Chicago River's main branch and west of the South Branch. This initial building was important in the city's history, but the market was open only for a decade. As the city further expanded, the other two markets also failed, competing unsuccessfully with neighborhood groceries and peddlers.

In general, compared to other large American cities, nineteenth-century Chicago became particularly dependent upon its grocery stores and peddlers.[48] While it was possible for consumers to patronize the wholesale markets, for the most part nineteenth- and early twentieth-century grocery shopping in Chicago consisted of visits to small local grocers, butchers, and produce shops, as well as buying from street peddlers. In relatively sprawling Chicago, street peddlers were an important conduit of foods from the central markets to the neighborhoods. Not only were peddlers convenient, they sold groceries in the small quantities that could be afforded by often cash-strapped families. Buying in small amounts also saved space in iceboxes and crowded apartments with no cold storage facilities, as well the cost of the ice itself. Peddlers provided great convenience. As economist Edward Duddy reported on lettuce sales in the South Water Market in 1926, "A carload of lettuce . . . is the unit of purchase for the (South Water Market wholesaler). The jobber buys ordinarily twenty crates or 1/16 of a car. The retailer buys one crate or 1/320 of a car, while the consumer buys one head or 1/7,680 of a car."[49] One of the most striking parts of this statement is that the retailer would only buy one crate of lettuce, showing the general small size of the retailers, whether peddler or store. Yet the importance of small vendors is highlighted in their total percentage of purchases at the Randolph Street and South Water Markets. Jobber peddlers, who resold commodities to small groceries and peddlers, and street peddlers together accounted for almost a third of the goods sold at the South Water Market in 1923, and peddlers accounted for 42 percent of the goods bought at the Randolph Street Haymarket. Peddlers also bought of 10,212 cartloads directly at the railroad team tracks from which perishable goods were distributed to the markets.[50]

Peddlers were part of the daily life of neighborhoods. As reported in Tracey Deutsch's excellent book *Building a Housewife's Paradise*, they brought an amazing variety of goods directly past consumer's doors, including "produce, ice, dairy goods, prepared foods, clothing, . . . or rags."[51] Even fish was peddled. Peddlers often negotiated for long periods with consumers. As one woman remembered from the 1930s, peddlers would go down streets and alleyways: "From my porch, I could see the mothers streaming out of the back doors . . . crowded around the produce truck."[52] Peddling was a hard life. Peddlers earned little, and were subject to anti-immigrant and anti-Semitic behavior, particularly as Jewish, Italian, and Greek peddlers entered Polish, Irish, and native-born communities. Even German Jews looked down on Jewish Russian immigrant peddlers, as did U.S.-born Greeks on immigrant Greek peddlers, calling them "parasites." In *So Big*, Edna Ferber characterizes the peddlers as shrewd, crafty, and dishonest," and she highlights a peddler named Luigi: "A swarthy face had Luigi, a swift brilliant smile, a crafty eye . . . When prices did not please Luigi he pretended not to understand."[53] When Ferber's heroine Selina decides to peddle her produce door to door in the wealthy Prairie Avenue neighborhood where she once lived, she feels the call of her patrician Vermont forebears telling her not to, embarrassed by her fall in class.[54] Grocers particularly complained about the competition peddlers presented. Such feelings led to strict regulations on peddlers that were often difficult to enforce, although the city tried, particularly in terms of food safety regulations, for which peddlers were particular targets. In general, peddlers represented a difficult-to-control, as well as a poor and immigrant, group that few with power would promote. Even so, the prices and convenience they offered led to their persistence into the 1930s.[55]

As previously mentioned, Chicago's relative sprawl compared to other American cities, as well as congestion along the bridges over the Chicago River and its branches, impeded the success of its central markets. Issues with Chicago's central markets continued long into Chicago's history, partially due to their ethnic and racial issues. South Water Market, the Randolph Street Haymarket, and Fulton Market were primarily wholesale markets, but they were open to individual shoppers. However, buying at the wholesale markets could be intimating. Tracey Deutsch quotes a 1913 housekeeping expert describing the sellers at these markets as "a class of dealers with the ugliest of social qualities, who hold food for a price while it wilts or deteriorates or spoils."[56] Traveling to the central markets was also difficult for most Chicago residents, and prices were difficult to negotiate for the uninitiated. All of this made peddlers and neighborhood groceries particularly important. Different from the wholesale markets was the famous Maxwell Street Market, developed around the turn of the twentieth century and formalized in 1912. It was a general peddler market that eventually focused more on clothing than food, although a section of Maxwell Street west of Halsted had a concentration of food stores and restaurants, mainly serving the local area from the fixed stores along the street.[57]

While small grocers complained about peddlers, the products the grocers and peddlers sold often came from the same place, and elements of risk were present in food buying for consumers, wherever they purchased food. In the nineteenth and early twentieth centuries, milk was also sold directly by street vendors and small stores, often "loose," dipped out of the dealer's jars into bottles and jars provided by the consumer. In the nineteenth century, this milk often came from "swill dairies," but the issues related to the milk consumed probably came as much from the delivery method and additives meant to keep the milk, whether from a swill dairy or a local farm, fresh smelling, such as formaldehyde, as from the cows themselves.[58] As the knowledge of the germ theory of disease developed, this open-air method was eventually deemed dangerous to public health, but it persisted into the twentieth century, both at vendors and in small stores. In 1913, the Chicago Health Department's *Bulletin of the Chicago School of Sanitary Instruction* guided housewives to never "buy milk served from a can."[59] In New York, a 1908 study estimated that half of all milk sold in the city was "loose," and a 1930s report continued to investigate the health issues of loose milk.[60] While loose milk was made more difficult to sell as health and regulations increased, an increasing focus on cleanliness in the selling of groceries, in particular perishables, influenced the rise of chain stores and supermarkets.

THE RISE OF CHAIN GROCERIES

In addition to peddlers and wholesalers, Chicago also featured many small neighborhood groceries, both independent and chain. In 1871, in the immediate wake of the Chicago fire, the Great Atlantic and Pacific Tea Company (A&P) opened its first store outside of New York, at 114–116 W. Washington Street in downtown Chicago, removing still-hot bricks to do so. The opening was attended to great fanfare, and great advertisement, by the Russian grand duke Alexis. It was extremely successful and led to a quick expansion of A&P in Chicago and other cities outside of New York.[61] Like Steele-Wedeles, A&P specialized in teas and coffees, advertising "the choicest new crop teas in every variety," as well as freshly roasted coffee.[62] Despite the growth of A&P and other chains, independent grocers held their own for many years. In 1923, according to historian Lizbeth Cohen, chains only operated 18 percent of all Chicago groceries.[63] While grocers of the late 1800s did not generally carry fresh produce, this increased over time, as evidenced by the large number of "peddler jobbers" that provided produce both to peddlers and to small groceries.

Until the 1930s, both chains and independents in general remained very small in size. The "model" grocery store of the 1920s was just 1,134 square feet, and most were probably smaller. Most lacked refrigeration, generally not selling meats and other refrigerated goods. Small stores such as this depended on personal relationships and often were focused on serving particular ethnic groups within the surrounding neighborhood. Prices were not posted, and items were kept behind the counter and were retrieved by clerks or by clerks accompanying customers. What people actually paid was subject to a great deal of bargaining and haggling. Sales were often on credit, and managing this credit was often a great challenge for storeowners. Stores often served a very limited number of customers, generally a few dozen, who lived in the immediate district. Stores generally had a limited life expectancy. A grocer on Chicago's North Side boasted that "my grocery is the oldest on the street" after having been open thirty years.[64]

South Shore neighborhood grocer Arthur J. Barnsback, owner of the 1907 grocery seen in figure 4.3, may have a typical life story, and the story of his store shows how many times stores could change hands, while generally staying within the same ethnic group. Barnsback, of old

Figure 4.3. Interior of Barnsback's Grocery in Chicago's South Shore neighborhood, 1907, photographer unknown. Chicago Public Library, Special Collections and Preservation Division, SSCC 1.4.

German stock, moved to Chicago around the age of eighteen, having worked in a country store in downstate Mattoon for three years previously. He found a position as a clerk in a store in the Windsor Park section of the then newly built and well-off South Shore neighborhood. He worked at this store for eleven years and then left to start his own business. He bought this new store from his employer Mr. Hecker (who may have purchased it to sell to Barnsback). Mr. Hecker had purchased it from a Mrs. Price, who ran it for a short amount of time. Mrs. Price had purchased it from the Gottwald family, who ran it successfully for six years. According to Barnsback, at the Gottwald's store: "Prices were low, for Thanksgiving turkeys—heavy ones, sold at ten cents a pound." The Gottwald family had bought it from the Huntschmidt family, the original grocers on the site (it had been a drug store previously), who ran it for just two months.[65]

The number of chain stores in Chicago expanded greatly during the 1910s through the 1920s, as they did elsewhere in the United States. This was the result of many factors, one being the rise of discount chains. A&P, for instance, in 1913 developed a smaller-model store with a limited selection that was specifically focused on discounts. The number of these discount A&P stores expanded rapidly, and A&P became a marketing juggernaut, holding down prices for particular items to near cost, which was impossible for independent grocers to compete with.[66] Soon thereafter, a rise in food prices surrounding World War I helped lead to a newspaper-promoted revolt against grocers, focusing on the independents, a situation that was not helped by the somewhat secretive way pricing was customarily done. The *Chicago Tribune* published a comic comparing grocers to armed robbers. In the 1920s, chains opened an amazing amount of stores. National Tea, the third largest grocery chain in the United States and headquartered in Chicago, grew the number of stores it operated in the area from 120 to 598 between 1920 and 1923 alone through acquisitions and new store openings. Kroger, A&P, and Piggly Wiggly followed similar patterns. In the Hyde Park community, A&P had a store on every corner of Lake Park Avenue, even having two on one corner.[67]

Finally, in the late 1920s and especially into the 1930s, self-service groceries, where customers chose their own items rather than asking for

Figure 4.4.   A Grocery Store in Chicago's "Black Belt," 1941. Library of Congress, Prints & Photographs Division, FSA/OWI Collection, LC-USF33-005142-M2.

clerks to assist, began to open. With this, large independents, such as Dawson's Trading Post on the South Side, opened the first supermarkets. Dawson's, located on the far South Side at 8200 S. South Chicago in an old bag factory, sold mainly groceries but was somewhat like today's Costco, selling furnishings and clothes in addition to groceries.[68] While they resisted at first, chains such as A&P and Jewel Tea were soon to enlarge their own locations. Individual chain stores grew in size, the intense covering of the retail landscape by small-scale chain stores lessened, and the era of the supermarket had begun.

JEWEL, CHAIN SUPERMARKETS, AND URBAN DEVELOPMENT

It is fitting that the most successful supermarket chain in Chicago's history spent its first thirty-three years as a mail order and door-to-door grocery company. Jewel began basically as a one-wagon peddler. In 1899, Frank Vernon Skiff used a rented horse and a secondhand wagon to peddle coffee, tea, and spices in the Back of the Yards neighborhood. In typical Chicago hustler tradition, Jewel grew through a method called "advancing the premium." Many door-to-door grocery salesmen generally would give a gift, such as china, to loyal customers who purchased a certain amount of groceries, in a way that was very similar to today's loyalty programs. In 1901, Skiff and his partner and brother-in-law, Frank Ross (by legend after Ross was hit with a broom by an irate housewife), decided to give consumers the premium gift up front if they would promise to buy products in the future. This new sales method was very popular, and Jewel, then called Jewel Tea, grew quickly.[69] By 1905 it had leased a three-story building to roast coffee. While Jewel Tea sold many items, its focus was on coffee. Since 1905, the company had roasted its own coffee in Chicago, and by 1909 it had added vanilla extract and baking powder to the products it manufactured. Later, Jewel Tea operated a coffee-roasting factory in Hoboken, New Jersey, and later in Los Angeles as well as in Barrington, Illinois. In 1916, the company was capitalized at $16 million, and it became listed on the New York Stock Exchange. At the time, it had 1,645 grocery routes that covered a large area of the country.[70]

World War I brought troubles, with higher raw material prices, many route drivers being conscripted, and the federal government taking over the Hoboken plant. The company contracted, but survived. In 1932, Jewel Tea purchased seventy-seven Loblaw Grocerterias, a Canadian chain that had decided to get out of the Chicago market. The same year, the town of Green River, Wyoming, passed an ordinance outlawing unsolicited door-to-door sales calls. Some four hundred other towns followed suit. The age of the door-to-door grocery peddler was coming to an end. Jewel, however, continued to maintain home grocery routes into the 1950s. In 1949, the company had 1,876 route managers serving "more than a million customers in 43 states."[71] It also had a large Art Deco headquarters building in suburban Barrington (it moved to Melrose Park in 1955), and a large warehouse at 3617 S. Ashland, in the "Central Manufacturing District," next door to the Chicago stockyards.

As a supermarket chain, Jewel initially struggled, partially because they were trying to build a company during the Depression. In 1933, the company surveyed Chicago housewives about the characteristics they desire in a store. The results led to the "Ten Commandments" of service for the company, including such things as self-service, fresh produce, honest weights, high-quality service, and low prices. Over time, the company grew, particularly in fresh items such as meat and produce, which grocers had just started to carry. Produce was delivered daily. While Jewel closed many of the original Loblaw stores, by 1949 the company operated 154 groceries in the Chicago area.[72] Jewel continued to grow throughout the twentieth century, but, in a piece of history that typifies Chicago supermarket chains, it was purchased by a number of national grocery chains and investors, beginning with American Stores in 1984, by Idaho-based Albertson's in 1999, SuperValu in 2006, and in 2013 New York investment firm Cerberus Capital Management. While Jewel's Chicago focus has increased in the past ten years, the Jewel brand no longer exists outside of the Midwest.

Jewel's progression from one peddler to a large-scale grocery delivery business to a local supermarket chain, and then being owned by a series of out-of-town corporations, and today, an investment firm, parallels many changes in Chicago's mainstream consumer food market, as well as its greater history of urban renewal and suburbanization. Supermarkets were often part of the urban renewal plans of the 1960s and later, as well as promoters or followers of gentrification. A Dominick's that opened in the 1990s across from the Cabrini-Green housing project was heralded both as a sign of the city assisting the Cabrini-Green residents and as part of the general urban renewal and gentrification of the neighborhood. Outside the city, sparkling supermarkets were, and remain, a mark of suburbanization. A 1973 magazine article described Golf Road beyond Woodfield Mall, the largest in the country at the time, as having "as many supermarkets as there are gas stations. A&P, National, Jewel, Eagle, Dominick's, . . . and others follow each other like covered wagons, each with its right of small storefronts (often new and empty) surrounding a tarred parking lot." Such new suburban supermarkets were also social centers. A "Jewel village" in suburban Westmont included "a pharmacy, a dry cleaner, a bakery, a florist, a card and gift shop . . . a variety store, and . . . a huge dress shop," in addition to the Jewel supermarket itself.[73] It is interesting that a decade later, A&P and National were no longer in the Chicago market. In addition, national retailer Kroger left the Chicago market in the early 1970s. By the 1990s, the Chicago market was uncommonly concentrated, with just two brands, Jewel and Dominick's, controlling most sales.

SUPERMARKETS GO GOURMET AND ETHNIC

While the "foodie culture" of the twenty-first century may seem like something new, there have been grocers providing upscale food to Chicago's elites throughout the history of the city. Early commentators remarked on the contrast between the muddy and unpleasant town of Chicago as a whole and the opulence of the food, including oysters and other seafood, served at the Lake House Hotel. Such food would have been provided by grocers such as Charles L. Harmon. In *So Big*, Edna Ferber mentions that grocers dotted the street corners of the Prairie Avenue district. One of these, Stop and Shop, began in 1872 (as Tebbets and Garland) at 18th and Wabash, moving in 1890 to 16th and Calumet, just next to Prairie Avenue, serving the trade of the wealthy with everyday and unusual foods, including hippopotamus meat and shark's fin soup. In the early twentieth century, Stop and Shop moved downtown. It evolved into a high-end grocer that survived in Chicago's Loop through to the 1970s. In 1972, it celebrated its one-hundredth anniversary with a ribbon-cutting event presided over by Chicago celebrity Irv Kupcinet and Mayor

Richard J. Daley, who declared January 19, 1972, "Stop and Shop Day in Chicago."[74] Stop and Shop as a retail operation was seemingly small, but it offered rare quality to high-end customers: "Because of our size, we're able to provide quantities of high-quality perishables that the bigger chains can't because there isn't enough to go around" the owner stated in a 1978 interview. They also had a large catering business and specialized in prepared foods, as well as specialty candies and deli items. The produce included "grapefruits the size of watermelons . . . mangoes, papayas . . . turnips, anise, leeks, dry shallot, okra, dill." The deli counter was "a veritable U.N. of deli delectables," and specialty sausage and cheese sections and an upscale meat counter with active butchers also graced the store.[75]

Stop and Shop's Loop location closed in 1983. The upscale urban grocery market was also served by Treasure Island, a small chain of supermarkets, specializing in European and prepared foods but also offer-

Figure 4.5.   Upscale Loop grocery store Stop and Shop, 16 W. Washington, 1957.
Chicago History Museum, ICHi-69984.

ing a full line of groceries, at locations on the Near North Side, Lincoln Park, Lake View, and also in upscale suburbs (their lone remaining suburban store is in Wilmette) and Hyde Park. An article in *The Chicagoan* (a predecessor of *Chicago* magazine) wrote of Treasure Island: "Slender matrons from the high rises seem to glide behind their shopping carts, past stalls of Belgian, French, Swiss, Danish, Puerto Ricans, Mexican, Italian, Japanese, and even Brazilian imports."[76] At least one Treasure Island even had a theater where children could be left to watch movies while their parents shopped.[77] Today, Treasure Island does not have a theater, has aged a bit, and has competition from many other upscale groceries, including Whole Foods and the new Italian megagrocery and eating place Eataly (its first location outside of New York). Mrs. Green's, a specialty organic/natural chain from the East Coast, has locations in Lincoln Park and Winnetka. These are upscale groceries in the tradition of Stop and Shop. However, Chicago foodies go out beyond these to search and discover ethnic groceries, butchers, and specialty stores throughout the city and suburbs. Stores such as Gene's Sausage Shop and Delicatessen in Lincoln Square, Marion Street Cheese Market in Oak Park, or the Fishguy Market in Albany Park cater to urban gourmets. Large ethnic supermarkets, catering mainly to locals but also sought out by gourmets, are opening all over the city and suburbs. These include chains that specifically target Latinos, such as La Justicia, stores such as Bobak Sausage Shop near Midway Airport, and Wally's International Market in the northwest suburb of Mt. Prospect that cater to Polish and other Eastern European populations. In the northwest and western suburbs, large Asian-oriented markets, including Mitsuwa Marketplace in Arlington Heights and Super H Market in Naperville, cater to the growing Asian populations in the suburbs. The Indian-Pakistani corridor of Devon Avenue and the Mexican Marketplace on 26th Street are the largest in the Midwest. The size of some of these stores may be new, but urban hipsters have long searched the city for unusual ethnic foods. A 1970s recipe book sponsored by the Old Town Triangle Association, Chicago's first modern gentrified neighborhood, not only included an unusually cocktail party–oriented set of recipes such as "Easy Whiskey Sour," but also a "Gourmet Shopping Guide," including a list of gourmet and ethnic groceries from all around the city.[78] Many of these have now closed, but the new larger ethnic stores, plus the growth of local farmer's markets, Community Supported Agriculture projects, and upscale co-ops, shows that Chicago is in a true heyday for chefs and others who like to find unusual groceries, whether they be produce, imported cheeses and meats, or packaged items.

THE FALL OF DOMINICK'S AND THE FUTURE

Like in many American cities, the period after 2000 has been a time of growth of large ethnic markets, upscale markets such as Whole Foods, discount chains such as Aldi, and supercenters such as Walmart. It has been a difficult period, however, for mainline full-service supermarkets. Jewel has survived, although it has closed stores and has been bought and sold numerous times. Chicago's longtime second largest chain, Dominick's, closed its remaining seventy-two stores in December 2013. Dominick's was founded in 1918 by Sicilian immigrant Dominick DiMatteo, who opened a deli in 1918 in a small storefront at 3842 W. Ohio Street. Over time, Dominick's Supermarkets became one of the Chicago area's largest grocery chains. When supermarkets began to close down corner stores during the 1950s, historian Dominic Candeloro notes that Dominick's offered employment to "Italian Americans whose corner stores were being knocked out of business."[79] The company became a small local chain and then opened its first supermarket in 1950. The company grew, taking over Eagle stores, among others, in the 1980s. At the time, Dominick's had about a quarter of the grocery market in the Chicago area and 116 stores. It focused mainly (but not only) on suburban locations, and it made its market generally as a slightly more upscale version of Jewel. The DiMatteo family operated or owned Dominick's until the 1990s, when it was sold to an investment firm, and then, in 1998, to Safeway. Chicago-native and Italian American Robert Mariano was hired by DiMatteo in 1968 as a deli clerk, and worked his way to becoming CEO until the company was sold to Safeway in 1998. Safeway, over time, closed stores and tried to model the remaining stores on Safeways elsewhere, a plan that did not succeed in increasing sales, which was probably predictable since Dominick's had for years marketed itself as a higher-quality Chicago institution and Safeway had little name recognition in the city and has generally been a middle-level supermarket chain.

What is perhaps more interesting about the closing of Dominick's is the fate of its final seventy-two stores. Instead of selling Dominick's as a whole, Safeway is attempting to sell the stores individually. When Safeway closed all the Dominick's grocery stores in December 2013, Mariano, as CEO of Roundy's Supermarkets, parent company of Mariano's Fresh Market, announced the company would buy eleven of his former employer's stores.[80] Mariano aims at a somewhat more upscale experience, an evolution of the 1970s and 1980s Dominick's concepts. Seven were purchased by Whole Foods. Nine of the stores were bought by Jewel. The rest of the stores that have been sold are split between smaller local chains, including some, like Joe Caputo & Sons and Cermak Fresh Market, that have generally in the past focused more on serving particular ethnic groups. In general, the outlook for the Chicago grocery market looks much more interesting than it has been, with independents and ethnic-oriented stores having a larger presence and Mariano's being a new chain in the region. Still, a few stores remain unsold, in particular Dominick's one location in the African American South Side in the South Shore neighborhood. The closure of Dominick's may proceed to show us both how quickly the grocery business is changing as well as the continuing of the processes that have caused food-access issues in many Chicago African American communities for the past century.

FOOD DESERTS, FOOD PRICES, AND INEQUITY IN CHICAGO'S RETAIL FOOD LANDSCAPE

On July 18, 2006, consultant Mari Gallagher presented her report, *Examining the Impact of Food Deserts on Public Health in Chicago*, to a packed audience at the Palmer House Hilton in downtown Chicago. The report, sponsored by LaSalle Bank and based on data from agencies and researchers from throughout the city and state, highlighted the inequity in access to supermarkets in Chicago and correlations between these inequities and health outcomes. The findings of the report were front-page news in the *Chicago Tribune* and led to reports on CNN and elsewhere.[81] Since Gallagher's report, food deserts have stayed in the news both in Chicago and elsewhere in the United States. President Obama has made addressing food deserts an important part of his administration's health and community development policy. Chicago mayor Rahm Emanuel included addressing food access issues one of the key foci of his administration, including inviting First Lady Michele Obama to a high-level summit

designed to attract new stores into underserved areas as well as to promote expanding fresh produce offerings in existing stores. A new focus
has also been placed on promoting urban agriculture and community
gardens, in particular developing new zoning codes that make urban agriculture a legal land use.

Results of these efforts in Chicago are mixed. On the one hand, urban
agriculture is growing in the city, and is now at levels most likely not
seen since at least World War II. On the other hand, while stores such as
Walgreen's have expanded their produce sections and a number of smaller discount stores such as Save A Lot have opened, the number of full-
service supermarkets that have opened in "food desert" communities is
small. The *food desert* term has also been attacked for being too dismis-
sive of the power of community foodways within areas with few supermarkets. In addition, some researchers and activists have questioned the
presence of food deserts in general (although not in Chicago) and their
relationship to health in particular.

While the relationship between food access and health remains difficult to trace, it is not surprising that Chicago, a city that frequently rates
as one of the most segregated in the United States, is a place of great
inequity in the number and types of grocery stores available to residents
of different communities. In particular, inner-city, African American
communities of Chicago's South and West sides, as well as African
American suburbs such as North Chicago, Maywood, and Robbins, tend
to have fewer full-service grocery stores than communities of other races.
Predominately Latino communities tend to have fewer full-service national chains but have somewhat smaller local chains that particularly
cater to Latinos. White communities, in particular wealthy ones, tend to
have a broad variety of grocery stores, with the exception of few discount
chains.[82] While the interest in this food desert pattern has grown since
Gallagher's 2006 article, food access, including both issues of geography
and price, has been an area of concern in Chicago almost since its beginning, one particularly heightened by the rise of chain stores in the 1920s
and supermarkets in the post–World War II era.

As discussed above, soon after its founding as a town, in the 1830s
Chicago went through a period of food shortage. Prices for goods such as
flour, butter, cheese, apples, and even salt skyrocketed in 1835 as people
poured into the city, and it rose even more with the winter close of
navigation later that year.[83] While this situation was temporary, the route

of the Chicago River and its branches, often depicted as an upside-down Y inside a circle, divides the city into three parts: the West Side; the North Side; and the Loop and South Side. These divisions and the relative low density of the city made peddlers and small neighborhood groceries of paramount importance in the provision of food to Chicagoans through World War II. With the decline of the peddlers and the rise of chains and supermarkets, food in large part stopped coming to neighborhoods and instead consumers had to go to larger, but fewer, stores.

Accelerating and confusing these changes were the price hikes surrounding World War I. The period 1913 to 1920 was a time of great inflation in the United States. Prices of food, as well as other basic needs, doubled, on average. Even in Chicago, with its large meatpacking plants and local wholesalers, the food price index doubled between 1914 to 1920. The city responded in many ways. One response by the city government and activists was to further promote the development of community gardens and urban agriculture. Another response was to promote farmer's markets. A city Market Commission was created to set up a new set of outdoor food markets at sites around the city. These were initially successful, but they did not sustain long term. Numerous city commissions investigated the high costs of living, in particular food prices, but actual interventions were few. A city investigation into the high cost of milk, for instance, attributed the issue largely to redundancies in milk delivery routes, with numerous milk companies delivering to any one block.[84] Similar patterns existed for peddlers or the jobbers who delivered to small stores. Solving such "inefficiencies" was a difficult thing for a government in a capitalist economy to do, unless (as was later suggested) foods such as milk were to be treated like utilities and each delivery company be given its own zone of monopoly. Chain stores, however, could limit inefficiencies by running their own distribution systems and later by limiting distribution distance by operating fewer, but larger, stores.

As mentioned in chapter 3, the largest racial upheaval in Chicago's history occurred in 1919, sparked by a black teenager being killed by a rock thrown by a white man at an informally segregated 31st Street beach and the subsequent refusal of a white policeman to arrest the perpetrator. It built on tensions for jobs following World War I, as veterans returned to find new migrants in their old positions. There were also issues of the control of space between blacks, who were outgrowing the overcrowded

Black Belt area that they were confined to by the Chicago Real Estate Board, and ethnic Irish and other whites, who fiercely defended the boundaries of their neighborhoods. Groceries and other retailers were greatly affected. In Chicago's Black Belt, the area now called Bronzeville that stretched south along State Street and what was then called South Park Boulevard (now Martin Luther King Jr. Drive), there were many groceries owned by African Americans, as well as many owned by whites, in particular Jews. In the Black Belt, Jewish grocers in the area formed a protective association to protect from looting. Following the 1919 upheaval and into the 1920s, black-owned newspapers such as the *Chicago Whip* and the *Chicago Defender* organized boycotts of the white-owned businesses in their midst. Blacks were not unique—Lithuanian, Slovakian, and Yugoslavian papers expressed similar sentiments, and native-born Americans stereotyped independent stores as "dirty" and "illiterate."[85] All of this built upon the general mistrust of independent grocers that rose in the World War I era.

Chain groceries built on the anonymous nature of the chain-store transaction, which were increasingly self-service, as well as on advertising prices and standardizing the clean nature of the stores. In an environment where grocers were not to be trusted and often, particularly in African American neighborhoods, did not live in the community, chains had many attractive features. They were, however, not available equally to all. Chains were placed, then as now, by assessing available information about communities. New housing developments on the outskirts of the city and in the suburbs, as well as the presence of young families and existing chain stores, tended to attract chain groceries. Chains did begin to move into immigrant communities during the 1920s as high rents in the most attractive areas forced them to look elsewhere. Chains were also cheaper. A 1930 comparison of grocery prices in Chicago chains, independent cash-and-carry groceries, and independent full-service groceries showed that chains were on average at least 10 percent less expensive for nine of twelve produce groups (all but crackers, seafood, and shortening) than independent full-service groceries, and at least 10 percent less expensive than cash-and-carry independents for seven of the twelve. While there were independents that had prices below chains for particular items, overall, chains were much lower.[86]

This obviously gave chains an advantage, but it led to an impression among some that chains were "cheap" and more suited to densely populated urban areas than suburban zones. Responding to this impression, part of the idea of the new, larger supermarkets that chain stores began to build in the 1930s was to create a middle-class or even upper-class shopping experience. National Tea and A&P opened their first expanded stores in the then upper-class South Shore community. As researched by historian Tracey Deutsch, while National Tea and Jewel and its predecessor Loblaw were split about evenly in Chicago between stores in average or below-average income customers between 1928 and 1930, by .1939 to 1940, over 80 percent of these company's stores in the city were in above-average income neighborhoods. High-Low, a new supermarket chain, opened eighteen of its twenty stores in above-average income neighborhoods.[87] These patterns mattered to average Chicagoans because of the relationship between independents and price. During the price-control period in World War II in 1945, 48 percent of small independents were selling groceries above wartime ceiling prices, while only 18 percent of large independent and chains did.[88]

In the postwar period, such patterns persisted, combined with a general movement of both Chicago's population and its retailers toward the suburbs and the very outer ring of the city. A 1954 study of Chicago shopping districts indicates that while the total sales in the city at food stores was up 24 percent between 1948 and 1954, of the six South Side African American districts of Douglas, Fuller Park, Grand Boulevard, Kenwood, Oakland, and Washington Park, all but Oakland and Grand Boulevard declined in sales, and only Oakland rose above the Chicago average. The largest gains were in outer-ring Chicago neighborhoods, particularly on the Southwest Side. Sales at food stores in the Loop declined over 20 percent in the period.[89] A 1964 University of Chicago study shows a net loss in the number of retailers in nearly all areas of the city between 1948 and 1958, and net gains in nearly all suburban areas except a few inner-ring suburbs.[90] While these changes went beyond food, a 1963 Super Market Institute report encourages supermarket chains to pay attention to both the rise in discount retailers and the movements of population in the cities they serve. The report suggests closing most or all stores in inner-city areas or areas of declining populations or converting them to discount stores (ignoring the large number of people still present) while at the same time opening stores in growing suburban areas.[91]

Commercial corridors in neighborhoods undergoing racial shifts show particular declines in sales between 1948 and 1954. Madison Street between California and Central Park in East Garfield Park on the West Side, an area that was becoming predominately African American at the time, declined in sales. The number of groceries on this strip dropped from seventy-one to forty-eight. The number of fish and meat markets dropped from twelve to five. While this shows the still-high number of stores even in this area of retail decline, this is a precipitous decline in a short period. The same report shows that 63rd and Halsted, in the Englewood neighborhood, remained the second largest retail zone in the city in terms of dollars spent. As Englewood began to shift racially, however, 63rd and Halsted was down 19 percent in sales in six years, more than any other district. While this was a general marketplace with numerous department stores, the number of grocery stores dropped from eighty-one to fifty-three and sales of groceries dropped 2 percent.[92] While the number of groceries was declining quickly citywide overall, in most areas sales were growing. Drops in store numbers with declines or stable amounts of sales (while other communities had rising sales) indicate that older stores closed while new, often larger stores were not moving in.

In 1968, in the three days following the assassination of Martin Luther King, an urban insurrection occurred in Chicago. Grocery stores in predominantly African American areas such as Madison Street on the West Side and 63rd Street in Woodlawn were the site of extensive looting, fires, and destruction. This destruction in many areas was not temporary. Many blocks remained vacant a year, or even decades, after 1968. Even before this time, there was a rise of interest in how groceries and other retailers were serving low-income consumers. "Do the Poor Pay More?" was a major question.[93] For African American leaders, the focus was often on local, and in particular African American, ownership. The price issue has been difficult to chart. The expected differences in price, with predominantly African American communities being higher than white communities, are overwhelmed by differences between store types and, in general, the expected differences have not been identified. The relationship between store type and price also is not straightforward. A 1980 Urban League study, for instance, found that prices in black communities overall were slightly higher than in white communities, but when location, store type, and specific neighborhood type were taken into account, black areas were somewhat lower. The major differences, though, were between store type and neighborhood type. Small chains, rather than large chains, were cheapest overall. Convenience stores were highest. The neighborhood type variable looked at the differences between older African American neighborhoods, that had been predominantly African American in 1970, newer black and mixed communities, and nonblack neighborhoods. Older black neighborhoods were by far the most expensive, with nonblack communities cheapest.[94] The complicated nature of this result parallels a 2006 study of the Austin neighborhood of Chicago's West Side and neighboring Oak Park. The key differences between the communities were in the mix of stores in them, with Austin having many small corner stores but only one chain supermarket. Price was complicated, with discount stores like Aldi having by far the lowest prices but limited selection. Local chains had lower prices than national chains for fresh items such as produce and meat, but national chains had the best selection. Talking to Austin residents, many of them used a number of different stores in a particular month or week, which makes sense due to the differences in prices, but it highlights the difficulty in provisioning for one's family in an area with limited larger stores, particularly with limited income.[95] In a later interview with a carless Englewood woman with limited mobility, she described taking the el train from Englewood seven miles north to the South Loop to a Jewel store on Roosevelt Road near an el stop with an elevator.[96] This interview highlights that the food desert issue is not just about geography. While neighborhoods in Chicago do differ greatly, both today and in the past, in terms of the kinds of stores present accessing food often has to do with a particular person's wealth or mobility. Black ownership of stores is also a major concern for many in the community. While whites and immigrants have always owned and operated groceries in African American communities, the number of African Americans owning supermarkets in Chicago has fallen today to zero. Farmer's Best Market in New City opened in 2008 and closed within five years.

FARMER'S MARKETS AND THE FUTURE

Today, much of Chicago is in the midst of a food renaissance. Beyond the flowering of upscale groceries, there has been a growth of farmer's markets, which in some ways has given current Chicagoans better access to local (meaning within three hundred miles or so) farm-grown produce and meats than at any other time since the mid-1800s. While with few exceptions, the markets are not open during the winter and are only open at most two days a week, they are spread throughout much of the city as well as many suburbs. There are markets two to three days a week in the Loop Monday through Friday, as well as in neighborhoods throughout the city. Many suburbs also have markets, led by Evanston's and Oak Park's, which were founded in the late 1970s. Patrons of these neighborhood and suburban markets are often as much about social interaction as food, although the fresh, local produce certainly helps. The leading market is Green City Market at North and LaSalle, at the very south end of Lincoln Park. It is an independent nonprofit, supported by many local chefs, that is particularly focused on sustainable food as well as education, sponsoring weekly events with local chefs during the summer. Founded in 1998, since 2009 it has also run an indoor market at the Peggy Notebaert Nature Museum during winter months. Farmer's markets have also been added more recently in many of Chicago's minority communities, with varying success. Opening new markets often is a chicken-and-egg situation. At first few vendors come, and customers are not impressed and may not return. Many markets have started only to last one season or not even a season. Through the help of groups like Growing Power, Experimental Station, and others, as well as programs such as coupons to double SNAP (food stamp) benefits used at the markets, particular markets such as the 61st Street Market in Woodlawn have survived and even thrived to start to become the kind of social food spaces that exist in places like Evanston, Oak Park, and Logan Square. In other cases, African American pastors have worked with African American farmers from the South and Pembroke Township, Illinois, to sell fresh produce out of trucks directly after church services.

In general, the farmer's market situation parallels that of Chicago's market and agricultural history as a whole. Chicago has a vibrant farmer's market scene, but Chicago takes up a large area and its former market garden ring is mainly gone. While local producers just outside and even within the city are growing, markets still struggle somewhat to find farmers to fill the available market slots. This is particularly the case in "nonpremier" markets that tend to be in areas with lower incomes, or even just in areas outside of the upper-income urban core. Beyond farmer's markets, Chicago's retail food scene today is one that features amazing diversity and innovation as well as one that continues to feature great differences between neighborhoods.

5

FROM FRONTIER TOWN TO INDUSTRIAL AND COMMERCIAL FOOD CAPITAL

From its days as a frontier town, Chicago has been a place where people have brought ideas for mixing capital and labor to produce goods to be sold elsewhere. Chicago's early food producers thought big and saw retail and wholesale markets as lying well beyond the city's limits. Waves of diverse migrants would not only produce the city's unique foodways but would also fuel a workforce that would produce regional, national, and eventually global food companies. In many ways, Chicago can be thought of as one of the places where the contemporary food corporation was invented, initially from raw materials transformed from nature and then eventually through some of the most creative food marketing on the planet. The city's food companies would expand far beyond grain stacking and meatpacking. Chicago would become host to a variety of raw commodities processed into a myriad of invented foods and brands that would change what and how people eat across the country and world.

WHEAT, CORN, AND MEAT

It could be argued that the history of Chicago's food economy begins with grains. Indigenous populations of the region proved for centuries that the fertile prairies of Illinois could be fruitful suppliers of corn and other cultivars that could, in turn, be dried and stored in pits for winter, transformed into merchandise, and used for trade. At the beginning of the nineteenth century, Chicago's economy was dominated by the Euro-American fur trade and increasingly by land speculation from East Coast investors. In a matter of a couple of decades, investors began to build the city's grain trade, the foundation of which was the removal of indigenous populations and the opening up of Illinois prairies to white settlement. The 1833 Treaty of Chicago formalized an ongoing process by which agricultural settlement by whites, including many new immigrants, cleared much of Central and Northern Illinois prairies for agriculture. The first shipment of wheat was sent from Chicago by steamship to Buffalo in 1838, five years after the treaty and only a year after the city's official charter. In 1839, some 3,678 bushels of wheat left Chicago for the East Coast; four years later that number would reach more than 628,000 bushels. By midcentury, Chicago exported more than two million bushels of wheat and over a million bushels of corn, and it was emerging as the national grain capital. [1]

When the Illinois and Michigan Canal was completed in 1848—connecting Lake Michigan to the Illinois River and ultimately to the Mississippi River and beyond—farmers in Central Illinois had a waterway into Chicago's marketplace. Previously, grains would arrive in Chicago in sacks by wagon from distant towns, often taking many days to reach the marketplace near the south bank of the Chicago River. Trips to Chicago that once took days turned into a matter of hours. Even while the city struggled with mud and poor drainage, making movement on its streets appear impossible, Chicago developed a comparative advantage over St. Louis and other river towns because of higher prices paid to farmers by buyers serving the demand for grain from the East. [2] Prior to the railroad, Chicago had the advantage of Lake Michigan as an inexpensive transport to the East. "An eastern-oriented economy," notes historian William Cronon, "'naturally' looked across the lakes to Chicago as the western most point of cheap water access to the agricultural heartland of the interior." [3]

Chicago and Illinois may have remained somewhat inconsequential in U.S. history had it not been for two key inventions linked to the city's growth. In 1836, New Englander John Deere moved to the town of Grand Detour along the Rock River southwest of Rockford in the Northern Illinois prairielands, a hundred or so miles west of Chicago. The tall prairie grass with deep roots meant strenuous animal-powered plowing, a long, tedious process that required continuous stopping and cleaning of the plow. In 1837, responding to concerns by local farmers, Deere manufactured a steel plow that cleanly turned the sticky Illinois prairie soil. By 1856, he was producing ten thousand plows annually, and the roots of the agricultural machinery corporate giant Deere & Company had been established. Over the next hundred years, Deere & Company would emerge as the largest farm equipment manufacturer in the world.

Clearing land and tilling the soil for planting upper Midwestern prairies was, however, half the battle. Reaping the benefits from regional grain agriculture required tools for efficiently harvesting crops from the fields. Chicago's early boom as an agricultural commodity-trading city built on grain transport and storage can be partly traced to Cyrus McCormick, son of Virginia inventor Robert McCormick. Drawn to the prospects of Midwestern agriculture, Cyrus McCormick relocated to Chicago in 1847, where he built a factory to produce his famous mechanical reaper. The original McCormick reaper factory was located on the north bank of the Chicago River east of the Michigan Avenue Bridge—interestingly, at the site of John Kinzie's property purchased from Chicago's first settler Jean Baptiste Point du Sable. The factory produced 450 reapers in the first year and, drawing on demand by Illinois wheat farmers, it tripled that number in the next two years, producing 1,500 per year by 1849.[4] Ten years later the McCormick Reaper Works had five buildings along the river and was making over five thousand reapers a year.[5] Before the end of the century, McCormick would have forty acres of factories and warehouses at Western Avenue and Blue Island Avenue in Chicago's Lower West Side.

The boom in reaper sales during the 1850s, along with the rapid expansion of Midwestern wheat production and ultimately Chicago grain markets, were largely made possible by railroads. When the Illinois and Michigan Canal opened in 1848, the canal's central importance to Chicago was quickly curtailed by the emergence of rail transportation. That same year, William Ogden orchestrated the construction of the Galena and Chicago Union Railroad, and in November the line carried its first cargo of wheat from the Des Plaines River to the corner of Halsted at Kinzie outside the city limits. Unconvinced by Ogden of the railroad's importance, the City Council forbade construction into the city.[6] The president of the railroad was Walter Newberry (whose bequest established Chicago's Newberry Library), who with his brother Oliver, a steamship builder in Detroit, collaborated to accelerate grain shipments via the Great Lakes to the eastern seaboard.[7] The success of Chicago's first rail line convinced naysayers of the importance of railroads, leading to a boom in construction that would turn the city into the world's largest railroad hub. During the 1850s, new rail lines fanning out from Chicago would spur growth in McCormick reaper sales and expand wheat production in western Illinois, Wisconsin, and Minnesota.[8]

By the mid-nineteenth century, settlers were flocking to the Midwest seeking to carve out farms in the fertile prairies of the Upper Mississippi Valley. While Midwestern prairies were rapidly converted into fields of grain, the presence of canals, trains, and steamships lured investors to build enormous grain transport and storage systems in Chicago. Trains left the city with new settlers and returned with grain, the vast majority of which was stored in elevators for export to the east. Chicago's first traffic jams involved freight cars filled with grains, and the city's first skyscrapers were constructed along the Chicago River not as offices but for grain storage. During the 1840s, horse-powered elevators stored grain brought to Chicago by wagons in sacks, but by 1848 the first steam-powered elevator was built. With the advent of railroads and expanded storage capacity, Chicago attained an advantage over grain ports such as St. Louis, where higher prices incorporated additional human labor at port. By the mid-1850s, the grain trade had shifted toward Chicago and the Great Lakes and away from the southern route through New Orleans. By 1857, a dozen multistoried automated grain elevators, many built by railroad companies, lined the river, giving Chicago the capacity and efficiency to move and store more grain than anywhere else in the world.[9]

The Chicago Board of Trade was also established in 1848, mainly as a member organization in support of the city's growing commercial and industrial sector. More than acting as a centralized trading space, the board's most important task in its first decade was to address the need for rules stemming from the rapidly expanding grain trade. In addition to a lack of agreement on uniform weights and measures at the city's grain elevators, challenges emerged from new transportation and storage processes that made shipping grains in sacks obsolete. The new aggregation system no longer identified the harvest crops with specific farms but mixed grains in large, vertical bins that would hold thousands and eventually millions of bushels. Grain arrived to Chicago's elevators from a vast array of farms in proximity to rail lines that jetted out from Chicago. Grain was transported in rail cars to the elevator and lifted by steam-

Figure 5.1. Sterographs of one of the two huge Buckingham grain elevators along the Chicago River at the lake, showing Chicago as a multimodal transportation transfer point. Copelin and Melander, photographers. Chicago Public Library, Special Collections and Preservation Division, CCW 5.7.

powered belts into enormous bins. A receipt was provided to the vendor that could, in turn, be sold, traded, or used to withdraw the specified amount of grain. Gravity and chutes allowed buyers to fill steamships bound for the East. Complaints about the system of mixing wheat of variable quality led the Board of Trade to implement a grading system that would establish standards for quality and a language of trade. In 1856, three wheat categories were defined: "White Wheat," "Red Wheat," and "Spring Wheat." In 1857, more grades were defined for Spring Wheat ("Club Wheat," "No. 1 Spring," "No. 2 Spring"), and in 1858 a "rejected" category was added.[10] In time, similar grading structures were applied to corn, oats, and other grains. The first wheat receipts that contained a grade were issued in 1857, ushering in a system by which grains of a specific grade could be speculated upon based on their "future" delivery date.[11] In 1859, the Illinois State Legislature gave the Board of Trade legal authority to establish a grading system and to hire inspectors whose grading decisions and trading rules were considered legally binding.[12]

As Chicago's grading systems and trading rules were formalized, receipts from grain sales emerged as a form of currency, "monetary abstractions," to be traded and speculated upon.[13] Along with the buying and selling of grain came the buying and selling of elevator receipts in what was seemingly an unending process of expansion in Chicago's grain storage. In 1858, the city had the capacity to store just over four million bushels of grain. By the time of the Chicago fire in 1871, that number had reached over eleven million.[14] The epicenter of the city's grain trade was along the Chicago River, with the largest elevators located near the mouth within the vicinity of the McCormick Reaper Works. In 1855, Solomon Sturges, C. P. Buckingham, and Alvah Buckingham constructed the largest elevator of the time, storing as much as seven hundred thousand bushels on land leased from the Illinois Central Railroad on the south bank of the Chicago River.[15] By 1858, the company had two elevators among the twelve grain elevators that made up Chicago's original skyline.[16] When the company's lease expired in 1865, John Buckingham and his brother Ebenezer (whose son Clarence is the namesake of Chicago's Buckingham Fountain) leased the same property from the railroad for ten additional years. When the Chicago fire destroyed one of the elevators, the Buckinghams rebuilt, expanding their capacity to 2,850,000 bushels.[17] In general, even after the fire destroyed six elevators, Chicago's location—mixing railroads, the lake, and access to agricultural lands of the West—led investors to rebuild towering structures that reflected expectations for future growth. Grain speculation became a national practice, and in 1865 the Board of Trade established rules for trade in contracts for future delivery of grains with specific grades. By the mid-1870s, Chicago had spurred a global trade in grain futures, a market made possible by combining grades with elevators and receipts. Chicago was not only at the heart of the nation's grain trade but also served as the largest market for gambling on future grain prices.

Most of the actual wheat traded in Chicago during the mid-nineteenth century would leave the city unmilled on lake boats headed for eastern flour milling cities such as Buffalo, Oswego, and Montreal. By the 1880s, Chicago's elevator and grading system had become highly developed, and the city's rail lines made transport possible to cities and towns on both coasts. So important were the Chicago grain elevators that one of the largest was purchased in 1889 by an English company in order to capture some control of grain trade from the Americans.[18] Yet even while Chicago's wheat and corn reserves provided the financial foundation of world grain trade, milling in the city developed as a secondary industry of less importance. From 1852 to 1871, the majority of flour in Chicago was produced elsewhere. The flour that was produced in the city was a small portion of overall stocks.[19] Most of the city's flour was shipped elsewhere, and the flour-milling business would never become a major Chicago industry. Mills that did succeed in the city reflected more about Chicago's location as a trade and transportation hub with an exploding population than as a sustainable flour-milling center. For example, following the completion of the Illinois and Michigan Canal (I & M), the canal town of Lockport benefited from the waterway's grain trade. During the 1850s, Hiram Norton founded the town's flour mill aided by hydraulic power from the canal.[20] By the early 1880s, Norton became the largest manufacturer of flour in the Chicago area.[21] Even so, the company fell into bankruptcy by 1896 and subsequently closed in 1902 when the new Sanitary and Ship Canal replaced the I & M, decreasing waterpower from the older canal.[22]

Norton's profound but short-lived success was only topped by the Star & Crescent Milling Company. During the early 1870s, Clinton Briggs and Thomas Heermans operated Star & Crescent Mill on Randolph Street within the vicinity of Chicago's towering grain elevators. The mill was the region's largest until Norton's exceeded it in 1880.[23] By that time, the city's flour milling business was miniscule in comparison to Minneapolis, in the heart of the country's richest wheat-growing region. During the 1880s, Minnesota was the country's most important wheat-producing region. With little interest in Chicago as a stopping point, suppliers sent trains directly from Minneapolis to buyers on the East Coast and then on to the United Kingdom. Known as "Mill City," Minneapolis emerged as the "Flour Milling Capital of the World."[24] In Chicago, Star & Crescent Mill continued production downtown until 1903 when the company moved to a new South Side plant in the South Deering neighborhood along the Calumet River. In 1922, Washburn Crosby Company, one of Minneapolis's oldest and largest flour milling companies, bought Star & Crescent, seeking to take advantage of Chicago's location in respect to growing competition from wheat grown in the Southwest.[25] The company proceeded to build a subsidiary packaged food company called Gold Medal Food Products, in which they experimented with pancake and cake mixes and breakfast cereal. By 1929, the Minneapolis firm had renamed itself General Mills, and two of its products, Silkasoft Cake Flour and Wheaties Cereal, emerged as brands from the Chicago plant.[26] The South Deering factory would go on to produce Bisquick baking products as well as Cheerios, Kix, Total, and Trix cereals. In 1997, General Mills closed its oldest food manufacturing plant, leaving the massive grain silos at

104th Street and Calumet River as artifacts of Chicago's contribution to breakfast cereal history.[27]

While wheat was important to Chicago's nineteenth-century economy, corn played an especially critical role in making the city the world grain capital. During the 1830s and 1840s, most of Chicago's corn supplies were consumed locally and fed to livestock. This pattern changed dramatically with opening of the Illinois and Michigan Canal, connecting Lake Michigan to ancient corn-producing soils of the Illinois River Valley and rapidly initiating Chicago's dominance in the corn trade. Farmers in the valley quickly saw the city as an alternative to St. Louis.[28] The transition was extraordinary. Chicago exported 67,315 bushels of corn in 1847, a year before the canal was complete. The following year when corn began flowing up the canal, the amount jumped to 550,460 bushels. By the 1850s, Chicago had become the largest corn market in the United States.[29] Developments in rail transportation had expanded the city's corn exports to more than eleven million bushels in 1856, a number that would reach more than thirty-six million by 1871.[30] Those numbers would continue to increase as railroads opened the West to settlement, dramatically increasing the demand for corn as animal feed to fatten cattle driven on their journey East. Before the end of the century, the North Central Region—from Ohio to Nebraska and Missouri to Minnesota—was producing the vast majority of U.S. corn, and Chicago had emerged as the most important corn-trading city in the world. It was not a coincidence, for example, that in 1910 the president of the New York–based Corn Products Refining Company (CPRC) chose southwest suburban Summit, Illinois—near rail and water in the heart of the Corn Belt—to build the world's largest corn–wet milling plant to produce Argo Corn Starch and Mazola Corn Oil (still produced in Summit).[31] During the 1950s, researchers hired by the company quietly completed a study illustrating the chemical production of high fructose corn syrup (HFCS) and published the results in *Science*.[32] When HFCS was commercialized in the 1970s and 1980s, CPRC went on to become one of the top distributors of the syrup produced at its Argo plant.

Chicago thus played a central role in the history of corn as a global commodity. During the last two decades of the nineteenth century, corn demand for human consumption increased both in the United States and Europe to the benefit of Chicago grain warehouses and commodity traders. By the early 1890s, the U.S. Department of Agriculture advertised corn as a staple food across Europe, European cookbooks began to include recipes with corn, and Europe's militaries began including corn in rations.[33] In 1893, at the World Columbian Exposition in Chicago, McCormick and Deering exhibited their newest corn-harvesting machinery, the state of Iowa built a "Corn Palace" for its exhibit, and visitors to the Model Kitchen in the Women's Building were provided with a recipe book titled *Recipes Used in Illinois Corn Exhibit* (see chapter 7).[34] Corn from Midwestern prairies was shipped by carload to Eastern seaboard states and then across the Atlantic with increasing efficiency. Most important to the future of corn, Chicago emerged as the U.S. meatpacking capital, a status partly attributed to the abundance of Midwestern corn as animal feed.

Midwestern farmers had produced corn for raising livestock since the early nineteenth century. During the latter half of the nineteenth century, however, Chicago's location and railroads lured investor capitalists to increasingly make the city a meeting point for cattle from ranches across the new Western frontier. Chicago's first stockyard, "Bull's Head," opened in 1848 at the corner of Madison Street and Ogden Avenue. The railroads transformed what was a regional industry into one that turned Chicago into a national transfer point for cattle fattened for butchering and consumption elsewhere. As livestock feeding moved West, Chicago's stockyard investors—largely railroads—had their eyes set on making the city the primary transfer point for livestock from the West. Consolidation occurred with the opening of the Union Stock Yards in 1865 on land jointly purchased by railroad companies.[35] The site south of Chicago became known as "Packingtown" and was the largest stockyard in the world. Meatpacking produced tens of thousands of jobs over time, drawing largely on the labor of European immigrants, African Americans, and eventually immigrants from Mexico. By the end of the century, the Stock Yards would spur the birth of the modern labor movement and, along with lumber and steel, solidified Chicago's role as a national transportation hub.

Next to Chicago's train system, availability of corn was a key factor in the city's burgeoning meatpacking industry. Early on it was realized that the grain would became most profitable in the national food economy as meat. The price of meat depended upon a fluid supply of animal feed, and farmers had to either grow corn or buy it; Chicago's elevators had the largest reserves. The feedlot system, prevalent across Illinois and Iowa,

Figure 5.2.   A busy morning at the Union Stock Yards, Chicago, ca. 1905. Library of Congress, Prints & Photographs Division, Stereograph Collection, LC-USZ62-55745.

engaged farmers in purchasing "stockers" from western ranchers and then raising cattle ("feeders") and hogs together on hay and corn, either bought or cultivated.[36] This meant that farmers made decisions on whether corn was more valuable at market or in animals. When prices of corn were higher than those of livestock, they could sell their corn at elevators instead of using it as feed. Chicago's birth as a meatpacking metropolis, "hog butcher for the world," benefited from the high demand for meat in the East and Europe; profits from meat were thus high relative to the value of corn as food (as it remains today through corn subsidies).

The U.S. pork industry, initially centered in Cincinnati (the original "porkopolis"), began moving to Chicago during the 1860s as a result of the railroad and movement of corn production West (salt resources, as we shall see, also played an important role). Most importantly, demand for pork by Union soldiers in the Civil War spurred the production of hogs raised on Midwestern corn that, as a result of a Union blockade of the Mississippi River, could not be shipped South and through the Port of New Orleans.[37] Farmers fed their corn to hogs and sent them off to Chicago and Milwaukee, where production skyrocketed during the war years.[38] By the 1880s, the Chicago meatpacking plants, led by the "Big Three," Philip Armour (Armour and Company), Gustavus Swift (Swift and Company), and Nelson Morris (Nelson Morris and Company), were processing millions of animals a year and shipping meat East in refrigerated railcars. Between 1872 and 1892, hog receipts in Chicago jumped 137 percent and cattle 422 percent.[39] The incredible rapidity of growth in Chicago meatpacking was highlighted by historian Bessie Louise Pierce in her 1957 *A History of Chicago*:

> The measure of growth evidenced in the dollar value of the packers' products was equally impressive and prophetic. The $19,152,851 of 1870 appeared insignificant indeed in the light of the $85,324,371 of 1880 and the $194,337,838 of 1890—an expansion of over 900 per cent in twenty years! At the same time capital mounted 511 percent.[40]

This expansion may not have happened had it not been for ice-cooled railcars commissioned by Gustavus Swift during the late 1870s. The invention spurred massive development of ice harvesting, an industry already in service to Chicago's bustling lager beer breweries. Giant ice-houses with steam-powered elevators were constructed in Northern Illinois and Wisconsin and linked by rail lines to Chicago. Convinced that sending "dressed" meat in refrigerated railcars was far more profitable than shipping live ones, Chicago meatpackers invested in icing stations along Eastern rail lines so that cars could be replenished along their journey.[41] By the 1890s, Chicago's dressed meats could be shipped across the country and to British, French, and German markets.[42]

Refrigeration turned Chicago meatpacking into a year-round business, requiring more butchers, slaughterhouses, and pens at the Stock Yards. By the late 1870s, the multitude of butchers in the meatpacking houses was complaining about long workdays and low wages. Packinghouse butchering had been transformed from a skilled craft to an enormous assembly-line operation where low-wage workers conducted one task hundreds of times per day. The long hours and working conditions of the Chicago slaughterhouses, processing hundreds of animals per hour, gave rise to worker discontent. As early as 1877, laborers expressed frustration by striking in demand of a $2 per day wage increase. On one occasion, persistent protests prompted police to shoot into a crowd, resulting in numerous deaths and injuries.[43] Discontent continued, and on May 1, 1886, packinghouse butchers joined tens of thousands of laborers in a national strike for an eight-hour workday. Within a couple of days, meatpacking plant owners, the largest employers in Chicago, agreed to the same pay for an eight-hour day as was paid for ten hours for thirty-five-thousand workers.[44] On May 4, 1886, violence broke out at a nonviolent protest at the Haymarket on Des Plaines Street north of Randolph. When police ordered the crowd to disperse, a bomb was thrown and police began firing. The Haymarket Affair ended with numerous deaths in the crowd and eight dead officers. Within months, Philip Armour organized meatpacking plant owners into the National Independent Meatpackers Association, and the eight-hour workday was rescinded.[45]

Meatpacking workers continued to agitate throughout the 1890s into the 1900s, through support from the Amalgamated Meat Cutters and Butcher Workmen of North America, an affiliate of the recently created American Federation of Labor (AFL). Through a series of strikes, owners mastered the art of using race and ethnicity as a tool for dividing workers.[46] Like most craft unions that made up the AFL, the Amalgamated Meat Cutters was predominantly white, and when packinghouse workers walked off their jobs in 1894 calling for higher wages, owners proceeded

Figure 5.3.   Manicurists in the Canning Department of Armour Foods, ca. 1909. Library of Congress Prints & Photographs Division, Stereograph Collection, LC-USZ62-80737.

to hire Polish immigrants and black workers as replacements. In 1904, twenty-eight thousand workers walked off the job, and owners proceeded to transport trainloads of African Americans from the South to replace the striking workers, establishing racial divisions on the Chicago South Side that linger to the present.[47] If there were any justice for workers, white or black, it would come two years later in 1906 when novelist Upton Sinclair published *The Jungle*, articulating the horrifying conditions of meatpacking plants and the inhumane exploitation of workers. Following the release of the novel, President Theodore Roosevelt sent his labor commissioner to Chicago to investigate the meatpacking plants, which since 1902 had consolidated into the National Packing Company, a merger primarily of the "Big Three." Through the court case *Swift and Co. v. United States*, Roosevelt had already succeeded in forcing the packers to discontinue price fixing. After the commissioner's visit, congress passed the Federal Meat Inspection Act and the Pure Food and Drug Act, the latter leading to the formation of the U.S. Food and Drug Administration. Four years later, Swift, Armour, and Morris were indicted by a grand jury in Chicago for conspiracy and illegal monopoly, and by 1912 their conglomerate was forced to dissolve.[48] *The Jungle* went on to become a standard novel in English and social studies curriculums in U.S. schools.

By the time *The Jungle* was published Chicago's meatpacking industry was massive in scale, producing the vast majority of meat consumed in the United States. The packing plants set the standard for the industry in terms of operations, products, and labor relations. The Armour, Swift, and Morris families were among the wealthiest Americans, not only because of their ascendancy as meatpackers but also because of investments in commodity futures for goods they produced or controlled. During the 1890s, Phillip Armour controlled a good portion of Chicago's grain elevators, having built the city's largest elevators at Goose Island on Chicago's North Side. If Armour wasn't cornering the market for pork, wheat, or corn, he was using his massive storage capacity to ward off others from doing so.[49] No less important than making money from grain futures markets was the meatpacking magnate's efforts to control the price of animal feed.

Chicago meatpackers were the first to establish the concept of vertical integration within the food industry. Through vertical integration, a company controlled all phases from supply of raw ingredients to production and distribution, reducing costs and creating efficiencies wherever possible. Swift and Armour were particularly shrewd at this practice, exhibiting an obsession for controlling costs and streamlining purchasing, production, distribution, sales, and waste. From the grains that fed livestock to the trains that transported them to the by-products of the slaughterhouse, the meatpackers sought profit. Indeed, without profits from by-products, at the prices the meatpackers were selling meat they would lose money.[50] For example, during the 1880s, the meatpackers produced oleomargarine as a butter substitute from by-products of meat processing; they produced "leather, soap, fertilizer, glue, imitation ivory, gelatin, shoe polish, buttons, perfume, and violin strings," establishing a production framework by which entire nonfood industries would be developed from the slaughtering process.[51] Every part of an animal was used, and waste products were purchased from smaller packinghouses. In Sinclair's fictional account, he describes how

> out of the horns of the cattle they made combs, buttons, hairpins, and imitation ivory; out of the shinbones and other big bones they cut knife and toothbrush handles, and mouthpieces for pipes; out of the hoofs they cut hairpins and buttons, before they made the rest into glue. From such things as feet, knuckles, hide clippings, and sinews came such strange and unlikely products as gelatin, isinglass, and phosphorus, bone black, shoe blacking, and bone oil. They had curled-hair works for the cattle tails, and a "wool pulley" for the sheepskins; they made pepsin from the stomachs of the pigs, and albumen from the blood, and violin strings from the ill-smelling entrails.[52]

One of the most lucrative products of Chicago's meatpacking industry was canned pork and beef, whether for humans or nonhumans. In 1868, Libby, McNeill & Libby ("Libby's") began packing beef in brine into barrels. Seven years later the company started packing corned beef in pyramid-style cans at their factory on State and 16th Street. During their first year they slaughtered some forty-five thousand cattle, a number that would reach more than nine hundred thousand by 1884.[53] By that time half of their production was going to Great Britain and another 20 percent to Germany. The national and international popularity of canned beef prompted Armour, Swift, and Morris to enter the canning business. They especially had their eyes on international markets as European orders for "compressed beef" surged during the colonization of Africa and Asia. The demand for beef over pork was, however, a concern for the Chicago meatpackers, who made the most money from pork.[54] More than a hundred years before the European Union banned U.S. beef over concerns about excessive hormones (and later mad cow disease), U.S. meatpackers struggled with European governments' and the public's perception that canned U.S. pork would cause illness; bans of U.S. canned pork led the Chicago's Board of Trade and meatpackers to call for U.S. retaliation during the early 1880s.[55]

Driven largely by international demand, Libby's built an enormous beef slaughterhouse facility at the Union Yards, and by the mid-1880s the company's production was approaching thirty-six million cans per year, packing over two hundred thousand cattle annually.[56] When the company incorporated in 1888, Gustavus Swift quickly purchased stock, making his son Edward vice president and essentially giving the family control of the company for decades.[57] At the beginning of the twentieth century, Libby's continued to expand, eventually diversifying into canned fruits and vegetables, among other products. In 1918, the company built a large plant in suburban Blue Island when the town south of Chicago was still in proximity to fruit and vegetable farms.[58] During the 1970s, Libby's became a subsidiary of Nestlé, and by the end of the twentieth century, ConAgra, one of the largest U.S food companies, owned Libby's canned meat division.

Meat canners would venture beyond human food, especially as access to fresh meat became more widespread among the U.S. populace during the twentieth century. The meat canning industry, initially spurred by wars and colonial endeavors, led to the development of a U.S. market for "canner cows" considered less suitable for packaging as dressed meat. During World War I, "canner cows" brought high prices to ranchers and recharged the canned meat business in Chicago.[59] But when business slumped following the war, meatpackers turned to canning pet food to profit from packinghouse remains, including "ground bone, meat scraps, and 'tankage' (a liquid slurry of meat particles and water)."[60] Armour and Company began to market Dash dog food during the 1920s, and Swift and Company introduced Pard, a "scientifically balanced dog food" that claimed to reduce "nervousness in dogs."[61]

Regardless of attempts to revive it, Chicago's dominance in meatpacking would slowly diminish during the mid-twentieth century largely due to the decentralization of meatpacking operations and the introduction of refrigerated trucking. During the early 1920s, Morris and Company was acquired by Armour and Company, and the latter continued to package meat at the Union Stock Yards throughout the 1950s. The Union Stock Yards closed all meat processing in 1971. A year earlier, Chicago-based Greyhound Corporation bought Armour, and in 1983 it sold the company's meatpacking division to ConAgra and the canned meats division to Pinnacle Foods.[62] Ironically, by the end of the 1980s ConAgra had purchased Swift and Company and, in theory, once again reunited the "Big Three" (albeit for a short time). ConAgra would eventually sell all its meat processing operations in 2002, and by 2007 the remnants of Chicago's meatpackers were owned by the Brazilian company JBS, which claimed in 2014 to be "the world's largest exporter of animal protein." ConAgra also sold its refrigerated meats division, primarily consisting of Armour brand deli meats, to conglomerate Smithfield Foods, the largest pork producer in the world, which was acquired in 2013 by a Chinese firm named Shuanghui. By 2014, a relatively few corporations—JBS, Shuanghui, Cargill, and Tyson—practiced vertical integration at a depth and breadth that would have been likely unimaginable to nineteenth-century Chicago meatpackers who established the model now used to control most meat on the planet.

SALT, "SUGAR," AND OATS

Chicago's nineteenth-century meatpacking industry would not have been possible without salt. Salt was the most basic ingredient in preservation because its use in curing and packing prevented the development of microorganisms. The practice was commonplace for centuries, allowing for meat (e.g., "salt pork") to be stored and rationed in times of war and to use while traveling long distances, for example, in colonial expeditions and outposts. Partly because of salt interests, in 1818 Illinois became the twenty-first U.S. state. Only two years after the rebuilding of Fort Dearborn when Chicago barely had a single settler, the majority of the state's inhabitants lived in southern Illinois, where the largest enterprise was salt production. Illinois's salt industry developed over a decade earlier when the federal government created a salt reserve along the Saline River near the Ohio River at the present-day border of Kentucky. The government's salt interests were intricately tied to meat production in order to feed troops garrisoned in forts across the Ohio River Valley and across the new Western frontier of the U.S. territories. Rights to salt production were leased by the government to individual investors, and by the time of statehood, the thriving industry used as many as two thousand slaves at a time to produce more than one hundred thousand bushels of salt per year outside Shawneetown, Illinois.[63] The issue of slave labor in Illinois salt production remained important enough that the state's first constitution of 1818 included the provision that " no person bound to labor in any other state, shall be hired to labor in this state, except within the tract reserved for the salt works near Shawneetown."[64] The provision continued until 1825, and the state would eventually ban slavery in 1848.

The story of Illinois's early salt industry illustrates the important role of salt in the early nineteenth-century geography of U.S. meat production. By the 1830s, Illinois salt producers faced mounting competition from salt mines in Kanawha County, Virginia (eventually West Virginia), the largest salt producer west of the Appalachian Mountains. Shawneetown's salt works went into severe decline and essentially vanished by the time the Union Stock Yard opened in 1865.[65] Nevertheless, Illinois salt producers were important players in the nascent Ohio River Valley meatpacking industry. The meat industry was dependent on slave labor for one of its primary ingredients, a product second in importance only to the hog itself. Antebellum Virginia salt producers would build a robust industry fueled by West Virginia coal and, most importantly, the slavery system. By 1850, Virginia salt producers generated over three million bushels, making it by far the largest supplier to the Ohio River Valley, and the river city of Cincinnati turned into "porkopolis."[66] Prerailroad and canal meatpackers in Chicago were at a disadvantage to Cincinnati, a river city with vital proximity to Kanawha County salt. Midwestern grain and livestock farming and Chicago's railroads would become the major impetus for Chicago's meat industry, but it wasn't until a military assault on the South and development of the New York State salt industry that Chicago would emerge as a meatpacking empire and, interestingly, the headquarters for the country's leading processor and distributor of salt.

Early in the Civil War, Union troops gained control of the Kanawha Valley, which had emerged as the second largest salt-producing center in the country.[67] The Union troops maintained the salt works with slave labor intact until the fall of 1862 when Confederate soldiers succeeded at invading the region and raiding the salt works (oddly enough, liberating the slaves).[68] Moreover, throughout the war, Union forces carried out regular attacks on salt works across the South, along the East Coast and the Gulf of Mexico, and into Louisiana and Texas. Perhaps most importantly, a naval blockade of the Atlantic and Gulf of Mexico ports deeply hindered the ability to import salt and other necessities needed by the Confederate army. Toward the end of the war, salt shortages across the South made it virtually impossible to cure sufficient meat for provisioning the troops, posing a substantial blow to the Confederacy.[69]

In contrast, by the early 1860s, New York State had become the largest supplier of domestic salt, an important source for the developing Northern Illinois and Wisconsin meatpacking industry that proved vital to Union victory. New York State's salt industry developed around Lake Onondaga near the city of Syracuse (known as "Salt City"). In 1797, the state created Onondaga Salt Springs Reservation and began leasing land to producers, who by the middle of the eighteenth century had significantly expanded production. Construction of the Erie Canal immediately accelerated shipments from Upstate New York to Northern Illinois and Wisconsin ports, and by the 1850s Onondaga salt was an important supplier to Chicago meatpackers. Chicago hosted meatpacking houses since 1827 when Archibald Clybourne built a slaughterhouse on the North Branch of the Chicago River to supply Fort Dearborn.[70] The industry grew steadily during the 1830s and 1840s, mostly through local consumption but also from shipments to the East through Detroit. By the end of the decade, Chicago beef packers had regular contracts from Boston and England and could be found all along the city's river banks as far south as Bridgeport.[71] After costs incurred for cattle and labor, the packers' primary expense was for salt and barrels used in packing. Between 1850 and 1865, some 628,776 barrels of salt were transported on the Illinois and Michigan Canal largely to support meatpackers; the 1919 Illinois State Geological Survey reported that "the canal gave an important impetus to the salt industry of New York, Onondaga salt competing with Kansas salt as far west as St. Louis."[72] In 1862, the City of Chicago reported "not less than 1,360,000 bushels were shipped to Chicago and Milwaukee," much of which likely went into meatpacking.[73] One of those Milwaukee meatpacking plants was co-owned by a young Philip Armour, who reportedly got his start in the business selling salt and pickled pork to migrants traveling West.[74]

By the early 1860s, Northern Illinois and Wisconsin meatpackers had become important suppliers to the Union army, and New York's salt industry was critical for the military's most important source of protein: salt pork. In 1862, at the heat of war, Onondaga Salt Springs produced a century high of more than nine million bushels of salt; this was by far more salt produced than anywhere else in North America. The number of barrels of salt shipped to Chicago reached 668,000, an increase by 58 percent from before the war. Even after the war, salt continued to flow into Chicago as the city's meatpacking industry consolidated at the Union Stock Yards. By the end of the 1870s, packers such as Armour, Swift, and Morris were turning Chicago into a meat metropolis, and by default one of the saltiest cities on the planet. Indeed, salt would become one of the city's most important industries.

In 1880, a young man named Joy Morton moved to Chicago from Nebraska and became a supply agent at the Burlington & Quincy Railroad Company southwest of Chicago in Aurora, Illinois. Within a short time he joined E. I. Wheeler and Company, a Chicago agency engaged in the salt trade. The company dated back to the opening of the Illinois and Michigan Canal in 1848 when Alonzo Richmond started Richmond and Company, a sales office for Onondaga Salt of Syracuse, New York.[75] The Chicago salt business expanded with the settlement of the West as settlers required salt, most importantly for raising and slaughtering livestock.[76] The canal provided the waterway to ship salt to the Mississippi and beyond, and railroads and the Civil War turned Chicago into a key salt transfer point. Since the Civil War, Michigan salt edged out Onondaga Salt Springs as the primary supplier to Chicago, and the Michigan Salt Association, a pool of producers, maintained enormous control over prices and distribution.[77] Richmond became the Midwest supplier for the association, and Wheeler took over the company from Richmond just prior to hiring Morton. When Wheeler died in 1885, Morton took over the firm, renaming it Joy Morton and Company. In 1888, Morton built a seventeen-acre warehouse and packaging facility along the pier at Randolph Street at the mouth of the Chicago River. The operation provided efficient transportation to salt buyers from Chicago, the Midwest, and beyond. By the mid-1890s Joy Morton and Company was also the western sales agent for Retsof Mining Company, owner of the largest salt mine in the United States, and one of the largest in the world. Morton would become a board member.[78] In Chicago, meatpacking companies such as Armour, Swift, and Morris were expanding, as were their salt needs, and Morton would become an important supplier.

During the 1890s, Morton also diversified his investments, including his influence over production of starch at Argo Manufacturing Company in Nebraska City. The company was renamed Argo Corn Starch, which it popularized through an exhibit at the 1893 Columbian Exposition in Chicago. In 1899, Morton orchestrated a deal to merge Argo with New York–based United Starch Company. The latter was in turn sold in 1900 to National Starch Company that was itself sold in 1902 to the Corn Products Refining Company of New York (CPRC). Morton remained as one of the company's board members. Eight years later, as previously noted, CPRC's president would select to build the Argo corn refinery in Summit, Illinois, less than twenty miles from Morton's new Thornhill Estate where he lived for the remainder of his life and which became the 1,700-acre Morton Arboretum (Morton's father, J. Sterling Morton, established Arbor Day).

In addition to Argo, Morton became the principle investor in the United States Sugar Refinery—producing glucose products from corn syrup—on 140 acres of Lake Michigan property in Waukegan, Illinois. The company took advantage of the growing demand for corn-based sweeteners as a less expensive alternative to cane sugar for candy making, preserving fruits and jellies, beer brewing, and as a substitute for maple syrup. Corn-derived glucose also had a wide variety of industrial uses. The Waukegan "sugar" plant was incorporated into the United Starch Company deal and would operate as part of the Corn Products Refinery Company. In 1912, the Waukegan plant had a massive explosion, considered to be the worst in the county's history, killing fourteen workers. The following year it was closed. The Argo plant in Summit would continue to produce glucose products, including the popular Karo syrups that claimed in 2014 to be the only corn syrup "available across the United States" (the product was still produced in Summit by a subsidiary of a British company).[79] Largely because of the Argo plant, Corn Products Refining Company went on to become the largest producer of glucose in the country, drawing attention in 1913 from the Interstate Commerce Commission for complaints about industry price fixing.[80]

Morton invested in starch, glucose, meatpacking, oats, and railroads, among other industries, but his primary focus always remained on salt. Like his peers in meatpacking, he attained dominance through vertical integration of production, distribution, and marketing. Investments were made in salt production in Michigan and Kansas, and Morton gained influence over the New York–based National Salt Company, a conglomerate of salt-producing companies across New York, West Virginia, and Ohio. By the end of the nineteenth century, Joy Morton and Company was the sole western supplier for National Salt Company where Morton had become vice president and a board member.[81] In 1901, National Salt went bankrupt, and its properties were placed under the newly incorporated International Salt Company of New Jersey.[82] Morton proceeded to reposition Joy Morton and Company under a separate company called International Salt Company of Illinois, and he made it a subsidiary of the New Jersey firm. Eight years later the New Jersey firm failed and Morton acquired its holdings, renaming the new corporation Morton Salt Company.

Less than a decade after renaming the company, Morton Salt would become the exclusive agent for a large salt producer in Utah near Salt Lake City.[83] In doing so, the company would become the largest salt dealer in the United States. Moreover, the Chicago salt giant would become a household name across the country after adding magnesium carbonate to a dark blue, round, cylinder-shaped paperboard container that said "Morton Salt." The anticaking additive forever changed the nature of pouring table salt, as did the girl in the yellow dress carrying an umbrella to protect her from raining salt with the underlying slogan "when it rains it pours." The marketing campaign contributed to making Morton's table salt an indispensable staple worldwide, especially after 1924 when the company developed iodized salt as an approach to reducing iodine deficiency and related illnesses. Morton Salt was sold in the 1980s (for a while becoming a subsidiary of Dow Chemical), and in 2014 it was owned by K+S, a German company and the largest salt company in Europe.

Joy Morton's role in defining Chicago's foodways went far beyond salt and its deep influence on industries such as meatpacking. In 1905, Morton moved his offices to the new Railway Exchange Building on Jackson and Michigan Avenue, overlooking the still-undeveloped Chicago lakefront. In the building's penthouse, Daniel Burnham designed himself a studio, where he developed his famous 1909 *Plan of Chicago*. Having interest in transportation (for obvious reasons) Morton became chair of Burnham's committee on railway terminals.[84] In addition to Burnham, neighbors included the newly formed Quaker Oats Company, one of Morton's chief competitors.

The country's oats trade had grown during the latter half of the nineteenth century along with the expansion of cities that depended on oats for horse feed.[85] During the 1850s, an Akron, Ohio, grocer by the name of Ferdinand Schumacher began to hand-grind oats at his grocery store to be sold for human consumption; he sold the by-products from the operation as feed. Schumacher proceeded to open an oat mill that invented a process to significantly reduce waste and preparation time for preparing oatmeal. In 1891, the mill was part of a set of mergers and consolidations across Iowa, Illinois, and Ohio, resulting in the formation of the American Cereal Company in Akron, Ohio. One of those consolidated companies was Quaker Mill Company, owned by Henry Parsons Crowell from Ravenna, Ohio. Quaker Oats became American Cereal's oatmeal brand, with Crowell as company vice president. Building their product's image at the 1893 Columbian Exposition, the company erected a large pavilion of "antique oak with a stained glass cornice" with depictions of American-grown cereals.[86] Meanwhile, during the same decade, Joy Morton had entered the cereal business, gaining control of Nebraska City Cereal Mills in his former hometown. He proceeded to popularize the brands Quail Rolled Oats and Mother's Oats as he built a portfolio of grain mills across the Midwest. In 1901, Crowell became president of the American Cereal Company, and before long the company was fully transferred under the name Quaker Oats, and was headquartered in Chicago.[87] Staunch competitors, Crowell and Morton became neighbors in the Railway Exchange Building.

Through the first decade of the century, Morton built his grain milling business into a sizeable corporation, Great Western Cereal Company, with ten mills across Nebraska, Iowa, Illinois, Minnesota, and Ohio and a headquarters at Jackson and Dearborn streets in the now demolished Great Northern Building (also designed by Burnham).[88] The company had a Chicago-area plant along the Illinois and Michigan Canal in Joliet, Illinois. The now popularized Mother's Oats cereal brand, a product ironically developed in Akron, Ohio, competed with Quaker Oats and its popular trademarked man dressed as a colonial-era Quaker. In comparison, Mother's Oats's label had a nurturing scene of a mother with a bowl of oatmeal holding a spoon up to feed a waiting child. After several years of heavy competition, Morton sold the company to Quaker Oats in 1911. Reflecting on the success of Mother's Oats, Quaker Oats kept the cereal's marketing image and included it in a revised form on their famous paperboard cylinder container that set the standard for oatmeal packaging to the present. For more than half a century, the two products were advertised side by side with slogans such as "Quaker Oats and Mother's Oats are the same."[89] When consumer interest shifted toward natural foods during the 1980s, Quaker turned Mother's Oats into one of the first brands of "natural" cereals with packaging that included an updated image of a mother and child. While Morton Salt would forever leave the cereal business, Quaker Oats would go on to become one of the most successful and recognized packaged cereal companies in the world, largely due to the marketing savvy of Henry Crowell.[90]

Quaker Oats took what was considered to be a product sold out of barrels to the level of a packaged food product with colorful marketing and creative design. In doing so, the company contributed to transforming the way people in the United States bought food at the turn of the century. Over twenty years before Quaker Oats bought Mother's Oats, American Cereal Company introduced the first trial-size promotional package and shipped enough to supply every household in Portland, Oregon, before continuing the campaign in other cities.[91] The company used premiums, including them on cereal boxes, and mail-order exchanges using cut outs from the package (i.e., the first cereal-box-top cutouts). They were the first to launch a national magazine cereal advertisement, to use incentive marketing with merchandise coupons on cereal containers, and to feature recipes—oatmeal bread and oatmeal cookies—on the cereal container. By the end of the first decade of the twentieth century, Quaker Oats was mass-producing the first puffed rice and puffed wheat cereals. Later in the century, the company would introduce Life and Cap'n Crunch cereals, thrust into national popularity during the early 1970s by creative advertising campaigns that captured broad public attention. Quaker Oats would also produce the first instant oatmeal, later enhancing it with a variety of flavors in individually packaged servings. By the end of the twentieth century, the company was one of the largest breakfast food producers in the world and owned nonbreakfast brands such as Rice-a-Roni and Gatorade. With eyes on the latter, PepsiCo purchased Quaker Oats in 2001.

DAIRY AND BAKERIES

Quaker Oats may have made its headquarters in Chicago, but most of its production occurred in plants with proximity to large-scale grain agriculture in towns such as Akron, Ohio, and Cedar Rapids, Iowa. Like the meatpackers, grain mills produced by-products referred to as midds, hulls or chaff, shorts, and bran, from which they sought profit often by selling them as animal feed. Mill by-products were fed as rations to cattle and hogs in addition to grasses, hay, alfalfa, and clover, as well as to horses in bustling preautomobile cities like Chicago. Livestock farmers also added supplements to feed including gluten, linseed, and cottonseed meal, and distillers' grains, a practice carried over from swill milk farms connected to distilleries during the nineteenth century. By the early twentieth century, grain milling companies began to make their by-products an industry, branding and patenting them and employing university scientists to conduct studies to prove the benefits of feed mixes on livestock health and productivity.

Quaker Oats was an early innovator in the development of branding animal feed from oats, dating back to Ferdinand Schumacher's mill in Akron. The company continued to tout the value of their brand "Schumacher Feed," and in time they developed an entire line of animal feeds marketed directly to dairy farmers. Before 1920, the company had its own dairy demonstration farm, Monona Farms, outside Madison, Wisconsin—the heart of Wisconsin dairy country—where they collaborated with the University of Wisconsin Agricultural Experiment Station to conduct studies to illustrate the success of their products for increasing milk production. A 1928 silent film produced as a marketing instrument illustrates how the company was employing agricultural scientists to prove the positive impact of Quaker products on milk production and how the company's animal feeds were supporting the country's milk consumption by helping "the dairyman supply that market."[92] Interestingly, later in the century Quaker Oats (PepsiCo) launched its "Milk Chillers" flavored milk drinks in 2005, and a campaign in 2014, funded by the milk industry, promoted swapping milk for water in preparing oatmeal. Quaker Oats oatmeal also became the first grocery store product to use the "Got Milk" mustache on packaging: the Quaker Oats man.[93]

A hundred years before milk appeared in flavors, the majority of dairy consumed by Chicagoans was delivered to the city from regional farms by rail, and within a couple of decades by truck. By that time, milk production had firmly been separated from consumption, and dairy farms used intermediaries to broker the relationship with urban consumers. Horse-drawn milk delivery wagons delivered products directly to households, and bottling and processing facilities were built along rail lines. A network of dairy farms, bottlers, and processors serving Chicago emerged along rail lines across Northern Illinois and Wisconsin. The railroad, for example, would transport hundreds of thousands of gallons of milk a year from Northern Illinois towns such as Bensenville, founded by German dairy farmers and cheesemakers. Morton Salt, in the meantime, had become the region's largest supplier of the dairy salt needed for butter and cheese production, and Quaker Oats, among others, marketed heavily to individual dairy farmers its line of cattle feeds, "scientifically prepared" to improve milk production.

In response to depressed milk prices after World War I, dairy farmers began organizing cooperative associations supported by the U.S. Capper–Volstead Act that exempted dairy associations from antitrust laws. These associations were mainly concerned about prices and growing competition from large dairy companies. In 1920, Chicago had 2.7 million people, second in population to New York. Its proximity to dairy farms, role in the grain trade, and network of railroads made the city an important center for development of the U.S. dairy industry. The "Chicago Dairy District," as it was called, became a magnate for corporate dairy companies.[94] In 1922, *Prairie Farmer* newspaper, a highly popular advocate for small farmers headquartered in Chicago, advocated for farmers to build an association to serve the Chicago Milk District or "let the Bowman Dairy Company reign supreme and pay any price they see fit."[95]

Bowman Dairy Company was one of the first corporate dairy companies in Chicago, opened in 1885 by St. Louis dairy owner J. R. Bowman. Bowman bought M. A. Devine, one of the oldest and most successful dairies in Chicago, and built the company into the city's largest home supplier. To do so, they bought dairies across the Midwest and opened bottling operations in cities and in "country plants" in proximity to suppliers.[96] In 1966, as consumers increasingly moved from home delivery to buying milk from supermarkets, the company struggled and was bought by local rival Dean Milk Company. Sam Dean started Dean Milk Company in 1925 in Pecatonica, Illinois, in Northern Illinois dairy country. Originally called Dean Evaporated Milk Company, the company expanded to sell fluid milk and eventually ice cream from its headquarters in the Chicago suburb of Franklin Park. Like Bowman, by midcentury Dean bought up several smaller dairies before buying Bowman and vastly expanding its business. Before the end of the century, Dean was the largest dairy company in the country and one of the largest in the world. In 2001, the company was bought by Suiza Foods, which proceeded to change its own name to Dean Foods.

Chicago's size and location also made it a magnate for corporations manufacturing butter, cheese, and ice cream. One of those companies, Blue Valley Creamery Company, relocated its headquarters from St. Joseph, Missouri, to Chicago during the 1920s. Blue Valley was considered a "centralizer," a creamery producing butterfat from raw materials sourced over a wide radius of "as much as 500 miles" in contrast to local creameries and cooperatives that sourced from farms in close proximity.[97] In 1918, Blue Valley was the fourth largest butterfat marketer in the country, trailing behind three other Chicago centralizers: Swift and Company, Armour and Company, and Beatrice Creamery.[98] Meatpackers Swift and Armour got involved in butterfat with their entrance into the oleomargarine (butterine) business back in the 1880s. Beatrice Creamery, which bought Blue Valley in 1939, moved to Chicago from Beatrice, Nebraska, in 1913 and established its headquarters at 1526 South State Street.[99] The company had built a well-known brand of dairy products, Meadow Gold, which already had a market west of the Rockies and would soon become nationally recognized. Like its competitor, Dean Milk, Beatrice purchased other companies, eventually changing its company name to Beatrice Foods. In 1986, the company was sold to another corporate dairy giant, Borden.[100] Borden was established in Connecticut during the 1850s as one of the first producers of condensed milk. Their "Eagle Brand" canned milk got a slow start, but its resistance to spoilage made it an important part of Civil War provisions (especially for use with coffee), leading to opening a plant in the Northern Illinois town of Elgin, Illinois, forty miles west of Chicago.[101] One hundred years later, Borden built the largest milk processing plant in U.S. history, twenty-five miles north of Elgin in Woodstock, Illinois.[102] The company and its brands were broken up and sold during the 1990s, including the Meadow Gold products earlier attained from Beatrice. Its founding product, Eagle Brand, was sold to J. M. Smucker Company (of peanut butter fame), which also owns PET Milk products, founded in 1885 as Helvetia Milk Condensing Company in the Chicago suburb of Highland Park.

Ten miles south of Highland Park in the suburb of Northfield, Illinois, the company Kraft Foods established its headquarters in 1992. Founded by James L. Kraft in 1903, J. L. Kraft and Bros. sold cheese wholesale by wagon to Chicago grocers. A separate but related company, Kraft Bros. Cheese, was headquartered in Plymouth, Wisconsin, west of Sheboygan, the cheese capital of the Midwest.[103] The company owned a patent to sterilize and pack cheese in tin containers that in time were sold throughout the United States. World War I orders for the cheese boomed at the cheese factory built in the Northern Illinois town of Stockton. In 1928, the company merged with Phenix Cheese Corporation, the maker of Philadelphia Brand cream cheese. Two years later, National Dairy Products Corporation, owner of Breyers ice cream and Breakstone cottage cheese, bought Kraft-Phenix. Kraft had already created Miracle Whip and purchased the Velveeta Cheese Company. Within a decade the company produced Kraft Macaroni and Cheese dinners and Parkay margarine, products that also become staples across U.S. households. In 1950, the company produced the first processed sliced cheese and a couple of years later Cheez Whiz spread. National Dairy Products changed its name to Kraftco in 1969, and by the 1980s Kraft was one of the largest packaged dairy companies in the country. By the end of the decade, tobacco giant Philip Morris bought the company, adding numerous brands to its portfolio. Kraft then oversaw products such as Kool-Aid, Post Cereals, and Oscar Mayer meat products, to name a few. The list of brands was extensive, and in 2000 it got even larger with the full acquisition of Nabisco.

During the 1950s, Nabisco built a plant on the South Side of Chicago considered to be one of the largest bakeries in the world, but the company already had a deep historical connection to the city. American Biscuit Company opened in Chicago in 1890 and grew to numerous bakeries across the Midwest. Before the end of the century, the company would join a large East Coast conglomerate called National Biscuit Company (eventually Nabisco), with its headquarters in Chicago in the Home Insurance Building (considered Chicago's first skyscraper). Though the headquarters would move to the East within a decade, the initial choice of Chicago aligns with the city's status as a transportation hub with connections to all points of the country and to rich grain and dairy resources of the Midwest. Nabisco would be the first company to produce individually packaged crackers (or biscuits), and those crackers were made in its Chicago bakeries.

When National Biscuit Company first settled in Chicago, the city was already steeped in a long history of cracker baking. Perhaps one of the most significant transformations in baking occurred in Chicago with the opening in 1858 of the Mechanical Bakery, built on a model developed in Brooklyn destroyed by fire in 1856. Located on Clinton Street between Lake and Randolph, the bakery was built on a system of chains, tracks, and cars that carried dough into the ovens with doors that opened and closed automatically. Machines were used for kneading and shaping dough into loaves or crackers.[104] Flour went in from one end of the building and products were shipped out the other. The company's business grew swiftly during the 1860s with contracts from the Union army for hardtack, a cracker made of flour and water. At one point, the bakery was manufacturing "as high as one hundred barrels of flour every twenty-four hours" in its nonstop operation.[105] In 1864, bakery workers were so upset with the long hours and low wages that they went on strike—"Chicago's first significant bakers' strike."[106]

Cracker baking has an even deeper history in Chicago. Chicago continued its role as an incubator of corporate bakeries when in 1927 the United Biscuit Company was organized out of a consolidation of Midwestern bakeries. From its headquarters in Chicago, and with one of its many bakeries on the city's West Side, the company established plants across the country. By the 1950s, United Biscuit had built a large bakery and headquarters in suburban Melrose Park, and the following decade it renamed itself Keebler. In 2001, as a primary competitor of Nabisco (Kraft) in the cracker and cookie business, Keebler was prime for purchase by Kellogg Company.

Chicago's history of industrial bread and cake baking is equally noteworthy. Paul Schulze opened Schulze Baking Company during the 1890s and eventually built a large bakery at 40 East Garfield Boulevard in Chicago's South Side Washington Park neighborhood. Schulze invented Butternut Bread before he sold the company to Interstate Bakeries Corporation, which continued to bake the bread at the Garfield Boulevard plant until closing it in 2004.[107] A decade earlier Interstate had bought Continental Baking Company, maker of Wonder Bread and Hostess products. About seventy years earlier while working at Continental's bakery in the Chicago suburb of Schiller Park, a baker named James Dewer started filling shortcakes with cream rather than strawberries and proceeded to create Twinkies.

While the Twinkie proceeded to become a national sensation, Chicago built its reputation for the famous Chicago hot dog served on a poppy seed bun invented by Louis Kuchuris, owner of Mary Ann's Bakery. Kuchuris had to significantly expand his operations during the mid-1950s when the company became a bun supplier for a new fast food chain called McDonald's.[108] Around the same period, Consolidated Foods Corporation, a Chicago grocery wholesaler with origins dating back to the Civil War, purchased Kitchens of Sara Lee from Charles Lubin, who started his pastry bakery a half a decade earlier and named it after his daughter. In 1964, Kitchens of Sara Lee opened a five-hundred-thousand-square-foot bakery in suburban Deerfield, Illinois.[109] By the mid-1980s the Sara Lee brand had become so successful that Consolidated changed its own name to Sara Lee Corporation, with headquarters in Deerfield. In 1989, Sara Lee bought Ball Park Franks, archrival to Chicago's Oscar Mayer hot dogs that had been recently acquired by Kraft. Two decades later, with headquarters less than five miles from one another, the two corporate giants started a two-year battle in what newspapers called the "Wiener War." In typical Chicago style, the companies flung lawsuits at each other over claims about which had the number-one dog.[110]

CANDY AND CHOCOLATE

Arguably, Chicago emerged as a (or *the*) hot dog capital of the United States during the twentieth century, but at the beginning of the century the city was the country's candy capital, or at least Chicagoans thought themselves as such. Their belief was based on the many candy makers and wholesale dealers that produced and distributed candy locally and across the continent. Undeniably, Chicago's railroads again gave it the advantage not only for shipping but also through the relatively easy access to the aforementioned raw materials—corn syrup, milk, salt, cornstarch, and even meatpacking by-products such as lard and gelatin. Before corn syrup and the availability of beet sugar, sugarcane and its by-product molasses (also used in making rum) were key ingredients in the developing candy industry. Sugarcane is grown in tropical climates, making Chicago far less than ideal for a candy industry. That all changed in 1848 with the building of the Illinois and Michigan Canal linking Chicago to the Mississippi River and ultimately to sugar from slave plantations in Louisiana and Cuba, the world's largest sugar producer. The first year the canal opened it brought close to five million pounds of sugar to Chicago. Four years later that number was more than fifteen million pounds.[111] Built largely out of a by-product of the slave system, small and large confectionaries proliferated during the 1850s, and Chicago had a growing candy industry until the Chicago fire destroyed many factories. At the time of the fire, some of the largest companies were already distributing to eastern and southern states.[112]

Chicago's role as a candy capital truly emerged around the turn of the century. Corn-based sweetener was increasingly available thanks to investors like Joy Morton, Corn Products Refining Company, and beet sugar from Michigan that provided a Midwestern alternative to sugarcane. During the 1890s, Chicago became the birthplace of a new popular treat made from a mix of popcorn, peanuts, salt, and molasses. The city's confectionary company of F. W. Rueckheim & Bros. sold Cracker Jack. Later on when the company started inserting toys into the box, sales took off and the brand became a national phenomena. Soon Cracker Jack would have free advertising through the popular "Take Me Out to the Ball Game" song with its lyrics "buy me some peanuts and Cracker Jack," chanted ritually during the middle of the seventh inning of baseball games. The company grew into and out of several factories, eventually landing on Cicero Avenue just south of Midway Airport. Borden bought the Cracker Jack Company in 1964, eventually selling it to Frito-Lay, a division of PepsiCo.

Shortly after Cracker Jack got its start, in 1904, Emil J. Brach opened his candy store (Palace of Sweets) on the north side of the city where he sold his popular caramels. Brach moved his candy into department stores, and the company grew out of multiple facilities before moving to its West Side plant where it operated for decades. During the 1950s the company introduced "Pick-A-Mix" kiosks into grocery stores, allowing customers to mix a variety of candies in their own bag. The strategy paid off, and Brach's gained national recognition while creating havoc for generations of parents at grocery stores. The company was sold in 1966, and when owners closed the Westside plant in 2001 Chicagoans felt a loss, as did over a thousand employees. A few years later in 2004 another Chicago candy icon, Fannie Mae, shuttered its doors.

Stories such as Cracker Jack, Brach's, and Fannie Mae are many in Chicago's candy history, a past riddled with growth, buyouts, closures and/or relocations, eventually weakening the city's "candy capital" status. Nonetheless, in retrospect, the region can lay claim to creating and/or producing many of the most well-known brands: Wrigley (chewing gum), Baby Ruth, Tootsie Roll and Tootsie Pops, Oh Henry!, Milk Duds, Red Hots, Jaw Breakers, Jelly Belly (also the maker of the original "chicken feed" later renamed "candy corn"), and Milky Way. Mars, the maker of Milky Way, continues to operate a manufacturing facility on the city's Northwest Side, where in 1929 it moved its operations from Minneapolis and building one of the country's largest candy factories at the time. In addition to the original Milky Way, the factory manufactured some of the most profitable chocolate candy bars in the history of candy, including 3 Musketeers, Snickers, and Mars Almond Bar. [113]

Chocolate manufacturing by itself is not a stranger to Chicago. The city has a profound relationship with cocoa beans through Blommer Chocolate Company. On any given day if the wind is blowing in the right

Figure 5.4.   Brach's first store. Candy was manufactured in back, ca. 1910s. Chicago Public Library, Special Collections and Preservation Division, ACC 2.15.

direction, visitors to downtown Chicago can't miss the smell of Blommer located at 600 West Kinzie Street just west of the historic juncture of the Chicago River's north and south branches. Established by Henry Blommer in 1939, the company began selling wholesale cocoa products when Chicago was still the candy capital. As Chicago's role in candy making diminished, Blommer's chocolate making expanded, eventually becoming the largest cocoa processor in the country. The company not only stayed in the heart of Chicago when most food industries left, but they also bucked the trend toward selling out to larger corporate interests. Blommer maintained a fading tradition in Chicago food manufacturing: they remained family run as recent as 2014.

Chicago continues to be a city of visionary food manufacturing companies, often family-run businesses such as Azteca Foods, opened in 1969 and now one of the largest manufacturers of tortilla and Mexican food products in the country. In 2014, the company was still run by the Velasquez family on Chicago's Southwest Side. The city also remains an incubator for some of the most inventive new food companies, such as Upton's Naturals, a seitan producer manufacturing a variety of meat alternatives including "bacon" in a nine-thousand-square-foot factory a little over a mile west of Chicago's historic Fulton Street Meat Market.[114] Established in 2006 and playfully named after novelist Upton Sinclair, by 2014 the company distributed its packaged seitan "meats" across the country to natural food stores and restaurants. Chicago may no longer be "hog butcher for the world," but it continues to be a place of innovation where small ideas turn into larger productions that increasingly seek to scale up beyond the city limits, giving credence to the designate "city of big shoulders."

6

EATING AT THE MEETING PLACE

A Short History of Chicago's Restaurants

In 1828, James Kinzie, the son of John Kinzie, established the Wolf Point Tavern on the west bank of the confluence of the north and south branches of the Chicago River. The next year Mark Beaubien, the brother of early trader Jean Beaubien, and his wife, Monique, opened the competing Eagle Exchange Tavern on the southeast bank of the confluence. In 1831, the Beaubiens built the first frame building in what was to become Chicago, the Sauganash Hotel, on this site, named after Sauganash, or Billy Caldwell, a Métis Pottawatomi warrior and interpreter. There, Mark Beaubien would entertain locals and travelers with his violin while patrons danced. [1]

The trading posts of Kinzie and du Sable, as well as the establishment of Fort Dearborn, are usually pointed to as the sites of Chicago's origin. However, Chicago's beginning as a town, rather than a trading post or fort, lies in the confluence of taverns that grew up around Wolf Point. These were the gathering points and entertainment venues for the new community. They (in particular the Sauganash) were also places where races and ethnicities mixed. The Sauganash had a central place in early Chicago that it would be hard to imagine one establishment playing in later years. While the Beaubiens only owned the hotel until 1834, and it burned down in 1851, it served as the site of the new town's first election (where the vote to incorporate the new town of Chicago was held) in 1833, as well as its first theater in 1837. Its multiple roles demonstrate three themes that run through the history of Chicago food and its eating (and drinking) establishments. First, Chicago is a destination and a way-station for travelers. It is a meeting place, and its food and restaurants reflect this. Chicago's hotels have played a significant role in its gastronomic history, being the site of many of its best eating places, particularly during the city's early history. From the late 1800s until the 1970s, many Chicago restaurants catered to those switching between trains going to or from the West and the East, who either raced from one station to another or spent an evening in the city between trains. In addition, many restaurants, in particular the city's famous steakhouses, greatly relied on tourists and business travelers. Second, eating out in Chicago is also a focus of the city's entertainment offerings. This evolved from connections between restaurants and theaters in the 1800s, to big bands and other formal entertainment in the first half of the twentieth century, to the current Lettuce Entertain You chain, which creates and runs themed restaurants in Chicago and around the country. Third, Chicago has a huge variety of restaurants featuring the food of its immigrant populations. These often serve as local meetinghouses of neighborhoods, although some were also destinations for tourists or others wanting to try something new and different. These ethnic restaurants varied greatly, from diners and hot dog stands to ethnic restaurants of almost every type. As Chicago's gourmet culture has developed, some ethnic restaurants now feature fine dining, at both the quality and price point that characterize it. Finally, food and entertainment combine in Chicago's recent fine dining movement, such as immensely creative and entertaining destination restaurants as the recently closed Charlie Trotter's and, more recently, Alinea and Grace. This chapter and the following investigate the history of Chicago's public eating places, with chapter 6 focusing on restaurants and hotels and chapter 7 focusing on street food and fast food, leading into a discussion of classic Chicago recipes and cookbooks.

THE MEETING PLACE: COMING TOGETHER AND INDULGING AT CHICAGO'S HOTELS AND RESTAURANTS

Hotel Eateries

The Sauganash Hotel and its competitors around Wolf Point are famous in Chicago history for being places of refuge for the widely varied travelers that came into the city. The site of Chicago was not particularly inviting at the time. Entering the Chicago River from Lake Michigan in 1829, the traveler encountered Fort Dearborn, a mark that the area was controlled by the U.S. government. The fort greeted visitors with stockades rather than open arms. Trader John Kinzie's compound, which earlier had been du Sable's, was across the river from the fort, but it was a house and small farm. It was only after passing the fort and arriving at the forks of the north and south branches at Wolf Point that the traveler encountered the heart of the (still unincorporated) settlement of Chicago. There, travelers found often rough rest and entertainment, with innkeepers including not only the Beaubiens and James Kinzie but also Elijah Wentworth, who arrived with his family in the fall of 1829, decided to overwinter, and then took over the rent of the Wolf Point Tavern in 1830. These innkeepers often went onto other jobs, and were essential in founding the city. Wentworth did not stay a tavern owner for long, but he remained in the city and became its first coroner and an early mail carrier.[2] Like Beaubien and Kinzie, running a tavern was only part of Wentworth's career. Across the river, Samuel Miller and Archibald Clybourne operated another store and tavern, next to which, in 1831, Chicago's first church was established. Next door to the Sauganash, Mark Beaubien operated the community's first drug store. Beaubien later was the keeper of the Chicago lighthouse.

The little community that formed around Wolf Point was based on service to travelers and newly arrived settlers, although they mixed with more permanent residents. The Sauganash in particular appears to have been a place of mixing, named after a famous, and still living, Métis man. It was a rough spot for the uninitiated and closed minded. A prominent Scottish agriculturalist, Patrick Shirreff, who visited the hotel during the Indian negotiations of 1833, describes being given a board in a corner of the loft to sleep on and then being ordered, unsuccessfully, to abandon this rough bed in the middle of the night by a pair of French traders. In general, he seems disgusted by the presence of the French traders: "They are a swarthy scowling race, evidently tinged with Indian blood, speaking the French and English languages fluently, and much addicted to swearing and whisky." However, his view of the food was better, if qualified: "The table was amply stored with substantial provisions, to which justice was done by the guests, although indifferently cooked, and still more served up."[3] The key attraction of the Sauganash, although probably not for Shirreff, was Beaubien himself. Nineteenth-century Chicago historian Alfred T. Andreas describes Beaubien as "a jolly host," famous for entertaining guests on his fiddle: "After having given his guests the best his larder afforded, he would of evenings tune up his violin, . . . and often, till late at night, amuse and entertain them with his melody. Dancing too, generally formed no small feature of these sports."[4] Another traveler described a dance scene in 1834, greatly amused by the mixing of officers from the fort with the mixed-race daughters of traders.[5]

The particular foods that were served at the Sauganash and the surrounding early hotels are not entirely clear, but it is evident that the food was plentiful. A typical tavern meal at the time, said Charles Cleaver, a prominent early Chicagoan, was "bread, butter, potatoes, and fried pork."[6] Early twentieth-century historian M. M. Quaife quotes an 1835 traveler to a tavern near what is now suburban Riverside: "The call to breakfast disclosed an abundance of food." There was no milk, and only poor-quality butter, but "the coffee . . . was excellent, the pork steaks 'tolerable,' and the bread, both corn and wheat, was good." In the middle of the table was a pot of rabbit stew.[7] In the next few years, many more hotels sprung up, mainly along the south bank of the main branch of the Chicago River, along Lake Street, the historic core of the city, in the area between Wolf Point and Fort Dearborn. Beaubien himself opened a new hotel at Lake and Wells. Provisions at these hotels during the overcrowded shortage years of the mid-1830s were spare. Joseph Balestier, an 1840 observer, perhaps exaggerating in order to emphasize subsequent changes in the city, described the situation in 1835 as "miserable in the extreme . . . the strangers and the scarcity of provisions rendered every tavern in the place an abode of misery. The luxury of a single bed was almost unknown and the table had no charms to the epicure."[8]

An exception to the low levels of luxury and the development on the south bank of the Chicago River was the Lake House, opened in 1835, which looked over the lakeshore (which now is a half-mile of this point east due to sand accumulation and landfill) at what is now the north end of the Michigan Avenue bridge. The Lake House was Chicago's first brick hotel, and the most luxurious place to stay in the new town. James Silk Buckingham, a publisher, reformer, and former member of the British Parliament, was impressed with the Lake House when he visited in 1840, calling it "equal to that of any house we had met with since leaving Baltimore." The area surrounding the Lake House, north of the river along the lakefront, contained many "pretty villas, some of them large and elegant." The food served at the Lake House included live oysters, provided for the first time during the winters of 1838 and 1839, shipped from New Haven on sleighs.[9] Printed menus and napkins were also provided.[10] By 1840, Balestier could state that travelers could now "indulge in all the luxuries of the east."[11]

The importance of hotel restaurants persisted. In 1846, what was then the largest and most well-appointed hotel in the west, the Sherman House, opened. From its tall cupola, the managers would search for incoming boats and then (along with other hotels) send runners down to meet those who came off, attempting to cajole them to the hotel.[12] It also was one of the downtown Chicago buildings famously raised, through a hydraulic process led in part by George Pullman of passenger car fame, to a higher, less likely to flood level, while guests still were in the hotel. After burning in the Great Chicago Fire of 1871, the Sherman House survived through multiple rebuilds until 1973. It was the site of Chicago's most famous hotel restaurant, the College Inn, which stayed open for more than 130 years. Like many downtown hotel restaurants, the College Inn became an entertainment destination as well as a restaurant, with nightly shows (often recorded for radio and later television) along with the food. The College Inn's food was fancy and expensive for the time, yet still accessible for tourists and nightclub visitors. A Thursday night menu from 1938 features Lake Superior whitefish, Louisiana shrimp, a Vienna rostbratan with noodles, and prime rib. This accompanied Frankie Masters and His Radio Orchestra and, in particular, the Inn's ice-skating show.[13] In addition, like such restaurants as Frontera Grill today, in the 1920s College Inn began to use its reputation with travelers by marketing its food beyond the restaurant by creating items to be sold, in this case canned, at the local grocery. It was famous for its Chicken á la King, made with house-made chicken broth. A story in the January 1922 issue

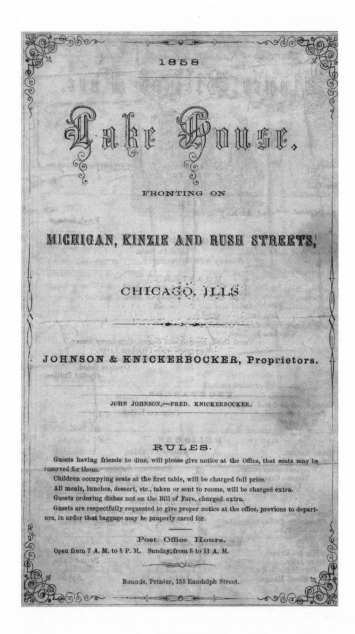

Figure 6.1.   Menu cover from the Lake House, Chicago's first upscale hotel, 1858. Chicago History Museum, Commerical Menu Collection, ICHi-69986.

of *Canning Age* raves about College Inn's decision to can its product as an opening to a new gourmet market for canned foods. College Inn products were, at the time, made in a kitchen next to the Sherman House. The article describes the "plump, young chicken, tender mushrooms" and "delicate Spanish pimentoes" in the canned Chicken á la King.[14] College Inn brand chicken broth is still available today in supermarkets. College Inn's forays into canning did not mean that it down-classed its restaurant, though. The 1922 New Year's menu is written in French, and it features sea bass and Poitrine de Pintade (stuffed breasts of guinea fowl).[15] Later, the Sherman House housed the College Inn Porterhouse, a steak house, and College Inn Well of the Sea, an upscale seafood restaurant sporting a menu cover that echoed Miro.

With the possible exception of the Sauganash, Chicago's most legendary now-gone hotel is the Edgewater Beach. Located along the lakefront on the city's far North Side, the Edgewater presented Chicago as a beach resort rather than a busy trading and industrial center. Opened in 1916 and famous for its festive pink color and its private beach, the Edgewater hosted famous live shows with big bands such as Tommy Dorsey. It was also the Chicago home of many traveling movie stars and athletes such as Babe Ruth. While the Edgewater Beach, as well as other fancy Chicago hotels, were places for tourists, they also hosted numerous everyday and special events for wealthier Chicagoans. Emily Frankenstein, an upper-middle-class Hyde Park girl, described an Independence Day 1918 visit with her family and her sweetheart in glowing terms in her diary: "We were given a table in the beautiful dining-room just in front of the door out of which we could look and see Lake Michigan shimmering and rippling before us only a few yards away . . . the scene was festive with the many brightly colored lights—softened yet gay, and the ochestra [*sic*] playing beautiful selections . . . and the meal was delicious. I had soft shelled crabs, combination salad and chocolate ice-cream."[16]

Downtown, the Stevens Hotel's Boulevard Room and the Palmer House's Empire Room had similar floor shows to the College Inn, including live radio broadcasts and ice shows, during the first half of the twentieth century. The Boulevard Room, now part of the Conrad Hilton (Hilton had bought the Stevens), switched to ice shows in 1948 so as not to compete with the Empire Room since both were Hilton hotels.[17] Large hotels such as the Sherman, Palmer House, and the Stevens/Conrad Hilton also offered a variety of restaurant styles, from simple cafes to haute cuisine. Upscale hotels competed for the luxury market while attempting to cater to everyday tourists as well as with restaurants such as the Shera-

Figure 6.2. Independence Day menu from the Edgewater Beach Hotel, 1938. Chicago History Museum, Commerical Menu Collection, ICHi-69987.

ton-Blackstone's Cafe Bonaparte, which in 1956 featured both a list of French specialties based on recipes made famous by Marie-Antoine

Carême, including Let Filet de Sôle Walewska and Let Filet de Boeuf à la Talleyrand, as well as a V-8 cocktail and a toasted cheese sandwich.[18] Similarly, the long-standing Drake Hotel offers a classic high tea, a holiday tradition for many families, as well as the long-standing Cape Cod Room, a faux authentic down-home New England seafood restaurant at non-down-home prices. Hotel restaurants such as these in the Drake are still today an important place for Chicagoans to celebrate, and they are points where Chicagoans and travelers mix. Like Cafe Bonaparte, today's hotel restaurants, especially in luxury hotels, are still split between serving the everyday needs of travelers and being fine dining establishments on their own.

Chicago as the Railroad and Shopping City: Changing Trains, Eating Food, and Tourism

In very early Chicago, there were few stand-alone restaurants. Mark Beaubien opened a "coffee house" in 1834. Despite Balestier's enthusiasm for Chicago cuisine in 1840, the Lake House and other upscale hotels seem to have been more indicative of the rise of an upper-class community and its visitors in Chicago rather than a thorough evolution in tastes than ran throughout the population. Many travelers were confined to boarding houses with accommodations similar to the Sauganash Hotel but lacking Mark Beaubien's fiddling and entertainment, a situation that remained true long into the twentieth century. Despite this, some Chicagoans attempted to bring their cuisines up to the level of the gourmet food appearing at the time in New York and Europe. While most were not as plush as the Lake House, in 1847 the city boasted twenty-five hotels and taverns, eighteen of them large enough to be considered hotels, and nine free-standing restaurants. The rise of an epicurean class was evident in 1842, when "intense excitement" was exhibited by local epicureans about an effort to bring live Maine lobster to Chicago. Unfortunately, the lobster died in Cleveland and was cooked and shipped to Chicago on ice.[19] Despite this failure, it is clear that there was an increasingly successful effort to bring East Coast luxuries and food to Chicago, which makes sense given that many Chicagoans were from New England and the Middle Atlantic. Stand-alone restaurants included coffeehouses for lighter fare, male-oriented restaurants that focused on alcohol, and ice cream "saloons" for women and children.[20] Still, having only nine restaurants in

1847 for a quickly growing population of around seventeen thousand (growing from about twelve thousand in 1845 to about thirty thousand in 1850) indicates that eating at them was still somewhat rare for most Chicagoans.

By the 1870s, while its hotels were still the focus of fine dining, Chicago had become a city of restaurants, serving both travelers and Chicagoans. As reported by Perry Duis, by the late 1870s Chicagoans were eating out at twice the daily per-capita rate of St. Louis, Cincinnati, and Boston.[21] Many of these restaurants were working-class diners and neighborhood haunts, catering to locals, but some were specifically designed for those switching between, arriving, or departing on one of the many railroads that linked Chicago with the rest of the country. They can be divided into fancy places to see and be seen, in particular the Pump Room, and less fancy restaurants in and next to train stations. Chicago, the hub of the U.S. train system, once had numerous hotels that catered to train travelers, stopping over for a night between trains. Train departure times were important in a similar way as at airport hotels today. Departures were listed on the back of the 1866 menus of the Metropolitan Hotel, along with the locations of nearby amusements. Railroad ticket offices were available in the lobbies of other large downtown hotels such as the Tremont and the Gardner House. On the other hand, the first (and sometimes only) experience many travelers had with Chicago was the restaurants in one of the lobbies of its six downtown railroad terminals. Many of the restaurants in these locations were run by Kansas City–based Fred Harvey, and these restaurants also expanded beyond its base in railroad terminals and dining cars to also include stand-alone restaurants and, in the 1950s, the iconic Illinois Tollway oases, located on bridges spanning the tollways. The oldest train traveler–oriented restaurant still operating is Lou Mitchell's, which graces the cover of this book. Lou Mitchell's opened in 1923 during the heyday of long-distance train travel. Located on Jackson Boulevard a half block from Union Station, in what is now called the West Loop, Lou Mitchell's serves homemade breakfast and lunches to travelers and Chicagoans. Amtrak travelers still stop there for a meal, often seated next to large suitcases, while transferring between trains from the East and West coasts, or other destinations. Lou Mitchell's is a favorite stop of campaigning politicians. Diners are offered a delicious cake doughnut hole upon seating, and women and children are given boxes of Milk Duds. Within the large menu, specialties include

Greek and Greek-inspired dishes, an apple and cheese omelet, and house-made bread and baked goods. In general, Lou Mitchell's is a high-quality Greek diner, an icon of a restaurant type still seen across Chicago and other large cities such as New York. Beyond being near Union Station, its link to transportation is also furthered by its location on Jackson Boulevard, the previous route of U.S. Highway Route 66, which ran from Santa Monica to Chicago. While Route 66 began (or ended, as Jackson now is a one-way street toward the east) at Michigan Avenue, Lou Mitchell's is often pointed to as the first (or last) iconic restaurant along the route by those who continue to trace its historic path.

At the opposite end of the traveler's restaurant spectrum is the Pump Room. While not at all a traditional train-oriented restaurant, the Pump Room, located in the Ambassador East Hotel in the Gold Coast, was known as a place to see stars passing through Chicago on their way between Los Angeles and New York, often seated at Booth 1. Opening in 1938, the Pump Room was one of Chicago's first post-Depression upscale restaurants, but, like many Chicago midcentury fancy restaurants, it was always at least as much about show as about fine cuisine. Main courses from a postwar menu include blini and caviar, a Indonesian rijst-tafel (probably related to the South Pacific themed–restaurant craze occurring at the same time), king crab, capons, as well as a choice of meats and seafoods served "on the flaming sword." Desserts also included flamed options such as crepes Suzette and cherries jubilee.[22] Showing its connection to travel, the Pump Room was chosen to create the menu for American Airlines' first dinner service in flight (for a route from Chicago to London) on November 19, 1945, starring caviar and stuffed squab.[23] The Pump Room declined in the 1960s, then was taken over in the 1970s by Chicago chain Lettuce Entertain You as their first white-tablecloth restaurant. During this period, it maintained its link to the stars with continuing classic portraits taken at Booth 1, including a particularly famous one of John Belushi (in a T-shirt) and Roger Ebert. Finally, in 2011, it reopened, by boutique hotelier and cofounder of New York's Studio 54 Ian Schrager, with Booth 1 still present but with a much more understated menu and atmosphere.

A focus on star (as well as politician) gazing was also a strong draw at another classic restaurant, Fritzel's. Located just north of Chicago's theater district, as well as just northwest of City Hall, at 201 N. State, Fritzel's opened just after World War II, in 1947. Fritzel's was somewhat of an upscale Jewish-style diner, although it was nowhere near kosher.[24] It was famous for its onion bread, and for the celebrities that ate there, including Mayor Richard J. Daley, Tony Bennett, and nearly the entire roster of the New York Yankees when they were in town, in particular Joe DiMaggio. Joe Jacobson, the longtime owner (original co-owner Mike Fritzel, who had owned a series of nightclubs with possible mob connections, retired in 1953), was a celebrity himself. Fritzel's closed in 1972, but its clout was measured by what a former police officer said in a 1972 grand jury: "It is taboo for policemen to write tickets for autos parked illegally in front of Fritzel's restaurant."[25]

Chicago's business district is not only a place for entertainment and business, it was (and remains) a retail center. Marshall Field's on State Street was one of earliest and largest department stores in the world. The wide range of products offered at Field's in the 1800s was like all the offerings at a current mall, placed in one store. Other department stores lined State Street, including Carson Pirie Scott, the Fair, Sears Roebuck, Montgomery Ward, and many others. In 1890, Marshall Field's opened a small tearoom, inspired (at least in legend) by Mrs. Hering, a salesclerk, who, when hearing two customers in the millenary department complaining about the lack of decent food available for women on State Street, offered them her chicken pot pie lunch. The customers said the next day they would bring their friends to try to the pie (and presumably buy some hats). Mrs. Hering set up a few tables the next day, which inspired the opening of the tearoom. Even though Marshall Field's is now Macy's, Mrs. Hering's chicken pot pie still highlights its menu.[26] Field's and other stores soon learned that offering food, at a variety of prices, made sense as both a way to keep customers, particularly women, in the store and as a revenue stream. Some stores, such as the Fair, used outside contractors, especially the informal Chicago chain Harding's. Marshall Field's created its own food lines. The seventh floor of its downtown location was filled with restaurants and specialty groceries, including its own baked goods and the famous Frango candies (most famously mints), made until 1999 at Marshall Field's own confectionary just above, on the thirteenth floor. Dining options at Marshall Field's included the Narcissus Room, which was most famous for its afternoon teas, a men's grill complete with a Tiffany Dome, and the spectacular Walnut Room, with dark-wood-paneled walls and a two-story atrium, famous as the site of the Marshall Field's Christmas tree and for Mrs. Hering's pot pie. In addition to the

Frango mints, Marshall Field's was also famous for its potato flour muffins, which James Drury called "an epicurean thrill of the highest order" in 1931.[27] Despite Marshall Field's rebranding as Macy's, a visit to the Walnut Room is still an annual holiday tradition for many Chicago families, who dress their children in their best holiday outfits and stand in long lines for the tables closest to the tree.

Steak and Game: Meat at the Meeting Place

Chicago's role as the city in the center of a country where thousands switched between trains, or today, planes, grew from its earlier history as a city on the edge of the frontier. In addition to the focus of the wealthy on sourcing luxuries from the East Coast, Chicagoans and visitors also focused on foods sourced from, or at least representing, the Western frontier. Chicago's role as a meatpacking center also came from its situation on the edge of the frontier, and it helped lead to the many Chicago steakhouses and the focus many travelers have on seeking out a fine steak when visiting the city. Beyond steak, Chicago restaurants maintained a particular focus on game that highlighted its status as a frontier city and a place to consume the bounty of the West, even as the city grew further and further from the frontier. For instance, the New Year's menu at the Briggs House Hotel in 1859 featured an impressive selection of game, including loin of bear, two types of wild duck, venison, pheasant, a choice of roast or broiled quail, wild turkey, wild goose, grouse, prairie chicken, rabbit, and broiled squirrel. The Thanksgiving 1858 menu from the competing Clifton House highlighted a similar selection of game, as does an 1860 Christmas menu from the Tremont House. Even an everyday menu at the Lake House in 1858 included mallard duck and rabbit, although an everyday Briggs House menu does not. These menus also featured a variety of beef, pork, and poultry dishes; a variety of organ meat, including liver, heart, brains, and sweetbreads; seafood, including both raw and cooked oysters; vegetables; cold relishes; and dessert.[28] The Drake Hotel in 1855 began a famous annual game dinner that by 1888 included more than sixty-eight different dishes and was served to more than five hundred people.[29]

The most famous game restaurant in Chicago history was Café Bohemia. Located near Union Station from 1936 until 1986, Café Bohemia was a favorite for tourists and locals, and it billed itself as "Chicago's game restaurant." While its most popular dish was crisp duck with wild rice, it also featured a huge variety of game, most of which bore little geographic relationship to Chicago. A 1971 menu includes moose, elk, Western buffalo (bison), bear, Western antelope (pronghorn), lion, jaguar, and Bengal tiger, along with a variety of fish, fowl, and steaks.[30] The Chicago focus on game and the connection between eating game, traveling to Chicago, and special and luxurious dinners continues to today, although even with the eat-local movement, the idea that the game is from Chicago's hinterlands is not generally followed. Frontier in Bucktown offers sausages including alpaca, wild boar, and venison, and game meats including rabbit, bison, elk, and alligator. Game is also being popularized today at restaurants such as the Gage that attempt to create a new prairie cuisine highlighting the bounty of the original Midwestern prairie landscape, although there is no indication that the elk and venison served is local.

The focus on game took a more accessible turn, at least to today's palates, with the development of the Chicago steakhouse. While Chicago was certainly not unique in catering to the American focus on eating large pieces of meat, the fact that one could do it in the shadow, or even looking out at, the Chicago stockyards made the experience particularly attractive, at least to some. A visit to a Chicago steakhouse is still a must for many Chicago conventioneers and tourists, as evidenced by the concentration of them in the tourist-oriented River North area. These steakhouses are part of a long legacy in the city. As early as 1837, Willard F. Myrick opened a small, fenced area for fattening livestock next to his boardinghouse, and many other such combination hotels/saloons/stockyards followed, specializing in serving the drovers who delivered the animals.[31] While it is not known specifically what was eaten at these establishments, it is very likely that a selection of the animals being butchered nearby appeared on the table. When the Chicago Union Stock Yards opened in 1865, its showpiece for travelers was the Hough House Hotel, a six-story hotel on South Halsted Street, bordered on the west by the stockyard and on the east, when it opened, by open prairie and fields. From the cupola, guests received a wide view of the nearby city as well as the stockyards. Later renamed the Transit House, it was famous for its food. An example of its tie to the stockyards occurred in 1878, when John B. Sherman, the superintendent of the stockyards, bought the winner of "The Fast Stock Show," the first livestock show in the city featuring thoroughbred, fattened animals, for $1,000 and served it for Christmas at the Transit House.[32] This incident highlights the importance of the hotel, as well as the Union Stock Yard itself, in popularizing the consumption of grain-fed fattened beef. In 1912, the Tudor-style Stock Yard Inn replaced the Transit House, and it remained open until the stockyards closed in 1971. It was next door to the International Amphitheatre, a large convention hall focus on the stockyards but also hosting a variety of other events including political conventions and boxing matches. The cowboy-themed Sirloin Room at the inn was a model Chicago steakhouse. Uncooked steaks were displayed on ice to patrons on a "steak throne" for choosing, and their customers "branded" their individual steak. It was "very dark, crowded, and smoky," Janet Davies, a local television host, remembered from her childhood, and "the wait staff made me feel like a little princess."[33] By 1954, the Stock Yard Inn added the separate Matador Room, still specializing in prime rib, steaks, and chops, but also serving yellow rice, arroz con pollo, and beef tenderloin in a wine sauce.[34]

While the Stock Yard Inn was early to the steakhouse game, many other classic steakhouses opened during the first half of the twentieth century. An early steakhouse, Abson's English Chop House, was founded in late 1800s in a small building (that still stands and is now a coffee shop) at the end of a downtown alley off Jackson east of State Street known as Pickwick Lane. It catered to "the sporting crowd" and politicians.[35] Johnny's and George Diamond were situated opposite each other on either side of the el tracks on the Wabash. Gene and Georgetti was founded in 1941 by Italian immigrant Gene Michelotti and partner Alfredo Federighi, in what is now the tourist-oriented neighborhood of River North but was then part of Chicago's red-light district. It was, and remains, a spot for business lunches, high-quality steaks, and cocktails. Other famous Chicago steakhouses include Morton's, which is now an international brand owned by Texas-based Landry's (which also owns Rainforest Cafe, among other brands), but it originated in Chicago. In the 1970s, Arnie Morton, the son of the owner of Morton's, "Hyde Park's best steakhouse" on the South Side, opened a number of restaurants including Morton's steakhouse, after leading the development of the Playboy Clubs. Gibson's, which competes with Gene and Georgetti's and Morton's for the most famous Chicago steakhouse, opened in 1989 on the site of Mister Kelly's, a famous Rush Street nightclub. Rush Street soon underwent a transformation from its red-light-zone status to a more gentrified eating and drinking zone, and Gibson's is in the center of this reborn Rush Street area.[36] While Americans today eat less beef than thirty years ago, Chicago steakhouses remain extremely popular, both for visitors and Chicagoans. Beyond those already mentioned, such restaurants as Chicago Chop House and Harry Caray's help make the River North and Rush Street areas a prime destination for consumers of large portions of beef.

DINING, ENTERTAINING, AND SHOPPING

Dinner Accompanies the Band . . . and the Puppets

Providing an entertaining experience is often an essential part of dining. Many Chicago restaurants, however, have been about entertaining the diner, either through performances or by creating closely themed dining experiences that take customers into alternate times and/or locations. The Sherman and similar hotels were only one group of Chicago venues that offered dinner and a show. During Prohibition in particular, entertainment was an essential profit source with the lack of money available from liquor or an essential front for gambling or liquor sales. At many of these, the food was an afterthought, but in others it became an essential part of the show. Perhaps the most famous of these was the Blackhawk, named after the famous Sac and Fox warrior. Opened in 1920 in the middle of downtown, across from Marshall Field's on the Wabash, in 1926 the Blackhawk added a live orchestra that hosted radio big band broadcasts over local stations WBBM and later, WGN. The Blackhawk became famous throughout the nation, and it was a key tourist stop as well as a site for local nights out. The site was often a showcase for bands recording for MCA. Bandleader Ben Pollack's band featured local musicians Benny Goodman and Glenn Miller. In 1935, the Blackhawk began a Monday night music quiz show that aired at midnight on WGN (later on CBS and NBC) called Kay Kyser's Kollege of Musical Knowledge, which became extremely popular in its own right. Food at the Blackhawk was not overly creative, but it was not an afterthought. A 1949 lunch menu featured a variety of classic sandwiches; fried oysters; a tuna-stuffed tomato; salads featuring shrimp, crab, lobster, or chicken; and a variety of desserts.[37] In 1953, the Blackhawk stopped being a musical venue and turned the entertainment toward the food. Today, the Black-hawk is remembered as much for the integration of entertainment into dining as for being a musical venue. In the 1950s the Blackhawk pioneered the spinning salad bowl complete with a well-rehearsed script, as well as a rolling prime rib cart. The Blackhawk also included the Indian Room, which catered to children. Disturbingly by today's standards, it featured Native Americans in traditional dress who roamed the room, providing photo opportunities with dining families similar to the character meals at Disney World. The original location of the Blackhawk closed in 1984, while additional locations remained open later, the one in suburban Wheeling finally closing in 2009.[38]

The Blackhawk was a core venue for music, in particular Chicago's white dance bands, but ballrooms sprang up all over Chicago, not just in the Loop, in the early and mid-twentieth century. Before the late 1920s, black musicians were kept out of white venues by the white musician's union local (black musicians had a separate local), but these barriers started to break down both due to demand and because of a case involving a black group that was accused of working under the union rate when it turned out that they were not but white musicians at the same venue frequently were. Louis Armstrong did play the Blackhawk briefly in 1927, but more often black artists such as Louis Armstrong and others were featured at venues along "The Stroll" between 26th and 39th streets along State Street, and, later, at clubs such as the Savoy Ballroom at 47th and South Parkway (now King Drive), and the neighboring Regal Theater.[39] Such clubs included "black and tans" that welcomed both blacks and whites, and clubs catering only to black audiences. These were music venues, but eateries lined the streets surrounding them as well. Unlike most of the clubs, these were often owned by blacks.[40]

Restaurants focusing on live entertainment also included those specializing in Chinese and Italian food, which were both growing quickly in popularity in the 1920s. Large Chinese venues with live entertainment included the Shangri-La and the Canton Tea Garden downtown and, in particular, the huge Golden Pumpkin on the West Side, opened in a located next to Garfield Park, which combined Chinese food with big band jazz music and a giant dance floor. It could accommodate one thousand diners.[41] More notorious was Colosimo's. Located in the South Loop, Colosimo's was originally opened in 1914 by gangster "Big Jim" Colosimo, a founder of the Chicago "outfit." Colosimo was gunned down in 1920 in the foyer of the restaurant, reportedly by associates of fellow gangster Johnny Torrio (perhaps by Al Capone, a mentee of Torrio).[42] Despite this (or maybe even because of this), Colosimo's thrived long afterward. Colosimo's featured a small band with four floor shows a night, the last beginning at 4 a.m. A 1939 menu and program features "N.T.G. and His Fairest of the Fair" revue, including Eve Arden in "the Temptation of Eve" and Yvette Dare in "Dances of Bali," as well as eighteen "Colosimo Cuties." The Italian food was also very important to the experience. The menu stated, "One million five hundred thousand yards of spaghetti always on hand." Food writer James Ward reports in 1931 there was "a seven-course table d'hote dinner for $1.50, featuring a whole baby lobster."[43] Colosimo's was a favorite stop for tourists at the 1933 World's Fair eager to experience a touch of Chicago's gang culture.

A completely different kind of entertainment was available at the Kungsholm restaurant.[44] Opening in 1937 in the Leader McCormick mansion on the Gold Coast, the Kungsholm was a Swedish smorgasbord, but it was more interesting for the performance after the meal, the "Chicago (or Kungsholm) Miniature Grand Opera," a puppet opera in a scale representation of the Royal Opera House in Stockholm. The Kungsholm performed such classics as *Tosca* and *Aida* with elaborate puppet performers and fifty-two puppet musicians in full dress, run by a staff of up to ten people.[45] Created by Chicagoan Ernest Wolff, the miniature opera had toured the country from the mid-1930s through World War II, when Wolff was drafted. Kungsholm then brought the company into its restaurant, where it stayed (despite fires and losing a suit to Wolff) until 1971. The Kungsholm introduced both opera and lingonberries to many Chicago children. After a while, the entertainment was prioritized over the food, with Fred Harvey buying the Kungsholm in 1957, and the Kungsholm closed in 1971.[46]

Conceptualizing Restaurant Experiences as Entertainment: Lettuce Entertain You Enterprises and Levy Restaurants

In 1971, Richard Melman, the son of a Skokie restaurant owner, and his partner, Jerry Orzoff, opened their first restaurant, R. J. Grunts, a relatively small restaurant with a relatively short menu, just west of Lincoln Park. The focus of R. J. Grunts was its salad bar and its irreverent atmosphere. Salad bars may not seem particularly exciting now, but in 1971, R. J.

Grunts had one of the first salad bars in the county at a sit-down restaurant, and certainly one of, if not the, largest salad bars in the country, with up to fifty items. The menu itself featured just ten additional entrees, most "from our charcoal hearth," including steak, Long Island duck, and liver steak, as well as a selection of sandwiches, including hamburgers and roast beef. Additional entrees included frog legs and Dungeness crab. The menu itself was highlighted by wry commentary and a cartoony look, including such statements as "'happy grunts'—the customary sounds of digestive happiness," and, on a 1972 menu, "Catering to the neurotic compensation of eating."[47] Patrons could (and still can) write on the tables. R. J. Grunts was not the only restaurant in town selling a hip atmosphere to a new class of young urbanites. Chances "R," a bar and burger-oriented restaurant on Wells in the heart of late 1960s and early 1970s hip Chicago, Old Town, encouraged patrons to throw peanut shells on the floor, which, like the salad bar, was adopted at many other restaurants afterward. But R. J. Grunts's fun and approachable theme, quality salad bar and food, and reasonable prices led it to stand out among these new hip and urban restaurants, and it sparked Chicago's most successful sit-down dining chain, Lettuce Entertain You.[48]

True to its name, Lettuce Entertain You has always focused on the dining experience as a whole, with carefully themed restaurants that, like R. J. Grunts, are approachable yet have a particular theme that allows the restaurant to stand out from other similar venues. At first, Lettuce Entertain You kept its irreverent attitude with restaurants such as Fritz That's It!, an Evanston restaurant that was somewhat similar to R. J. Grunts, and then Lawrence of Oregano, an Italian-themed eatery with a menu that featured a song called "Follow the Bouncing Meat Ball." Lettuce restaurants soon became more traditional, but they were still carefully themed. Bones was a barbecue restaurant in predominantly Jewish Lincolnwood that became perhaps the best place in the country to get ribs (either beef or pork) served with a variety of hard rolls reminiscent of a Manhattan deli.[49] Cafe Ba-Ba-Reeba! is a long-standing Spanish restaurant that helped bring tapas and small plates to Chicago in 1986. Lettuce Entertain You also branched out into fine dining restaurants, reopening the Pump Room in 1976, then opening Ambria with chef Gabriel Sotelino in 1980, an influential Chicago French restaurant that operated through the 1990s, which acted as a incubator for many other restaurants. Today, Lettuce Entertain You owns or is in partnership with fine dining establishments including Michelin-starred Everest and Tru. Lettuce Entertain You has also founded much less fancy restaurant concepts, including Corner Bakery, a quick, casual restaurant chain geared toward downtown lunches that is now spun off, M Burger, a gourmet burger stand, and foodlife, a food court providing a huge variety of food types inside Chicago's Water Tower Place. In addition, the company now runs restaurants in the Twin Cities, Las Vegas, Arizona, Washington, D.C., and Southern California.

Somewhat similar to Lettuce Entertain You, but eventually following a very different strategy, is Levy Restaurants. Levy started in the 1980s with D. B. Kaplan's, a hip, Jewish-style deli with a hugely long menu, in Water Tower Place, which was then the center of Chicago in-city shopping. D. B. Kaplan's was wildly successful, but the popularity of Water Tower Place eventually began to wane, and Levy opened a large French bistro just across from the Water Tower called Bistro 110, and, in 1984, Spiaggia, which, with its somewhat less fancy sibling, Café Spiaggia, at the very tony corner of Oak and Michigan. Spiaggia is Levy's flagship and Chicago's most highly reviewed, as well as most expensive, Italian restaurant.[50] A 2013 *Chicago* magazine article described one Spiaggia dish as "a wondrous truffle-tinged raw lamb loin sandwiched with deep-fried focaccia and slices of grappa-poached pears is a miracle that stays crunchy in spite of wet Castelmagno fonduta and light despite the truffle decadence."[51] Also available was a $95 pasta tasting. Spiaggia chef Tony Mantuano won a James Beard award for Best New Chef in 1986 and Best Chef Midwest in 2005. Spiaggia and Café Spiaggia are expensive, and *Chicago* argues, tourist oriented and somewhat overpriced, but the food is delicious, and Spiaggia anchors the reputation of Levy Restaurants as a whole, much of which now rotates around catering at stadiums and amusement parks, a focus that started with the skyboxes at Comiskey Park, the former home of the White Sox, in 1983.[52] In addition to its restaurants, Levy is now the foremost restaurant caterer for stadiums in the United States—all of this from a funky Jewish deli in a mall.

DINERS AND MIDDLE-CLASS DINING IN THE CITY

While Spiaggia and similar restaurants bring gourmets in from around the globe, Chicago is also filled with places for the middle class to enjoy a special dinner and the elites and powerful to lunch or dine on a more regular basis. There were also, and remain, many everyday eateries throughout the city that catered to those simply in need of a meal. After Mark Beaubien's Exchange Coffee House, which closed in 1836, there was the City Refectory, open in the mid-1840s, serving a large variety of unpretentious food, including, according to an advertisement, "Mush and Milk, Pickled Tripe, Pig's Feet, Tounges, &c." as well as "Buckwheat Cakes with Maple Molasses."[53] In the late 1800s, as Perry Duis states: "Chicago dining was undergoing another transformation in hundreds of eateries located outside the Loop."[54] Duis refers here to the growth of ethnic restaurants around the city, including Chinese, German, Italian, and many others. Interest was piqued by the 1893 World's Fair, and again by the 1933 World's Fair, which both heightened Chicagoans' and travelers' interest in cooking from around the world. Downtown and elsewhere, serving lunch to workers became particularly important for restaurants as, by the 1850s, many people could not go home from their work for lunch. While many working-class people took their lunch to work, lunchrooms also opened next to employers from the Union Stockyards to City Hall. At the low end, lunch counters thrived, having begun in 1858 at the Chicago Rock Island railroad station.[55] Later, the "free lunch," taverns where a patron would receive a small free lunch if they paid for a drink, developed. Beginning just after the fire in 1871, Chicagoan Joseph Chesterfield Mackin offered a free hot oyster with each drink, inventing the free lunch, an idea that spread quickly and only truly stopped with Prohibition, although it is carried on in such things as free peanuts, chips, and happy hours.[56] Soon, temperance forces, as well as business owners afraid of long worker lunchtimes, were up in arms about the proliferation of taverns offering free lunches, and churches and others offered cheap lunches themselves. While wealthy women could find sustenance in the women's dining rooms downtown, working-class women found little food available in the Loop, outside of the candy or drug store. In the 1890s, women's clubs formed around the Loop, serving lunch, one of which decided to get rid of the servers and serve themselves. Soon this was adopted by a commercial eatery, and then was quickly given the name *cafeteria*.[57]

At the same time, lunch chains proliferated in the Loop. Offering an alternative to street peddlers as well as more expensive restaurants, they focused on cleanliness, convenience, and simple preparations. One, H. H. Kohlsaat, claimed to have invented the lunch counter in the late 1800s.

Chicago-based Walgreen's helped build its brand by having a lunch counter with hot and cold items, rather than just the traditional soda fountain. A 1938 Walgreen's menu included a variety of traditional diner items such as a BLT, spaghetti, and a Hawaiian salad. Slightly fancier were the white-tiled Childs restaurants, part of a national chain based in New York, of which there were numerous locations around the Loop. Harold Spender, an English visitor to America in 1920, stated that Childs restaurants were "full of a profusion of cheap, great food, an immense boon to the workers of this great city."[58] John Drury stated that Childs in the theater district was popular with actors, "nighthawks, and *bon vivants*" eager for well-prepared, reasonably priced food.[59]

In and beyond the Loop, the menus of diners and "family restaurants" show Chicago and America's changing tastes. In 1934, the Cascades diner included, along with other things, a menu of "foreign dishes," from France, Italy, Germany, China, Spain, England, and Russia. While the nationality of the owner is unknown, the Russian dishes seem particularly authentic. A 1937 menu for the Old Hickory Inn, the "meeting place of the silver shore set," located in Lake View, offered a large variety of dinners from ravioli to beef tenderloin, a variety of sandwiches and meat dishes, choices of cheese, and, of course, a selection of oysters. Like the Old Hickory, Paul Feltman's Grill in 1942 featured a wide variety of foods, from peanut butter sandwiches to filet mignon.[60] Much later, in 1992 the Oak Tree, a Gold Coast diner now located in the upscale 900 N. Michigan shopping center, still featured a BLT, but also a veggie sandwich, a Belgian endive salad with tomatoes and watercress, as well as matzo ball and kreplach soups. Diners keep up with, and even sometimes help drive, neighborhood change.[61]

EATING THE WORLD FROM THE MIDWEST: ETHNIC RESTAURANTS IN CHICAGO

One of the many ways that the World's Columbian Exhibition of 1893 is a key event in Chicago's history is that it brought food, as well as people, from all over the world to the city, in a setting in which experiencing new cultures and foods was part of the Fair experience. The Fair included, as described by a French consul: "The Tunisian and Algerian café of Sifico . . . the restaurant of Mora, a Marseillais who fears nothing . . . a street in Cairo. China has its corner and its tea-house."[62] There was also a French restaurant run by the creator of the Paris Cafe Americain.[63] Outside the fairgrounds, the fare might have been somewhat less "themed," as Richard Melman would say, but the immigrant city was full of exotic foods for those who wanted to look for them.

By 1931, ethnic restaurants had become an important part of the Chicago restaurant scene. Guidebook author John Drury included a section titled "Around the World," in which restaurants specializing in Chinese, Arabian, Japanese, Greek, Mexican, Italian, Jewish, Roumanian [sic], Bohemian, Russian, Polish, German, Swedish, and Filipino restaurants were described. Elsewhere in the book, Hungarian, Spanish, French, and British eateries are detailed, and an entire chapter is devoted to Chicago's South Side Black Belt. The Russian restaurant in the "Russian Workers' Co-operative" featured American and Russian dishes, including beet borscht, kasha, and golupste (stuffed cabbage), to a clientele including "comrades reading *The Daily Worker.*" "Russian goluptse, Bohemian roast goose with sauerkraut, Greek lamb chops, Polish beef filet à la Nelson with mushrooms, Filipino adobo—foreign and exotic edibles of all kinds you may eat in this 'melting pot' of the middle west."[64] Eating out was an important part of Chicago ethnic life. Neighborhood eateries, such as saloons, were centers of community life, "a kind of communications center," as Perry Duis says about them.[65] In some cases, such as the Russian Workers' Co-Operative, this was quite explicit. A similar restaurant, the Idrott Swedish Co-Operative Café, served meatballs and salt herring and other Swedish specialties, but also had a library, a lecture hall, rooms for playing cards, as well as a public bakery.[66]

In addition to this importance in community life, "eating ethnic" also became part of the general culture of Chicagoans, who began, through such events as the 1893 Fair, to look beyond remaking Chicago cuisine in the vision of New York and Paris to the consumption of a variety of cuisines from around the world. The presence of a relatively wide variety of ethnic restaurants in Drury's 1931 book is evidence that Chicago food did go beyond American standards, and beyond the Italian and Chinese foods that were the first non-Western European cuisines adopted into Anglo-Saxon American culture. As Donna Gabaccia states, Americans by 1930 were "crossing the boundaries of taste."[67] By doing so, consumers also often crossed the physical boundaries between neighborhoods and cultures. In other cases, ethnic restaurants themselves moved across the borders, into Anglo-dominated and tourist areas such as the Loop and the Near North Side, or ethnic cuisines were adopted as themes by restaurateurs of different ethnicities.

Germania West: Berghoff, Red Star Inn, and Golden Ox

For Chicagoans of the late twentieth century, Berghoff was *the* classic Chicago restaurant. The Berghoff has served Chicagoans since 1898, except for a brief "closing" in 2006. It was a large space, in the middle of the Loop, with multiple dining halls and an abundance of wood and historical murals. The Berghoff began, however, as a saloon, set up to sell Berghoff beer, then made in Fort Wayne, Indiana, to thirsty Chicagoans. As an out-of-towner, founder Herman Berghoff could not get a wholesale liquor license to sell his beer to Chicago restaurants and hotels, so he opened his own "café" but was given a retail license, at which he could sell his beer (and whiskey) along with food. He had earlier set up a beer stand outside the 1893 World's Fair when he was unable to get a license to sell on the grounds. Originally located at Adams and State, in the midst of Chicago's shopping district, beer was served for "five cents a glass and ten cents a stein, and (included) a free sandwich."[68] The restaurant moved immediately after the Chicago Fire of 1871 to its current location a half-block west of State Street on Adams in what are now two connected buildings both dating from 1872. The original Berghoff Café was male only, and the bar at the Berghoff remained that way until 1969 when members of the National Organization for Women demanded service, although it was male dominated long after that.

Berghoff was originally a somewhat typical "free lunch" bar. It truly expanded its food operations, however, during Prohibition. In addition to brewing near beer and a line of soft drinks called Bergo, Herman Berghoff turned the bar into a full-service restaurant, adding wiener schintzel, sauerbraten, apple streudel, and other German specialties. In 1933, when Prohibition ended, Berghoff showed off his increased clout by getting Chicago retail liquor licenses numbers 1 and 2 for his bar and restaurant.[69] Over time, the restaurant grew, and was known not only for its food but also for its waiters, who were mainly careerists, often German or European, and were unionized. Their uniforms were starched, and they were clad in tuxedos and aprons.[70] For decades, they used a European system of pay, where they "bought" food from the restaurant using tokens and "resold" it to the customers at a somewhat higher price. When Berghoff closed in 2006, these waiters were laid off, as well as its unionized cooks, and when it reopened a year later, it was with a nonunionized staff. While this may or may not have been the reason for the closing (current owner and operator Carlyn Berghoff seemed somewhat confused about what was going to happen to the Berghoff during the time, trying a number of different business models), the episode and the announced closing and then reopening did greatly affect the restaurant. It now serves much of the same food as before, but with added less heavy and more modern specialties including a gluten-free menu, but it has lost some of the intimate connection it had for generations of Chicagoans.

The history of German restaurants in Chicago goes far beyond Berghoff. For many years, the most famous downtown German restaurant was Eitel's Old Heidelberg. Located on Randolph Street in Chicago's theater district or "Rialto," Old Heidelburg was a restaurant and nightclub, offering "entertainment, lunch, dinner, supper." A 1951 menu did offer sauerbraten, a German pancake, as well as smoked or fresh Theuringer sausage, but it also offered a variety of American dishes, including a side of pineapple cream cheese with jello.[71] Outside of the Loop, German restaurants were part of the large North Side German community that stretched from the Near North and Lincoln Park just north of downtown to Lincoln Square further north. Further to the west, in Norridge, the large German restaurant and market Edelweiss offers German American cooking and culture. Earlier eateries included Zum Deutschen Eck, which stood on Southport Avenue in Lakeview for almost fifty years, closing in 2000, and the Golden Ox, a beer hall on Clybourn Avenue near the Cabrini-Green housing project known for its dark German decor and its waitresses in provocative German-style costumes. However, the most long-lived German restaurant was the Red Star Inn. The Red Star Inn opened in 1899 as Zum Roten Stern and closed in 1970. It was always a restaurant, rather than beginning as a tavern like the Berghoff. In addition to a variety of American offerings, Red Star served a large variety of German dishes at relatively low prices, including the usual schnitzels and sausages, but also including such items as a Braised Fresh Calf's Tongue with Raisin and Almond Sauce and Grilled Fresh Pig's Feet, Deviled, Sauerkraut and Boiled Potato. The Red Star Inn, located in the middle of the North Side German district on Clark Street just south of North Avenue, across from the Germania Club, was known for its quality, as John

Drury wrote: "a menu equal to that of any first-class café in Berlin." The
Red Star Inn was one of Chicago's greatest losses from urban renewal. Its
original building, a replica of a tavern in Bavaria, was torn down as part
of the building of the Sandburg Village redevelopment in 1970. In a great
example of Chicago's mixing of cultures, the Red Star Inn was purchased
in 1968 by the Riggio family, who still run an Italian restaurant in suburban Niles. A new Red Star Inn location run by the Riggio family closed in
1982.[72]

Chinese, Thai, and Other Asian

On Randolph Street in the heart of Chicago's early twentieth-century
entertainment district was Hoe Sai Gai, an American Cantonese emporium with a huge marquee that dominated a very bright block and lavishly
decorated Art Deco interior. Owned by Chinese American restaurateur
Harry Eng, who also owned the Golden Pumpkin, among other restaurants, Hoe Sai Gai was an entertainment center, hosting big bands and
many tourists and locals out for a big night. From the 1930s until the
1960s when the block was torn down for the construction of the Daley
Center, Hoe Sai Gai was "large, impressively decorated, and first-class in
all respects."[73] A 1944 menu includes a wide variety of Chinese dishes,
starting with Americanized dishes such as chop suey and chow mein, but
the menu also includes a variety of Cantonese dishes as well as an
American menu. As discussed in chapter 3, Hoe Sai Gai was neither the
only large Chinese restaurant downtown, nor the first. Following the
1893 Century of Progress exhibition, Chinese food was one of many
global cuisines that appeared around the Loop and the city as a whole,
concentrating in Chicago's first Chinatown, around the corner of Clark
and Van Buren Streets (home to at least one Chinese restaurant currently,
although many were torn down in the 1960s with the building of a new
federal jail). In the early 1900s there were over one hundred Chinese
restaurants in the city, all or almost all owned by Chinese. In Chinatown
itself, centered around Cermak and Wentworth, the oldest restaurant is
Won Kow. Open since 1927, Won Kow has always catered both to the
local Chinese American community and tourists. John Drury in 1931
stated: "Observing discreetly the manner in which the Chinese diners eat
is an interesting diversion—and might be of help to you in using the
sticks."[74]

The idea of eating Asian food as a diversion and vacation was stretched almost to its limit with the Polynesian craze of the mid-twentieth century. The craze itself was nationwide, but Chicago was one of its centers. At the 1933 World's Fair, the Hawaii Room, "Paradise of the Fair," offered dinner "Ai Ahi Ahi" with a menu that in general bore more resemblance to a typical diner except for a banana and pineapple cocktail available as a relish. The star was the entertainment, including "Lee Makea and His Royal Hawaiians," two different orchestras, and a twice-nightly "Sacrifice to Pele" featuring "Princess Ahi."[75] In 1940 the Chicago branch of Don the Beachcomber, originally a Los Angeles chain, opened, serving Chinese food with some Hawaiian components and a variety of rum drinks and fresh pineapple.[76] The restaurant was copied by many, especially becoming popular during World War II and after the opening in 1949 of the musical stage play *South Pacific*. Most famous was the Chicago branch of Trader Vic's in the basement of the Palmer House, which opened in 1957 and lasted into the 2000s and had a menu that in 1976 was graced with drawings of seminaked "island girls" flaunting, dancing, and being beaten in front of white "Trader Vic." The Cantonese restaurant Shangri-La was one of many that tried to copy these trends into a more traditional Chinese menu, serving rum drinks along with Cantonese food between 1944 and 1968, calling itself "America's most romantic restaurant."[77]

During the late twentieth century, Chinatown expanded into Bridgeport to the south as well as in a new development to the north in what was an old railroad yard, including a new two-level outdoor mall, Chinatown Square. Opened in 1993, Chinatown Square is full of small businesses and many restaurants, including the original Lao Sze Chuan, often thought of as the best Chinese restaurant in Chicago and the core of the "Tony Gourmet Group," a small chain of Chinese restaurants around the Chicago area and beyond that specialize in fresh ingredients and authentic cooking.

While Chinese food long dominated the Asian food selections in the city, Chicago is today dotted with restaurants from around the continent, highlighted by the Indian and Pakistani cuisines present along Devon Avenue and elsewhere, as well as the concentration of Korean foods in Albany Park and Vietnamese food in the Argyle Street area and elsewhere. While Chicago is certainly not the center of Japanese cookery that many coastal U.S. cities are, there are plenty of storefront and upscale sushi restaurants, as well as Japanese-inspired upscale cuisine. While takeout chop suey shops still persist, the number of Americanized Chinese restaurants has declined, and, in many neighborhoods, Thai restaurants dominate the Asian food scene. While these vary greatly in quality, Chicago is home to what might be the best Thai restaurant in the country, Arun's, a high-end Thai restaurant in a storefront in Albany Park with no printed menu, which serves exquisitely prepared twelve-course prix fixe dinners and changed how Chicagoans and others envisioned the possibilities of Thai food. Open since 1985, Arun's was first somewhat ignored by Chicagoans, including *Chicago* magazine reviewers, who found it "pretty but overpriced."[78] Over time, Arun's became a go-to restaurant for chefs all over the country, who were wowed by the exquisite food and preparations. While people still wonder about the price, and there are complaints that the decor is now out of date, Arun's is now one of Chicago's oldest gourmet restaurants, still serving such gems as spring rolls "filled with tofu and cucumber, drizzled with a punchy sweet-sour tamarind sauce, and draped with Dungeness crabmeat."[79] Owned by chef Arun Sampanthavivat, who grew up on a Thai rubber plantation, Arun's is an American immigrant success story.

Italian Restaurants

American cuisine in general is the outcome of the influences of the people of the many cultures that are indigenous or moved to the United States, either forcibly or of their own volition. Like the Chinese, Italian immigrants first came to Chicago during the late 1800s, but the largest movement of Italians to the United States and Chicago in particular was in the first two decades of the twentieth century. Even before this, however, Italian cuisine had entered into the American mainstream, with macaroni in particular being offered at a wide range of restaurants, although its preparation likely was not particularly Italian in origin. Madame Galli was a long-standing Italian restaurant located near the Water Tower that opened around the World's Fair in 1893 and introduced spaghetti to a large number of non-Italian celebrities and everyday Chicagoans. Madame Galli had no menu—customers were simply asked what they wanted as a main dish from a variety of meats, which was then served with a series of courses, including appetizer, soup, spaghetti, salad, and dessert.[80] In 1910, immigrant Italians were concentrated on the city's near

West Side focused on Taylor Street, near Jane Addams's Hull House, as well as the near Northwest side, along Grand Avenue. Both of these areas house small "Little Italy" sections today, mainly distinguished by their restaurants rather than their residents. Over time, both groups moved west, many following Grand Avenue. Today, the core Italian neighborhood is the far Northwest side community of Montclare and its neighboring suburb Elmwood Park, although Italians have spread throughout the metropolitan area. Italian bakeries and restaurants dot the region, including such spots as Ferrara's in Little Italy, which has been open since 1908 and which led to the opening of the Ferrara Pan Candy Company in nearby Forest Park, maker of Lemonheads and Atomic Fireballs. Freddy's Pizza in Cicero is a crowded and delicious Italian deli and grocery with seemingly hundreds of prepared food options. Many of Chicago's more famous Italian restaurants that catered to the general population opened in the 1920s and 1930s, including Colosimo's, discussed before, as well as the Como Inn and Italian Village. The Como Inn, which closed in 2001, near the Northwest Side Grand Avenue Italian neighborhood, was a darkly lit place frequented by celebrities, politicians, and businessmen. It had fourteen rooms, and it was particularly popular for business meetings due somewhat to its variety of intimate rooms and also to its parking lot.[81] Italian Village, which is still open, is squeezed between office buildings on Monroe in the middle of the Loop. The "Village" is actually three restaurants on separate floors, the most famous of which is "The Village," which serves northern Italian food in a kitschy yet pleasant setting made to look like an Italian village. The food is traditional Chicago Italian, with "generous platters of richly sauced pasta," a style that defined Italian food for generations of Chicagoans and was part of a standard American image of a red-and-white-checkered-tablecloth Italian restaurant with hearty and reasonably priced food, but not at all gourmet.[82] This changed during the 1980s, as Italian restaurants countrywide focused more on fresh ingredients, more flavorful sauces, and more traditional Italian preparations sourced from throughout Italy. While traditional Italian restaurants remain throughout the Chicago region, many upscale restaurants now either focus on Italian food or incorporate it into their menus.

Bringing the OPA!: The Parthenon and Greek Restaurants in Chicago

Greek immigrants to the United States focused on food, opening restaurants and groceries wherever they went. They did not, however, always or even usually sell Greek food. The typical twentieth-century Greek diner carried a wide variety of food, but usually only a few, or even no, Greek items. Donna R. Gabbacia reports that in "Charlotte, North Carolina, Greek restaurateurs sold a lot of grits, but they eventually removed moussaka from the menu, since few customers were interested."[83] In the 1950s, 85 percent of restaurants in the Loop were owned by Greeks, an amazing number that occurred due to "chain migration," where relatives or acquaintances would bring over and support new immigrants, often bringing them into the family business.[84] In Chicago, Greeks owned, and still own, a large percentage of diners and related restaurants. In addition to Lou Mitchell's, another well-known Greek-owned restaurant is Miller's Pub, which opened in 1935 but was bought in 1950 by three Greek American brothers who supposedly did not have enough money to buy a new sign. Miller's is a restaurant rather than a diner, but like many Greek American restaurants, it has a very large menu, with only a few Greek specialties, including a variety of lamb dishes.[85]

The cuisine was different in Greektown, the "Delta," located just to the west and south of the Loop, along Halsted Street between Randolph and about Polk, extending to the west into what is now the University of Illinois at Chicago (UIC) as well as the Eisenhower Expressway and the Circle interchange. Greektown moved to the north following the building of UIC and the expressway. The intersection of Halsted, Harrison, and Blue Island, which would now be just south of the Eisenhower Expressway (Blue Island no longer extends to Halsted), was the center of the community. At Greektown's height, approximately thirty to forty thousand Greek Americans lived in the area. Today, however, Greektown is mainly a place to go eat. While there are many Greek restaurants up and down Halsted, both new and old, perhaps the most famous is the Parthenon, which opened in 1968 and introduced flaming saganaki, with its signature *OPA* to the world. While saganaki itself is a long-standing Greek food, the idea of flaming it made it into a show, following in the tradition of entertainment that had long characterized Chicago food.[86] The Parthenon also claims to have introduced gyros sandwiches to the world, although this claim is disputed by many, and a recent *New York Times* article claims that the Parkview Restaurant, a diner, served gyros in 1965.[87] Down the street is Greek Islands. Open since 1971, Greek Islands, with its second location, claims to be the most popular Greek restaurant in the United States, serving over a half a million customers annually.[88] While few Greeks still live in the area and much of the original Greektown has been demolished, what is left is thriving. The National Hellenic Museum is now open in the heart of the neighborhood, and the area is now part of the thriving West Loop restaurant scene.

Eating Out in the African American Community

Along the "Stroll," the famous entertainment district of the early twentieth-century Chicago African American community, black-owned restaurants featuring "down-home" Southern cooking dotted the streets, long before the term *soul food* was invented. They varied from neighborhood spots that were also community meeting places to places for special nights (or days) out. Drury in 1931 pointed to Chapman's, at 37th and Indiana, "a table lunch room" serving a variety of southern dishes, as well as the somewhat more upscale Duck Inn, that served roast duck and frog legs along with a mix of southern dishes. "Most of her patrons belong to the professional and commercial classes on the south side," states Drury. The Poro Tea Room at 44th and South Parkway (now King Drive) was "where the wealthier class of colored people dine and lunch." Unlike the Poro, most restaurants in the African American community were not upscale but were instead neighborhood spots offering hominess both in terms of food offerings and community. Such places were especially important in Bronzeville, which during segregation was extremely overcrowded, with many people living in apartments that lacked proper kitchens. Into this void came restaurants such as Gladys' Luncheonette on South Indiana, which was open from 1946 until 2001. Gladys' purveyed both quality food and a sense of community, although it also hosted many African American celebrities. A *Chicago Tribune* article from 1987 raved: "The corn muffins are moist, the biscuits more tender than flaky. The coffee's great. For Brenda's style of service of 'finish your carrots or no dessert' as well as her smile, we'd return."[89] In the 1940s and 1950s, Gladys' was a frequent stop for Negro League baseball players, who could not patronize white establishments. In owner Gladys Holcomb's

2003 obituary, African American activist, historian, and teacher Timuel Black stated, "I guess you could say my favorite is the fried chicken. . . . But the biggest thing about Gladys' is that it is a very friendly place, laid out physically so that you couldn't help but pass by people and say hello."[90]

Perhaps the most well-known soul food restaurant was Army and Lou's, which opened at the end of World War II in 1945 and closed in 2010. Army and Lou's was originally located at 39th and Indiana, in the heart of the "Black Metropolis," and it was an upscale restaurant serving home-style southern food. As one of its partners recalled upon its closing: "It was a fine dining establishment, and the first place that a lot of middle-class African-American families back then were taking their children where there were linen tablecloths and napkins, and there was live music."[91] Among others, Army and Lou's catered to many of the jazz musicians who played in the neighborhood. In the 1970s, Army and Lou's

Figure 6.3. Dining at the Perfect Eat Shop, a black-owned restaurant on 47th Street near South Parkway (now King Drive), 1942. Library of Congress, Prints & Photographs Division, FSA/OWI Collection, LC-USW3-001469-D.

moved to the middle-class African American community of Chatham, on 75th Street just east of King Drive. It was hurt somewhat by a return of upscale African Americans to the Bronzeville neighborhood in the past twenty years, but discussion of reopening Army and Lou's is still occasionally in the air. Along with Army and Lou's, the first decades of the twenty-first century were characterized by the closing of a number of well-known soul food establishments, including Edna's on the West Side and Izola's and Soul Queen on the South Side. Edna's reopened with the same staff, as Ruby's, but is now closed. There has definitely been a recent decline in "classic" soul food restaurants in Chicago. At the same time, new black-owned restaurants are opening, particularly in Bronzeville, where such places as Norman's Bistro on 43rd Street are attempting to anchor a neighborhood culinary revival. Along 75th Street, near where Army and Lou's was located, a string of restaurants and a bakery have now opened, including the Original Soul Vegetarian, mentioned in chapter 3, a vegan soul food restaurant operated by the Black Hebrew community which is a haven for vegetarians missing barbecue, and 5 Loaves, a breakfast and lunch soul food storefront.

Mexican and Latin American Restaurants

The Chicago area, as discussed earlier, has one of the largest Hispanic populations in the United States; about two million of the metropolitan area's 9.2 million inhabitants were of Hispanic origin in 2011, the fifth most of any U.S. urban area, and the largest population by far outside of border states, Miami, and New York.[92] Unlike some other cities in the middle of the county, Chicago's Hispanic population is also long standing. The Mexican government opened a consulate in 1884, and Mexican immigrants, mainly male, flowed into the city during the early parts of the twentieth century, escaping work with Midwestern railroads and sugar beet farms and finding work in steel mills and meatpacking plants. They mainly concentrated near the factories in the South Side communities of South Chicago, Back of the Yards, and on the West Side.[93] Many Mexicans returned to Mexico during the Depression, but during and after World War II, changes in policies and a booming economy enticed many immigrants. In the 1950s, Puerto Ricans began to arrive in large numbers as well, building to a population in the metropolitan area of above one hundred thousand.[94] Today, Chicago has thriving Mexican and Puerto

Rican communities that now extend well beyond the city borders, as well as groups of people representing many other Hispanic nationalities.

What may be most surprising, even for Chicagoans, is that Mexican restaurants, and not just neighborhood ones, have existed in Chicago since the early twentieth century. As mentioned in chapter 3, John Drury described in 1931 El Puerto de Vera Cruz, across from Hull House on Halsted. Specialties there sound much like a high-quality storefront Mexican restaurant today, serving rice soup in a meat broth, gallina con molle poblado (chicken in a mole sauce), "the familiar frijoles refritos, and tortillas," which Drury describes as "like very thin pancakes made of corn flour."[95] Ten years later, a 1941 menu from the Costa Rican, located in the Loop on South Clark Street near the old Chinatown, reads very much like an Americanized Mexican restaurant today, although the food is called "Spanish" or Costa Rican. Offerings include a mix of American specialties such as a BLT, turkey with cranberry sauce, and chicken fried steak. "Spanish" specialties include cheese enchiladas, chicken tacos, chicken tamales with Yucateca sauce, rice, and fried banana, a chicken tostada, black bean soup, arroz con camerones, and, oddly, Boston clam chowder.[96]

Today, Chicago Mexican food is split into small neighborhood restaurants and a new class of gourmet Mexican restaurants, epitomized by Rick Bayless's Frontera Grill and Topolobampo. Chicago's neighborhood Mexican restaurants and taquerias are excellent, and many consider Chicago's Mexican cuisine more "authentic" than the more derivative cuisines common in Texas and California. Places such as Nuevo Leon on 26th Street are core centers for Chicago's Mexican community for important and everyday dinners and events. To the many in the outside world, Chicago became particularly known for gourmet Mexican food with the opening of Frontera Grill in 1987. Rick Bayless, now a star chef known around the world for popularizing both high-end Mexican cuisine and "authentic" Mexican cuisine through his restaurants, products, and TV show, *Mexico, One Plate at a Time*, Bayless was an anthropological linguistics student at the University of Michigan who wrote, with his wife, Deann, *Authentic Mexican: Regional Cooking from the Heart of Mexico*. The same year, Bayless opened Frontera Grill in the River North neighborhood. Two years later, he opened the fine dining restaurant Topolobampo next door.

Bayless is a controversial figure in the Mexican American cooking world. A white Oklahoma native and a member of a family that owned barbecue restaurants, Bayless's claims about "finding" authentic Mexican food and introducing it to the United States is considered insulting to some in the Mexican American community that owned, cooked, and served food in restaurants and at home long before 1987. Bayless's first cookbook, which slightly predated his first restaurant, was called *Authentic Mexican*, and it was the result of an exhaustive search (originally begun while he was working toward a doctorate in anthropology) for authentic Mexican recipes, not touched by "Americanization," throughout Mexico.[97] The food he found and then translated to a Chicago audience, now showcased at Frontera Grill and Topolobampo, is exquisite. A May 2014 Topolobampo dish on a $120 prix fixe menu is "creamy tamal colado, tepary beans, garlic chive oil, homemade lardo, allium in various guises." Frontera Grill menus are less fancy and less pricy, and feature a large selection of "street food, for sharing," including tamales, quesadillas, sopes, and taquitos, all with fresh ingredients. Among other awards for Bayless and his restaurants, Frontera Grill was named outstanding restaurant by the James Beard Foundation in 2007. Bayless is also a local leader of the farm-to-table movement, and he works with local farms in and outside of the city to provide ingredients for his restaurants. Finally, he is a master marketer and is open to a whole variety of restaurant formats. You can buy Frontera products at grocery stores, and Frontera restaurants are also located at O'Hare Airport and at Northwestern University and the University of Pennsylvania. Overall, Bayless is likely Chicago's leading celebrity chef, although it is a closely contested race.

Polish, Jewish, and Eastern European Specialties

An often-quoted statement about Chicago is that more Poles live in the Chicago area than anywhere outside of Warsaw. While New York may have recently overtaken Chicago as a current Polish immigrant destination, and with Chicago's recent economic downturn many Poles have moved back to Poland, there is no denying that Poles have a very strong presence in the Chicago area, with almost a million people of Polish descent in the metropolitan area. Their migration is also long standing, from the 1800s to the World War II era to the late twentieth century. Chicago's strong Eastern European influences go far beyond the Poles,

however. The Chicago area has the largest community of people of Lithuanian extraction outside of Lithuania, as well as one of the largest number
of Ukrainian, Czech, Serbian, Bosnian, and Croatian residents of any
other city in the United States. In addition, Chicago's Jewish population
also arises largely from Eastern Europe, although early Jewish immigrants were mainly from Germany.

While Eastern Europeans did not have the kind of influence some
other ethnicities did in terms of the creation of large, tourist-oriented
restaurants in the Loop, they did open hundreds of storefront restaurants
catering mainly to people within their communities as well as some larger
places that reached out beyond. Along Milwaukee Avenue on the northwest side as well as along Archer Avenue on the southwest side there are
concentrations of Polish restaurants, either buffet style or sit-down, serving pierogis, kielbasa, stuffed cabbage, and other specialties. Standouts
include Andy's Deli, which has been open since 1918. Andy's is a deli
and wholesaler on North Milwaukee Avenue that produces a variety of
authentic Polish sausages and other products that they sell at the deli and
to stores all over the United States. Kasia's Polish Deli, located in the
now hip Ukrainian Village area, specializes in pierogis, made famous
partially by their appearance at Taste of Chicago. They are sold not only
at the deli but also as a frozen item in supermarkets throughout the region. Red Apple is probably the quintessential Polish smorgasbord, with
a large selection of Polish specialties.[98]

The Czech/Bohemian population traditionally was centered in the Pilsen community, then moved west to what is now Little Village and then
Cicero. While Cicero has become more Hispanic, it is still the site of the
large eating emporium Klas, which has served Czech food since 1922,
and neighboring Berwyn is the home of rival Czech Plaza. A perhaps
more famous place, Old Prague Restaurant, burned down in the 1990s.
The Lithuanian community was originally sited in Bridgeport, alongside
an older Polish community. Over time, they moved further southwest, to
the area around Marquette Park, and today, even further southwest into
West Lawn and the southwest suburbs. Lithuanian restaurants are not
plentiful, but can be found; for instance, Grand Duke's in Summit, which
serves Lithuanian food in a castle atmosphere, or the less pretentious
Mabenka in Burbank. While many Ukrainians have moved on from gentrifying Ukrainian Village, the area remains the center of cultural Ukrai-

nian life, with many churches and civic organizations, as well as a small number of delis and restaurants.

While the Jewish community has a very different history of immigration than the other predominantly Eastern European groups, the history of their movements within the city is somewhat similar, starting in immigrant "ghettos," largely on the West Side, and then moving out toward the suburbs, in this case the far North Side and northern and southern suburbs as they assimilated. The Jewish influence on Chicago food has been large, but specifically Jewish restaurants have generally not been as prevalent as in New York. Drury did list a few Jewish and kosher spots in 1931, including Barron's, on Roosevelt near Halsted, which in particular catered in Jewish artists and writers. Longtime deli Ashkenaz lasted a hundred years, moving from the immigrant North Lawndale community, north to Rogers Park, and then back into the Gold Coast. It closed in 2012 and was replaced by a low-priced place specializing in lobster rolls. Today, while there is a growth of interest in kosher gourmet food, and a few longtime Jewish restaurants such as the Bagel remain, the most well-known Jewish-style deli in Chicago is Manny's, a favorite of politicians, UIC professors, and lunchers in general, which serves enormous deli sandwiches with a potato pancake side, kreplach and matzo ball soup, and many other specialties in a cafeteria setting. Manny's is located in what used to be the Maxwell Street district (although not on Maxwell Street) in an area of the South Loop that today is somewhat off the beaten path. In general, it is a place to go to get a little feel of a bygone era in Chicago as well as to perhaps overhear some political wheeling and dealing and eat a pretty good pastrami sandwich.

UPSCALE DINING IN THE CITY

While Chicago today is dotted with restaurants and smaller eateries that provide sustenance to get people through the day (often in delicious ways), the city has also long been home to destination restaurants, either where eating is part of an overall entertainment package or where the meal and dining experience is a destination. While many of these were and are upscale, middle-class Chicago families also had traditions of attending a show at the Blackhawk, Christmas dinner at the Walnut Room, or seeing the Kungsholm miniature opera theater as well. On the

South Side, early twentieth-century African Americans patronized restaurants and clubs along the State Street "Stroll" between 26th and 39th streets. While gastronomes were present in Chicago almost from the beginning, a new kind of gourmet began to appear during the post–World War II period in the city, and it truly grew in the 1960s and 1970s, inspired by the renaissance of American cooking sparked by Julia Child and the response to postwar industrial food, of which Chicago was a center of production. These new gourmets patronized Louis Szathmary's the Bakery and restaurants such as Le Français and Gordon, followed in the late 1980s by the opening of Charlie Trotter's and Frontera Grill, and in the 2000s by such restaurants as Alinea, L2O, and Girl and the Goat. While many high-end Chicago restaurants originally attempted to be fairly true to traditional French cooking, Chicago has a particular style, including artisan meat-focused restaurants such as Publican, high-end ethnic cuisines such as Frontera Grill and the Thai restaurant Arun's, and the "molecular gastronomy" (a somewhat controversial term) of Alinea and Moto. In 2011, Michelin decided that Chicago was enough of a food destination that it became only the third American city, after New York and San Francisco, worthy of the creation of a city Red Restaurant Guide. While the city has always been a place to get a good steak, Chicago has become a global eating destination.

Henrici and Late Nineteenth-Century Chicago Upscale Restaurants

In early Chicago, fine eating, for the most part, was done at hotels such as the Lake House, Sherman Hotel, and others. Besides this, in general, Chicago's eateries were taverns and less fancy "eating houses." In the years following the Civil War, and particularly following the Chicago Fire of 1871 into the late 1890s, a number of downtown restaurants opened that focused on special-occasion dinners for middle-class Chicagoans, as well as catering to lunches for politicians and businessmen. The most famous and longest lasting of these was Henrici's. Henrici's was opened by Austrian immigrant Philip Henrici in 1868 as a pastry shop. Following its destruction in the Chicago fire and several moves (the last in 1894), Henrici's expanded to be a restaurant patterned on elegant Viennese dining halls. It seated five hundred people, often serving nearly two thousand people in a day, with an adjoining smoking room (for men) that seated one hundred. The open eating space had walls painted light green and purple and white tablecloths. "All the work was executed . . . by firms who are artists in their respective lines," ran a promotional brochure. Henrici's promoted itself as a restaurant with "no orchestral din."[99] Henrici's survived at 71 W. Randolph Street, in the midst of Chicago's original theater and entertainment district, until it was torn down in 1962 to make way for the Daley Civic Center. The Austrian food remained relatively stable through the years, although it was certainly an Americanized version of a Viennese menu. In 1894, the menu was long and featured a variety of croquettes, meats and sausages, oysters, "game in season," and canned fruits. Much of the focus was on the extensive cake and pastry menu, including such things as baumkuchen. A 1930 menu included a variety of steaks and meats, fish, roasts, and entrees including Austrian specialties such as Hungarian beef goulash and chicken croquettes. Fish focused on lake fish such as whitefish, lake trout, and sturgeon (although the source of these was not given except for the whitefish), as well as finnan haddle. Sauces and even salad dressings were à la carte. Soon before its closing, in 1958, the menu had become shorter, and had been updated with three dishes "finished to perfection on a plank of hickory," but it still included a variety of meats, whitefish, and lake trout. Desserts were highlighted by Henrici's Austrian pastries, including a flaming pancake. Henrici's special Austrian pancake was also available (now also for dinner) rolled either with apples or blueberries. Henrici's menu and marketing were enwrapped in its status as a historic restaurant. It emphasized its long life and the changes to Chicago on the menu. The 1930 menu included a patriotic description of the evolution of the United States since 1868, with a hint of manifest destiny: "It is interesting to recall that the first railroad to the Pacific Coast had not then been completed. Buffaloes roamed the western plains in herds of thousands. General Custer and his devoted band had yet several years to live before showing, as Americans have shown before and since, that the last drop of their hearts' blood was not too precious to be shed willingly in the service of their country."[100]

While Henrici's was unusual in its longevity and its menu may not seem overall original to today's tastes, Chicago, in its phoenix-like renewal following the fire and its late nineteenth- and early twentieth-century dreams to be the largest and greatest city in the world that peaked in the 1893 Columbian Exhibition, did have a class of gourmets that were particularly interested in bringing European cuisine to the city from the

Figure 6.4. Crowds lining up the last day Henrici's was open, August 15, 1962. Chicago History Museum, ICHi-69985.

mid-nineteenth century. This is not surprising in a city that was also building Parisian-style boulevards and bringing art from Europe to help found the Art Institute. As early as 1867, the Brunswick Restaurant featured such items as frenchified dishes Filet de Beuf, au Champignons and Omelet Souffleve. The Brunswick was not an establishment just for the wealthy, judging by the fact that officers of the Chicago police were complementary (at least on October 22, the day of the menu).[101] Founded in 1877, the Meat Cooks', Pastry Cooks and Confectioners' Cosmopolitan Society held an annual banquet designed to convince Chicagoans that fine cooking could thrive in their city.[102] French restaurants, however, had difficulty surviving, at least until the World's Fair of 1893, and an undated menu from the 1890s for Malatesta and Cella's French Restaurant has no French language writing at all and is very similar to other menus of the time, with the somewhat unusual inclusion of brains.[103] Like

Henrici's Viennese dining hall, most of the large downtown restaurants focused on atmosphere as much as food. They were usually bright, with elaborate ornamentation. The largest, such as H. M. Kinsley's or Rector's Oyster House, had multiple dining rooms, including ladies and gentleman's lunch rooms, a bar, as well as a large main dining room. Many of these late nineteenth-century restaurants focused on seafood, often trying to create a New England experience. One of the most well known of these was the North American Oyster House, located at State and Monroe, featuring a huge dining room that seated one thousand people.[104] The DeJonghe Hotel and Restaurant was famous for its shrimp sautéed in herbs and butter, still called Shrimp DeJonghe.[105] The most famous, however, was Rector's, which went on to spawn a second and also well-known location in New York. A Rector's Oyster House menu from 1893 featured a wide variety of oysters and other seafood, in addition to the usual steaks, chops, an impressive game menu, and a selection of omelets. Rector's also ran the Café Marine at the 1893 World's Fair.[106] Even nonseafood restaurants almost always had seafood (particularly oysters) available. Burcky and Milan Ladies' and Gents' Restaurant, founded just after the fire downtown on Clark Street, in 1884 featured a menu of raw, fried, and stewed oysters, in addition to the standard roasted and boiled meats, vegetables, and a large selection of pies. The oyster focus lasted into the twentieth century. In addition to the usual chops, breakfast items, and Viennese fare, a 1917 Henrici's menu featured an oyster menu, "in season all months containing the letter 'R.'"[107]

TWENTIETH-CENTURY REVIVAL OF FINE DINING

Despite the fact that Chicago had a class of gourmands almost from its beginning and despite the 1931 promotion by John Drury of Chicago as a city where a world of cuisines could be visited within a ten-mile distance from the Loop, mid-twentieth-century Chicago was still considered a second-class city in terms of the availability of haute cuisine. While places such as the Kungsholm and the Blackhawk thrived, visitors and locals in 1950s and 1960s Chicago were more focused on eating steaks at places such as Stock Yards Inn, or game at the Café Bohemia, than on spending large sums for a exquisitely prepared and presented meal. New York critic Jorie Graham summed the situation up thusly in 1968: "Don't look for haute cuisine. The natives won't . . . pay the price it requires, and neither the expense-account crowd nor . . . conventioneers . . . want it."[108] This does not mean, however, that Chicagoans would not spend a lot of money on food, or try to push the limits a bit. There were a variety of restaurants with French names on the Near North Side that provided them with the opportunity to do so. The most famous of these was the Chez Paul, located after 1964 in the old McCormick mansion on Rush Street. Chez Paul is famous for its appearance in the Blues Brothers movie (actually a replica built in California), where Jake Blues (John Belushi) convinced ex-band member and now maitre'd Mr. Fabulous to come back to the band by stating that he and partner Elwood would return to the restaurant every day unless he agreed. Chez Paul was known as the fanciest restaurant in town, but by 1985, as a *Chicago Tribune* reviewer put it, "Chez Paul's unremittingly heavy, rich food is decidedly out of fashion." The article was titled "Chez Paul Still Fancy (But Predictable) After All These Years."[109] A 1988 menu included "Le New York Sirloin."[110] Chez Paul closed in 1995. A similar restaurant was Jacques, which was famous for being a place for "ladies who lunch" but served very Americanized French cuisine.

The revival of the Chicago fine dining scene is often traced to the 1963 opening of the Bakery, located in the Lincoln Park neighborhood, which at the time was still a middle-class Chicago community rather than the upscale place full of high-end restaurants it is today. The Bakery stood out compared to other Chicago restaurants of the time in that it was chef owned, by the charismatic Louis Szathmary, a Hungarian immigrant. There was no printed menu, only one seating a day, mismatched plates, a bring-your-own-alcohol policy, and a comfortable and creative atmosphere. It was almost the absolute opposite of imposing places such as Chez Paul. Szathmary was essential in American cookery in promoting the place of the executive chef as a professional, as well as training numerous future chefs at his restaurant. He also was a celebrity, with his own cookbooks, television shows, and even a frozen food line. Customers could receive recipes by request for the food they ate, which included Hungarian-inspired specialties such as a pork and sausage goulash with sauerkraut, and chicken paprikash with spaetzles, as well as beef Wellington.[111] For today's diners, these dishes might seem heavy, but Szathmary's genius was to create continental European dishes that appealed to Americans yet stayed true to their European roots.

The Bakery closed in 1989. By the late 1970s and early 1980s, however, French haute cuisine had truly begun to enter Chicago life, at least for those who had enough money. Many of these chefs focused on staying true to the French cooking traditions, rather than creating fusion cuisines with Asian and other influences, which became more popular later. At the same time, "Contemporary American" cuisine, that often used French sensibilities but focused on high-quality takes on American cuisine, developed. An early practitioner was Gordon Sinclair, owner of Gordon, which became a nursery for Chicago chefs. In the French restaurants, the particular kind of French cuisine served often varied from the traditional. Café Provençal in Evanston featured southern French cooking. Everest, run by Alsatian chef Jean Joho, which is still a top restaurant in the city, focused on Alsatian cooking. Many other restaurants began to create "fusion" cuisines between cultures, particularly Asian, such as Yoshi's, a longtime Japanese fusion restaurant in Lake View.

Perhaps the pinnacle of Chicago dining in the last quarter of the twentieth century was Le Français, run by chef Jean Banchet in suburban Wheeling. Le Français was the first Chicago restaurant to vie for the title of "best restaurant in America." Jean Banchet opened Le Français in northwest suburban Wheeling, not at all a foodie destination, in 1973. In 1975, the restaurant burned down and had to be rebuilt. In 1980, Le Français was named the best restaurant in America by *Bon Appetit*. In many ways, Le Français was a traditional French restaurant with impeccable standards but used fresh and new ingredients. Banchet spent his teenage years apprenticing at restaurants around France, and then by twenty-one was chef at a London casino. Banchet then was enticed to the Midwest by future steakhouse owner Arnie Morton to run the kitchen in the Playboy Club in Lake Geneva, Wisconsin, in 1968. At Le Français, "(h)e created a temple of gastronomy," said Everest chef Jean Joho in Banchet's 2013 obituary. "He did something different from what everybody did at the time. Most of the food (elsewhere) was really conservative; Jean brought a new way to run restaurants and prepare foods. He used ingredients and preparations people hadn't seen before. He gave you a lot for the eyes before you ate."[112] Ingredients came from all over the world. His sous chef remembered, "The pheasant came from Scotland. The duck was from Canada."[113] Banchet left Le Français in 1989, returning briefly ten years later. By that time, Le Français had made Chicago a global restaurant destination, a designation that continues today.

In 1987, two years before Jean Banchet started his extended break from Le Français, a young University of Wisconsin graduate from a wealthy North Shore family named Charlie Trotter opened his self-named restaurant in rapidly gentrifying Lincoln Park. Between 1982 and 1987, Trotter worked at forty restaurants building his skills. His restaurant continued Le Français's traditions of focusing on a large variety of fresh ingredients from around the world, but Charlie Trotter's was not specifically French; instead, the food was creative American food, using influences from around the world, eschewing traditional heavy sauces. Trotter also began a specific focus on local sourcing. He would create tasting menus in the morning and serve them in the evening and claimed that he never repeated a dish. Trotter also led the revival of foie gras in Chicago and American restaurants, but famously later he took it off his menu after visiting some foie gras farms, inspiring public arguments with other Chicago chefs and Chicago's short-lived ban on its sale.[114] Trotter was a very demanding chef who could be very difficult, but he also started a foundation that, among other things, brought Chicago students in for meals and a discussion of excellence in the culinary environment. In 2012, he closed Charlie Trotter's, which was still very popular and was one of the first Michelin two-star restaurants in the city, saying he needed to focus on other parts of his life. One year later, a couple of weeks before the death of Jean Banchet, Trotter unexpectedly died. In his obituary, the *New York Times* wrote that Trotter had made Chicago "a must."[115]

Today's Cuisine: Paul Kahan, Stephanie Izard, Alinea, Molecular Gastronomy, and Next

Today, Chicago is a culinary destination. While Charlie Trotter's is now gone, other fine dining restaurants have opened, many operated by chefs trained at restaurants such as Charlie Trotter's and Le Français or other top-notch Chicago restaurants such as Grace, Moto, Trio, and Everest. Chef Paul Kahan revolutionized restaurant design with the opening of the modernist Blackbird and its neighbor Avec, which brought the idea of serving patrons at long, shared tables to the United States. Kahan also opened Publican, one of a number of restaurants in the Fulton/Randolph Market area, tying in to the area's previous, and still existing, role as a wholesale food market. Many of these restaurants, including Publican and Stephanie Izard's Girl and the Goat, focus particularly both on local ingredients and locally raised and restaurant-prepared artisan sausages and other meat products, tying both to the heritage of the neighborhood and of Chicago as a whole.

While the presentation of meals at fine dining (and many other) restaurants has always been a performance, and top chefs carefully work on presentations, Grant Achatz's Alinea, which opened in 2005, took the idea of presentation and "taking food apart" and then combined them into delicious and extraordinary dishes. Alinea became an international sensation, often labeled one of the world's best restaurants, and sometimes (such as in a 2014 *Elite Traveler* list) the best. Even more than its predecessors such as Charlie Trotter's, Alinea is a destination restaurant with a distinctive style that is almost unique not only in Chicago but also in the world. It is specifically modern, leading the American version of what is called "molecular gastronomy" or "deconstructivist" cooking, which experiments and takes apart foodstuffs in attempts to find their essences, then, using techniques such as presenting foods on pillows of scented air, or encapsulating flavors into orbs, creates unexpected and new combinations. Chef Achatz was trained at the French Laundry in Napa Valley, as well as Trio in Evanston, where he created a half-inch square of paper on a pin called "pizza" that tasted just like pepperoni pizza.[116] At Alinea, Achatz was able to create an entire dining experience that allows diners to experience such dishes as part of a prix fixe suite, of course. There is no typical Alinea dish, but PB&J is a fine example of a simple idea, peanut butter and jelly, torn apart by Achatz. It includes a peeled grape, still attached to its stem, coated with custom-made peanut butter and wrapped in an oval piece of a baguette, then toasted and served on a "vase" of wire-thin metal that holds it vertically. Another dish is wild turbot, served with shellfish, water chestnuts, fennel, and tarragon, in a sunchoke custard, surrounded by a larger bowl in which whole hyacinth flowers and leaves are placed, then boiling water poured over, to provide a vapor of hyacinth to the eater while they consume the turbot, shellfish, and custard.[117]

Alinea is also known for its somewhat controversial reservation system, in which tickets for a particular seating are paid for in advance for the prix fixe dinners (which in 2014 ran from about $215 to $275, depending on the day and time). Tickets are transferable, much in the way that tickets to concerts or sports events are, but not refundable. Achatz took this idea further in 2011 with Next, which serves a particular cuisine for four months, takes a month off, then switches to a new cuisine, so that gourmands sign up for a series, in a similar way to a theater series. These series tickets for a particular year sell out within minutes, although additional tables are available through the restaurant's Facebook site on a daily basis. Next's cuisines dive into particular times or places. The initial menu returned to Paris 1906, and later menus focused on Thailand, childhood, the famed Spanish restaurant El Bulli, the hunt, vegan, Chicago steak, and others. While reviews of particular Next meals vary, the idea of an ever-changing subscription restaurant takes the link between fine dining and theater to new heights.

Chicago today is truly a center of culinary innovation, bringing together eclectic cuisines, science, and presentation to create restaurants that often approach theater. At the same time, Chicago life is often centered around neighborhood restaurants, many of them serving food representing ethnicities from around the globe. In addition, Chicago is also characterized by hot dog stands, rib tip joints, and other purveyors of street food as well as local recipes that change much more slowly than those at gourmet restaurants but may be just as delicious, if not quite as unique, as those presented at Alinea and other upscale spots. We now turn our attention to Chicago's street food and the places that prepare and serve it.

7

CHICAGO STREET FOOD, RECIPES, AND COOKBOOKS

While gourmets may travel to Chicago to eat at Alinea or Girl and the Goat, if you ask most Americans what typical Chicago food is, you are likely to be told hot dogs and deep-dish pizza. Chicago's street food is the source of many of its local specialties, although today it is usually served not on the street but in hot dog stands and other small, casual restaurants. This is where classic Chicago foods such as Chicago hot dogs, Italian beef, and deep-dish pizza, as well as ethnic specialties and more common American fare, were served and developed. Such restaurants helped influence the development of national fast food chains such as McDonald's and local favorites such as Harold's Chicken and Portillo's.

Not all classic Chicago foods were birthed in informal settings, however. Shrimp DeJonghe, for instance, has its roots in a late nineteenth- and early twentieth-century downtown hotel. Chicken Vesuvio is a rustic-style dish and its origins are a mystery, but it is served at Chicago restaurants from corner pizza takeouts to homestyle Italian restaurants throughout Chicago to somewhat fancier spots such as Harry Caray's. However, since many of Chicago's classic dishes are street foods, a discussion of street foods leads to a collection of Chicago recipes. Chicago's foods, both fancy and plain, are also detailed in cookbooks, both historic and more recent, that show the general population how to cook Chicago specialties, the food of a particular popular restaurant, or less Chicago-specific goals such as healthy eating or eating on a budget. In the final chapter of this food biography of Chicago, we turn our attention to what

Chicagoans eat and ate on the streets, recipes for these foods and other classic foods that typify Chicago, and finally relate a short history of Chicago cookbooks.

CHICAGO FAST FOOD: THE HOME OF MCDONALD'S . . . AND HAROLD'S CHICKEN

When Michelin chose Chicago as its third Red Dining Guide city in the United States, they were probably not thinking of Chicago's role in the history of fast food. However, a food biography of Chicago would be incomplete without a discussion of McDonald's, the world's largest hamburger chain, as well as some of Chicago's local chains. While McDonald's began in Southern California, McDonald's Corporation has been headquartered just outside of Chicago in suburban Oakbrook since the late 1950s. The original concept for the restaurant was put into place by the McDonald brothers in San Bernardino in 1948. The brothers had transformed their restaurant from being a successful, but ordinary, drive-in to an efficient, modern, fast food restaurant, with a limited menu, no carhops or other waiters, an assembly-line kitchen, no dishes, and most importantly, low prices. Famously, Ray Kroc, from the Chicago suburb Oak Park, was selling milkshake makers and came to San Bernardino to find out why McDonald's needed eight of them. Impressed with their "Speedee" system, Kroc convinced the McDonald brothers to let him handle nationwide franchising (the McDonald brothers already were franchising their system in Southern California and Arizona).[1] Kroc opened a McDonald's in suburban Des Plaines in 1955, began the McDonald's Corporation, and then in 1960 purchased the naming rights from the McDonald brothers. By this time, there were over a hundred McDonald's nationwide. By 1965, there were over seven hundred locations.[2]

It is difficult to say how "Chicago" McDonald's actually is. It was not a local chain that grew up from the Chicago area, and the goal was never to focus just on the Chicago area. The original idea was from Southern California, and the concept of a cheap and fast dinner served in disposable packaging, originally without even an indoor place to sit, does seem to fit the wide-open suburbanization that 1950s Southern California epitomizes. But Kroc, who was a salesman and marketing genius much more than a restaurant man, had the idea, or the good fortune, to note that

Figure 7.1. The crew at an early Chicago-area McDonald's, c. 1960s. Note the limited menu. Chicago History Museum, ICHi-36310.

suburbs were growing everywhere, particularly middle-class ones such as Des Plaines (San Bernardino itself was a small, working-class city rather than a suburb), and that these new suburbs were empty slates in their foodways and that quick "street food" would be needed, just like in more densely populated urban communities. McDonald's also quickly went into the more densely populated areas themselves, to either replace or compete with existing fast food operations, although hot dog stands and other independent "street food" restaurants have persisted in most parts of the city. Despite the weakness of original specific Chicago ties, Chicago, as the "most American city," was a great place to base the world's largest hamburger chain. Franchisees could easily access Chicago to attend "Hamburger University," and the company had access to a wide range of agricultural and commodity companies that supplied the raw ingredients for the food. Chicago is also still the center of the pricing of U.S. agricultural goods. McDonald's, in a sense, continued what the Chicago meatpackers had begun in the late nineteenth century by taking the assembly line all the way to the consumer.

Besides McDonald's, Chicago also is the home of many regional fast food chains, including Portillo's and Buona Beef, as well as local sandwich chain Mr. Submarine. The most interesting, however, may be Harold's Chicken Shack. Harold's is a mainstay of Chicago's African American neighborhoods. Opened first in 1950 by Harold Pierce, one of many black southerners who migrated to Chicago during the World War II era, Harold's is a predominately local chain that specializes in made-to-order fried chicken. A half chicken is served over fries and a slice of white bread, with a side of cole slaw. Harold's chicken and fries are cooked in a half beef tallow/half vegetable oil mix, somewhat similar to the original practice at McDonald's. The chicken is served with Louisiana-style hot sauce. Pierce's first restaurant was in the Kenwood neighborhood. It was the result of a partnership with Gene Rosen, who had a nearby poultry shop. Harold's began franchising almost immediately, before either McDonald's or Kentucky Fried Chicken, but he maintained a relatively loose franchising structure so Harold's locations varied quite a bit in quality, and many opened and closed over the years. As Pierce's daughter recalled in 2006 about early franchisees: "He put $50 in their registers, told them to get their chickens from Rosen, and expected them to pay him a 42-cent royalty per bird."[3] Harold's now charges franchisees 6 percent of their overall revenue. Harold's outlets vary so much that *Chicago Reader* columnist and food critic Mike Sula even developed a rating system purely for Harold's locations. Despite this, Harold's has been successful. By 2006, there were sixty-two Harold's locations, including ones in Minneapolis, Milwaukee, and Atlanta.[4]

STREET FOOD

Chicago has an amazing variety of low-cost food served along its wayfares. However, the nature of these establishments differs from many cities. In most cities, street food is actually sold on the street. New York is famous for its pretzel, hot dog, and knish stands. Portland, Oregon, is well known for its food trucks. While Chicago does have a growing number of food carts as well as food trucks, since the early 1900s regulations on selling food on the street have been stricter than in most cities in the United States. As discussed earlier, early twentieth-century food carts came under fire from public health agencies along with peddlers and were regulated for health concerns, such as the lack of running water, and they were also attacked verbally and in print by grocers and restaurants whose concerns were economic but were often expressed in terms of anti-immigrant fears. In African American communities, new migrants were criticized by more established blacks for their habits of eating on front stoops, as well as their "sidewalk barbecue pits" and "chicken shacks."[5] While both of these still exist, sidewalk carts peddling hot or prepared food are rare in Chicago's African American communities. While Chicago does have a mix of food carts, some of which are officially licensed and some of which have operated for years outside of the law, Chicago street food is generally sold at permanent locations, in particular, hot dog stands. Foods involving preparation, including cooking and slicing, has generally been forbidden at food carts and food trucks, although currently "mobile food dispensers" are allowed to do "final preparation" on foods with an upgraded license, available since 2012. At a higher level, food preparation is now allowed, but the license is difficult to obtain. The new license for food trucks requires $1,000 for every two-year license and a $350,000 liability insurance policy, even if the mobile food vendor is only serving items that arrived packaged and is not doing preparation. Additional requirements are in place for mobile food vehicles (food trucks) and those that have heating elements, including fire inspections (which add additional fees) as well as a large number of public health requirements. Finally, for food trucks, they cannot park near "competitive businesses"—restaurants—meaning that a large area of Chicago's central area is out of bounds. There are also some areas that are particularly set aside for food trucks, but they cannot stay there longer than two hours.[6]

It was not always this way. At lunch in particular, in the 1800s thousands of peddlers were located outside of factories and schools and near boarding houses. Waffles were sold for breakfast, and hand-edible food such as sausages, sandwiches, watermelon, and popcorn balls were available for lunch.[7] At night, "night wagons" would sell sweets and more food. In the 1890s, a tamale craze struck the country, beginning in Chicago and San Francisco, and "tamaleros" became a noted part of Chicago's street scene. The tamales were not yet the current Chicago variety, sold in plastic wrappers. These were more traditional cornhusk tamales. A tamalero (who looks more Eastern European than Latino, although his ethnicity is not known) was pictured in Krausz's *Street Types of Chicago* selling a "California" chicken tamale in a plain, white outfit indicating purity, in the same way that many restaurants did at the time.[8] Despite efforts such as this to maintain a clean visage, street vendors came under attack by restaurants and public health officials worried about disease control, and by 1902 their numbers were in great decline.[9]

While tamales may still be found occasionally at Chicago street vendors, on the streets today the most distinctive Chicago item is the elote. Also found throughout Mexico and in cities such as Los Angeles, an elote is corn on the cob, grilled or boiled, eaten either on the cob or in a bowl and topped with a large variety of toppings, often all together. Toppings include squeeze margarine, mayonnaise, cotija cheese (somewhat like Parmesan), salt, chili powder, lime juice, and Mexican-style sour cream. With all the toppings, an elote tastes somewhat like a delicious chili-and-lime-laced corn pudding. It is also a somewhat perfect food to represent Chicago's Mexican community, many of whom are from the central Mexican states of Michoacán, Guerrero, and Jalisco, where elotes is a popular street food. In addition, many of the first wave of Mexicans, who arrived in Chicago in the early 1900s, had come from working on Midwestern farms to Chicago to work in the steel mills or meatpacking plants. The connection between corn, the staple of Mexico, and the position of Chicago in the middle of the Corn Belt, where many Mexicans worked then and still, make the presence of elote as a popular Chicago street food not at all surprising.

Other than elotes, many other foods are sold by street vendors in Chicago's Mexican community, including tamales, chicharrons (fried pork rinds), paletas (popsicles), fruit, and many other treats. The city has also promoted the sale of whole and cut-up produce at food carts as a response to food access issues through a privately funded program called "Neighbor Carts." Neighbor Carts places sturdy, well-maintained produce carts at sites across the city, many along "el" lines. The number of carts, however, at the moment remains somewhat limited compared to New York and elsewhere. In addition, trucks selling watermelon (often delivered straight from farms in the South) and sometimes other fruits frequent the city, especially the South Side, during the summer.

The Chicago Hot Dog

The most famous Chicago street foods are sold not from street vendors but from the many permanent hot dog stands that dot the city and suburbs. There are estimated by food historian Bruce Kraig to be between 2,500 and 3,000 stands in Chicago and the suburbs.[10] Perhaps the most iconic Chicago food, a Chicago hot dog is usually (but not always) an all-beef hot dog with natural casing and a variety of spices made by Vienna Beef or Red Hot Chicago, nestled in a poppy seed bun, which is usually made by local bakery S. Rosen, and topped with mustard, chopped onion, bright green pickle relish, a kosher pickle wedge, sliced fresh tomatoes, Louisiana "sport" peppers, and usually celery salt. The bright green food coloring likely developed as a way to hide color changes that occurred over time to cold-packed pickle relish. They are generally "bathed," heated to a little under boiling, although grilling is also acceptable. Chicago hot dogs were an outgrowth of a move to place German sausages on a bun that was occurring in many parts of the country in the late nineteenth century. The term *hot dog* can be traced to an earlier term *dachshund sausages*, which was used in college humor magazines of the 1890s.[11]

Kraig notes that the hot dog itself was one of the first portion-controlled, mass-produced foods, but by topping it so generously, hot dog vendors such as Fluky's, the vendor who probably constructed the first Chicago hot dog, were able to make the relatively small hot dog into a meal. In 1932 in the Maxwell Street area, Fluky's mixed the ingredients on the "garden" that tops a Chicago hot dog, and they sold it with fries for a nickel. This "Depression sandwich" caught on during the 1930s, and hot dog stands multiplied throughout the region. Abe "Fluky" Drexler probably did not just come up with this on his own. The all-beef, kosher hot dog (Vienna Beef hot dogs are not currently kosher but were at the time) certainly came from a Jewish tradition, but as Kraig writes, "If Jews made hot dogs, Greeks, Macedonians, Bulgarians, Italians, and Mexicans dressed them."[12] The relish and sport peppers are Italian in origin (although Mississippi peppers are often used), and mustard, pickles, and celery salt are German or Eastern European Jewish. While Drexler and the founders of Vienna Beef were Jewish, hot dog stand owners came from a wide range of ethnicities.

The hot dog stands themselves are often neighborhood landmarks. Most are brightly colored, most often yellow and red, the colors of Vienna Beef, and often (but certainly not always) have "cute" names such as "The Wiener's Circle." Many are famous in the city, and even throughout the nation. The Wiener's Circle is famous for its late hours and the sarcastic, sometimes intentionally rude behavior, or just funny banter, of the late-night employees. Superdawg on the far Northwest Side is a drive-in known for its distinct take on the hot dog itself, serving it in a box with a side of fries and a picked tomato, as well as the statues of "Morrie" and "Florrie," a hot dog couple, on its roof.[13] Gene and Jude's, in west suburban River Grove, does not even serve the full Chicago hot dog—just mustard, onions, relish, and peppers—but the dogs are topped with delicious, freshly made fries in a concoction that brings lines of customers to its offbeat location.[14] Portillo's has evolved from a hot dog stand in west suburban Villa Park to a small national chain of fast casual restaurants with an Americana theme.

For the last twenty years, perhaps the most famous stand was Hot Doug's, which closed in 2014. Hot Doug's was a gourmet stand, a "sausage emporium," making its own sausages but combining the basics of a hot dog stand including hot dogs, Polish sausages, and Italian sausages, with a whole variety of gourmet meats, most famously a "fois gras and sauternes duck sausage with truffle aioli, foie gras mousse and fleur de

Figure 7.2.   Legendary Chicago drive-in Superdawg. Richard L. Block, 2014.

sel." For this sausage, Hot Doug's defied the 2006 ordinance, which is now repealed, outlawing the sale of fois gras within the city, calling the sausage the "Joe Moore" after the alderman who advocated for the ban.[15] Hot Doug's also served sausages made out of rattlesnake, gyros, and escargot, among others, and always had a game option. Despite this focus on unusual ingredients, Hot Doug's was neither expensive nor unapproachable. A hot dog was just $2.50, and the decor mirrored those of other Chicago hot dog stands. Kid-friendly items such as bagel dogs and corn dogs were available. Even the foie gras sausage was $11, a lot for a sausage on a bun but not a lot for any dish featuring foie gras. When owner Doug Sohn announced that Hot Doug's would close, long lines developed, at their highest over six hours, with people sleeping out overnight to be the earliest into the restaurant. While this may seem like a long time to wait for a hot dog, the line itself became a community and even an attraction. Many people in line came to experience the line as much as the sausages, and it was covered by news agencies around the country, many focusing on the oddity of people waiting so long for such a seemingly common food. In a way, though, the popularity of Hot Doug's seems like a particularly Chicago phenomenon, built out of love for one of its signature foods combined with the new foodie interest in gourmet sausages and cured meats that builds off its history as the "Hog Butcher to the World."

Recipe: Chicago Hot Dog

Makes one hot dog .
1 beef, natural-casing hot dog, such as Vienna or Red Hot Chicago. Other non-Chicago brands will work but may not produce the Chicago experience "exactly" due to differences in the spice mix used. The Chicago brands themselves are often smaller when sold retail.
1 poppy seed bun, preferably S. Rosen "Mary Sue" brand
Yellow mustard, such as French's or Plochman's
Green pickle relish. Any sweet pickle relish will do in a pinch, but for the authentic experience, use the bright green relish marketed by Vienna or the Puckered Pickle
2 tomato wedges or 3 tomato slices (wedges are more common)

Chopped onions, generally raw but may also be grilled. Amount can vary based on personal preference.
1 kosher large dill pickle spear, should be crisp
2 sport peppers, such as the Del'Appe or Vienna brand
Dash of celery salt (optional)
Directions
Boil or grill hot dog. Steam bun over boiling water, using a steamer rack or a cooling rack placed over a pot. Place hot dog in bun. Squirt a line or squiggle of mustard on top of hot dog. Spoon pickle relish over hot dog. Place chopped or grilled onions on top of hot dog. If using tomato wedges, fit wedges along the side of hot dog. Place pickle spear on opposite side of hot dog. Fit sport peppers alongside of hot dog as well. If using tomato slices, place on top of dog. Sprinkle with dash of celery salt. Eat immediately.

Polish Sausage, Italian Beef, and Tamales

Chicago hot dog stands do not just sell hot dogs. They also usually sell a variety of other Chicago street foods, most notably Polish sausage, Italian beef, and, often, gyros. Even Gene and Jude's, the most basic of hot dogs stands, sells one other item, Chicago-style precooked tamales, steamed in a plastic bag. Such favorites as Polish sausage and Italian beef in particular have their own origin stories and famous stands. Like with hot dogs, which stand is best is a question for great and frequent debate. The Polish sausage sandwich was developed not by a Pole, but by Jim Stefanovic, the Macedonian owner of Jim's Original on Maxwell Street at Halsted. Opening in 1939, in 1941 Stefanovic worked with a Polish sausage company to create a sausage that was much larger than the Chicago hot dog.[16] It was cooked using the deep fryer and paired with caramelized onions and mustard, and soon it also was available in an all-beef form, and could also be served with the standard Chicago hot dog toppings. Jim's also featured a pork chop sandwich, on a bun and with the bone. It was, and still is, juicy and greasy and almost impossible to eat without getting your hands messy. In the 1950s, a relative of Jim's opened a very similar stand across the street, Express Grill. Jim's Original and Express Grill had to relocate in 1994 when the University of Illinois-Chicago, along with the city, redeveloped the neighborhood and moved Maxwell Street Market itself. Maxwell Street Polish sausages, or Polishes, are now available at hot dog stands all over the city and are made "Maxwell Street" style, or boiled and served like a hot dog.[17]

While hot dogs and pizza are perhaps more renowned outside of the city, if you ask a Chicagoan what the quintessential Chicago food is, they will often say the Italian beef sandwich. Most often just called a "beef" by Chicagoans, an Italian beef is similar to a French dip sandwich, which was invented in Los Angeles in the early twentieth century. It consists of thin slices of lean roast beef on a fresh, soft Italian roll, usually from Turano Bakery in Berwyn. However, the Italian beef differs in many ways from the French dip. First of all, the meat is seasoned with Italian herbs and spices, then slowly roasted over (or slightly in) a pan, which collects the "juice" or drippings. In addition, it is thinly sliced with a commercial meat slicer (not a knife), and then placed back in the juice, which has been reseasoned and combined with broth or water to reheat. It is then served either "dry" or "wet," where the sandwich is dipped back into the juice.[18] Another option is a "combo," with Italian beef and an Italian sausage on one sandwich. A final option is to forgo the meat altogether and instead eat bread dipped in the fragrant and delicious gravy. Either way, the sandwich may be topped with sweet or hot peppers, the sweet being sautéed bell peppers and the hot being giardiniera, which has become a Chicago specialty in its own right, available as a topping for pizza or even as a sandwich topping at Chicago-area Subway sandwich restaurants. Giardiniera is a preserved vegetable relish, soaked in brine and then packed in oil. The specific vegetables may vary but generally include hot peppers (thus "the hot"), olives, carrots, and cauliflower. Giardiniera was one of many pickled vegetable and fruit products introduced to Chicago by new immigrant populations, in this case Italians. Giardiniera is basically a pickled side dish, which can involve a whole range of vegetables. Today, it generally refers to a mix of peppers, olives, carrots, celery, and spices but may also include cauliflower and many other vegetables. The vegetables are pickled in vinegar, then packed in oil. Companies such as E. Formella and Sons and V. Formusa have been making and/or importing giardiniera into the country for over a hundred years.[19]

The origin of the Italian beef is somewhat shrouded in mystery. It may have been an attempt for an Italian meatpacker, Scala (who currently is the leading supplier of Italian beef to restaurants), to capture a new market. It may have also been a response of Italian restaurant owners to the cheaper and more abundant beef that was available in Chicago compared to Italy. In any case, the Italian beef is, like the Chicago hot dog, a Depression-era sandwich designed to feed a person or family at a relatively low price. Like with hot dogs, Chicagoans debate the best beef sandwiches. Al's Beef, located in Little Italy on the Near West Side, is now a small chain, and it claims to have originated Italian beefs. Other well-known locations include Johnnie's Beef in Elmwood Park, and Buona Beef, which has now expanded to become a fast casual small chain, much in the way that Portillo's expanded from its original hot dog stand. This recipe combines recipes from a variety of sources, including Mike Baruch's *Street Food Chicago*.

Recipe: Italian Beef

Makes about 10 sandwiches with about a 1/4 pound of meat on each
    About 3 pounds beef, either a small sirloin tip roast, top sirloin butt roast, rump roast, or rib roast
    Vegetable oil
    Meat Rub Seasonings
    1/2 teaspoon garlic powder
    1/2 teaspoon salt
    1/2 teaspoon dried basil
    1/2 teaspoon dried oregano
    1/2 teaspoon crushed red pepper
    "Juice"
    2 teaspoons olive oil
    3 cups beef stock
    2 garlic cloves, chopped
    1 small onion, chopped
    1/2 teaspoon dried basil
    1/2 teaspoon dried oregano
    1/4 teaspoon salt
    1/2 teaspoon paprika
    1/4 teaspoon garlic powder
    1 teaspoon Worcestershire sauce

Directions

Preheat oven to 350°. Heat the vegetable oil in a large skillet. When it is hot, brown the roast on all sides. Remove roast and let cool slightly, until it can be touched. Combine "meat rub" seasonings and rub over roast. Put meat into a shallow pan. Roast for 35 to 40 minutes or when the internal temperature reaches 130 to 135 degrees. Rely on the thermometer rather than the timing, and add more liquid if the pan starts to dry out. When done, take out and chill the beef. Reserve the drippings. Slice the beef once chilled (at least overnight), very thin (preferably with an electric meat slicer).

Separately, heat and add olive oil. Add the onion and garlic and saute until lightly brown. Add dry seasonings and saute for an additional minute. Add the drippings, beef stock, and Worcestershire sauce. Bring the juice to a simmer, reduce the heat, and simmer for at least an hour. Cool. Skim any grease off the top. Strain juice, using a wooden spoon to push juice through the onions and garlic.

Finally, reheat the juice until warm (about 140°), place sliced beef in the juice for about a minute to rewarm (DO NOT leave beef in the juice for longer than about 10 minutes—it will fall apart). Serve on opened (but not split) Turano or other high-gluten rolls. Place a little juice inside the roll before putting in the beef. After placing the beef in the sandwich, dip the sandwich into "juice" if desired. Top with a choice of hot giardiniera or sauteed sweet bell peppers.

The Chicago tamale is probably the most surprising of the foods served at Chicago hot dog stands. It has an interesting history, as does its presence at hot dog stands. On the South Side, a few hot dog stands serve a sandwich called a mother-in-law, which consists of a Chicago tamale, topped with chili, onions, peppers, and sometimes cheese and tomatoes, served on a hot dog bun. The inclusion of tamales may seem odd at Chicago hot dog stands, but their presence is an outcome of history, marketing, and ease of cooking. The widespread presence of tamales in America began with the 1890s tamale fad, which, by 1904, was in great decline over most of the country, although the legacy of the popular "tamale men" were still seen and heard in popular song and film for decades thereafter. The tamales they sold were a particular American type, larger than the Mexican variety, stuffed into a cornhusk and tied on both ends. Vendors would carry three-layered pails with fire in the bottom layer, boiling water in the middle, and placing tamales on top. Vendors for San Francisco's Putnam Company sold tamales at sites across the nation, most importantly for our story at the 1893 Chicago World's Fair. Putnam incorporated a separate tamale company, called California Chicken Tamale, in Illinois, which was then undercut in price by a new company founded by one of his workers, creating an ongoing battle between the companies. After the Fair, these companies disappeared for a while, but a new class of tamale men appeared in 1896.[20] They were often African American, and they were probably selling a new type of tamale, a "Delta" or "Mississippi" tamale, made with corn meal rather than masa and stuffed with beef or pork. It was also spicy. As the Great African American Migration occurred from the South, and particularly the Mississippi Delta, began, people brought the Delta tamale north. African American tamale men were a presence in Chicago in the 1920s, as seen through a 1921 *Tribune* article about their efforts to unionize.[21] However, the Chicago tamale, mass-produced, shaped like a perfect cylinder, made of corn meal and stuffed with ground beef, and wrapped in paper, was introduced later, probably in 1937, with the creation of the Tom Tom tamale, still manufactured on the Southwest Side near Midway Airport. Supreme Tamale further industrialized the Chicago tamale, mass-producing them and today providing most of the tamales to vendors around Chicago. Tom Tom is owned by a Greek American and Supreme by an Armenian American.[22] These tamales may seem to be a pale imitation of the original dish, but they meet the needs of hot dog vendors well in that they are easy to prepare by steaming, in the same way a hot dog is generally made, and are a small food that can be eaten with the hands or a fork.

Gyros, Rib Tips, Tacos, and Jibaritos

Beyond hot dogs, Italian beef, and Polish sausage, gyros are also available at many hot dog stands. Gyros are now eaten nationwide, but mass-produced gyros were invented, and still mainly originate, in Chicago. Gyros are ground and pressed lamb slowly cooked on a vertical broiler. The meat is on a "cone," in which lamb and beef trimming have been ground; mixed with bread crumbs, water, and seasonings; pushed through a machine checking for bones; and then formed into a cone shape. The "cone" itself was patented by Chicago vendor Kronos (although the question of who was first is debated by competitor Central Gyros), and the spit was also locally invented.[23] A gyro itself is made of browned slices of the ground and pressed lamb, served on a warm pita, with tomatoes, onions, and tzatziki sauce.[24] What specifically Chicago added to make gyros so popular was the mass-production method, developed in the mid-1970s, of making the "cones," as well as the vertical broiler. Once again, Chicago was a pioneer in food mass production, leading in this case to a new fast food.

As mentioned in chapter 3, as a city that once hosted the largest stockyards in the world, it is not surprising that Chicago has its own particular brand of barbecue, most often ribs, with a thick and somewhat sweet sauce, marinated for about three days in the sauce before cooking. The cooking itself traditionally goes on in an "aquarium style" box of steel and aluminum with a see-through glass cooking chamber. The base of the box is where the fire is built. The meat is placed in the main chamber, which can be adjusted for size. Although whole slabs are usually on the menu (particularly baby back), in the African American community, especially on the South Side, the true street food is Chicago-style rib tips. Rib tips are a by-product, or waste, from a slab of spare ribs, the "trimmed flap pieces from the sternum and cartilage of the . . . rack."[25] Rib tips are chewy, cartilaginous, and fatty, but when slow-cooked and covered with sauce, they are also often delicious. Traditionally, they are often served with a hot link—a course ground, spicy sausage. Barbecue places in Chicago split into two groups: South and West side stands that have generally been open for many years, and newer spots, mainly on the North and Northwest sides that often offer a variety of barbecue styles, including Chicago. In 1931, John Drury focused on King George's, "the big thrill in the Black Belt," which, according to him, was "a dingy one-story nondescript shack . . . but it houses the first and only authentic barbecue pit in town."[26] Today, great debates occur around which is the best, but the most well-known South Side locations include Lem's, Leon's, and Barbara Ann's, all of which specialize in rib tips, hot links, whole slabs, and chicken, served with white bread and a choice of sides. These are all true takeout places, often with no sit-down tables at all. Barbara Ann's also is a motel, which is connected to the rib joint. On the North Side, barbecue tends to be a sit-down affair. The most well-known newer barbecue outlet is Smoque on the Northwest Side, which, like many newer barbecue places in the city, does not strictly serve Chicago style, but instead offers a variety of barbecue styles from around the country.

While hot dog stands and Italian beef may be the most famous, and people travel for miles for the best rib tips, the streets of Chicago are also filled with taquerias, submarine sandwich shops, and Chinese and Thai takeout. The taquerias usually focus on the central Mexican cuisine that is the core heritage region of Chicago's Mexican community. A taco is two warm corn tortillas (Chicago is the leading producer of corn tortillas in the United States), topped with chopped steak (asada), ground beef, barbecued beef, chicken, pork, or tongue, or at many taquerias, a whole variety of different meat options including brains and other organ meats, then topped with onions and cilantro or, if requested, tomatoes, lettuce, and sour cream. Taquerias usually also offer tortas, served on large rolls, with meat, lettuce, tomato, and sour cream, and burritos. In Chicago, tacos on corn tortillas are usually the king. Chicago sub shops often highlight Italian cold cut sandwiches, best when served with lettuce, tomato, seasonings, and giardiniera. In general, Chicago street food is typified both by the variety of options and regional influences that appear along its streets and by the presence of very specific Chicago specialties such as Chicago hot dogs and Italian beef. Chicago is again both a patchwork of ethnicities and regional influences and a creative city in its own right, whose long-time residents swear by not only their particular ways of serving these specialties but also particular places that serve them the best.

Chicago's newest widespread street food creation is the jibarito—a Puerto Rican sandwich, traditionally of steak, lettuce, tomato, and garlic mayonnaise, served between two deep-fried plantains. Chicken or pork can be substituted for the steak, and sweet, grilled onions and cheese may also be added. While the sandwiches are made with plantains substituting for the bread at times throughout the Caribbean and northern South America and a similar sandwich is available at one restaurant in Puerto Rico, the sandwich took off in Chicago. In Chicago, the jibarito was introduced by Juan C. Figueroa at his Borinquen Restaurant in Humboldt Park in 1996. A few years later, his small stand was selling between five hundred and one thousand jibaritos a day. As other stands and restaurants copied the idea, it soon became a staple of Chicago Puerto Rican fast food. The sandwich has now been adopted into other Chicago Latino cuisines, including Cuban, Dominican, and Venezuelan restaurants, among others, although when Figueroa tried to open a jibarito stand in Puerto Rico itself, it failed.[27] The jibarito is also spreading outside Chicago, including a newly opened Manhattan food truck and a popular Cleveland Puerto Rican restaurant. Unfortunately, the sandwiches tend to be marketed as a Puerto Rican specialty and the Chicago roots tend not to be on display outside the city, but the jibarito is a new addition to the list of foods Chicago has had a part in popularizing in the United States.

COME IN AND STAY A WHILE . . . CHICAGO DISHES THAT TAKE A LITTLE MORE TIME

Pizza

In 1943, a ex-University of Texas football lineman named Ike Sewell partnered with Chicago artist and restaurateur Ric Riccardo to open a pizza restaurant, Pizzeria Uno, at which they or their chef created perhaps Chicago's most famous local dish, deep-dish pizza. The new dish came out of thicker-crusted pizzas such as those in Sicily, but also it was an outcome of the pushing of ingredients that were easily available during World War II, in particular flour, to create a thick, doughy crust that could be combined with cheese and tomato sauce and then whatever happened to be available.[28] Not surprisingly, the filling and tasty pizza were popular, so much so that deep-dish pizza was copied by many other Chicago restaurants, such as Gino's East. Restaurants often pushed the thickness of the crust and toppings until, in 1974, current chains Nancy's and Giordano's placed a second crust above the cheese and meats and below the tomato sauce (based on, according to Giordano's website, an Italian Eastertime tradition) in order to support an even thicker pizza. Giordano's claims that its stuffed pizzas are "40% bigger than our top competitors' deep-dish pizzas."[29]

While reheated versions are sold over the counter, unlike the pizzas of Naples and New York, Chicago deep-dish pizza is not a street food. It is a sit-down restaurant meal that can take up to forty-five minutes to prepare and bake. Some pizza aficionados claim that deep dish is not a pizza at all, but a sort of pizza-inspired casserole. With the rise of gourmet thin-crust, Neapolitan-style pizzas around the country and in Chicago itself,

Chicago deep dish often gets derided as heavy and somewhat old-fashioned. When it is well made, however, it is delicious, and it is undeniably a Chicago invention. It is, in addition, typical of many Chicago food themes. Like Chicago hot dogs, Italian beef, and Polish sausage, Chicago pizza was a response to the need to provide hungry Chicagoans with hearty food from limited ingredients. Also like these foods, it (at least the original deep-dish pizza) became popular in the mid-twentieth century, and it is an extension of existing ethnic traditions.

Whether a deep-dish pizza is delicious or not is all about the crust, of which there is plenty (although not as much as some non-Chicago chains serve on a "pan" pizza). While deep-dish chains also compete on the sauce, a cardboard-tasting crust will kill off an aspiring pizza joint owner. Gino's East and Lou Malnati's have a cornmeal crust; others put a bit of tomato sauce in. Whichever it is, the long preparation time means that in Chicago "going out for pizza" often involves a trip to a restaurant rather than a fast food joint. Oddly, though, Chicagoans today eat more thin crust than thick. While there is a growth of more traditional Italian pizzas and a good number of New York–style "foldable" pizzas available, Chicago has a style of thin crust pizza all its own (although it is similar to pizza sold throughout the Midwest). It is generally more heavily topped than the New York variety, with a crackery crust that can be loaded with a large amount of toppings (but not folded). Most typically, it is cut into square "party slices" rather than wedges.

Homestyle Chicago: Chicken Vesuvio

One of the great mysteries of Chicago food is the origin of the chicken, garlic, potato wedges, herbs, and peas dish known as Chicken Vesuvio that is served at Italian restaurants and diners around the city and has inspired related dishes such as Vesuvio potatoes and Steak Vesuvio. On a 1939 menu from the infamous Colosimo's was Unjointed Chicken, Vesuvio Style, presumably the now-classic Chicago dish. A dish by this name was also featured on a 1934 menu from the San Carlo Ristorante at the Century of Progress World's Fair, which was located near Colosimo's.[30] Italian Village also served Chicken Vesuvio in 1939 and is thought by many Chicagoans to have originated the dish (served at Italian Village famously without peas). There was also a downtown Chicago Italian restaurant called Vesuvio during the 1930s that could be the origin, but while it is described in John Drury's 1931 guidebook, there is no discussion of a special baked chicken dish. While the true origins of the name Chicken Vesuvio remain a mystery Italian Village, Colosimo's and the San Carlo Ristorante are certainly possibilities. *Chicago Sun-Times* reporter Tom McNamee looked into it, stating finally that while Colosimo's or Italian Village might have served Chicken Vesuvio in the 1920s, the earliest evidence is the 1934 World's Fair menu.[31] Mike Baruch in his book *Street Food Chicago* separates the Vesuvio recipes into their own chapter and heading in the index (separate from chicken recipes), and he has an alternative origin story of a rivalry between Vic Giannotti, who owned a suburban Italian steakhouse and for years claimed to have originated the dish, and Petros Kogiones, who owned a Greektown restaurant, competing to make the best chicken dish. According to the story, ultimately the recipes merged into today's Chicken Vesuvio. Supporting the story is the similarity of the dish to Greek Lemon Chicken, another dish present at diners throughout Chicago. However, while the combination of Italian and Greek recipes could have happened (as well as the perfecting of the dish), Chicken Vesuvio appeared on many menus long before this supposed competition occurred in the 1960s.[32] Whatever the origins, baked chicken with potatoes, garlic, and herbs is certainly not an entirely Chicago creation. McNamee quotes the co-owner of an Italian steakhouse that "ultimately, these were recipes invented by people's moms."[33] Unlike most other famous "Chicago" foods, Chicken Vesuvio could very well come from a home kitchen. However, "Vesuvio" is now also a Chicago food, available since the 1950s all over the city. It is a specialty of the house at Harry Caray's restaurants. It also makes appearances in neighborhood recipe books, showing that it remains a recipe that is also made at home. The 1980s Old Irving Park (a Northwest Side neighborhood) Association cookbook features two Chicken Vesuvio recipes, including a very simple one written by then 38th Ward alderman Joseph S. Kotlarz. The fact that an alderman with a non-Italian name in a multiethnic Chicago neighborhood would choose to publish a Chicken Vesuvio recipe says something about its tie to Chicago, and its ability to move from the restaurant to the home chef.[34] In 2014, the *Chicago Tribune* even published a recipe for vegetarian Chicken Vesuvio using seitan.

The key to a good Chicken Vesuvio lies in the garlicky olive oil and wine-based sauce that surrounds the chicken and vegetables (or whatever other food is cooked in it), and browning the chicken before baking. The potatoes wedges are also a key element, and many restaurants serve Vesuvio potatoes as a potato option (along with mashed, baked, etc.). Peas are a generally accepted component, but some recipes, particularly Italian Village's, do not use peas. In general, reflecting its home-cooked origins, the recipe for Chicken Vesuvio varies greatly, contrasting with such food as the Chicago hot dog or the Maxwell Street Polish sausage, where the mix of ingredients (at least besides the sausage) is quite prescribed. Here is one recipe, based on the one Tom McNamee found at Vic's Classic Italian Steakhouse, a now-gone restaurant that was the descendent of Giannotti's in the western suburbs, combined with one from the *Chicago Tribune's Ethnic Chicago Cookbook.*

Recipe: Chicken Vesuvio

Makes 4 servings

   1 boiler/fryer chicken (3 to 4 pounds), cut up, rinsed under cold water, and dried

   3 large russet potatoes, cut into wedges

   1/3 cup olive oil

   1/3 cup flour (leave out for a thinner but clearer sauce)

   1 teaspoon dried basil

   3/4 teaspoon dried oregano

   1/4 teaspoon dried thyme

   1 teaspoon garlic powder

   Pinch of dried rosemary

   Pinch of dried sage

   1/4 teaspoon ground black pepper

   1/2 teaspoon salt

   Dash of Tabasco (optional)

   6 garlic cloves, minced

   1/2 cup dry white wine

   3 tablespoons fresh parsley, chopped

   OPTIONAL: 2/3 cup peas (fresh preferred, frozen OK), lightly cooked

   Preheat oven to 425°. Mix flour, basil, oregano, thyme, garlic powder, rosemary, sage, black pepper, and salt, and roll chicken pieces in mixture. Set aside. Heat olive oil in oven-safe pot or 12-

inch cast iron skillet over high heat. Sautée potato wedges until golden brown. Remove and set aside. Place chicken pieces in pot/ skillet and brown until golden on all sides. Add garlic cloves and continue to saute for two to four minutes. Remove chicken and drain on paper towels. Return chicken and potatoes to pot/skillet. Sprinkle with parsley. Pour wine over dish. Cover and bake chicken for 10 minutes. Uncover and cook until chicken is cooked and potatoes are fork-tender (about 20 minutes). Add peas and parsley and bake an additional 5 minutes. Remove from oven and let stand 5 minutes before serving. Serve on a platter with peas and potatoes surrounding. Top with the pan juices.

Chicago's Most Enduring Signature Dish: Shrimp DeJonghe

While Chicken Vesuvio and deep-dish pizza are relatively hearty home-style recipes that are served at family restaurants (or in the case of deep-dish pizza, local chains) across the city, other signature city foods, Shrimp DeJonghe and Chicken a la King being two of the most famous, have got their start at fancier downtown establishments. While over time these dishes may have made their way into homes and neighborhood diners, and in the case of Chicken a la King, lost their Chicago connection, they remained "fancy" dishes, if a little old-fashioned.

Shrimp DeJonghe originated at the DeJonghe Hotel and Restaurant, which was a hip, upscale Loop establishment at the turn of the twentieth century. The DeJonghe Hotel was started by a pair of Belgian immigrants who came to Chicago to run a restaurant at the 1893 World's Fair. Like many others, they used the momentum gained through the Fair to start restaurants in the city, including the DeJonghe Hotel and Restaurant, which opened in 1899. The restaurant thrived, and its signature dish, a rich, baked, shrimp dish that combined Chicago's love of seafood at the time (evidenced by large restaurants such as Rector's Oyster House and others) and the love of rich, hearty food. The DeJonghe Hotel and Restaurant closed during the 1920s due to liquor violations. Its manager and another worker had earlier been cited for vice. However, its signature dish, likely originated by Chef Emile Zehr or by DeJonghe brother Henri remains, although the hotel's secret recipe was never revealed. Many

Chicago restaurants have made approximations of the original, and recipes have been published by the *Chicago Tribune*, among others. Preparations differ. In general, they involve boiling raw shrimp in water seasoned with salt, pepper, celery, and a bay leaf. Next, the cooked shrimp is peeled and then tossed with melted butter and a little sherry. Following this, it is combined in a casserole with more butter, breadcrumbs, shallots, garlic, and a little hot pepper, covered with more breadcrumbs, and baked.[35] Other recipes such as one from the Greektown restaurant Sabatini's calls for sautéing peeled shrimp before baking in seasoned butter and crumbs.[36] Either way, the goal is to create a seasoned, baked, butter and shrimp casserole, delicious as an appetizer or a heavy main course.

BAKERIES, POPCORN, AND CHEESECAKE

Chicago's neighborhood bakeries are often a cornerstone of its ethnic identity and are an important part of its street food scene. North Side Andersonville, which is not really particularly Swedish anymore, is the home of Swedish Bakery, an almost always crowded wonderland full of limpa and other breads, as well as a large variety of marzipan-topped deserts, among others. Lutz is an old-time "continental" bakery and coffee shop, with delicious apple streudel and coffee settings out of 1950s Vienna. Reuter's and Dinkel's are long-standing North Side German bakeries. Italian bakeries serving cannoli cake and other Italian specialties are highlights of the Northwest Side/Elmwood Park Italian community, and Ferrara Bakery (owned by the same family as Ferrara Pan candy) is still a cornerstone of what remains of the Taylor Street Little Italy community. Polish and Czech bakeries highlight kolachky (either the cookie dough Polish style or the yeast-based Czech style) and many other specialties. Mexican bakeries such as the La Baguette chain and El Nopal on 26th Street sell a variety of Mexican pastries, breads, and cakes. These ethnic bakeries often cross-pollinate. Pączkis, a traditional Polish filled doughnut, made with a rich dough, has become especially popular on Mardi Gras, when lines form out the door of the Chicago bakeries that carry them, which include many non-Polish ones who have stepped in to capitalize on the sweet's popularity. Chicago also sports many newer, somewhat fancier, bakeries and pastry shops, such as Kristoffer's, a Mexican bakery in Pilsen and Bridgeport (and now South Florida) that Rick

Bayless says makes the best tres leches cake he has ever had. Brown Sugar Bakery on 75th Street is part of the growing restaurant (and bakery) row in the longtime African American Park Manor community, and it specializes in caramel cake and huge cupcakes. Another new South Side bakery, Jimmy Jamm, specializes in all things sweet potato, including sweet potato pies, ice cream, and sandwiches served on sweet potato bread. On the North Side, there are a variety of hip new bakeries specializing in pie, including Bang Bang Pie, which specializes in over-the-top indulgences such as chocolate creams, and Hoosier Mama, which focuses on more "old time" farmer's-market-style pies.

Given this large variety of sweets, it is perhaps unfortunate at the terminals at O'Hare you can only buy two particularly Chicago deserts: Eli's cheesecake and Garrett's popcorn. These items, though, are in many ways typical of many Chicago foods. Like Kronos gyros and Vienna sausages, Eli's is a local business that has expanded by applying industrial baking techniques to the production and development of a modified ethnic recipe that originated at a restaurant. Chicago Mix, a mixture of caramel and cheese popcorn, is part of a long history of Chicago popcorn innovations that included the popcorn machine, Cracker Jack, and "TV Time" popcorn, innovations that were originally rooted in Chicago's location in the middle of the Corn Belt. They are also some of the most recently invented of Chicago's signature foods—Eli's cheesecake in the early 1970s, and the "Chicago Mix" in the 1980s (although Chicagoans ordered and created it earlier). Both also are notable by being called "Chicago," unlike such foods as gyros or Polish sausage. Eli's cheesecake now typifies Chicago-style cheesecake, even though it was a recipe invented for a restaurant just forty years ago.

Garrett's Popcorn opened its initial store in the Loop in 1949. At the time, it was one of a number of boutique popcorn shops open around the country.[37] Garrett's now has eleven Chicago locations, plus shops in New York and Las Vegas and in eight countries within Asia and the Middle East. What Garrett's is particularly known for, however, the "Chicago Mix," is a relatively new creation. According to Garrett's website, what is now known as the "Garrett Mix" was created and requested by customers. The origins of Chicago Mix are somewhat obscure. Brenda Lamb, co-owner of small Minnesota company called Candyland, claims that she came up with the cheese and caramel corn mix in 1988. She claims she called it "Chicago Mix" because "if I had put Minneapolis Mix or St.

Paul Mix, would it be popular in another state? A big-city name usually draws attention to a product." Candyland applied and received a copyright for Chicago Mix in 1992. Recently, Candyland sued Garrett's, along with two companies marketing packaged popcorn, to stop using the term *Chicago Mix*. Garrett's has taken the term off its website, although the term *Chicago Mix* may still be on Chicago store menus. The other companies, Snyder's-Lance, which now owns former Chicago brand Jay's O-KE-DOKE popcorn, and Cornfields, Inc., which markets G. H. Cretor's popcorn, still are selling Chicago Mix. [38]

Garrett's claims that it changed from Chicago Mix to Garrett Mix because it is now selling popcorn all over the world. The idea that the term arose in Minneapolis in the late 1980s and then spread to Chicago seems pretty far-fetched, but Garrett's never applied for a copyright. Garrett's website implies that Chicago Mix was invented by its fans who asked for the combination. Whichever occurred, Garrett's and Chicago Mix comes out of a long tradition of innovations in popcorn that are Chicago centered. Chicago was the center of the popcorn processing and marketing industry during the late 1800s. Grocers in the city and elsewhere sold half-pound boxes of Snowdrift and Snowflake, Chicago-manufactured products that were simply popped and ground popcorn, and could be eaten somewhat like cereal, with milk and sugar, or as a savory supper dish. Tastier-sounding dishes such as popcorn bricks, which combined popcorn, corn syrup, and molasses, led to a variety of popcorn concoctions available at the 1893 World's Fair, the most long lasting being a mix of popcorn, molasses, and peanuts introduced by the Reuckheim Brothers that by 1896 was called Cracker Jack. Cracker Jack became a best seller, especially after the innovation of putting it in a triple-sealed, moisture-proof package in 1902; the inclusion of Cracker Jack in "Take Me Out to the Ball Game" in 1908; and finally the insertion of toys into the Cracker Jack boxes in 1912. [39]

From 1966 to 2005, Eli's the Place for Steak was a well-known Chicago restaurant located in Streeterville near Northwestern Medical Center. Its owner, Eli Schulman, was a classic restaurateur, hobnobbing with Chicago's rich and famous, including members of the Chicago Bears, politicians, journalists, and TV and radio personalities. The atmosphere at Eli's helped inspire such restaurants as Morton's and the Lettuce Entertain You chain. However, its most lasting contribution to Chicago's cuisine is the development of the Chicago cheesecake, introduced at the restaurant during the late 1970s and outside the restaurant at Taste of Chicago, at which Eli's was an original participant, on July 4, 1980. Eli's became the most popular desert at the "Taste," and in 1996 the company opened a cheesecake bakery, Eli's Cheesecake World, on the Northwest Side.[40] The factory is open for tours to the public and to school groups. Eli's cheesecake is a cream-cheese-and-sour-cream-based cheesecake that is baked and is firm on the outside and creamy on the inside, with a cookie crust. Eli's makes over twenty thousand a day, including related deserts, and slices of cheesecake can be bought at grocery stores around Chicago.

CHICAGO HISTORIC COOKBOOKS AND HOME RECIPES

While this has declined somewhat in recent years, Chicago has been a center for publishing, printing, and advertising. This characteristic has meant that the city has been the site for the publishing of many cookbooks. Quite a few of these are general cookbooks that were published in Chicago, but otherwise have few Chicago connections. In addition to publishing many early cookbooks, Chicago printing giant R. R. Donnelley also had a specialty in advertising cookbooks, showcasing brands from around the country. Other Chicago-published cookbooks were more Chicago centered. These included charity cookbooks, compiled and sold by a church, neighborhood organization, or other charitable association; cookbooks focused on the food served at a particular restaurant or hotel; and cookbooks that compiled recipes from newspapers and other media. In addition, many cookbooks attached to government or organizational exhibits or nutritional lessons were published in the city. While there are many collections of cookbooks in the city, we owe a debt to Louis Szathmary, who in addition to being the chef of the Bakery and a TV personality, was also a culinary historian who collected a large number of cookbooks, many of which had Chicago connections. In addition to cookbooks, historic Chicago home recipes exist, either in archives or in compilations. Many of these highlight the lives of those who wrote them and the art of living in Chicago at the time they were written, in ways that cookbooks from an established publisher do not. Here, we highlight the variety of cookbooks with connections to Chicago and focus on a few particularly interesting examples, as well as discuss some historic Chicago home recipes.

Nineteenth-Century Beginnings

The book that is probably the first American cookbook printed west of Indiana is an example of a book printed in Chicago but having little other connection to Chicago, *The Cake Baker*, published in 1857. *The Cake Baker* was a short volume of cake recipes from bakeries in New York City and Albany. By 1872, Chicago printer R. R. Donnelley published *The Cuisine*, a small cookbook "prepared under the supervision of an eminent French caterer," which was one of the first of the mass-produced cookbooks meant to be given away as premiums by companies and stores. In 1877, one of the first of many Chicago newspaper cookbooks was published by the *Chicago Tribune*. In 1878, the first of a series of product-oriented recipe books for Dr. Price's Baking Powder was published.[41]

The most popular early Chicago cookbooks were the *Lakeside Cook Book*, volumes one and two, published by Donnelley, Gassette, and Lloyd (the predecessor of printer R. R. Donnelley) in 1878, and compiled by Naomi Donnelley, wife of founder Richard Robert Donnelley. These cookbooks were relatively cheap, costing only ten cents (about $2.40 today), published on cheap paper with a weak binding in paperback. But they were jam packed with a wide selection of recipes, written in paragraph form with a mix of specific and general measurements, for dishes from soups to breakfast, dinners, and deserts, as well as preserved food, and household recipes and instructions. In general, recipes are relatively simple and with few exceptions are not specifically "ethnic," but occasionally they have interesting features. For instance, one recipe for chicken soup features raw egg added just before serving:

> To the broth in which chickens have been boiled for salad, etc., add one onion and eight or ten tomatoes, season with pepper and salt; boil thirty minutes; add two well beaten eggs just before sending to table.[42]

One of two recipes for eggplant prescribes boiling the eggplant, and then deep-fat frying in lard. Another recipe in the vegetable section is for "macaroni," which is actually baked macaroni and cheese. While there are some more complex dessert recipes, this recipe for sugar cookies epitomizes the cookbook's general simplicity:

> COOKIES: Two cups sugar, on cup butter, one cup milk, three eggs, flour enough to make a soft dough, two teaspoons baking powder; roll thin; sift over with sugar and bake.[43]

An interesting recipe for pickled nasturtium seeds (then called nasturtions) links to a current revival of the use of the seeds as a substitute for capers:

> Take those that are small and green, put them in salt and water, changing it two in the course of a week; when you have done collecting them, turn off the brine and turn on scalding vinegar, with a little alum in it.[44]

Finally, directions for testing milk for watering were placed in the "Miscellaneous" section:

> A well polished knitting needle is dipped into a deep vessel of milk, and immediately withdrawn in upright position; when, if the sample be pure, some of the fluid will be found to adhere to it, while such is not the case if water has been added to the milk.[45]

The success of the two *Lakeside Cook Book*s was an important step in Donnelley's ability to spread beyond its initial core business of directory printing. Among other things, they stand out in that, despite the directions for testing milk, the *Lakeside Cook Book* was not a general guide for housewives. It was first and foremost a cookbook with relatively easy to follow recipes. However, the milk-testing instructions do show the increasing focus on adulterated food items in Chicago and other U.S. cities. In 1880, another Chicago publisher published a book with a title that sounds very modern day, J. T. Pratt's *Food Adulteration: Or, What We Eat, and What We Should Eat!*, although the concerns included the selling of margarine. Examples of early Chicago-published household guides and general-purpose cookbooks include the 1891 *Dining Room and Kitchen: An Economical Guide in Practical Housekeeping for the American Housewife* by Mrs. Grace Townsend and the 1894 *Dr. N. T. Oliver's Treasured Secrets: The Century Cook Book.* In 1892, the Chicago-based Regan Printing House published *The Every-Day Cook-Book* *and Encyclopedia of Practical Recipes*, an early general cookbook (similar to a *Joy of Cooking*) published in 1892 in Chicago. This was full of "everyday" recipes, as well as health advice, advice on marketing (advising to pay cash rather than buying on account), and rules for eating (including "never sit down to a table with an anxious or disturbed mind").[46] The interest in foreign, specifically French, cuisines around the time of the 1893 World's Fair is evidenced by the Chicago publishing of *La Cuisine Francaise: French Cooking for Every Home, Adapted to American Requirements*. The growth of the temperance movement and Chicago's central role in it is shown in *The White Ribbon Cook Book: A Collection of Original and Revised Recipes in Cookery and Housekeeping*.[47]

Chicago also was the publishing site of one of the earliest children's cookbooks, *Six Little Cooks or Aunt Jane's Cooking Class*, first published in 1877 and going through many later editions. It is told as a narrative children's story, with recipes interspersed. For instance, a recipe for Boiled Custard is presented thusly:

> One quart milk, six eggs, two teaspoonfuls vanilla extract; sweeten to taste. "That's another thing I am sure would drive me distracted," said Grace. "How can you know that sugar enough for your taste would be enough for anybody else's?"
> "Only by practice my dear," answered her aunt.

Her aunt then goes on to instruct Grace and her friends on how to make "Tipsy Cake" by topping slices of sponge cake (for which a recipe was also provided) with blanched almond slices, "pour over it as much wine as it will absorb," followed by the boiled custard described above. A narrative describing the group making the concoction follows, including Grace saying how much she loves Tipsy Cake.[48]

Chicago continued to be a center of cookbook publishing throughout into the twentieth century. Industry-oriented cookbooks published in the city such as *Hotel Meat Cooking: Comprising Hotel and Restaurant Fish and Oyster Cooking. How to Cut Meats, and Soups, Entrees, and Bills of Fare*, as well as numerous cookbooks published by Chicago and later Evanston-headquartered *Hotel Monthly*. In addition, there were many standard cookbooks such as the *Twentieth Century Cook Book*, published in 1921 and given away by banks and other businesses, and *Mrs. Anna J. Peterson's Simplified Cooking: Handbook of Everyday Meal Prepara-*

tion, published by the Chicago-based American School of Home Economics in 1924. The school also published a correspondence course on cooking and menu preparation. A number of cookbooks also were published by Chicago-based *Woman's World* magazine, including the 1930s *The Woman's World Cookbook*, which included references to the use of electric appliances. Many of these cookbooks seem to have been oriented toward middle-class women with lessening amount of servant help but with increasing kitchen technology and increasing amounts of cooking responsibility.

Chicago newspapers have long seen publishing cookbooks as a way to build extra interest in themselves as well as to make a little extra money either from recipes that were already created by their staff or by holding recipe contests among their readers and then publishing the results. These cookbooks sometimes were specialized in one area of cooking, such as the *Chicago Tribune*'s recently released collection of the last twenty-five years of its holiday cookie contest, but in general newspaper cookbooks are eclectic collections. As mentioned above, as early as 1877, the *Chicago Tribune* (then called the *Daily Tribune*) published a collection of recipes and "Hints, Pertaining to Cookery" suggested by "500 Ladies."[49] The 1896 *Chicago Record Cook Book*, reprinted as *The Daily News Cook Book* (the *Chicago Record* was owned by the *Daily News* at the time) was organized by day of the year and contained menus for every meal of each day. Menus and recipes for each day were contributed by a particular woman reader. The cookbook was "designed to furnish a good living in appetizing variety at an expense not to exceed $500 for a family of five," catering to middle-class women readers. It contained over a thousand recipes, contributed by over five hundred women. In addition to special meals such as a New Year's Day dinner, there is an interesting seasonality to the menus, particularly the vegetables included. June 8 features strawberries for breakfast, strawberry dressing with rice as a side for lunch, and cucumber salad and new potatoes for dinner (the main dinner dish for this day, a Friday, was baked halibut). January 5 features celery as a lunch side, and cream of celery soup as well as a side of parsnips for dinner (the main dinner dish was beef roulette).[50] The 1930 *Chicago Daily News Cook Book* had some similarities to its predecessor in that it was based on a contest (with more than twenty thousand recipes submitted this time) and focused on cooking on a budget, this time $4 per person per week. While it was not organized by day-of-the-year menus, it did

have a section outlining seasonal menus by day of the week, in addition
to a chapter titled "10 Minute Menus." The cookbook was cowritten by
Herman Bundesen, who was the former and future Commissioner of
Health for the City of Chicago, as well as a nationally known health
expert for hire. Bundesen contributed a section on "Eating for Health." In
addition to this section, there were also chapters on "Balancing the Budget" and "Kitchen Science," both fronted, like the other chapters, by
beautiful art deco illustrations.[51] Another Chicago-published general
cookbook of note included the *United States Regional Cook Book*, published first in 1930, one of a number of cookbooks published by the
Chicago-based Culinary Arts Institute. This particular volume included a
variety of regional dishes from around the country, including Russian
borscht and Armenian eggplant. A final Chicago-published cookbook of
interest was Henri Charpentier's self-published *Food and Finesse: The
Bride's Bible*, which includes chapters for every American state.[52]

Advertising, Government, Organizational, and
Product-Centered Cookbooks

As evidenced by the 1878 Dr. Price's Baking Soda cookbook, Chicago
was a center of the printing of product-centered cookbooks and pamphlets from an early period in its history. Some of these full cookbooks,
given away by companies as premiums, did not necessarily have alle-
giances to any one product. An example of this was the 1870 *The Cuisine*
discussed above. The copies of *The Cuisine* in the Szathmary collection
were "presented" by a china firm and a clothing store. In 1928, George
Rector published *The Rector Cook Book*, based on the success of his
Chicago and New York restaurants, although the cookbook contained
recipes from many restaurants. It appears to have been given away by the
Chicago, Milwaukee, and Pacific Railroad (the Milwaukee Road) for
which Rector also worked at the time, in addition to other businesses.[53]

   Chicago was a particular center for the production of product-focused
recipe booklets. Many featured one of the industrial food products Chicago was famous for. Besides the numerous Dr. Price booklets, another
early example was *Culinary Wrinkles*, a short recipe book published in
Chicago in 1901, focused on the use of Armour's Extract of Beef in the
cooking of foods for "bachelor maids, men, and others."[54] A 1910 recipe
booklet featured Chicago-based Moxley's Special Oleomargarine. Reci-

pes ranged from breads, cookies, cakes, and pies, including items such as Parker House rolls and hard sauce, to main dishes including Potatoes au Gratin and Hamburg Beef Cakes.[55] In 1919 Swift and Company published *Jewel Menus with Tested Recipes Using Jewel Shortening*. In 1927, Chicago-headquartered Quaker Oats published *America's Most Famous Recipes*. Subtitled "new ways in which millions of women are using it to make delicious pancakes, waffles, and muffins," it focused on Aunt Jemima mix.[56] These are just some of many examples that continue today, as Kraft Foods in particular continues to publish product-centered recipe pamphlets, in addition to Internet recipes. R. R. Donnelley in particular focused on printing such pamphlets, and in the late 1940s and early 1950s it promoted such projects to advertising agencies and food processors through vividly colored samples in a monthly packet called "Ways to a Women's Heart."[57]

Recipe pamphlets and short cookbooks were also produced outside of the advertising world, specifically by government and nonprofit organizations. One of the most interesting nineteenth-century Chicago cookbooks is *Favorite Dishes: A Columbian Autograph Souvenir*, featuring recipes from the lady managers and alternates from each state, Alaska, and England, of the Women's Department of the 1893 World's Fair, with signatures for each of the recipe providers. Recipes are separated by type and are presented in paragraph form. Other than the eminence of many of the contributors, the mixture and variance of the recipes themselves is similar to a community cookbook. Many women contributed typical recipes of their home states, but the recipes do not always match expected states since many are favorite household recipes. There are three different recipes for gumbos, one each from Alabama, Kentucky, and Connecticut. Clam chowder recipes come from Nevada and Georgia. A set of lobster recipes comes from the lady manager and alternate lady manager of Idaho. Illinois suffragist and president of the Women's Christian Temperance Union, Frances Willard, claimed to have little interest in cooking, but she sent her mother's doughnut recipe.[58]

Beyond the souvenir cookbook published by Women's Department, another product of the 1893 World's Fair was a short recipe booklet promoting the consumption of corn meal, published by the Illinois Women's Exposition Board and accompanying the Illinois Corn Exhibit in the Women's Building. As befitted the official exhibitions of the Fair, the booklet combined science with promotion of an Illinois product, comparing the content of wheat and corn, for instance, for water, ash, oil, carbohydrates, and albuminoids (protein). The author, cookbook writer Sarah T. Royer, argues that corn meal should be emphasized in the diets of soldiers and that "(a)s a food for cold climates, (fresh) corn is most valuable, being rich in fatty and starchy matter, two heat-giving elements." Royer also suggests that Irish peasants switch from the potato to corn as their main source of carbohydrates, stating that "he would without doubt be a much better fed individual, consequently a much more contented one." Recipes include those for three Zuni breads, collected by the Smithsonian, as well as seven different cornbread recipes, recipes for corn meal scones, grits, and a number of puddings using cornstarch. An example of the Zuni bread is "Zuni mù-we," a hot cake recipe. Greased paper is substituted for cornhusks used by the Zuni:

> 1 cup white corn flour, 1 cup yellow meal, 1 cup water, 1 teaspoon salt, 1/8 teaspoon cayenne, 1 cup chopped suet. Mix all well together, form into rolls about five inches long, roll in greased paper, and bake in a moderate oven one hour. Serve hot.[59]

An interesting Chicago-based governmental recipe booklet was published during World War I by the State Council of Defense of Illinois. Titled *What to Eat: How to Cook It*, it was the official recipe book of a "Patriotic Food Show" held in Chicago in 1918. Subtitled "Win the War in the Kitchen" and containing a forward by U.S. Food Commissioner Herbert Hoover and "The President's Call to the Women of the Nation" from Woodrow Wilson, the booklet focused on substitutions of more abundant products for those needed to feed the army, including corn meal for wheat, vegetable oil for butter and lard, molasses and honey for sugar, and eggs for beef. A recipe section called "Meatless Meats" contains recipes for poultry, a fish section highlights "new fish" such as whiting and carp, and a legumes section contains recipes for stews and loafs made from such things as lentils and peas.[60] Short product-centered cookbooks were also published by standard Chicago publishers. An example is *The Book of Potato Cookery*, published by Chicago publisher A. C. McClurg during World War I as part of its "Dame Curtsey's" series of short books on household subjects from etiquette to games for children. The book was dedicated to "those woman patriots who are helping win the war."[61]

Two very different kinds of government-published cookbooks were *Mayor Byrne's Chicago Heritage Cookbook* and *The Taste of Chicago*

Figure 7.3.   Cover from a recipe book accompanying the Illinois corn exhibit at the 1893 Chicago World's Fair. University of Illinois-Chicago, Special Collections.

Cookbook. While *The Taste of Chicago* cookbook focuses on a particular event, both cookbooks were spiral-bound volumes meant to showcase

Chicago's ethnic diversity. Both also include a mayoral recipe. Mayor Byrne's is "Snow Birds," chicken salad served in a pineapple and banana "bird," while Richard M. Daley submitted his wife Maggie's beef stew. The *Chicago Heritage Cookbook* publishes submitted recipes from a list of ethnicities from around the city. The *Taste of Chicago* cookbook is a collection of recipes submitted by the festival participants. It contains many classic recipes such as Harry Caray's Chicken Vesuvio and peach cobbler from classic West Side soul food restaurant Edna's.[62]

Hotel, Restaurant, and Chef Cookbooks

The earliest Chicago cookbooks were generally not focused on a particular eatery or a star chef. An 1887 to 1888 catering guide for the huge downtown restaurant Kinsley's included some recipes, but true restaurant cookbooks did not become popular in Chicago until the twentieth century. The Congress Hotel in 1914 created a beautiful souvenir booklet containing deep descriptions, but not truly recipes, of a number of its most elegant dishes.[63] In 1926 hotel caterer Arnold Shircliffe wrote the Edgewater Beach Hotel Salad Book, which became a hit and went through over ten editions and was the most popular salad book of its time in the United States. While the recipes are, to today's eyes, of varying nutrition levels, the introduction to the book places it within the new nutrition of the early twentieth century, in which the discovery of vitamins furthered the idea of vegetables as being essential to health. The idea of the book, a large cookbook focused on salads, which were often ignored or at least not emphasized in earlier cookbooks, was both somewhat revolutionary and helped build the reputation of the Edgewater Beach as a healthy and pleasant place both to dine and to vacation. Salads ranged from very simple, such as the "Poor Man's Salad," which combined young, foraged dandelion greens and watercress, tossed in a bowl rubbed with a garlic clove and served with chopped chives and French dressing, to the complex, such as the namesake "Edgewater Beach," which looks like the hotel's monogram, a construction of lettuce, pineapple, grapefruit, oranges, watercress, cream cheese, red bell pepper, and green and ripe olives.[64]

In 1940, Palmer House chef Ernest E. Amiet wrote and compiled *The Palmer House Cook Book*. It was a general cookbook, organized by menus and featuring over a thousand recipes. Amiet wrote that the book featured "dishes that have proved to be popular in the dining-rooms of the Continental and American hotels with which I have been associated . . . reduced by actual testing and experimenting to proportions for use in the kitchens and dining-rooms of the average home." Menus (for which recipes are provided for all items) included common and uncommon hotel food, often with a fancy touch. One breakfast menu was Sliced Orange, Rolled Oats, and Fried Eggs au Beurre Noire. The eggs were served with capers and a butter and vinegar sauce. One dinner menu is Canapé Maine, Veal Steak Magenta, German Style Spinach, and Cocoanut [sic] Pudding. Veal Steak Magenta was a veal steak, covered and fried with salami, and served with a two-egg omelet on top. The Palmer House was, among other things, the inventor of the chocolate brownie, created by its pastry chef in 1893 at the request of Bertha Palmer, wife of hotel owner Potter Palmer, who was president of the Board of Lady Managers of the 1893 Columbian Exhibition and needed a portable desert that could be placed into box lunches. Topped with an apricot glaze, the unusual brownie is today highlighted on many current Palmer House menus, but it did not appear among the recipes in the 1940 Palmer House cookbook.

Since the 1970s and especially during the past twenty years, cookbooks highlighting restaurants and premier, or even not so premier, chefs have become common. Sometimes, such as in the case of Rick Bayless, the cookbook preceded the fame. Standouts such as Alinea and Charlie Trotter's have published associated cookbooks, as well as tradition-filled spots as Berghoff's. Many chefs such as Bayless and Trotter built off their restaurants to publish a series of cookbooks. Louis Szathmary, the first of Chicago's modern celebrity chefs, wrote *The Chef's New Secret Cookbook* in 1975, highlighting Szathmary's hearty continental cuisine but containing just black-and-white illustrations and limited commentary. By contrast, *Alinea* is almost more of a coffee table book than a cookbook, full of beautiful color illustrations but too large to be practical in many kitchens. The change highlights the transition of top chefs into a kind of performance artist working with an edible palette. There are also many less fancy restaurant cookbooks, such as the two *Chicago Diner* cookbooks, based on the food of Chicago Diner, a vegetarian diner that recreates many standard Chicago, American, and ethnic diner foods for vegetarians. Other cookbooks highlight farmer's markets and special events, such as the *Green City Market Cookbook* and the city-published *Taste of Chicago Cookbook*. In general, while general cookbooks still are published, in much of Chicago's recent cookbooks the chef, the restaurant, or even the farmer's market is the star. [65]

Charity and Neighborhood Cookbooks and Home Recipes

Some Chicago cookbooks, especially those focusing on Chicago foods, such as *Street Food Chicago* and the *Ethnic Chicago Cookbook* as well as cookbooks devoted to a particular ethnicity, give us an idea of what people ate at home, although many of the city's signature dishes are eaten mainly at restaurants. Newspaper compilations of contributed recipes include home recipes, but the nature of the contests from which these cookbooks arise makes them a very selective view of Chicago cooking.

Home recipes are found in diaries and other archival material, index card boxes handed down from generation to generation, which sometimes appear at antique stores, and other, more random locations. They also appear in charity and neighborhood cookbooks, something Chicago has a long history of. Contributors to these cookbooks, similar to *Favorite Dishes: A Columbian Autograph Souvenir* (which was basically a published fancy charity cookbook), as well as contributors to newspaper competitions, often will not choose an everyday recipe to send in. Charity cookbooks, however, are usually much less selective than the newspaper contests, and may even take all contributions. In addition, charity and neighborhood cookbooks often contain interesting material about the group that published them and the neighborhood they represent.

The recipes that survive in archives often are from Chicago's most prominent families. E. W. Blatchford arrived in Chicago in 1837 at the age of eleven, the son of John Blatchford, a pastor of the First Presbyterian Church. The family moved to Missouri, but E. W. moved back to Chicago with his St. Louis–based lead and linseed oil manufacturing plant. Blatchford and his wife built a large house on Chicago's North Side called Ulmenheim, which was destroyed in the Chicago Fire of 1871 but was rebuilt and stood at 1011 LaSalle until 1929. Included in the many documents from Ulmenheim was its cookbook, a book full of family recipes likely meant to be passed down, as well as perhaps used by servants. Many of the recipes appear to have been copied from older recipes, or perhaps from contemporary cookbooks, but others are passed down from a named person. A recipe for Smothered Prairie Chickens is marked "Mothers F.W.B." It reads:

Skin the chickens—just cook them in hot butter; and turn them often in the butter for 5 or 10 minutes. Then pour on boiling water sufficient to cover them. Add pepper + salt with the water—Cover closely until cooked. Serve in a nice brown gravy.[66]

The oldest recipe in the Blatchford files is claimed to be "Chowder for 20 Persons," which is a fish chowder recipe handed down by "the Blatchford family mothers." It is stated to be originally from Mrs. Francis, Wickes Blatchford, the wife of Presbyterian pastor John Blatchford, and the mother of E. W. This recipe is not actually in the Ulmenheim book, but it is included in the book on a separate page. Two versions are given, likely from multiple trials at making the recipe. They are both very basic boiled fish recipes, with layers of fish, potatoes, and crackers boiled in water and milk.

Recipe: Chowder for 20 Persons

2 lbs. of good pork to be fixed in the pot and let the fat only remain in

1 layer of fish
1 la. (layer) of potatoes
1 la. (layer) of crackers

add Pepper & salt on each layer & continue the layer till the pot is filled sufficiently full with fish, potatoes & crackers

When filled put in 1 pt. (pint) of water & cover the whole with milk.

Boil the same moderately about 20 minutes or till the potatoes are boiled which is good evidence that the chowder is done

1 cod 1 (illegible) & three haddock or from 8 to 10 (illegible) for the chowder

Chowder Second

1 lb. of fish prepared as above with a layer of fish, potatoes, crackers with pepper & salt.

After it boils add milk to cover it well over also put in 1/4 of a pound of butter

1 (illegible) of crackers which some put in on top of the whole.

Notes

The Chowder was good though <u>rather dry</u>.

July 1844

(Recipe for "Chowder for Twenty Persons," Blatchford Family, Ulmenheim Recipe Book, ca. 1850–1870, Blatchford Family Papers.)

The home recipes of a variety of prominent families living on upscale Prairie Avenue during the late 1800s and early 1900s were collected and studied by Carol Callahan and incorporated into *The Prairie Avenue Cookbook*, which is a social history in addition to a book of collected recipes, indicating life along Chicago's most upscale thoroughfare. Upscale events were highlights of the year. The intellectual Glessner family once hosted a reading of *Faust* with twenty-five Chicago Symphony musicians providing musical accompaniment. Following this, Robert Lincoln (the son of Abraham Lincoln and the manager of the Pullman Works) and Allison Armour made lobster Newburg. Day-to-day social interactions are also documented. A recipe for sweetbreads is credited to a neighbor. Recipes also show a wider variety, probably as a result of travel. Two families had recipes for risotto. The Glessner family (whose house still stands and is open for tours) in the early twentieth century had a recipe for Tamale Pie.

Irma Rosenthal, an educated and sophisticated German Jewish woman living in Chicago at the turn of the twentieth century, endeavored not only to learn to be an outstanding cook but also to create a cookbook. She never succeeded, but she put together a notebook full of manuscript recipes, some based on ones she found in newspapers and magazines, but others are likely hand-me-downs from her mother or even unique creations. Rosenthal married late for her time, at age twenty-seven in the year 1898, and had been a teacher previously, not focusing on cooking. When she got married, she set about learning to cook in a purposeful and almost academic way. Her cookbook was found in a box along with assorted diaries (including her daughter's, whose trip to the Edgewater Beach Hotel was described earlier). Rosenthal's recipe book is interesting both for its German Jewish recipes and the way it outlines the life of a housewife trying to build her skills and combine influences from her heritage and contemporary American upper-middle-class life, while at the same time attempting to limit spending. A menu of soup, veal, French potatoes, and green peas is written out on one page. A cutout recipe for "kisses," an economical meringue dessert that could be cooked in a still-warm oven after the evening's meal was prepared, is placed on another page. Elsewhere there is a recipe for "nasturtium sandwiches," white bread with butter and nasturtium flowers "seasoned with a dust of salt, pepper, and mustard, and . . . hid between the snowy slices."[67] Rosenthal undoubtedly grew the easily grown nasturtiums. A recipe for a more traditional German stuffed veal breast, using bacon both as a fat and as flavoring (Irma Rosenthal was a Reform Jew), also appears.[68]

While Irma Rosenthal's recipe book communicates much about the life and cooking habits of a Chicago housewife at the turn of the twentieth century, the life and cooking habits of Chicago communities are revealed in a different way in charity and community cookbooks. Charity cookbooks have a long history in Chicago. As early as 1891, a compilation of recipes from the South Chicago community was published for the benefit of its Congregational Church.[69] A recipe book benefiting the Chicago Women's Club kindergarten was released the same year. In the 1910s, two well-known charity cookbooks were published in Chicago. The *Bethany Union Cook Book*, first published in 1912, supporting the Bethany Union Church of the far South Side (and then relatively suburban) Washington Heights neighborhood, is conscious of its status as a community document as well as a cookbook. "As a neighborhood document, the careful reader may find in it material for many an interesting observation," reads the preface. The recipes from this upper-middle-class neighborhood are a mixture of standard fare, and recipes are included from the British, Irish, German, Dutch, Scandinavian, and other ethnicities that generally inhabited the community, and some newer recipes showing that food from other ethnicities was entering the community. In the meat section, for instance, there are recipes for Boiled Ham, Irish Stew-Mutton, Liver-Mexican Style, and Paprika Schnitzel. This is a particularly well-organized charity cookbook, organized and with an amount of recipes that mirrors encyclopedic cookbooks of the time. Interesting local advertisements are spread throughout, including one for a chain of four stores, all relatively nearby, selling chicken feed and supplies, indicating that many in the community were probably keeping chickens.[70] In 1919 the *Stevenson Cook Book* supported the Sarah Hackett Stevenson Memorial Lodging House for Women, a house for "the woman who is on the downward path of years, when it is so hard to find employment," as well as the "young girl who is alone" and "the mother who is alone." Located just to the south of the Prairie Avenue district, this book collects the recipes of a more urban upscale group of women than the *Bethany Union Cook Book*. There are recipes that seem to be focused on entertaining, including a variety of canapés including lobster, salmon, and salmon and tomato, as well as fancy main dishes such as Calve's [*sic*] Heart Stuffed and Braised. There are also a variety of Americanized ethnic recipes including three for chop suey, an Indian vegetable curry, Cuban rice, and Belgian Hare en Casserole. Despite this, many of the recipes are not at all fancy, such as Grandmother's Pork Noodles, pot roast, and luncheon beef.[71]

Charity and community cookbooks vary greatly in the quality of their recipes, but taken as a whole they give us a view of the variety of Chicago communities and their culinary histories, whether those communities were geographic communities or communities of interest. One particularly interesting example is *At Home on the Range*, a 1946 cookbook compiled during World War II by Chicago librarians to make money for gifts for soldiers but delayed in publishing due to short staffing during the war. An editorial note states a truth about many charity cookbooks: "The editors haven't the slightest idea as to what results you'll get by following Miss So-and-So's directions. All we can promise you is that none of the ingredients is immediately lethal." The recipes are interesting in that the librarians were from a variety of ethnicities from all over the city. They include both more ordinary recipes such as Chicken a la King, as well as gefilte fish and Norwegian pancakes.[72] The *Old Town Dusk until Dawn Cookbook*, mentioned earlier and published around 1970, was as much about the newly gentrifying urban North Side neighborhood. While there are everyday recipes, it contains recipes for a variety of cocktails, a variety of dishes for entertaining such as oysters Rockefeller and escargot, as well as a section titled "Dinners a Deux," which includes recipes for "a young man to serve a young lady of his choice."[73] Another community organization cookbook of note is the 1990s *Old Irving Park Association Cookbook*. In addition to featuring the alderman's recipe for Chicken Vesuvio described in chapter 6, it showed the variety of ethnicities living in the Northwest Side neighborhood at the time, from Grandmother's Buttermilk Pot Roast, contributed by a local resident who was also then the president of the National Livestock and Meat Board, to the Polish dish Zrazy Wrepczowezryzem (Pork and Rice Patties) to the Jewish meat, prune, carrot, and sweet potato specialty Tzimmes.[74] Church cookbooks, such as the 1994 *Irving Park Lutheran Church Cookbook*, often feature more specific ethnicities in addition to standard American dishes, in this case Swedish pancakes and other Scandinavian dishes.[75]

We will end this discussion, and this book, by highlighting two organizational cookbooks. Both of their subjects and the differences between them show Chicago as a place full of both wealth and poverty, with both signature events and foods, and people working hard to organize and improve the situation of their neighborhood or community. *One Magnificent Cookbook*, a hardcover and beautifully printed cookbook with many designer photographs, was released in 1988, one of a number of cookbooks released by the Junior League Club of Chicago to support their volunteer efforts. The cookbook was sponsored by companies such as Tiffany's and Bloomingdale's, and it features menus tied to particular Chicago events. Together, these menus suggest a year of social events for Chicago's wealthy, but it also mentions many of the city's landmark cultural institutions and traditions. They include an "Architectural Walking Tour Luncheon," an "After the Hockey Game Party," a "Chicago's Marathon Salad Buffet," and the "Lyric Opera Opening Late-Night Supper." While the cookbook may not celebrate Chicago's diversity, and such events as the opera opening or a "Fourth of July Sailing Party" to view the fireworks, are certainly not affordable to most Chicagoans, events such as the fireworks over the lake, cultural landmarks such as the city's famous architecture, the Lyric Opera (as well as the Chicago Symphony, which has its own meal), and Chicago sporting events would appear on the list of what many or most Chicagoans enjoy most about their city. Experiencing these events is often tied to particular culinary traditions, whether a picnic in Grant Park, dinner at a downtown restaurant before a concert, or going to a bar to watch a Blackhawks or Bears game.[76] At the other end of the organizational cookbook spectrum, at least for production value, is the typewritten 1970 *Chicago American Indian Center Cookbook*, created to support the center, located in the Uptown neighborhood, and to help establish a library and museum there. It was the result of a center-sponsored recipe contest to collect Native American recipes. The winners were a Chippewa (Ojibway), who submitted an Indian Wild Rice Hot Dish; an Oneida who submitted an Indian Plum Pudding; and a Winnebago (Ho-Chunk) who submitted Indian Corn Soup. The preface describes the center, which is the oldest Native American Center in the country and had then just recently acquired a permanent location, and its services, including summer programs for children, family counseling, sports leagues, and tribe-based social groups. The recipes include a variety of breads, including a number of recipes for fry bread; game recipes including porcupine, raccoon, and moose; soups; and a number of wild rice dishes.[77] The cookbook is interesting in that its use of food specifically for organizing, to help bring a community together, and to help support a community center, focused on a particular ethnic group. Such ties between food, organizing, and ethnicity are a Chicago tradition in the neighborhoods just as much as attending the opening of the Lyric Opera might be for the wealthy. Chicagoans are intensely proud of their cultural landmarks and events, and they flock downtown to take part in them. Back in the neighborhoods, though, people still often focus on their particular ethnic group, their church, or their neighborhood organization, and they continue to use food to organize, to accompany meetings, and to mark special events. The goal of this food biography of Chicago is to provide an introduction to the evolution of Chicago's culinary traditions across the multiplicity of scales in which they operate, and to reveal an unorthodox history of Chicago itself by pondering these culinary traditions.

NOTES

INTRODUCTION

1. Daniel H. Burnham and Edward H. Bennett, *Plan of Chicago*, ed. Charles Moore (Chicago: Commercial Club of Chicago, 1909; reprint, with an introduction by Kristin Schaffer, New York: Princeton Architectural Press, 1993).

2. Daniel H. Burnham Jr. and Robert Kingery, *Planning the Region of Chicago*, eds. John Barstow Morrill and Paul O. Fischer. Prepared under the direction of the Chicago Regional Planning Association (Chicago: Chicago Regional Planning Association, 1956).

3. Richard Florida, "What Is the World's Most Economically Powerful City?" *The Atlantic*, May 8, 2012, www.theatlantic.com/business/archive/2012/05/what-is-the-worlds-most-economically-powerful-city/256841/.

4. William Cronon, *Nature's Metropolis: Chicago and the Great West* (New York: W. W. Norton & Company, 1991).

I. THE MATERIAL RESOURCES

1. Libby Hill, *The Chicago River: A Natural and Unnatural History* (Chicago: Lake Claremont Press, 2000).

2. Dominic A. Pacyga, *Chicago: A Biography* (Chicago: University of Chicago Press, 2009).

3. Quoted in Bessie Louise Pierce and Joe Lester Norris, *As Others See Chicago: Impressions of Visitors, 1673–1933* (1933, reprint, with a forward by Perry Duis, Chicago: University of Chicago Press, 2004), 25.

4. Pacyga, *Chicago*; Robert A. Holland, *Chicago in Maps: 1612 to 2002* (New York: Rizzoli, 2005).

5. Holland, *Chicago in Maps*.

6. Bessie Louise Pierce, *A History of Chicago, Volume II: From Town to City* (Chicago: University of Chicago Press, 1940).

7. John C. Hudson, *Chicago: A Geography of the City and Its Region* (Santa Fe: Center for American Places and Chicago: University of Chicago Press, 2006).

8. William Cronon, *Nature's Metropolis: Chicago and the Great West* (New York: W. W. Norton and Company, 1991).

9. Pacyga, *Chicago*; Holland, *Chicago in Maps*.

10. Pierce, *A History of Chicago, Volume II: From Town to City*.

11. Holland, *Chicago in Maps*; Hill, *The Chicago River*.

12. Hill, *The Chicago River*.

13. Quoted in Pierce and Norris, *As Others See Chicago*, 14.

14. Hill, *The Chicago River*, 13.

15. Bessie Louise Pierce, *A History of Chicago, Volume I: The Beginning of a City, 1673–1848* (1937, reprint, Chicago: University of Chicago Press, 2007), 30.

16. Quoted in Bessie Louise Pierce, *As Others See Chicago: Impressions of Visitors, 1673–1933*, 45.

17. Charles Cleaver, *Reminiscences of Chicago during the Forties and Fifties*, with an introduction by Mabel McIlvaine (Chicago: Lakeside Press, 1913), 44.

18. *Reminiscences of Chicago during the Forties and Fifties*, 44.

19. Hill, *The Chicago River*, 113.

20. Richard Lanyon, *Building the Canal to Save Chicago* (Bloomington, IN: Xlibris Corporation, 2012).

21. Hudson, *Chicago: A Geography of the City*.

22. Holland, *Chicago in Maps*.

23. Pierce, *A History of Chicago, Vol. I: The Beginning of a City, 1673–1848*, 44.

24. Holland, *Chicago in Maps*.

25. Charles Bartlett Diaries, Chicago History Museum Archives and Library.

26. Pierce, *A History of Chicago, Vol. I: The Beginning of a City, 1673–1848*, 52.

27. *Reminiscences of Chicago during the Forties and Fifties*, with an introduction by Mabel McIlvaine (Chicago: Lakeside Press, 1913), 40.

28. Cronon, *Nature's Metropolis*; Pierce, *A History of Chicago, Volume II: From Town to City*.

29. Pacyga, *Chicago*.

30. Hill, *The Chicago River*.

31. Perry R. Duis, *Challenging Chicago: Coping with Everyday Life, 1837–1920* (Urbana and Chicago: University of Illinois Press, 1998).

32. Edna Ferber, *So Big* (1924; reprint, New York: Harper Perennial Modern Classics, 2010).

33. Joseph Calvin Buford, *Vegetable Production and Marketing in the Chicago Area—A Geographical Study* (Normal, IL: Illinois State Normal University Studies in Education 15, 1947).

34. Buford, *Vegetable Production and Marketing*.

35. Thomas McGowen, *Island within a City* (Harwood Heights, IL: Eisenhower Public Library District, 1989), 57.

36. McGowen, *Island within a City*, 58.

37. McGowen, *Island within a City*, 78.

38. Edward A. Duddy, *Agriculture in the Chicago Region* (Chicago: University of Chicago Press, 1929).

39. Quoted in R. U. Piper, *Diseased Milk and the Flesh of Animals Used for Human Food* (Chicago: Jameson and Morse, 1879). Chicago History Museum, 27–28.

40. Edward G. Ward, *Milk Transportation: Freight Rates to the Largest Fifteen Cities in the United States* (Washington, DC: U.S. Department of Agriculture, Division of Statistics Bulletin 25), 1903.

41. Daniel R. Block, "Protecting and Connecting: Separation, Connection, and the United States Dairy Economy, 1840–2002," *Journal for the Study of Food and Society* 6 (2002): 22–30.

42. Quoted in Judith Walzer Leavitt, *The Healthiest City: Milwaukee and the Politics of Health Reform* (Princeton, NJ: Princeton University Press, 1982), 169.

43. Milton J. Rosenau, *The Milk Question* (London: Constable, 1913), 261.

44. Rosenau, *The Milk Question*, 259.

45. Daniel R. Block, "Public Health, Cooperatives, Local Regulation, and the Development of Modern Milk Policy: The Chicago Milkshed, 1900–1940," *Journal of Historical Geography* 35 (2009): 128–53.

46. Block, "Public Health, Cooperatives, Local Regulation."

47. Heather Lalley and Brendan Lekan, *Chicago's Homegrown Cookbook: Local Food, Local Restaurants, Local Recipes* (Minneapolis: Voyageur Press, 2011), 76.

48. The South Fork of the South Branch of the Chicago River was called "Bubbly Creek" due to the bubbles that rose from the carcasses, offal, and other waste that was concentrated in it during the heyday of the Chicago Union Stockyards in the late 1800s and the early 1900s. Bubbles still occasionally rise to the surface, even though the stockyards have been closed since 1971. Michael Hawthorne, "A Truly Foul, Nasty River Ran Through It: Even Bubbly Creek, Worst of Worst, Was Never Cleaned Up." *Chicago Tribune,* June 25, 2011. articles.

chicagotribune.com/2011-06-25/news/ct-per-flashback-bubbly-0626-2-
20110625_1_offal-and-carcasses-bubbly-creek-chicago-river, accessed April 17,
2015.

2. INDIGENOUS FOODWAYS
OF CHICAGO

1. Helen Hornbeck Tanner, "Tribal Mixtures in Chicago Area Indian Villages," in *Indians of the Chicago Area*, 2nd ed., edited by Terry Strauss (Chicago: NAES College Press, 1990), 18–21.

2. Charles E. Cleland, "Indians in a Changing Environment," in *The Great
Lakes Forests: An Environmental and Social History*, ed. Susan L. Flader (Minneapolis, MN: University of Minnesota Press, 1983), 83–95.

3. Steven R. Kuehn, "New Evidence for Late Paleoindian-Early Archaic
Subsistence Behavior in the Western Great Lakes," *American Antiquity* 63, no. 3
(1998): 458.

4. Charles W. Markman, *Chicago Before History: The Prehistoric Archaeology of a Modern Metropolitan Area* (Springfield, IL: Illinois Historic Preservation Agency, 1991), 44–46.

5. Kuehn, "New Evidence for Late Paleoindian-Early Archaic Subsistence
Behavior," 468–71.

6. Markman, *Chicago Before History*, 47.

7. Kuehn, "New Evidence for Late Paleoindian-Early Archaic Subsistence
Behavior," 471.

8. Kathryn E. Parker, "The Archaeobotany of the Paleo-Indian and Archaic
Components at the Christianson Site," *Journal of the Illinois Archaeology Survey*
18 (2006).

9. E. Barrie Kavasch, *Native Harvests: American Indian Wild Foods and
Recipes* (Mineola, NY: Dover Publications, 2005).

10. Mary L. Simon, "A Regional and Chronological Synthesis of Archaic
Period Plant Use in the Midcontinent," in *Archaic Societies: Diversity and Com-
plexity across the Midcontinent*, eds. Thomas E. Emerson, Dale L. McElrath, and
Andrew C. Fortier (Albany, NY: SUNY Press, 2009), 81–114.

11. C. Russell Stafford, "Archaic Period Logistical Foraging Strategies in
West-Central Illinois," *Midcontinental Journal of Archaeology* 16 (1991):
212–46; Christopher R. Moore and Victoria G. Dekle, "Hickory Nuts, Bulk
Processing and the Advent of Early Horticultural Economies in Eastern North
America," *World Archaeology* 42 (2010): 595–608.

12. Markman, *Chicago Before History*, 54.

13. Moore and Dekle, "Hickory Nuts, Bulk Processing," 595–608; Stafford, "Archaic Period Logistical Foraging Strategies in West Central Illinois," 595–608.

14. Simon, "Archaic Period Plant Use in the Midcontinent," 94.

15. Simon, "Archaic Period Plant Use in the Midcontinent," 91.

16. Bruce D. Smith and Richard A. Yarnell, "Initial Formation of an Indigenous Crop Complex in Eastern North America at 3800 B.P.," in *Proceedings of the National Academy of Sciences* 106 (2009): 6564–65.

17. Parker, "Archaeobotany of the Paleo-Indian," 122–48.

18. Markman, *Chicago Before History*, 54–59.

19. Markman, *Chicago Before History*, 61.

20. David L. Asch and Nancy B. Asch, "Prehistoric Plant Cultivation in West-Central Illinois," in *Prehistoric Food Production in North America*, ed. Richard I. Ford (Ann Arbor: Museum of Anthropology Anthropological Papers 75, University of Michigan, 1985), 149–204. Production of some of these crops in Illinois date back to the Late Archaic period. Smith and Yarnell, "Initial Formation of an Indigenous Crop Complex," 6561–66; Parker, "Archaeobotany of the Paleo-," 122; Paula J. Porubcan, Peter J. Geraci, and Melissa L. Baltus, "The Bottlemy Site (11MH495): An Emerging and Mature Late Woodland Occupation in Northeastern Illinois," *Illinois Archaeological Survey, Inc., Illinois Archaeology* 22 (2010): 600.

21. Bruce Smith, *Rivers of Change: Essays on Early Agriculture in Eastern North America* (Birmingham: University of Alabama Press, 1992), 193–97; Patricia S. Bridges, John H. Blitz, and Martin C. Solano, "Changes in Long Bone Diaphyseal Strength with Horticultural Intensification in West-Central Illinois," *American Journal of Physical Anthropology* 112 (2000): 217–38.

22. Jared Diamond, *Guns, Germs, and Steel: The Fates of Human Societies* (New York: W. W. Norton & Company, 1998), 151.

23. Thomas J. Riley, Gregory R. Walz, Charles J. Bareis, Andrew C. Fortier, and Kathryn E. Parker, "Accelerator Mass Spectrometry (AMS) Dates Confirm Early Zea Mays in the Mississippi Valley," *American Antiquity* 59 (1994): 490–98.

24. Mary L. Simon, "Regional Variations in Plant Use Strategies in the Midwest During the Late Woodland," in *Late Woodland Societies: Tradition and Transformation Across the Midcontinent*, eds. Thomas E. Emerson, Dale L. McElrath, and Andrew C. Fortier (Lincoln, NE: University of Nebraska Press, 2000), 47–59.

25. Markman, *Chicago Before History*, 77.

26. Markman, *Chicago Before History*, 99.

27. "Hoxie Farm and Huber: Two Upper Mississippian Archaeological Sites in Cook County, Illinois," in *At the Edge of Prehistory, Huber Phase Archaeolo-*

gy in the Chicago Area, ed. James A. Brown and Patricia J. O'Brien (Kampsville: Center for American Archeology Press, 1990), 3–119; "The Oak Forest Site: Investigations into Oneota Subsistence-Settlement in the Cal-Sag Area of Cook County, Illinois," in *At the Edge of Prehistory: Huber Phase Archaeology in the Chicago Area*, ed. James A. Brown and Patricia J. O'Brien (Kampsville: Center for American Archeology Press, 1990), 241–65.

28. Brown and O'Brien, *At the Edge of Prehistory*, 91–98.

29. Charles M. Slaymaker III and Charles M. Slaymaker Jr., with appendices by Hugh Cutler and Leonard Blake and Charles F. Meres, "Au Sagaunashke Village: The Upper Mississippian Occupation of the Knoll Spring Site, Cook County, Illinois," in *Mississippian Site Archaeology in Illinois I, Site Reports from the St. Louis and Chicago Areas, Bulletin No. 8* (University of Illinois, Urbana: Illinois Archaeological Survey, Inc., 1971), 244–46.

30. Markman, *Chicago Before History*, 107.

31. Markman, *Chicago Before History*, 108.

32. Helen Hornbeck Tanner and Miklos Pinther, *Atlas of the Great Lakes Indian History* (Norman, OK: University of Oklahoma Press, 1987), 29.

33. Markman, *Chicago Before History*, 112.

34. Charles S. Winslow, *Indians of the Chicago Region* (Chicago: Charles S. Winslow, 1946), 10; William Duncan Strong, *The Indian Tribes of the Chicago Region* (Chicago: Field Museum of Natural History, 1938), 7.

35. Stewart Rafert, *The Miami Indians of Indiana: A Persistent People, 1654–1994* (Indianapolis: Indiana Historical Society, 1996), 10.

36. R. David Edmonds, "Chicago in the Middle Ground," in *Encyclopedia of Chicago*, encyclopedia.chicagohistory.org/pages/254.html, accessed August 23, 2013.

37. Milo Milton Quaife, *Chicago and the Old Northwest, 1673–1835: A Study of the Evolution of the Northwestern Frontier, Together with a History of Fort Dearborn* (1913, reprint, Urbana: University of Illinois Press, 2001), 42.

38. W. Vernon Kinietz and Antoine Denis Raudot, *The Indians of the Western Great Lakes, 1615–1760* (Ann Arbor, MI: University of Michigan Press, 1991), 172; Jay Miller, "Land and Lifeway in the Chicago Area: Chicago and the Illinois-Miami," in *Indians of the Chicago Area*, ed. Terry Strauss (Chicago: NAES College Press, 1990), 83.

39. Michigan Historical Commission, "Michigan Pioneer and Historical Society," in *Michigan Historical Collections 21* (Ann Arbor: University of Michigan Library, 2006), 491, quod.lib.umich.edu/cgi/t/text/text-idx?c=moa;idno=0534625.0021.001, accessed September 1, 2014.

40. Kinietz, *The Indians of the Western Great Lakes*, 173; Emma Helen Blair, trans., *The Indian Tribes of the Upper Mississippi Valley and Region of the Great Lakes* (Cleveland: Arthur H. Clark Company, 1911), archive.org/stream/

indiantribesofup01blaiiala/indiantribesofup01blaiiala_djvu.txt, accessed July 1, 2014.

41. Rafert, *The Miami Indians of Indiana*, 12.

42. Kinietz, *The Indians of the Western Great Lakes*, 175.

43. Janet C. Gilmore, "*Sagamité* and *Booya*: French Influence in Defining Great Lakes Culinary Heritage," *Material Culture Review* 60 (2004): 9.

44. Kinietz, *The Indians of the Western Great Lakes*, 175.

45. McCafferty notes that Chicago is "the word for the striped skunk (Mephitis) in Miami-Illinois," an Eastern Great Lakes Algonquian language, but that the term also refers to *Allium tricoccum* (wild leek) as determined by Swenson. Chicago today is commonly thought of as the place of the wild onion (or garlic). Michael McCafferty, "A Fresh Look at the Place Named Chicago," *Journal of the Illinois State Historical Society* 95 (2003): 117; John F. Swenson, "Chicagoua/Chicago: The Origin, Meaning, and Etymology of a Place Name," *Illinois Historical Journal* 84 (1991): 235–48.

46. Tanner, *Atlas of the Great Lakes Indian History*, 42.

47. Tanner, *Atlas of the Great Lakes Indian History*, 42.

48. Tanner, *Atlas of the Great Lakes Indian History*, 63; Quaife, *Chicago and the Old Northwest*, 83; Virgil Vogel, "The Tribes," in *Indians of the Chicago Area*, ed. Terry Strauss (Chicago: NAES College Press, 1990), 8.

49. Helen Hornbeck Tanner, "Tribal Mixtures in Chicago Area Indian Villages," in *Indians of the Chicago Area*, ed. Terry Strauss, 18–21 (Chicago: NAES College Press, 1990), 20.

50. Huron Smith, "Ethnobotany of the Forest Potawatomi Indians," *Bulletin of the Public Museum of the City of Milwaukee* 7 (1933): 104; Andrew Smith and Bruce Kraig, *The Oxford Encyclopedia of Food and Drink in America, Volume 1* (New York: Oxford University Press, 2004), 683.

51. Albert Ernest Jenks, "The Wild Rice Gatherers of the Upper Lakes: A Study in American Primitive Economics," *Annual Report of the Bureau of American Ethnology to the Secretary of the Smithsonian Institution* 19, Part 2 (Washington, DC: Government Printing Office, 1900), 1053–69.

52. James A. Clifton, George Cornell, and James M. McClurken, *People of the Three Fires: The Ottawa, Potawatomi, and Ojibway of Michigan* (Grand Rapids, MI: Michigan Indian Press, 1986), 43.

53. Ann Durkin Keating, *Rising Up from Indian Country: The Battle of Fort Dearborn and the Birth of Chicago* (Chicago: University of Chicago Press, 2012), 31.

54. Keating, *Rising Up from Indian Country*, 24; R. David Edmonds, "Chicago in the Middle Ground," in *Encyclopedia of Chicago*, encyclopedia. chicagohistory.org/pages/254.html, accessed August 23, 2013.

55. Keating, *Rising Up from Indian Country*, 56.

56. Keating, *Rising Up from Indian Country*, 65.

57. Keating, *Rising Up from Indian Country*, 119.

58. Jacqueline Peterson, "The Founding Fathers: The Absorption of the French-Indian Chicago, 1816–1837," in *Ethnic Chicago: A Multicultural Portrait*, edited by Melvin G. Holli and Peter d'A. Jones (Grand Rapids, MI: Wm. B. Eerdmans Publishing Company, 1995), 22.

59. Alfred Theodore Andreas, *History of Chicago, Volume I* (New York: Arno Press, 1884), 104–7.

60. Quaife, *Chicago and the Old Northwest*, 328.

61. Bessie Louise Pierce, *A History of Chicago, Volume I: The Beginning of a City, 1673–1848* (Chicago: University of Chicago Press, originally published 1937, reprinted 2007), 44.

62. Andreas, *History of Chicago*, 180.

63. Pierce, *A History of Chicago, Volume I*, 48–49.

3. MIGRATION AND THE MAKING
OF CHICAGO FOODWAYS

1. Bessie Louise Pierce, *A History of Chicago, Volume II: From Town to City, 1848–1871* (1940, reprint Chicago: University of Chicago Press, 2007), 44.

2. William Cronon, *Nature's Metropolis: Chicago and the Great West* (New York: W. W. Norton and Company, 1991), 45–46.

3. Saint Andrew's Day "Feast of the Haggis," Chicago Scots, www.chicagoscots.org/feastofhaggis/, accessed July 30, 2014.

4. Cronon, *Nature's Metropolis*, 54–93.

5. Tom Campbell, *Fighting Slavery in Chicago: Abolitionists, the Law of Slavery, and Lincoln* (Richmond, BC: Ampersand, Inc., 2009), 72–73.

6. Mike Danahey and Allison Hantschel, *Chicago's Historic Irish Pubs* (Mount Pleasant, SC: Arcadia Publishing, 2011), 7; Carlyn Berghoff, Jan Berghoff, and Nancy Ross Ryan, *The Berghoff Family Cookbook: From Our Table to Yours, Celebrating a Century of Entertaining* (Riverside, NJ: Andrews McNeel Publishing), 28.

7. Máirtín Mac Con Iomaire and Pádraic Óg Gallagher, "Irish Corned Beef: A Culinary History," *Journal of Culinary Science and Technology* 9 (2011): 27–43.

8. Berghoff Restaurant and Catering Group, www.theberghoff.com/berghoff-restaurant/, accessed July 30, 2014.

9. Danahey and Hantschel, *Chicago's Historic Irish Pubs*, 12.

10. Cronon, *Nature's Metropolis*, 318.

11. Irving Cutler, *The Jews of Chicago: From Shtetl to Suburb* (Champaign, IL: University of Illinois Press, 2008), 9–27.

12. Herbert Eiseman and Jerold Levin, "Hot Dog! Jewish Participation in Chicago's Meat Industry," *Chicago Jewish History*, Chicago Jewish Historical Society, 36 (2012): 6–7, chicagojewishhistory.org/pdf/2012/CJH-2_2012.pdf, accessed July 30, 2014; one of Morris's bookkeepers, Nicholas Pritzker, a Jewish immigrant from Kiev, was the grandfather to the founders of the Hyatt Hotel chain.

13. Susan Berger, "The End of a Chicago Tradition: Is Absolutely Nothing Sacred?," *Chicago Tribune*, January 23, 2009, www.bergerreport.com/chicago-tribune-oped-the-end-of-a-chicago-tradition-1.html, accessed July 30, 2014.

14. Eiseman and Levin, "Hot Dog!" 8.

15. Pierce, *A History of Chicago, Volume II*, 187.

16. Joseph Gustaitis, *Chicago's Greatest Year, 1893: The White City and the Birth of a Modern Metropolis* (Carbondale, IL: Southern Illinois University Press, 2013), 211.

17. Bob Skilnik, *The History of Beer and Brewing in Chicago, 1833–1978* (West Conshohocken, PA: Infinity Publishing, 2002), 122.

18. Bob Skilnik, "Building Chicago Was Thirsty Work: Brewers Rolled in with a Solution," *Chicago Tribune*, July 16, 1997, articles.chicagotribune.com/1997-07-16/entertainment/9707170336_1_beer-chicagoans-first-brew-pub, accessed July 30, 2014.

19. "German Industry and Its Results: A Visit to the Brewery of Mr. John A. Huck," *Illinois Staats-Zeitung*, May 16, 1863, flps.newberry.org/article/5418474_6_1468, accessed July 30, 2014.

20. Joseph C. Heinen, *Lost German Chicago* (Mount Pleasant, SC: Arcadia Publishing, 2009), 43.

21. Heinen, *Lost German Chicago*, 79.

22. Royal L. Melendy, "The Saloon in Chicago," *American Journal of Sociology* 6 (1900): 304.

23. "Marigold Arena Sold for Use as Church," *Chicago Tribune*, April 4, 1963, 2A, archives.chicagotribune.com/1963/04/04/page/105/article/marigold-arena-sold-for-use-as-church, accessed July 30, 2014.

24. Edward R. Kantowicz, "Polish Chicago: Survival through Solidarity," in *Ethnic Chicago: A Multicultural Portrait*, edited by Melvin G. Holli and Peter d'Alroy Jones (Grand Rapids, MI: William B. Eerdmans Publishing Company, 1995), 174.

25. Dominic A. Pacyga, *Polish Immigrants and Industrial Chicago: Workers on the South Side, 1880–1922* (Chicago, IL: University of Chicago Press, 2003), 251.

26. Royal L. Melendy, "The Saloon in Chicago, IL," *American Journal of Sociology* 6 (1901): 455.

27. Pacyga, *Polish Immigrants and Industrial Chicago*, 138.

28. Joseph W. Zurawski, *Polish Chicago: Our History, Our Recipes* (St. Louis, MO: G. Bradley Publishing, 2007), 170–74.

29. "Development of Polish Business in Chicago White Eagle Brewing Company Worth More Than Half Million Dollars," *Dziennik Związkowy*, August 11, 1917, flps.newberry.org/article/5423968_4_1721, accessed July 30, 2014.

30. Leon T. Zglenicki, *Poles of Chicago, 1837–1937: A History of One Century of Polish Contribution to the City of Chicago, Illinois* (Chicago, IL: Polish Pageant, Inc., 1937), 16.

31. Pacyga, *Polish Immigrants and Industrial Chicago*, xi.

32. Irving Cutler, *The Jews of Chicago: From Shtetl to Suburb* (Champaign, IL: University of Illinois Press, 2008), 222.

33. David R. Roediger, *Working toward Whiteness: How America's Immigrants Became White: The Strange Journey from Ellis Island to the Suburbs* (New York: Basic Books, 2006).

34. Christopher Robert Reed, *Black Chicago's First Century, Volume 1* (Columbia, MO: University of Missouri Press, 2005), 71.

35. David A. Joens, *From Slave to State Legislator: John W. E. Thomas, Illinois' First African American Lawmaker* (Carbondale, IL: Southern Illinois University Press, 2012).

36. Reed, *Black Chicago's First Century*, 67.

37. Reed, *Black Chicago's First Century*, 261–63.

38. Sidney Mintz, *Tasting Food, Tasting Freedom* (Boston, MA: Beacon Press, 1996), 33–49.

39. James R. Grossman, *Land of Hope: Chicago, Black Southerners, and the Great Migration* (Chicago, IL: University of Chicago Press, 1991), 155.

40. Andrew Warnes, *Savage Barbecue: Race, Culture, and the Invention of America's First Food* (Athens, GA: University of Georgia Press, 2008), 20–21.

41. Mary Owen, "Leon Finney Sr.: 1916–2008 Founded Leon's Bar-B-Q," *Chicago Tribune*, articles.chicagotribune.com/2008-04-06/news/0804050372_1_mr-finney-restaurants-eldest-son, accessed July 30, 2014.

42. "Lem's Bar-B-Q," www.youtube.com/watch?v=3FSKgNQO2sg or www.southernfoodways.org/interview/lems-bar-b-q/, accessed July 30, 2014.

43. Michael Gebert, "A Barbecue History of Chicago," *Sky Full of Bacon 17*, skyfullofbacon.com/blog/, accessed July 30, 2014. The increasing popularity of barbecuing among Americans in the 1940s and 1950s led to the invention of the kettle grill with a tight lid. In the early 1950s, George Stephen, an employee of the Chicago-based Weber Metal Works, cut a metal buoy in half to create the Weber grill now used by millions.

44. Mike Royko, "Erasing Thoughts of Meatless Ribs," *Chicago Tribune*, September 23, 1986, articles.chicagotribune.com/1986-09-23/news/ 8603110160_1_vegetarians-gluten-sauce, accessed July 30, 2014.

45. William Swislow, "Neighborhood Flavor Spices Up Restaurants," *Chicago Tribune*, March 17, 1993, articles.chicagotribune.com/1993-03-17/news/ 9303180061_1_bridgeport-prime-rib-neighborhood, accessed July 30, 2014.

46. Matthew Frye Jacobson, *Whiteness of a Different Color: European Immigrants and the Alchemy of Race* (Cambridge, MA: Harvard University, 1999), 3–4.

47. Robert M. Lombardo, "Chicago's Little Sicily," *Journal of the Illinois State Historical Society* 100 (2007): 41–56.

48. Vincenza Scarpaci, *The Journey of the Italians in America* (Gretna, LA: Pelican Publishing Company, 2008), 280; www.gonnella.com.

49. Diane Gannon, Gloria Baraks, Mark Weinstein, and Liz Roy, *The Foods of Chicago: A Delicious History* (St. Louis, MO: G. Bradley Publishing, 2007), 70; www.alsbeef.com.

50. Graydon Megan, "Sam Ricobene Sr., 1931–2011: Restaurateur Helped Build Ricobene's into Chain," *Chicago Tribune*, October 22, 2011, articles. chicagotribune.com/2011-10-22/news/ct-met-obit-ricobene-1023-20111022_1_ gonnella-baking-new-restaurant-twin-brother, accessed on July 30, 2014.

51. Huping Ling, *Chinese Chicago: Race, Transnational Migration, and Community since 1870* (Redwood City, CA: Stanford University Press, 2012), 33–34.

52. Ling, *Chinese Chicago*, 34–35.

53. Ling, *Chinese Chicago*, 38.

54. "1889, The Clark Street Chinatown Reaches Maturity," Chinese-American Museum of Chicago, www.ccamuseum.org/index.php/en/research/ research-before-1900/139-1889-the-clark-street-chinatown-reaches-maturity, accessed July 30, 2014.

55. "Gleeful Celestials Chicago Chinamen Celebrate Their New-Year's Festival," *Chicago Tribune*, January 20, 1890, Newberry Library, flps.newberry.org/ article/5418479_0251/, accessed July 30, 2014.

56. Chuimei Ho and Soo Lon Moy, *Chinese in Chicago, 1870–1945* (Mount Pleasant, SC: Arcadia Publishing, 2005), 60.

57. Susan Moy, "The Chinese in Chicago: The First One Hundred Years," in *Ethnic Chicago, A Multicultural Portrait*, edited by Melvin G. Holli and Peter d'A. Jones (Grand Rapids, MI: Wm. B. Eerdmans Publishing Co., 1995), 398.

58. Gabriela F. Arredondo, *Mexican Chicago: Race, Identity, and Nation, 1916–39* (Champaign, IL: University of Illinois Press, 2008), 171.

59. John Drury, *Dining in Chicago* (New York: John Day Company, 1931), 172.

60. Steven Pratt, "Hidden Gems: Smaller Firms Thrive with Loyalty, Quality Tortillas Became 'a Miracle' for an Immigrant," *Chicago Tribune*, May 6, 1993, articles.chicagotribune.com/1993-05-06/entertainment/9305070416_1_tortilla-factory-tortilleria-el-milagro, accessed July 30, 2014.

61. Judy Hevrdejs, "26th Street !sass! This Southwest Side Neighborhood Offers a Culinary Adventure for the Senses," *Chicago Tribune*, September 22, 1988, articles.chicagotribune.com/1988-09-22/entertainment/8802010409_1_street-vendors-main-shop, accessed on July 30, 2014.

62. Nilda Flores-Gonzalez, "Paseo Boricua: Claiming a Puerto Rican Space in Chicago," *Centro Journal* 2 (2001).

63. Milo Milton Quaife, "Property of Jean Baptiste Point Sable," *Mississippi Valley Historical Review* 15 (1928): 90–91.

4. MARKETS AND RETAIL

1. William Cronon, *Nature's Metropolis: Chicago and the Great West* (New York: W. W. Norton and Company, 1991).

2. Daniel Block, Noel Chávez, and Judy Birgen, *Finding Food in Chicago and the Suburbs* (Chicago: Chicago State University, 2008).

3. Bessie Louise Pierce, *A History of Chicago, Volume I: The Beginning of a City, 1673–1848* (1937, reprint Chicago: University of Chicago Press, 2007), 44.

4. A. T. Andreas, *History of Chicago, Volume I* (New York: Arno Press, 1884), 180.

5. Pierce, *A History of Chicago, Volume I*, 48–49.

6. Pierce, *A History of Chicago, Volume I*, 51.

7. Pierce, *A History of Chicago, Volume I*, 126–27.

8. Charles Cleaver, extracts from an article appearing first in the *Chicago Tribune*, in *Reminiscences of Chicago during the Forties and Fifties*, with an introduction by Mabel McIlvane (Chicago: Lakeside Press, 1913), 74–75.

9. Andreas, *History of Chicago, Volume I*, 458.

10. Andreas, *History of Chicago, Volume I*, 104–7.

11. Harmon Account Books and Papers, vol. 1, Mar. 1834–Jan. 1839, Charles L. Harmon Papers, Chicago History Museum, Chicago.

12. Andreas, *History of Chicago, Volume I*, 203.

13. Cleaver, Extracts, *Reminiscences of Chicago during the Forties and Fifties*, 74–75.

14. Harmon to Randall, Oct. 20, 1846, Charles L. Harmon Papers, Letter Books, vol. 8, Microfilm Reel 3 of 10, Chicago History Museum.

15. Harmon to Boyd, Dec. 4, 1848, Charles L. Harmon Papers, Letter Books, vol. 8, Microfilm Reel 3 of 10, Chicago History Museum.

16. Harmon to Montgomery, Oct. 13, 1846, Charles L. Harmon Papers, Letter Books, vol. 8, Microfilm Reel 3 of 10, Chicago History Museum.

17. Harmon to Howard, Nov. 3, 1846, Charles L. Harmon Papers, Letter Books, vol. 8, Microfilm Reel 3 of 10, Chicago History Museum.

18. Harmon to Waring, Feb. 7, 1848, Charles L. Harmon Papers, Letter Books, vol. 8, Box 2 of 7, Chicago History Museum.

19. Harmon to Panl?, Dec. 19, 1846, Letter Books, vol. 8, Microfilm Reel 3 of 10, Chicago History Museum.

20. Harmon to Bennett, Oct. 29, 1846, Letter Books, vol. 8, Microfilm Reel 3 of 10, Chicago History Museum.

21. Harmon to Kensett, Dec. 8, 1848, and Sales Statement, Nov. 30, 1848, Letter Books, vol. 8, Box 2 of 7, Charles Loomis Harmon Papers, Chicago History Museum.

22. Account Book for Schooner Racer, Harding and Hall Papers, Chicago History Museum.

23. "Chicago as a Jobbing Center," *The Grocer's Bulletin* 1, no. 1 (April 21, 1881), Chicago, IL: 1.

24. Cronon, *Nature's Metropolis*, 91–92.

25. Bessie Louise Pierce, *A History of Chicago, Vol. II: From Town to City, 1848–1871* (Chicago: University of Chicago Press, [1940] 2007), 111.

26. Perry R. Duis, *Challenging Chicago: Coping with Everyday Life, 1837–1920* (Urbana and Chicago: University of Illinois Press, 1998), 116.

27. "Review of the Markets," *The Chicago Grocer* 4, no. 24 (February 7, 1878): 10.

28. Edward M. Steele, "Great Oaks from Little Acorns Grow," Reprint from the *Wholesale Grocer News*, September 1942, Steele-Wedeles Papers, Chicago History Museum.

29. Chilton Gano, "Chicago Jobber Making History," April 1918, unknown newspaper, Steele-Wedeles Papers, Chicago History Museum.

30. Steele-Wedeles Company to Grocers, Dec. 1885, Steele-Wedeles Papers, Chicago History Museum.

31. Steele-Wedeles Company to Adler, Nov. 8, 1901, Steele-Wedeles Papers, Chicago History Museum.

32. *City within a City: The Biography of Chicago's Marina City: A Brief History of 300 North State Street.* www.marinacity.org/history/story/300_north. htm Accessed May 2, 2015.

33. Edna Ferber, *So Big* (New York: P. F. Collier and Son, 1924), 175.

34. Duis, *Challenging Chicago*, 116.

35. Duis, *Challenging Chicago: Coping with Everyday Life*, 116.

36. Bessie Louis Pierce, *A History of Chicago, Vol. III: The Rise of a Modern City, 1871–1893* (Chicago: University of Chicago Press, [1957] 2007), 184–85.

37. Ferber, *So Big*, 190.

38. *Chicago Tribune*, February 7, 1897, quoted in Duis, *Challenging Chicago*, 117.

39. Cronon, *Nature's Metropolis*, 107.

40. Duis, *Challenging Chicago*, 123.

41. James D. Butterworth, "A Study of the Changes in the Volume of Fresh Fruits and Vegetables Handled by Middlemen Operating in the Chicago South Water Market, 1939–1949" (PhD diss., Northwestern University, 1950), 21.

42. Special Announcement, May 19, 1909, Steele-Wedeles Papers, Chicago History Museum.

43. Duis, *Challenging Chicago*, 124.

44. U.S. Dept. of Agriculture, Bureau of Agricultural Economics in Cooperation with the University of Illinois Department of Agricultural Economics, *Traffic Survey in the South Water Market, Chicago* (Washington, DC, 1940).

45. Butterworth, "A Study of the Changes in the Volume of Fresh Fruits," 2.

46. Butterworth, "A Study of the Changes in the Volume of Fresh Fruits."

47. Melissa Harris, "West Loop Produce Wholesaler: Should I Stay or Should I Go?" *Chicago Tribune*, April 10, 2015.

48. Duis, *Challenging Chicago*, 114–15.

49. E. A. Duddy, "Distribution of Perishable Commodities in the Chicago Metropolitan Area," *University Journal of Business* 4, no. 2 (1926): 151–81.

50. Duddy, "Distribution of Perishable Commodities."

51. Tracey Deutsch, *Building a Housewife's Paradise* (Chapel Hill: University of North Carolina Press, 2010), 29.

52. Bertha Michaels Shapiro, "Memories of Lawndale," quoted in Deutsch, *Building a Housewife's Paradise*, 29.

53. Ferber, *So Big*, 186.

54. Ferber, *So Big*.

55. Deutsch, *Building a Housewife's Paradise*, 29.

56. Jane Eddington, "Economical Housekeeping," *Chicago Tribune*, September 16, 1913, 13. Quoted in Deutsch, *Building a Housewife's Paradise*, 27.

57. Edward C. Schulz, "A Functional Analysis of Retail Trade in the Maxwell Street Market Area of Chicago" (Master's thesis, Northwestern University, 1954).

58. Duis, *Challenging Chicago*. Daniel R. Block, "The Development of Regional Institutions in Agriculture: The Chicago Milk Marketing Order" (PhD diss., University of California-Los Angeles, 1997).

59. *Bulletin of the Chicago School of Sanitary Instruction (Bulletin of the Chicago Department of Health)*, vol. 7, ns, no. 25 (June 21, 1913): 98.

60. Alfred F. Hess, "The Incidence of Tubercle Bacilli in New York City Milk," in *Collected Studies from the Research Laboratory* (New York: Department of Health, City of New York), 64–80.

61. Marc Levinson, *The Great A&P and the Struggle for Small Business in America* (New York: Hill and Wang, 2011), 30.

62. Pierce, *A History of Chicago, Volume III: The Rise of a Modern City*, 185.

63. Deutsch, *Building a Housewife's Paradise*, 58.

64. Quoted in Levinson, *The Great A&P*, 81.

65. "The Bach, Berens, and Barnsbacks," in *Genealogical Charts of South Shore Families, 1934–1941*. Collected by David B. Bird Sr., Oversize, SSCC 1. Chicago Public Library Department of Special Collections.

66. Levinson, *The Great A&P*.

67. Deutsch, *Building a Housewife's Paradise*, 59–61.

68. "Super-Markets," *Time*, May 24, 1937.

69. Frank A. Bostwick, "Why Jewel Sparkles," *Central Manufacturing District Magazine*, December 1949, 23–31; Leanne Star, "The Story of Jewel: A Century of Fresh Ideas, *Chicago Tribune*," February 28, 1999, Special advertising supplement, 18–43.

70. Star, "The Story of Jewel."

71. Bostwick, "Why Jewel Sparkles," 27.

72. Bostwick, "Why Jewel Sparkles," 23.

73. Flora Johnson, "Superstars of Our Supermarkets," *The Chicagoan*, October 1973, 61.

74. *Stop and Shop 100th Anniversary Scrapbook*, Chicago History Museum Box Lot 1983.549.

75. Nobert Blei, "The *Super*market: A Rhapsodic Tribute to Stop and Shop," *Chicago*, December 1978, 176–81.

76. Johnson, "Superstars of Our Supermarkets," 63.

77. Old Town Triangle Association, *The Old Town Dawn Until Dark Cookbook* (Chicago: Old Town Triangle Association, ca. 1970s).

78. Old Town Triangle Association, *The Old Town Dawn Until Dark Cookbook*.

79. Dominic Candeloro, *Chicago's Italians: Immigrants, Ethnics, Achievers 1850–1985* (Mount Pleasant, SC: Arcadia Publishing, 2003), 128.

80. Emily Bryson York, "Former Dominick's CEO Opening More Grocery Stores Here," *Chicago Tribune*, February 11, 2013, articles.chicagotribune.com/2013-02-11/business/ct-biz-0211-executive-profile-mariano-20130211_1_bob-mariano-grocery-stores-roundy/2, accessed July 30, 2014.

81. Mari Gallagher Research and Consulting Group, *Examining the Impact of Food Deserts on Public Health in Chicago*, 2006, www.marigallagher.com.

82. Daniel Block, Noel Chávez, and Judy Birgen, *Finding Food in Chicago and the Suburbs* (Chicago: Chicago State University, 2008).

83. Pierce, *A History of Chicago, Volume I: The Beginning of a City, 1673–1848.*

84. Chicago City Council, Committee on Health, *Report on the More Economic Distribution and Delivery of Milk in the City of Chicago*, Municipal Reference Library Bulletin no. 8 (Chicago: City of Chicago, 1917).

85. Deutsch, *Building a Housewife's Paradise*, 59–61.

86. Einar Bjorklund and James L. Palmer, *A Study of the Prices of Chain and Independent Grocers in Chicago* (Chicago: University of Chicago Press, 1930).

87. Deutsch, *Building a Housewife's Paradise*, 142.

88. Deutsch, *Building a Housewife's Paradise*, 170.

89. Evelyn M. Kitagawa and De Ver Sholes, *Chicagoland's Retail Market* (Chicago: Chicago Association of Commerce and Industry and Chicago Community Inventory of the University of Chicago, 1957).

90. James Simmons, *The Changing Pattern of Retail Location*, University of Chicago Department of Geography Research Paper 92 (Chicago: University of Chicago Press, 1964), 115.

91. Thornton W. Snead, Charles F. Allison, and John C. Stetson, *Perspective for Decision Makers: A Study of the Emerging Retail Environment* (Chicago: Super Market Institute, 1963).

92. Kitagawa and Sholes, *Chicagoland's Retail Market.*

93. Charles S. Goodman, *Do the Poor Pay More? A Study of the Food Purchasing Practices of Low-Income Consumers* (Philadelphia: Self-Published, 1967).

94. Chicago Urban League, Research and Planning Department, *Grocery Food Prices: Race, Neighborhood, and Other Determinants* (Chicago: Chicago Urban League, 1980).

95. Daniel Block and Joanne Kouba, "A Comparison of the Availability and Affordability of a Market Basket in Two Communities in the Chicago Area," *Public Health Nutrition* 9 (2006): 837–45.

96. Alison H. Alkon et al., "Foodways of the Urban Poor," *Geoforum* 48 (2013): 126–35.

5. FROM FRONTIER TOWN TO INDUSTRIAL AND COMMERCIAL FOOD CAPITAL

1. Alfred Theodore Andreas, *History of Chicago, Volume I* (New York: Arno Press, 1884), 555.

2. William Cronon, *Nature's Metropolis: Chicago and the Great West* (New York: W. W. Norton and Company, 1991), 60.

3. Cronon, *Nature's Metropolis*, 63.

4. Cronon, *Nature's Metropolis*, 313; Dominic A. Pacyga, *Chicago: A Biography* (Chicago: University of Chicago Press, 2009), 38.

5. Gordon Winder, *The American Reaper: Harvesting Networks and Technology, 1830–1910* (Burlington, VT: Ashgate Publishing, Ltd., 2013), 81; in 1880, William Deering, McCormick's primary competitor, relocated his Deering Harvester Works plant from Plano, Illinois, to Fullerton and Clybourn on Chicago's North Side. The two companies spent two decades battling one another for sales in farm machinery, and they eventually merged in 1902 to form International Harvester Company that in 1986 became Navistar.

6. Donald L. Miller, *City of the Century: The Epic of Chicago and the Making of America* (New York: Simon and Schuster, 1996), 94–95.

7. Jack Harpster, *The Railroad Tycoon Who Built Chicago: A Biography of William B. Ogden* (Carbondale, IL: Southern Illinois University Press, 2009), 83.

8. Cronon, *Nature's Metropolis*, 316–17.

9. Cronon, *Nature's Metropolis*, 110–14.

10. Cronon, *Nature's Metropolis*, 118.

11. Andreas, *History of Chicago, Volume I*, 581.

12. Cronon, *Nature's Metropolis*, 119.

13. Cronon, *Nature's Metropolis*, 126.

14. Alfred Theodore Andreas, *History of Chicago, Volume II: From 1857 until the Fire of 1871* (Chicago, IL: A.T. Andreas Company Publishers 1885), 373.

15. Andreas, *History of Chicago, Volume II*, 581.

16. Miller, *City of the Century*, 107.

17. Andreas, *History of Chicago, Volume II*, 374.

18. Bessie Louise Pierce, *A History of Chicago, Volume III: The Rise of a Modern City, 1871–1893* (1957, reprint Chicago: University of Chicago Press, 2007), 74.

19. Andreas, *History of Chicago, Volume II*, 380; Alfred Theodore Andreas, *History of Chicago, Volume III: From the Fire of 1871 until 1885* (Chicago, IL: A. T. Andreas Company Publishers 1886), 324.

20. John Lamb, "Lockport, IL," in *Encyclopedia of Chicago*, edited by Janet L. Reiff, Anne Durkin Keating, and James R. Grossman (Chicago: Chicago Historical Society, 2014), www.encyclopedia.chicagohistory.org/pages/760. html, accessed September 1, 2014.

21. Andreas, *History of Chicago, Volume III*, 325.

22. Richard Helliger (with research assistance from John Lamb), *Lockport Historic District HAER No. IL-16 Bounded by: 8th, Hamilton, 11th Streets and*

the Illinois and Michigan Canal (Washington, DC: Historic American Engineering Record National Park Service Department of the Interior, 1979), lcweb2.loc.gov/master/pnp/habshaer/il/il0400/il0431/data/il0431data.pdf, accessed September 1, 2014; "Norton and Co. Go Under," *Chicago Tribune*, December 27, 1896, 5, archives.chicagotribune.com/1896/12/27/page/5/article/norton-co-go-under, accessed September 1, 2014.

23. Andreas, *History of Chicago, Volume III*, 325.

24. Guy A. Lee, "The Historical Significance of the Chicago Grain Elevator System," *Agricultural History* 11 (1937): 30.

25. James Gray, *Business without Boundary: The Story of General Mills* (Minneapolis, MN: University of Minnesota Press, 1954), 97.

26. Gray, *Business without Boundary*.

27. Jacqueline Fitzgerald, "General Mills Shuts Down Plant," *Chicago Tribune*, September 30, 1997, articles.chicagotribune.com/1997-09-30/business/9709300308_1_general-mills-shuts-wheaties-and-cheerios, accessed September 1, 2014.

28. Cronon, *Nature's Metropolis*, 64.

29. Harlan Harland Barrows, *Geography of the Middle Illinois Valley* (Champaign, IL: University of Illinois, 1910), 96.

30. Andreas, *History of Chicago, Volume 1*, 558–59; Andreas, *History of Chicago, Volume II*, 380.

31. Robert Kott, *Summit* (Mount Pleasant, SC: Arcadia Publishing, 2009), 69; Mark R. Wilson, "Corn Products Refining Co.," in *Encyclopedia of Chicago: Dictionary of Leading Chicago Businesses (1820–2000),* edited by Janet L. Reiff, Anne Durkin Keating, and James R. Grossman (Chicago: Chicago Historical Society), www.encyclopedia.chicagohistory.org/pages/2628.html, accessed November 1, 2014.

32. John W. Bode, Mark W. Empie, and Kyd D. Brenner, "Evolution of High Fructose Corn Syrup within the Sweetener Industry," in *Fructose, High Fructose Corn Syrup, Sucrose, and Health*, edited by James M. Rippe (New York: Humana Press, 2014), 140; Richard O. Marshall and Earl R. Kooi, "Enzymatic Conversion of D-Glucose to D-Fructose," *Science* 125 (1957): 648–49.

33. Pierce, *A History of Chicago, Vol. III*, 71.

34. Sarah T. Rorer, *Recipes Used in Illinois Corn Exhibit Model Kitchen, Woman's Building, Columbian Exhibition* (Chicago: University of Illinois-Chicago, Special Collections, 1893).

35. Pacyga, *Chicago: A Biography*, 60.

36. Cronon, *Nature's Metropolis*, 222–23.

37. Cronon, *Nature's Metropolis*, 230.

38. Andreas, *History of Chicago, Volume II*, 380–81.

39. Pierce, *A History of Chicago, Vol. III*, 108.

40. Pierce, *A History of Chicago, Vol. III*, 108.

41. Cronon, *Nature's Metropolis*, 235.

42. Pierce, *A History of Chicago, Vol. III*, 129.

43. Aaron Brenner, Benjamin Day, and Immanuel Ness, eds., *The Encyclopedia of Strikes in American History* (New York: Routledge, 2009).

44. Brenner, Day, and Ness, *Encyclopedia of Strikes*, 375.

45. Jackie S. Gabriel, "Unionizing the 'Jungle': A Century of Meatpacking Strikes," in *The Encyclopedia of Strikes in American History*, edited by Aaron Brenner, Benjamin Day, and Immanuel Ness (New York: M.E. Sharpe, 2009), 375–77.

46. Gabriel, "Unionizing the 'Jungle'"; David H. Bates, "Between Two Fires: Race and the Chicago Federation of Labor, 1904–1922" ([PhD dissertation], University of Illinois, 2012).

47. Bates, "Between Two Fires," 35–36.

48. "Ten Big Packers Indicted in Chicago: Heads of Swift, Armour, and Morris Concerns, query.nytimes.com/mem/archive-free/pdf?res= 9807E6DE1330E233A25750C1A96F9C946196D6CF; "Charged with Conspiracy and Monopoly," in *New York Times (1857*–1922) (New York: New York Times, September 13 1910), 1.

49. "The Chicago Man That Cornered the Pork Market," *True Republican*, September 25, 1880, Illinois Digital Newspaper Collections, idnc.library.illinois. edu/cgi-bin/illinois?a=d&d=STR18800925.2.37#, accessed September 15, 2013; Kara Newman, *The Secret Financial Life of Food: From Commodities Markets to Supermarkets* (New York: Columbia University Press, 2013), 51–52; Stephan Benzkofer, "The Great Grain Gamble," *Chicago Tribune*, July 29, 2012, articles. chicagotribune.com/2012-07-29/site/ct-per-flash-futures-0729-20120729_1_ wheat-market-actual-wheat-wheat-pit, accessed December 1, 2014.

50. Cronon, *Nature's Metropolis*, 251.

51. ChicagoHS.org, "Chicago: Slaughterhouse to the World," www. chicagohs.org/history/stockyard/stock2.html.

52. Upton Sinclair, *The Jungle* (Mineola, NY: Dover Publications, 2001, original 1906), 33.

53. Andreas, *History of Chicago, Volume III*, 757.

54. Pierce, *A History of Chicago, Volume III*, 131.

55. Pierce, *A History of Chicago, Volume III*, 133.

56. Pierce, *A History of Chicago, Volume III*, 117; Andreas, *History of Chicago: Volume III*, 757.

57. *States Federal Trade Commission Report of the Commissioner of Corporations on the Beef Industry*, March 3, 1905 (Washington, DC: United States Bureau of Corporations), 289, play.google.com/books/reader?id= NLpJAAAAMAAJ&printsec=frontcover&output=reader&hl=en.

58. *The Blue Island Story: An Historical Review of the First One Hundred and Twenty-Seven Years of Our City on the Hill, Blue Island, Illinois*, Lion Club of Blue Island, 53, archive.org/stream/blueislandstoryh00lion#page/52/mode/2up, accessed July 15, 2014.

59. "Butchers' Advocate: Dressed Poultry and the Food Merchant," 71, October 5, 1921, 19, in *Butchers' Advocate: Dressed Poultry and the Food Merchant Issues 1–14; Issues 19–20; Issues 22–25*, books.google.com/books?id= aZVCAQAAMAAJ&printsec=frontcover&source=gbs_ge_summary_r&cad= 0#v=onepage&q&f=false, accessed July 15, 2014.

60. Katherine Grier, "On the Material Culture of Petkeeping," in *Routledge Handbook of Human Animal Studies*, edited by Garry Marvin and Susan McHugh (New York: Routledge, 2014), 130.

61. Katherine C. Grier, *Pets in America: A History* (Chapel Hill, NC: University of North Carolina Press, 2006), 285–87.

62. Pamela G. Hollie, "Greyhound Selling Armour," *New York Times*, June 30, 1983, www.nytimes.com/1983/06/30/business/greyhound-selling-armour. html.

63. David Ress, *Governor Edward Coles and the Vote to Forbid Slavery in Illinois, 1823–1824* (Jefferson, NC: McFarland Press, 2006), 62; Isaac Lippincott, "The Early Salt Trade of the Ohio Valley," *Journal of Political Economy* 20 (1912): 1051.

64. "Illinois Constitution of 1818," Illinois Digital Archives, www.idaillinois. org/cdm/compoundobject/collection/isl2/id/12600, accessed December 15, 2014.

65. Lippincott, "The Early Salt Trade," 1051.

66. Lippincott, "The Early Salt Trade," 1051; Steven C. Gordon, "From Slaughterhouse to Soap-Boiler: Cincinnati's Meat Packing Industry, Changing Technologies, and the Rise of Mass Production, 1825–1870," *Journal of the Society for Industrial Archeology* 16 (1990): 55–67.

67. Lippincott, "The Early Salt Trade," 1030.

68. Cyrus Forman, *A Briny Crossroads: Salt, Slavery, and Sectionalism in the Kanawha Salines* (MA thesis, City University of New York, 2014), 43, dspace. cuny.edu/bitstream/handle/11049/24282/2014SpHu09.pdf?sequence=1, accessed December 1, 2014.

69. Andrew F. Smith, *Starving the South: How the North Won the Civil War* (New York: St. Martin's Press, 2011), 20–24.

70. Andreas, *History of Chicago, Volume I*, 560.

71. Andreas, *History of Chicago, Volume I*, 561–62.

72. Harlan Harland Barrows, *Geography of the Middle Illinois Valley* (Champaign, IL: University of Illinois, 1919), 95.

73. "The Necessity of a Ship-Canal between the East and the West. Report of the Committee on Statistics, for the City of Chicago" (National Ship-Canal Con-

vention, June 2, 1863), 16, quod.lib.umich.edu/cgi/t/text/text-idx?c=moa&cc= moa&view=text&rgn=main&idno=AJQ1175.0001.001, accessed December 15, 2014.

74. Harper Leech and John Charles Carroll, *Armour and His Times* (New York: D. Appleton-Century Company, Incorporated, 1938), 2.

75. James Ballowe, *A Man of Salt and Trees: The Life of Joy Morton* (DeKalb: Northern Illinois University Press, 2009), 75.

76. Ballowe, *A Man of Salt and Trees*, 75

77. Ballowe, *A Man of Salt and Trees*, 76; William G. Roy, *Socializing Capital: The Rise of the Large Industrial Corporation in America* (Princeton, NJ: Princeton University Press, 1997), 185.

78. Ballowe, *A Man of Salt and Trees*, 126.

79. Karo, karosyrup.com/about_us.html.

80. *Interstate Commerce Commission Reports: Decisions of the Interstate Commerce Commission of the United States Volume 24* (Washington, DC: L. K. Strouse Publisher, 1913), 135–36, play.google.com/store/books/details?id= qlEuAAAAYAAJ&rdid=book-qlEuAAAAYAAJ&rdot=1, accessed December 1, 2014.

81. Charles Jolly Werner, *A History and Description of the Manufacture and Mining of Salt in New York State* (Huntington, NY: Author, 1917), 135–37, archive.org/details/historydescripti00wern, accessed December 15, 2014.

82. *Poor's Manual of Industrials: Manufacturing, Mining and Miscellaneous Companies* (New York: Poor's Manual Company, 1916), 1873.

83. Ballowe, *A Man of Salt and Trees*, 193.

84. Ballowe, *A Man of Salt and Trees*, 162.

85. John T. Cumbler, *Northeast and Midwest United States: An Environmental History* (Santa Barbara, CA: ABC-CLIO, 2005), 108–9.

86. Stuart Charles Wade, *Rand, McNally & Co.'s Handbook of the World's Columbian Exposition* (Chicago, IL: Rand, McNally & Company, 1893), 110.

87. "The Economist: Investors Section," *The Economist: A Weekly Financial, Commercial, and Real-estate Newspaper, Volume 55* (Chicago, IL: Economist Publishing Company, 1916).

88. Charles M. Goodsell and Henry Edward Wallace, *The Manual of Statistics: Stock Exchange Handbook, Volume 29* (New York: Manual of Statistics Company, 1907), 525.

89. For an example from 1960, see the following commercial www.youtube.com/watch?v=eyNJEVobr8w.

90. Andrew F. Smith, *Eating History: Thirty Turning Points in the Making of American Cuisine* (New York: Columbia University Press, 2009), 105–11.

91. Smith, *Eating History*, 105.

92. *Quaker Oats Company, "Factory to Dairy"* (1928), Chicago Film Archives William O'Farrell Collection, www.youtube.com/watch?v= LAupzdTFqyQ, accessed December 15, 2014.

93. E. J. Schultz, "The Quaker Man Is Growing a Milk Mustache," *Advertising Age*, September 8, 2014, adage.com/article/cmo-strategy/quaker-man-growing-a-milk-mustache/294857/, accessed December 1, 2014.

94. H. A. Ross, *The Marketing of Milk in the Chicago Dairy District* (Urbana, IL: University of Illinois Agricultural Experiment Station, 1925), 469–73, babel. hathitrust.org/cgi/pt?id=mdp.35128001191129;view=1up;seq=19, accessed December 1, 2014.

95. "He Who Is Not for U," *Prairie Farmer* 94 (August 5, 1922): 8, play. google.com/store/books/details?id=5x4_AQAAMAAJ&rdid=book-5x4_ AQAAMAAJ&rdot=1, accessed December 1, 2014.

96. Frank Boles, Mary Janzen, and Richard Popp, "Descriptive Inventory for the Bowman Dairy Company Records at the Chicago Historical Society" (Chicago: Chicago Historical Society, 1981), chsmedia.org/media/fa/fa/M-B/ BowmanDairy-inv.htm, accessed December 1, 2014.

97. "Report of the Federal Trade Commission on Milk and Milk Products 1914–1918" (Washington, DC: United States Federal Trade Commission, June 6, 1921), 68.

98. "Report of the Federal Trade Commission on Milk and Milk Products 1914–1918," 73.

99. "Blue Valley Creamery Sold to Beatrice," *Chicago Daily Tribune*, February 18, 1939, 21, archives.chicagotribune.com/1939/02/18/page/21/article/blue-valley-creamery-sold-to-beatrice, accessed December 1, 2014.

100. John Gorman, "Borden Buys Beatrice's Dairy Group," *Chicago Tribune*, October 31, 1986, articles.chicagotribune.com/1986-10-31/business/ 8603210957_1_borden-spokesman-dairy-operations-meadow-gold, accessed December 1, 2014.

101. Deborah Valenze, *Milk: A Local and Global History* (New Haven, CT: Yale University Press, 2011), 185–86.

102. "People and Events," *Journal of Dairy Science* 48 (1965): 18, www. journalofdairyscience.org/article/S0022-0302%2865%2988348-5/pdf, accessed December 1, 2014.

103. "Corporate Affairs," *Milk Plant Monthly* 9 (1920): 42.

104. I. D. Guyer, *History of Chicago: Its Commercial and Manufacturing Interests and Industry* (Chicago: Church, Goodman & Cushin, 1862), 172–73, openlibrary.org/books/OL7052474M/History_of_Chicago, accessed December 15, 2014; Pacyga, *Chicago: A Biography*, 41.

105. Andreas, *History of Chicago, Volume II*, 87.

106. John B. Jentz and Richard Schneirov, *Chicago in the Age of Capital: Class, Politics, and Democracy during the Civil War and Reconstruction* (Champaign, IL: University of Illinois Press, 2012), 46.

107. John Schmeltzer, "Butternut Bread-Maker Closing Chicago Bakery," *Chicago Tribune*, September 24, 2004, articles.chicagotribune.com/2004-09-24/business/0409240329_1_interstate-bakeries-hostess-twinkies-wheat-bread, accessed December 1, 2014.

108. Ray Kroc and Robert Anderson, *Grinding It Out: The Making of McDonald's* (New York: Macmillan, 1992), 98–100.

109. "Vast Bakery Dedicated by Kitchens of Sara Lee," *Chicago Tribune*, September 2, 1964, archives.chicagotribune.com/1964/09/02/page/43/article/vast-bakery-dedicated-by-kitchens-of-sara-lee, accessed December 1, 2014.

110. "Kraft, Sara Lee Call Truce in Wiener War," *Chicago Tribune*, September 8, 2011, articles.chicagotribune.com/2011-09-08/business/chi-kraft-sara-lee-call-truce-in-wiener-war-20110908_1_national-taste-test-sara-lee-pure-beef, accessed December 20, 2014.

111. Andreas, *History of Chicago, Volume I*, 575.

112. Andreas, *History of Chicago, Volume III*, 753–54.

113. Leslie Goddard, *Chicago's Sweet Candy History* (Mount Pleasant, SC: Arcadia Publishing, 2012), 8–10.

114. Lorene Yue, "Go Gluten-Free? No, Eat More of It," *Crain's Chicago Business*, August 24, 2013, www.chicagobusiness.com/article/20130824/ISSUE01/308249977/go-gluten-free-no-eat-more-of-it, accessed December 20, 2014.

6. EATING AT THE MEETING PLACE

1. Alfred Theodore Andreas, *History of Chicago, Volume I* (New York: Arno Press, 1884), 629.

2. Fremont O. Bennett, *Politics and Politicians of Chicago, Cook County, and Illinois: Memorial Volume, 1787–1887: A Complete Record of Municipal, County, State and National Politics from the Earliest Period to the Present Time* (Chicago: Blakely Print Company, 1886).

3. Bessie Louise Pierce and Joe Lester Norris, *As Others See Chicago: Impressions of Visitors, 1673–1933* (Chicago: University of Chicago Press, 1933), 67–68.

4. Andreas, *History of Chicago, Volume I*, 633.

5. Pierce and Norris, *As Others See Chicago*, 72–73.

6. Milo Milton Quaife, *Chicago's Highways, Old and New, From Indian Trail to Motor Road* (Chicago: D. F. Keller & Company, 1923), 174.

7. Quaife, *Chicago's Highways, Old and New*, 174.

8. Joseph N. Balestier, *The Annals of Chicago: A Lecture Delivered before the Chicago Lyceum, January 21*, Republished from the Original Edition of 1840 (Chicago: Fergus Printing Company, 1876), 33.

9. Bessie Louise Pierce, *History of Chicago, Volume I: The Beginning of a City, 1673–1848* (Chicago: University of Chicago Press, [1937] 2007), 200.

10. Perry R. Duis, *The Saloon: Public Drinking in Chicago and Boston, 1880–1920* (Urbana and Chicago: University of Illinois Press, 1983), 146.

11. Balestier, *The Annals of Chicago*, 33.

12. Pierce, *A History of Chicago, Volume I*, 214.

13. Commercial Menu Collection, Chicago History Museum.

14. "An Experiment in Canning Strategies," *Canning Age*, January 1922, 34.

15. College Inn Chicago Menu, New York Public Library online menu collection, menus.nypl.org/menu_pages/69186/explore.

16. Emily Frankenstein Diary, pages 78–79, Chicago History Museum.

17. Robert V. Allegrini, *Chicago's Grand Hotels: The Palmer House Hilton, the Drake, and the Hilton Chicago* (Charleston, SC: Acadia Publishing, 2005).

18. Commercial Menu Collection, Chicago History Museum.

19. Duis, *The Saloon*, 146–47.

20. Duis, *The Saloon*, 147.

21. Duis, *The Saloon*.

22. Commercial Menu Collection, Chicago History Museum.

23. Commercial Menu Collection, Chicago History Museum.

24. Neal S. Samors, Eric Bronsky, Bob Dauber, and Penny Pollack, *Chicago's Classic Restaurants: Past, Present & Future* (Chicago: Chicago's Books Press, 2011), 91. .

25. George Estep, "State Street Special: For 25 Years Celebrities Were the Order of the Day at Fritzel's," *Chicago Tribune*, April 20, 1986.

26. Joan Greene, *A Chicago Tradition: Marshall Field's Food and Fashion* (Petaluma, CA: Pomegranate, 2005), 13.

27. John Drury, *Dining in Chicago* (New York: John Day Company, 1931), 229.

28. Commercial Menu Collection, Chicago History Museum.

29. Duis, *The Saloon*, 147.

30. Andy Knott, "Eatery Ends Wild, Grizzly Era," *Chicago Tribune*, May 23, 1986; BidStart, the Collectibles Marketplace, collectibles.bidstart.com/Cafe-Bohemia-Game-Restaurant-Menu-Chicago-IL-1971-/17020857/a.html.

31. William Cronon, *Nature's Metropolis: Chicago and the Great West* (New York: W. W. Norton & Company, 1991), 209.

32. Louise Carroll Wade, *Chicago's Pride: The Stockyards, Packingtown, and Environs in the Nineteenth Century* (Urbana and Chicago: University of Illinois Press, 1987), 85.

33. Quoted in Samors, Bronsky, Dauber, and Pollack, *Chicago's Classic Restaurants*, 31.

34. Commercial Menu Collection, Chicago History Museum.

35. Duis, *The Saloon*, 148.

36. Samors, Bronsky, Dauber, and Pollack, *Chicago's Classic Restaurants*, 173.

37. Commercial Menu Collection, Chicago History Museum.

38. Samors, Bronsky, Dauber, and Pollack, *Chicago's Classic Restaurants*, 81.

39. William Howland Kenney, *Chicago Jazz: A Cultural History, 1904–1930* (New York: Oxford University Press, 1993).

40. Allan H. Spear, *Black Chicago: The Making of a Negro Ghetto* (Chicago: University of Chicago Press, 1967), 184.

41. Charles A. Sengstock, *That Toddlin' Town: Chicago White Dance Bands and Orchestras, 1900–1950* (Urbana: University of Illinois Press, 2004), 166–67.

42. Charles A. Sengstock, *That Toddlin' Town*, 161–62.

43. Drury, *Dining in Chicago*, 245–46.

44. Samors, Bronsky, Dauber, and Pollack, *Chicago's Classic Restaurants*, 54.

45. "Programs and Tickets," Chicago Miniature Opera Company Collection, Chicago History Museum, Box 1.

46. Yasmin Rammohan, "Puppet Opera," *Chicago Tonight: Cultural Connections*, WTTW Chicago Public Television, December 29, 2011, chicagotonight. wttw.com/2011/12/29/puppet-opera.

47. Samors, Bronsky, Dauber, and Pollack, *Chicago's Classic Restaurants*, 112–13; Commercial Menu Collection, Chicago History Museum.

48. Samors, Bronsky, Dauber, and Pollack, *Chicago's Classic Restaurants*, 109–10.

49. Samors, Bronsky, Dauber, and Pollack, *Chicago's Classic Restaurants*, 114–21; "Lettuce Tell You Our History," Lettuce Entertain You Enterprises, www.leye.com/about-us/history.

50. Samors, Bronsky, Dauber, and Pollack, *Chicago's Classic Restaurants*, 131–35.

51. Jeff Ruby, "Has Spiaggia Sold Out?" *Chicago*, May 22, 2013.

52. Samors, Bronsky, Dauber, and Pollack, *Chicago's Classic Restaurants*, 131–35.

53. Quoted in Pierce, *A History of Chicago, Volume I: The Beginning of a City, 1673–1848*, 215.

54. Perry Duis, *Challenging Chicago: Coping with Everyday Life, 1837–1920* (Urbana and Chicago: University of Illinois Press, 1998), 149.

55. Bruce Kraig, "Restaurants," in *Encyclopedia of Chicago*, edited by Janet L. Reiff, Anne Durkin Keating, and James R. Grossman (Chicago: Chicago Historical Society, 2005), www.encyclopedia.chicagohistory.org/pages/1066.html.

56. Duis, *The Saloon*, 52.

57. Duis, *Challenging Chicago*.

58. Quoted in Pierce and Norris, *As Others See Chicago*, 473.

59. Drury, *Dining in Chicago*, 131.

60. Commercial Menu Collection, Chicago History Museum.

61. *Dish*, Spring 1992.

62. Statement of M. E. Bruwaert, in Pierce and Norris, *As Others See Chicago*, 335.

63. Statement of M. E. Bruwaert, in Pierce and Norris, *As Others See Chicago*, 331.

64. Drury, *Dining in Chicago*, 9.

65. Perry Duis, "The Saloon in a Changing Chicago," in *Wild Kind of Boldness: The Chicago History Reader*, edited by Rosemary K. Adams (Grand Rapids, MI: William B. Eerdmans Publishing Company and Chicago: Chicago Historical Society, 1998). Originally published in *Chicago History*, winter 1975–1976.

66. Drury, "The Saloon in a Changing Chicago," 180–81.

67. Donna R. Gabaccia, *We Are What We Eat* (Cambridge, MA: Harvard University Press, 1998).

68. Carlyn Berghoff and Jan Berghoff with Nancy Ross Ryan, *The Berghoff Family Cookbook* (Kansas City, MO: Andrews McMeel Publishing, 2007), 7.

69. Berghoff and Berghoff, *The Berghoff Family Cookbook*, 9.

70. Kathy Bergen, "Life's 'Perfect' Plate Being Carried Away," *Chicago Tribune*, January 15, 2006.

71. Commercial Menu Collection, Chicago History Museum.

72. Lost Recipes Found, "Red Star Inn–Style Sauerbraten Zwiebelfleisch," lostrecipesfound.com/recipe/red-star-inn-style-sauerbraten-zwiebelfleisch-onion-beef-roast/.

73. Samors, Bronsky, Dauber, and Pollack, *Chicago's Classic Restaurants*, 74.

74. Drury, *Dining in Chicago*, 169.

75. Commercial Menu Collection, Chicago History Museum.

76. Sengstock, *That Toddlin' Town*, 161.

77. Commercial Menu Collection, Chicago History Museum.

78. Jeff Ruby, "Arun's in Albany Park: The Accidental Masterpiece," *Chicago*, 2011.

79. Ruby, "Arun's in Albany Park: The Accidental Masterpiece."

80. Drury, *Dining in Chicago*, 47–48; Samors, Bronsky, Dauber, and Pollack, *Chicago's Classic Restaurants*, 43.

81. Ellen Almer, "Como Inn to Say 'Ciao' on Saturday," *Crain's Chicago Business*, June 28, 2001.

82. Samors, Bronsky, Dauber, and Pollack, *Chicago's Classic Restaurants*, 66.

83. Gabbacia, *We Are What We Eat*, 115–16.

84. Gabbacia, *We Are What We Eat*, 116.

85. Samors, Bronsky, Dauber, and Pollack, *Chicago's Classic Restaurants*, 75.

86. Alexa Ganakos and Katherine Bish, *Greektown Chicago: Its History, Its Recipes* (St. Louis, MO: G. Bradley, 2005), 166–67.

87. David Segal, "The Gyro's History Unfolds," *New York Times*, July 14, 2009.

88. Ganakos, *Greektown Chicago*, 154.

89. Margaret Sheridan, "It's Down Home Goodness at Gladys' Luncheonette," *Chicago Tribune*, May 1, 1987.

90. Celeste Garrett, "Gladys Holcomb, 96, Gladys' Luncheonette Owner," *Chicago Tribune*, May 3, 2003.

91. Maudlyne Ihejirika, "South Side Soul Food Legend Army and Lou's Closes," *Chicago Sun-Times*, February 4, 2011.

92. Anna Brown and Mark Hugo Lopez, *Mapping the Latino Population by State, County, and City*, Pew Research Center, 2013, www.pewhispanic.org/2013/08/29/iv-ranking-latino-populations-in-the-nations-metropolitan-areas/, accessed December 15, 2014.

93. Dominic A. Pacyga, *Chicago: A Biography* (Chicago: University of Chicago Press, 2009), 390.

94. Wilfredo Cruz, *City of Dreams: Latino Immigration to Chicago* (Lanham, MD: University Press of America, 2007).

95. Drury, *Dining in Chicago*, 172–73.

96. Commercial Menu Collection, Chicago Historical Society.

97. Rick Bayless with Deann Groen Bayless, *Authentic Mexican: Regional Cooking from the Heart of Mexico* (New York: William Morrow, 1987).

98. Joseph W. Zurawski, *Polish Chicago: Our History, Our Recipes* (St. Louis: G. Bradley Publishing, Inc., 2007).

99. Samors, Bronsky, Dauber, and Pollack, *Chicago's Classic Restaurants*, 42.

100. Commercial Menu Collection, Chicago History Museum.

101. Commercial Menu Collection, Chicago History Museum.

102. Duis, *Challenging Chicago*, 148.

103. Commercial Menu Collection, Chicago History Museum.

104. Samors, Bronsky, Dauber, and Pollack, *Chicago's Classic Restaurants*, 38.

105. Duis, *Challenging Chicago*, 148.

106. William Rice, "Oh, How Chicago Loved Its Oysters," *Chicago Tribune*, July 16, 1997.

107. Commercial Menu Collection, Chicago History Museum.

108. Quoted in Samors, Bronsky, Dauber, and Pollack, *Chicago's Classic Restaurants*, 85.

109. Mark Knoblauch, "Chez Paul Still Fancy (But Predictable) After All These Years," *Chicago Tribune*, June 2, 1985.

110. Chicago Menus, 1988, Advertising supplement to the *Chicago Tribune*, October 11, 1987.

111. Phyllis Hanes, "The Food Father: Chef Louis Szathmary of Chicago's Bakery is the Award-Winning Author of Five Cookbooks," *Christian Science Monitor*, June 1, 1988.

112. Chicago Culinary Museum and Chefs Hall of Fame, "Jean Banchet, Legendary Chef," www.thechicagoculinarymuseum.org/?page_id=310.

113. Phil Vettel, "Le Francais Chef Set High Standard for Fine Dining in Chicago," *Chicago Tribune*, Nov. 25, 2013.

114. Mark Caro, *The Foie Gras Wars* (New York: Simon & Schuster, 2009).

115. William Grimes, "Charlie Trotter Dies at 54; Chef Made Chicago a Must," *New York Times*, November 5, 2013.

116. Michael Ruhlman, "Toward Creativity," in *Alinea* by Grant Achatz (Berkeley, CA: Ten Speed Press, 2008), 1–6.

117. Grant Achatz, *Alinea* (Berkeley, CA and Toronto: Ten Speed Press, 2008), 102–3, 118–19.

7. CHICAGO STREET FOOD, RECIPES, AND COOKBOOKS

1. Eric Schlosser, *Fast Food Nation: The Dark Side of the All-American Meal* (Boston: Houghton Mifflin, 2001).

2. McDonald's Corporation, "McDonald's History," www.aboutmcdonalds.com/mcd/our_company/mcdonalds_history_timeline.html.

3. Mike Sula, "The First Family of Fried Chicken," *Chicago Reader*, April 14, 2006, 12–13.

4. Sula, "The First Family of Fried Chicken."

5. Tracy Poe, "African American Meals from Slavery to Soul Food," in *The Meal, the Proceedings of the Oxford Symposium on Food and Cookery*, edited by Harlan Walker (London: Prospect Books, 2001), 180.

6. City of Chicago Department of Business Affairs and Consumer Protection, "Mobile Food Vendor Licenses," www.cityofchicago.org/city/en/depts/bacp/supp_info/mobile_food_vendorlicenses.html, accessed November 14, 2014.

7. Perry Duis, *Challenging Chicago: Coping with Everyday Life, 1837–1920* (Urbana and Chicago: University of Illinois Press, 1998), 160.

8. Gustavo Arellano, *Taco USA: How Mexican Food Conquered America* (New York: Scribner, 2012).

9. Duis, *Challenging Chicago,* 160.

10. Bruce Kraig, *Hot Dog: A Global History* (London: Reaktion Books Ltd., 2009), 60.

11. Michael J. Baruch, *Street Food Chicago: A Complete Book of Original Recipes, History and Stories about the Most Loved Foods in the City* (Chicago: LBCM Publishing, 2007), 148.

12. Kraig, *Hot Dog,* 78.

13. Kraig, *Hot Dog,* 86.

14. Bob Schwartz, *Never Put Ketchup on a Hot Dog* (Chicago: Chicago's Books Press, 2008), 36.

15. Mark Caro, *The Foie Gras Wars: How a 5,000-Year-Old Delicacy Inspired the World's Fiercest Food Fight* (New York: Simon & Schuster, 2009), 199–201.

16. Kraig, *Hot Dog,* 90.

17. Schwartz, *Never Put Ketchup on a Hot Dog,* 31.

18. Mike Baruch, *Street Food Chicago* (Del Mar, CA: LBCM Publishing, 2007), 211.

19. Baruch, *Street Food Chicago,* 232–33.

20. Arellano, *Taco USA.*

21. Mike Sula, "Omnivorous: On the Trail of the Delta Tamale," *Chicago Reader,* May 15, 2008.

22. Leah Zeldes, "The Unique Chicago Tamale, a Tuneful Mystery," *Dining Chicago*, www.diningchicago.com/blog/2009/12/18/the-unique-chicago-tamale-a-tuneful-mystery/.

23. David Segal, "The Gyro's History Unfolds." *New York Times*, July 14, 2009, www.nytimes.com/2009/07/15/dining/15gyro.html?pagewanted=all, accessed January 27, 2015.

24. Baruch, *Street Food Chicago,* 293–94.

25. Baruch, *Street Food Chicago,* 168.

26. John Drury, *Dining in Chicago* (New York: John Day Company, 1931), archive.org/stream/dininginchicago00drur -page/n7/mode/2up, accessed July 30, 2014, 255–56.

27. Monica Eng, "Saga of a Sandwich," *Chicago Tribune*, June 18, 2003.

28. Neal S. Samors, Eric Bronsky, Bob Dauber, and Penny Pollack, *Chicago's Classic Restaurants: Past, Present and Future* (Chicago: Chicago's Books Press, 2011), 79.

29. Giordano's, "The Menu," giordanos.com/the-menu/.

30. Commercial Menu Collection, Chicago History Museum.

31. Tom McNamee, "Hunt's On, Chicago's Vesuvio's a Chicago Original, But Who Created It? A Stack of Menus, Claims of Invention and Missing Peas. Mystery Is Served . . ." *Chicago Sun-Times*, January 12, 2005.

32. Baruch, *Street Food Chicago*, 207.

33. McNamee, "Hunt's On, Chicago's Vesuvio's a Chicago Original."

34. *Old Irving Park Association Cookbook* (Chicago: Old Irving Park Association, n.d.).

35. Paul A. Camp and JeanMarie Brownson, "The Heavenly Recipe That Helped Make Henri De Jonghe Immortal." *Chicago Tribune*, January 27, 1985.

36. National Geographic Society, "Chicago Recipes," travel. nationalgeographic.com/travel/city-guides/chicago-recipes/, accessed October 8, 2014.

37. Andrew F. Smith, *Popped Culture: A Social History of Popcorn in America* (Columbia, SC: University of South Carolina Press, 1999), 145.

38. Mary Ellen Podmolik, "Garrett's Popcorn Sued over Chicago Mix," *Chicago Tribune*, September 2, 2014.

39. Smith, *Popped Culture*, 83–89.

40. Eli's Cheesecake Chicago, "Our Story," www.elicheesecake.com/about/ our-story/.

41. Louis Szathmary, *From Chicago Kitchens: A Checklist of Selected Cookbooks Collected by Chef Louis Szathmary on Exhibition with Menus and Other Culinary Memorabilia, June 26–Sept. 25, 1982* (Chicago: Chicago Public Library Cultural Center, Special Collections Division, 1982), 3.

42. Naomi Donnelley. *The Lakeside Cook Book No. 2: A Manual for Cooking, Pickling, and Preserving, and Other Useful Information for the Housekeeper* (Chicago: Donnelley, Gassette, and Lloyd, 1878), 3.

43. Donnelley, *The Lakeside Cook Book No. 2*, 29.

44. Donnelley, *The Lakeside Cook Book No. 2*, 41.

45. Donnelley, *The Lakeside Cook Book No. 2*, 46.

46. E. Neil, *The Every-Day Cook-Book and Encyclopedia of Practical Recipes* (Chicago: Regan Printing House, 1892), 10.

47. Szathmary, *From Chicago Kitchens . . .*

48. E. S. Kirkland, *Six Little Cooks or Aunt Jane's Cooking Class* (Chicago: Jansen, McClurg & Company, 1877), 24–26.

49. Chicago Daily Tribune, *The Home Guide; Or, a Book by 500 Ladies, Embracing about 1,000 Recipes and Hints, Pertaining to Cookery, the Household, the Sick Room, the Toilet, Etc.* (Elgin, IL: S. L. Taylor, 1877).

50. Mary Mott Chesbrough, *The Daily News Cook Book, being a reprint of The Chicago Record Cook Book* (Chicago: Chicago Daily News, 1896).

51. Edith G. Shuck and Herman N. Bundesen, *The Chicago Daily News Cook Book* (Chicago: Chicago Daily News, 1930).

52. Szathmary, *From Chicago Kitchens* . . .

53. Szathmary, *From Chicago Kitchens* . . .

54. Szathmary, *From Chicago Kitchens* . . .

55. Emily Riesenberg, *Original Recipes Compiled for Wm. J. Moxley, Chicago*, Special Collections (University of Illinois-Chicago, ca. 1910).

56. Szathmary, *From Chicago Kitchens* . . .

57. R. R. Donnelley Company, *Ways to a Woman's Heart*, Newberry Library, Special Collections (Chicago: R. R. Donnelly Company, 1948).

58. Carrie V. Shuman, compiler, *Favorite Dishes: A Columbian Autograph Souvenir* (Chicago: R. R. Donnelley & Sons, 1893).

59. Sarah T. Rorer, *Recipes Used in Illinois Corn Exhibit Model Kitchen, Woman's Building, Columbian Exhibition* (Chicago: University of Illinois-Chicago, Special Collections, 1893).

60. State Council of Defense of Illinois, *What to Eat. How to Cook It: Official Recipe Book*, Educational Document 5 (Chicago: State Council of Defense of Illinois, 1918).

61. Mary L. Wade, *The Book of Potato Cookery: More Than One Hundred Recipes Suitable for the Tables of Rich and Poor Alike, Showing How to Prepare Economical and Nutritious Dishes from the "Noble Tuber"* (Chicago: A. C. McClurg & Company, 1918).

62. City of Chicago, Mayor's Office of Special Events, *Mayor Byrne's Chicago Heritage Cookbook* (City of Chicago, 1979); City of Chicago, Mayor's Office of Special Events, *Taste of Chicago Cookbook* (City of Chicago, 1990).

63. Irving S. Paull, *Congress Hotel, Home of a Thousand Homes: Rare and Piquant Dishes of Historic Interest* (Chicago: Sleepick & Hellman, 1914).

64. Arnold Shircliffe, *The Edgewater Beach Salad Book* (Evanston, IL: Hotel Monthly Press, 1926), 11th printing, 1951.

65. Louis Szathmary, *The Chef's New Secret Cookbook* (Chicago: Henry Regnery Company, 1975); Jo A. Kaucher, *The Chicago Diner Cookbook* (Summertown, TN: Book Publishing Company, 2002); Grant Achatz, *Alinea* (Berkeley, CA and Toronto: Ten Speed Press, 2008); Green City Market, *The Green*

City Market Cookbook, with an introduction by Rick Bayless (Chicago: Midway, 2013).

66. Recipe for "Smothered Prairie Chickens," Blatchford Family—Ulmenheim—recipe book, ca. 1850s–1870s, Blatchford Family Papers, 1777–1987, Bulk 1839–1965, Box 102, Folder 1674, Newberry Library, Special Collections, Chicago, IL.

67. Ellen F. Steinberg with Eleanor Hudera Hanson, *Learning to Cook in 1898: A Chicago Culinary Memoir* (Detroit: Wayne State University Press, 2007), 61.

68. Steinberg and Hanson, *Learning to Cook in 1898*.

69. Szathmary, *From Chicago Kitchens . . .*

70. Women's Society of Bethany Union Church, comp., *The Bethany Union Cook Book* (Chicago: Martin H. Kendig, 1912).

71. Sarah Hackett Stevenson Memorial Lodging House Association, comp., *Stevenson Memorial Cook Book* (Chicago: Stevenson Memorial Lodging House Association, 1919).

72. Staff of the Chicago Public Library, *At Home on the Range or What Librarians Cook* (Chicago: Staff Association of the Chicago Public Library, 1946).

73. Old Town Triangle Association, *Old Town Dawn until Dusk Cookbook* (Chicago: Old Town Triangle Association, ca. 1970).

74. Old Irving Park Association, *Old Irving Park Association Cookbook* (Leawood, KS: Circulation Service, n.d.).

75. Irving Park Lutheran Church, *90th Anniversary Cookbook* (Collierville, TN: Fundcraft Publishing, 1994).

76. Junior League Club of Chicago, *One Magnificent Cookbook* (Chicago: Junior League Club of Chicago, 1988).

77. American Indian Center, *Chicago American Indian Center Cookbook* (Chicago: American Indian Center, 1970).

BIBLIOGRAPHY

"1889, The Clark Street Chinatown Reaches Maturity." Chinese-American Museum of Chicago. www.ccamuseum.org/index.php/en/research/research-before-1900/139-1889-the-clark-street-chinatown-reaches-maturity. Accessed July 30, 2014.

Account Book for Schooner Racer. Harding and Hall Papers, Chicago History Museum.

Achatz, Grant. *Alinea.* Berkeley, CA and Toronto: Ten Speed Press, 2008.

Alkon, Alison Hope, Daniel Block, Kelly Moore, Catherine Gillis, Nicole DiNuccio, and Noel Chavez. "Foodways of the Urban Poor." *Geoforum* 48 (2013): 126–35.

Allegrini, Robert V. *Chicago's Grand Hotels: The Palmer House Hilton, the Drake, and the Hilton Chicago.* Charleston, SC: Arcadia Publishing, 2005.

Almer, Ellen. "Como Inn to Say 'Ciao' on Saturday." *Crain's Chicago Business,* June 28, 2001.

"An Experiment in Canning Strategies." *Canning Age,* January 1922, 34.

Andreas, Alfred Theodore. *History of Chicago, Volume I.* New York: Arno Press, 1884.

Andreas, Alfred Theodore. *History of Chicago, Volume II: From 1857 until the Fire of 1871.* Chicago: A. T. Andreas Company Publishers, 1885.

Andreas, Alfred Theodore. *History of Chicago, Volume III: From the Fire of 1871 until 1885.* Salem, MA: Higginson Book Company, 1885.

Arellano, Gustavo. *Taco USA: How Mexican Food Conquered America.* New York: Scribner, 2012.

Arredondo, Gabriela F. *Mexican Chicago: Race, Identity, and Nation, 1916–39.* Champaign, IL: University of Illinois Press, 2008.

Asch, David L., and Nancy B. Asch. "Prehistoric Plant Cultivation in West-Central Illinois." In *Prehistoric Food Production in North America,* edited by Richard I. Ford, 149–204. Ann Arbor: Museum of Anthropology Anthropological Papers 75, University of Michigan, 1985.

"The Bach, Berens, and Barnsbacks," in *Genealogical Charts of South Shore Families, 1934–1941.* Collected by David B. Bird Sr., Oversize, SSCC 1. Chicago Public Library Department of Special Collections.

Balestier, Joseph N. *The Annals of Chicago: A Lecture Delivered before the Chicago Lyceum, January 21, 1840.* Chicago: Fergus Printing Company, 1876.

Ballowe, James. *A Man of Salt and Trees: The Life of Joy Morton.* DeKalb, IL: Northern Illinois University Press, 2009.

Barrows, Harlan H. *Geography of the Middle Illinois Valley.* Champaign, IL: Illinois State Geological Survey, 1910.

Bartlett, Charles. Charles Bartlett Diary. Chicago History Museum Archives and Library.

Baruch, Michael J. *Street Food Chicago: A Complete Book of Original Recipes, History and Stories about the Most Loved Foods in the City.* Chicago: LBCM Publishing, 2007.

Bates, David H. "Between Two Fires: Race and the Chicago Federation of Labor, 1904–1922." PhD dissertation, University of Illinois, 2012.

Bayless, Rick with Deann Groen Bayless. *Authentic Mexican: Regional Cooking from the Heart of Mexico.* New York: William Morrow, 1987.

Bennett, Fremont O. *Politics and Politicians of Chicago, Cook County, and Illinois: Memorial Volume, 1787–1887: A Complete Record of Municipal, County, State and National Politics from the Earliest Period to the Present Time.* Chicago: Blakely Print Company, 1886.

Benzkofer, Stephan. "The Great Grain Gamble." *Chicago Tribune*, July 29, 2012. articles. chicagotribune.com/2012-07-29/site/ct-per-flash-futures-0729-20120729_1_wheat-market-actual-wheat-wheat-pit. Accessed December 1, 2014.

Bergen, Kathy. "Life's 'Perfect' Plate Being Carried Away." *Chicago Tribune*, January 15, 2006.

Berger, Susan. "The End of a Chicago Tradition: Is Absolutely Nothing Sacred?" *Chicago Tribune*, January 23, 2009.

Berghoff, Carlyn, Jan Berghoff, and Nancy R. Ryan. *The Berghoff Family Cookbook: From Our Table to Yours, Celebrating a Century of Entertaining.* Kansas City, MO: Andrews McMeel Publishing, 2007.

Berghoff Restaurant and Catering Group. www.theberghoff.com/berghoff-restaurant/. Accessed July 30, 2014.

Bjorklund, Einar, and James L. Palmer. *A Study of the Prices of Chain and Independent Grocers in Chicago.* Chicago: University of Chicago Press, 1930.

Blair, Emma Helen, trans. *The Indian Tribes of the Upper Mississippi Valley and Region of the Great Lakes.* Cleveland: Arthur H. Clark Company, 1911. archive.org/stream/indiantribesofup01blaiiala/indiantribesofup01blaiiala_djvu.txt

Blatchford Family Papers, Newberry Library, Special Collections, Chicago, IL.

Blei, Norbert. *Chi Town.* Granite Falls, MN: Ellis Press, 1990.

Blei, Nobert. "The *Super*market: A Rhapsodic Tribute to Stop and Shop." *Chicago*, December 1978.

Block, Daniel R. "Protecting and Connecting: Separation, Connection, and the U.S. Dairy Economy, 1840–2002." *Journal for the Study of Food and Society* 6 (2002): 22–30.

Block, Daniel R. "Public Health, Cooperatives, Local Regulation, and the Development of Modern Milk Policy: The Chicago Milkshed, 1900–1940." *Journal of Historical Geography* 35 (2009): 128–53.

Block, Daniel, and J. Kouba. "A Comparison of the Availability and Affordability of a Market Basket in Two Communities in the Chicago Area." *Public Health Nutrition* 9, no. 7 (2006): 837–45.

Block, Daniel, Noel Chavez, and Judy Birgen. *Finding Food in Chicago and the Suburbs.* Chicago: Chicago State University, 2008.

The Blue Island Story: A Historical Review of the First One Hundred and Twenty-Seven Years of Our City on the Hill, Blue Island, Illinois. Blue Island, IL: Blue Island Publishing Company, 1962. catalog.hathitrust.org/Record/012103600. Accessed July 15, 2014.

"Blue Valley Creamery Sold to Beatrice." *Chicago Daily Tribune*, February 18, 1939, 21. archives.chicagotribune.com/1939/02/18/page/21/article/blue-valley-creamery-sold-to-beatrice. Accessed December 1, 2014.

Bode, John W., Mark W. Empie, and Kyd D. Brenner. "Evolution of High Fructose Corn Syrup within the Sweeteners Industry." In *Fructose, High Fructose Corn Syrup, Sucrose, and Health.* Edited by James M. Rippe. New York: Humana Press, 2014.

Boles, Frank, Mary Janzen, and Richard Popp. "Descriptive Inventory for the Bowman Dairy Company Records at the Chicago Historical Society." Chicago, IL: Chicago Historical Society, 1981. chsmedia.org/media/fa/fa/M-B/BowmanDairy-inv.htm. Accessed December 1, 2014.

Bostwick, Frank A. "Why Jewel Sparkles." *Central Manufacturing District Magazine* 33 (1949): 23–27.

Boyer, Barbara. *Mayor Byrne's Chicago Heritage Cookbook.* Chicago: City of Chicago, Mayor's Office of Special Events, 1979.

Brenner, Aaron, Benjamin Day, and Immanuel Ness. *The Encyclopedia of Strikes in American History*. Armonk, NY: M. E. Sharpe, 2009.

Bridges, Patricia S., John H. Blitz, and Martin C. Solano. "Changes in Long Bone Diaphyseal Strength with Horticultural Intensification in West-Central Illinois." *American Journal of Physical Antropology* 112 (2000): 217–38.

Brown, Anna, and Mark Hugo Lopez. *Mapping the Latino Population by State, County, and City*. Pew Research Center, 2013. www.pewhispanic.org/2013/08/29/iv-ranking-latino-populations-in-the-nations-metropolitan-areas/. Accessed December 15, 2014.

Brown, James A., and Patricia J. O'Brien. *At the Edge of Prehistory: Huber Phase Archaeology in the Chicago Area*. Kampsville, IL: Published for the Illinois Department of Transportation by the Center for American Archeology, 1990.

Bryson York, Emily. "Former Dominick's CEO Opening More Grocery Stores Here." *Chicago Tribune*, February 11, 2013. articles.chicagotribune.com/2013-02-11/business/ct-biz-0211-executive-profile-mariano-20130211_1_bob-mariano-grocery-stores-roundy/2. Accessed July 30, 2014.

Buford, Joseph Calvin. *Vegetable Production and Marketing in the Chicago Area—A Geographical Study*. Normal, IL: Illinois State Normal University Studies in Education 15, 1947.

Bulletin of the Chicago School of Sanitary Instruction Devoted to the Dissemination of Advice and Information of the Department of Health, volume 7, number 25. Chicago: City of Chicago, June 21, 1913.

Burnham, Daniel H., and Edward H. Bennett. *Plan of Chicago*. Chicago: Commercial Club of Chicago, 1909; reprint, with an introduction by Kristin Schaffer, New York: Princeton Architectural Press, 1993.

Burnham, Daniel H., and Robert Kingery. *Planning the Region of Chicago*. Chicago: Chicago Regional Planning Association, 1956.

"Butchers' Advocate: Dressed Poultry and the Food Merchant," 71, October 5, 1921, 19. In *Butchers' Advocate: Dressed Poultry and the Food Merchant Issues 1–14; Issues 19–20; Issues 22–25*. books.google.com/books?id=aZVCAQAAMAAJ&printsec=frontcover&source=gbs_ge_summary_r&cad=0#v=onepage&q&f=false. Accessed July 15, 2014.

Butterworth, James D. "A Study of the Changes in the Volume of Fresh Fruits and Vegetables Handled by Middlemen Operating in the Chicago South Water Market, 1939–1949." PhD Dissertation, Northwestern University, 1950.

Camp, Paul A., and JeanMarie Brownson. "The Heavenly Recipe That Helped Make Henri De Jonghe Immortal." *Chicago Tribune*, January 27, 1985.

Campbell, Thomas. *Fighting Slavery in Chicago: Abolitionists, the Law of Slavery, and Lincoln*. Chicago, IL: Ampersand, Inc., 2009.

Candeloro, Dominic. *Chicago's Italians: Immigrants, Ethnics, Americans, 1850–1985*. Mount Pleasant, SC: Arcadia, 2003.

Canning Age. Pontiac, IL: Vance Publishing Corporation, 1920.

Caro, Mark. *The Foie Gras Wars: How a 5,000-Year-Old Delicacy Inspired the World's Fiercest Food Fight*. New York: Simon & Schuster, 2009.

Charles L. Harmon Papers, Chicago History Museum, Chicago.

Chesbrough, Mary M. *The Daily News Cook Book, Being a Reprint from the Chicago Record Cook Book*. Ulan Press, 2012.

"Chicago as a Jobbing Center." *The Grocer's Bulletin* 1 (1881): 1.

Chicago American Indian Center. *Chicago American Indian Center Cookbook*. Chicago: Chicago American Indian Center, 1970.

Chicago Culinary Museum and Chefs Hall of Fame. "Jean Banchet, Legendary Chef." www.thechicagoculinarymuseum.org/?page_id=310. Accessed January 27, 2015.

Chicago Daily News, Inc. *The Daily News Cookbook*. Chicago: Chicago Daily News Company, 1896.

Chicago's Green City Market Program. *Green City Market Cookbook: Great Recipes from Chicago's Award-Winning Farmers Market*. Chicago: Agate Midway, 2014.

"The Chicago Man That Cornered the Pork Market." *True Republican*, September 25, 1880. Illinois Digital Newspaper Collections. idnc.library.illinois.edu/cgi-bin/illinois?a=d&d= STR18800925.2.37#. Accessed September 15, 2013.

"Chicago Menus." *Chicago Tribune*, October 11, 1987.

Chicago Miniature Opera Company Collection. "Programs and Tickets." Chicago History Museum, Box 1.

Chicago Public Library. *At Home on the Range; or, What Librarians Cook*. Chicago: Staff Association of the Chicago Public Library, 1946.

"Chicago Recipes." *National Geographic Society*. travel.nationalgeographic.com/travel/city-guides/chicago-recipes/. Accessed October 8, 2014.

Chicago Scots. "Saint Andrew's Day 'Feast of the Haggis.'" www.chicagoscots.org/feastofhaggis/. Accessed July 30, 2014.

Chicago Urban League, Research and Planning Department. *Grocery Food Prices: Race, Neighborhood, and Other Determinants*. Chicago: Chicago Urban League, 1980.

City within a City: The Biography of Chicago's Marina City: A Brief History of 300 North State Street. www.marinacity.org/history/story/300_north.htm. Accessed May 2, 2015.

Cleaver, Charles. Extracts from article appearing first in the *Chicago Tribune*. In *Reminiscences of Chicago During the Forties and Fifties*, edited by Mabel McIlvaine, William Bross, Charles Cleaver, Alfred Theodore Andreas, and Joseph Jefferson, 74–75. Chicago: R. R. Donnelley & Sons Company, 1913.

Cleland, Charles E. "Indians in a Changing Environment." In *The Great Lakes Forests: An Environmental and Social History*, edited by Susan L. Flader, 83–95. Minneapolis, MN: University of Minnesota Press, 1983.

Clifton, James A., George Cornell, and James M. McClurken. *People of the Three Fires: The Ottawa, Potawatomi and Ojibway of Michigan*. Grand Rapids, MI: Michigan Indian Press, 1986.

College Inn Chicago Menu. New York Public Library online menu collection. menus.nypl.org/menu_pages/69186/explore.

Commercial Menu Collection, Chicago History Museum.

Committee on Health, Chicago City Council. *Report on the More Economic Distribution and Delivery of Milk in the City of Chicago*. Municipal Reference Library Bulletin 8. Chicago: City of Chicago, 1917.

"Corporate Affairs." *Milk Plant Monthly* 9 (1920): 42.

Cronon, William. *Nature's Metropolis: Chicago and the Great West*. New York: W. W. Norton & Company, 1991.

Cruz, Wilfredo. *City of Dreams: Latino Immigration to Chicago*. Lanham, MD: University Press of America, 2007.

Cumbler, John T. *Northeast and Midwest United States: An Environmental History*. Santa Barbara, CA: ABC-CLIO, 2005.

Cutler, Irving. *The Jews of Chicago: From Shtetl to Suburb*. Champaign, IL: University of Illinois Press, 1996.

Danahey, Mike, and Allison Hantschel. *Chicago's Historic Irish Pubs*. Charleston, SC: Arcadia Publishing, 2011.

Danckers, Ulrich, Jane Meredith, John F. Swenson, and Helen Hornbeck Tanner. *A Compendium of the Early History of Chicago: To the Year 1835 When the Indians Left*. River Forest, IL: Early Chicago, Inc., 2000.

Deutsch, Tracey. *Building a Housewife's Paradise: Gender, Politics, and American Grocery Stores in the Twentieth Century*. Chapel Hill: University of North Carolina Press, 2010.

"Development of Polish Business in Chicago White Eagle Brewing Company Worth More Than Half Million Dollars." *Dziennik Związkowy*, August 11, 1917. flps.newberry.org/article/5423968_4_1721. Accessed July 30, 2014.

Diamond, Jared M. *Guns, Germs, and Steel: The Fates of Human Societies*. New York: W. W. Norton & Company, 1998.

Dish. Winnipeg: Studio Publications, 2009.

Donnelly, Naomi. *The Lakeside Cookbook No. 2: A Manual of Recipes for Cooking, Pickling, and Preserving, and Other Useful Information for the Housekeeper*. Chicago: Donnelley, Gassette & Loyd, 1878.

Drury, John. *Dining in Chicago*. New York: John Day Company, 1931. archive.org/stream/ dininginchicago00drur -page/n7/mode/2up. Accessed July 30, 2014.

Duddy, Edward A. *Agriculture in the Chicago Region*. Chicago, IL: University of Chicago Press, 1929.

Duddy, Edward A. "Distribution of Perishable Commodities in the Chicago Metropolitan Area." *University Journal of Business* 4, no. 2 (1926): 151–81.

Duis, Perry. *Challenging Chicago: Coping with Everyday Life, 1837–1920*. Urbana and Chicago: University of Illinois Press, 1998.

Duis, Perry. *The Saloon: Public Drinking in Chicago and Boston, 1880–1920*. Urbana, IL: University of Illinois Press, 1983.

Duis, Perry. "The Saloon in a Changing Chicago." In *Wild Kind of Boldness: The Chicago History Reader*, edited by Rosemary K. Adams. Grand Rapids, MI: William B. Eerdmans Publishing Company and Chicago: Chicago Historical Society, 1998. Originally published in Chicago History, winter 1975–1976.

"The Economist: Investors Section." *The Economist: A Weekly Financial, Commercial, and Real-Estate Newspaper, Volume 55*. Chicago: Economist Publishing Company, 1916.

Eddington, Jane. "Economical Housekeeping." *Chicago Tribune*, September 16, 1913.

Edmonds, R. David. "Chicago in the Middle Ground." In *Encyclopedia of Chicago*. encyclopedia.chicagohistory.org/pages/254.html. Accessed August 23. 2013.

Eiseman, Herbert, and Jerold Levin. "Hot Dog! Jewish Participation in Chicago's Meat Industry." *Chicago Jewish History*. chicagojewishhistory.org/pdf/2012/CJH-2_2012.pdf. Accessed July 30, 2014.

Emily Frankenstein Diary, Chicago History Museum.

Eng, Monica. "Saga of a Sandwich." *Chicago Tribune*, June 18, 2003. articles.chicagotribune. com/2003-06-18/features/0306180103_1_plantains-sandwich-puerto-ricans. Accessed January 15, 2015.

Estep, George. "State Street Special: For 25 Years Celebrities Were the Order of the Day at Fritzel's." *Chicago Tribune*, April 20, 1986. articles.chicagotribune.com/1986-04-20/ features/8601280625_1_nancy-jacobson-restaurant-meat-cutter. Accessed September 1, 2014.

"Feast of the Haggis." Chicago Scots. www.chicagoscots.org/feastofhaggis. Accessed July 30, 2014.

Ferber, Edna. *So Big*. New York: P. F. Collier and Son, 1924.

Fitzgerald, Jacqueline. "General Mills Shuts Down Plant." *Chicago Tribune*, September 30, 1997. articles.chicagotribune.com/1997-09-30/business/9709300308_1_general-mills-shuts -wheaties-and-cheerios. Accessed September 1, 2014.

Flader, Susan. *The Great Lakes Forest: An Environmental and Social History*. Minneapolis, MN: University of Minnesota Press in association with Forest History Society, Inc., Santa Cruz, 1983.

Flores-Gonzalez, Nilda. "Paseo Boricua: Claiming a Puerto Rican Space in Chicago." *Centro Journal*, vol. 2, January 1, 2001.

Florida, Richard. "What Is the World's Most Economically Powerful City?" *The Atlantic*, May 8, 2012. www.theatlantic.com/business/archive/2012/05/what-is-the-worlds-most-economic ally-powerful-city/256841/. Accessed January 27, 2015.

Forman, Cyrus. "A Briny Crossroads: Salt, Slavery, and Sectionalism in the Kanawha Salines." MA Thesis, City University of New York, 2014. dspace.cuny.edu/bitstream/handle/11049/ 24282/2014SpHu09.pdf?sequence=1. Accessed December 1, 2014.

Gabaccia, Donna R. *We Are What We Eat: Ethnic Food and the Making of Americans*. Cambridge, MA: Harvard University Press, 1998.

Gabriel, Jackie S. "Unionizing the 'Jungle': A Century of Meatpacking Strikes." In *The Encyclopedia of Strikes in American History*, edited by Aaron Brenner, Benjamin Day, and Immanuel Ness. New York: M.E. Sharpe, 2009.

Ganakos, Alexa, and Katherine Bish. *Greektown Chicago: Its History, Its Recipes*. St. Louis, MO: G. Bradley Publishing, 2005.

Gannon, Diane, Gloria Baraks, Mark Weinstein, and Liz Roy. *The Foods of Chicago: A Delicious History*. St. Louis, MO: G. Bradley Publishing, 2007.

Gano, Chilton. "Chicago Jobber Making History." April 1918, unknown newspaper, Steele-Wedeles Papers, Chicago History Museum.

Garrett, Celeste. "Gladys Holcomb, 96, Gladys' Luncheonette Owner." *Chicago Tribune*, May 3, 2003. articles.chicagotribune.com/2003-05-03/news/0305030177_1_restaurant-biscuits-fried-chicken. Accessed January 27, 2015.

Gebert, Michael. "A Barbecue History of Chicago." Blog. *Sky Full of Bacon*. skyfullofbacon.com/blog/. Accessed July 30, 2014.

"German Industry and Its Results: A Visit to the Brewery of Mr. John A. Huck." *Illinois Staats-Zeitung*, May 16, 1863. flps.newberry.org/article/5418474_6_1468. Accessed July 30, 2014.

Gilmore, Janet C. "*Sagamité* and *Booya*: French Influence in Defining Great Lakes Culinary Heritage." *Material Culture Review* 60 (2004): 9.

"Giordano's Menu." Giordano's. giordanos.com/the-menu/.

"Gleeful Celestials Chicago Chinamen Celebrate Their New-Year's Festival." *Chicago Tribune*, January 20, 1890. flps.newberry.org/article/5418479_0251/. Accessed July 30, 2014.

Goddard, Leslie. *Chicago's Sweet Candy History*. Mount Pleasant, SC: Arcadia Publishing, 2012.

Goodman, Charles S. *Do the Poor Pay More? A Study of the Food Purchasing Practices of Low-Income Consumers*. Philadelphia: Self-Published, 1967.

Goodsell, Charles M., and Henry Edward Wallace. *The Manual for Statistics: Stock Exchange Handbook, Volume 29*. New York: Manual of Statistics Company, 1907.

Gordon, Steven C. "From Slaughterhouse to Soap-Boiler: Cincinnati's Meat Packing Industry, Changing Technologies, and the Rise of Mass Production, 1825–1870." *Journal of the Society for Industrial Archeology* 16 (1990): 55–67.

Gorman, John. "Borden Buys Beatrice's Dairy Group." *Chicago Tribune*, October 31, 1986. articles.chicagotribune.com/1986-10-31/business/8603210957_1_borden-spokesman-dairy-operations-meadow-gold. Accessed December 1, 2014.

Gray, James. *Business without Boundary: The Story of General Mills*. Minneapolis, MN: University of Minnesota Press, 1954.

Greene, Joan. *A Chicago Tradition: Marshall Field's Food and Fashion*. Petaluma, CA: Pomegranate, 2005.

Grier, Katherine C. *Pets in America: A History*. Chapel Hill, NC: University of North Carolina Press, 2006.

Grimes, William. "Charlie Trotter Dies at 54; Chef Made Chicago a Must." *New York Times*, November 5, 2013. www.nytimes.com/2013/11/06/dining/charlie-trotter-chicago-chef-who-elevated-american-dining-dies-at-54.html?_r=0. Accessed January 27, 2015.

Grossman, James R. *Land of Hope: Chicago, Black Southerners, and the Great Migration*. Chicago: University of Chicago Press, 1989.

Grier, Katherine. "On the Material Culture of Petkeeping." In *Routledge Handbook of Human Animal Studies*, edited by Garry Marvin and Susan McHugh. New York: Routledge, 2014.

Gustaitis, Joseph A. *Chicago's Greatest Year, 1893: The White City and the Birth of a Modern Metropolis*. Carbondale, IL: Southern Illinois University Press, 2013.

Guyer, I. D. *History of Chicago: Its Commercial and Manufacturing Interests and Industry*. Chicago: Church, Goodman & Cushin, 1862. openlibrary.org/books/OL7052474M/History_of_Chicago. Accessed December 15, 2014.

Hanes, Phyllis. "The Food Father: Chef Louis Szathmary of Chicago's Bakery Is the Award-Winning Author of Five Cookbooks." *Christian Science Monitor*, June 1, 1988. www.csmonitor.com/1988/0601/hflou.html. Accessed January 27, 2015.

Harpster, Jack. *The Railroad Tycoon Who Built Chicago: A Biography of William B. Ogden*. Carbondale, IL: Southern Illinois University Press, 2009.

Harris, Melissa. "West Loop Produce Wholesaler: Should I Stay or Should I Go?" *Chicago Tribune*, April 10, 2015.

Hawthorne, Michael. "A Truly Foul, Nasty River Ran Through It: Even Bubbly Creek, Worst of Worst, Was Never Cleaned Up." *Chicago Tribune*, June 25, 2011. articles. chicagotribune.com/2011-06-25/news/ct-per-flashback-bubbly-0626-2-20110625_1_offal-and-carcasses-bubbly-creek-chicago-river. Accessed April 17, 2015.

Heinen, Joseph C., and Susan B. Heinen. *Lost German Chicago*. Mount Pleasant, SC: Arcadia Publishing, 2009.

Helliger, Richard. *Lockport Historic District HAER No. IL-16 Bounded by: 8th, Hamilton, 11th Streets and the Illinois and Michigan Canal*. Washington, DC: Historic American Engineering Record National Park Service Department of the Interior, 1979. lcweb2.loc.gov/master/pnp/habshaer/il/il0400/il0431/data/il0431data.pdf. Accessed September 1, 2014.

Hess, Alfred F. "The Incidence of Tubercle Bacilli in New York City Milk." In *Collected Studies from the Research Laboratory*. New York: Department of Health, City of New York.

Hevrdejs, Judy. "26th Street !sass! This Southwest Side Neighborhood Offers a Culinary Adventure for the Senses." *Chicago Tribune*, September 22, 1988. articles.chicagotribune.com/1988-09-22/entertainment/8802010409_1_street-vendors-main-shop. Accessed July 30, 2014.

"He Who Is Not for U." *Prairie Farmer* 94, August 5, 1922. play.google.com/store/books/details?id=5x4_AQAAMAAJ&rdid=book-5x4_AQAAMAAJ&rdot=1. Accessed December 1, 2014.

Hill, Libby. *The Chicago River: A Natural and Unnatural History*. Chicago: Lake Claremont Press, 2000.

Ho, Chuimei, and Soo Lon Moy. *Chinese in Chicago, 1870–1945*. Mount Pleasant, SC: Arcadia Publishing, 2005.

Holland, Robert A. *Chicago in Maps: 1612 to 2002*. New York: Rizzoli, 2005.

Hollie, Pamela G. "Greyhound Selling Armour." *New York Times*, June 30, 1983. www.nytimes.com/1983/06/30/business/greyhound-selling-armour.html. Accessed January 27, 2015.

The Home Guide: Or, a Book by 500 Ladies, Embracing About 1,000 Recipes and Hints, Pertaining to Cookery, the Household, the Sick Room, the Toilet, Etc. Chicago, IL: Chicago Daily Tribune, 1890. catalog.hathitrust.org/api/volumes/oclc/154502820.html. Accessed January 27, 2015.

Hudson, John C. *Chicago: A Geography of the City and Its Region*. Santa Fe, NM: Center for American Places and Chicago: University of Chicago Press, 2006.

Ihejrika, Maudlyne. "South Side Soul Food Legend Army and Lou's Closes." *Chicago Sun Times*, February 4, 2011.

"Illinois Constitution of 1818." Illinois Digital Archives. www.idaillinois.org/cdm/compoundobject/collection/isl2/id/12600. Accessed December 15, 2014.

Interstate Commerce Commission Reports: Decisions of the Interstate Commerce Commission of the United States, Volume 24. Washington, DC: L. K. Strouse Publisher, 1913. play. google.com/store/books/details?id=qlEuAAAAYAAJ&rdid=book-qlEuAAAAYAAJ&rdot=1. Accessed December 1, 2014.

Iomaire, Máirtín Mac Con, and Pádraic Óg Gallagher. "Irish Corned Beef: A Culinary History." *Journal of Culinary Science and Technology* 9 (2011): 27–43.

Irving Park Lutheran Church. *90th Anniversary Cookbook*. Collierville, TN: Fundcraft Publishing, 1994.

Jacobson, Matthew Frye. *Whiteness of a Different Color: European Immigrants and the Alchemy of Race*. Cambridge, MA: Harvard University Press, 1998.

Jenks, Albert Ernest. "The Wild Rice Gatherers of the Upper Lakes: A Study in American Primitive Economics." In *Annual Report of the Bureau of American Ethnology to the Secretary of the Smithsonian Institution, 19 (Part 2)*. Washington, DC: Government Printing Office, 1900, 1053–69. www.wisconsinhistory.org/turningpoints/search.asp?id=1065. Accessed September 1, 2014.

Jentz, John B., and Richard Schneirov. *Chicago in the Age of Capital: Class, Politics, and Democracy during the Civil War and Reconstruction*. Champaign, IL: University of Illinois Press, 2012.

Joens, David A. *From Slave to State Legislator: John W. E. Thomas, Illinois' First African American Lawmaker*. Carbondale, IL: Southern Illinois University Press, 2012.

Johnson, Flora. "Superstars of Our Supermarkets." *The Chicagoan* 1 (1973): 60–63.

Junior League of Chicago. *One Magnificent Cookbook*. Chicago, IL: Junior League of Chicago, 1988.

Kantowicz, Edward R."Polish Chicago: Survival through Solidarity." In *Ethnic Chicago: A Multicultural Portrait*, edited by Melvin G. Holli and Peter d'Alroy Jones. Grand Rapids, MI: W. B. Eerdmans Publishing Company, 1994.

Kaucher, Jo A. *The Chicago Diner Cookbook*. Summertown, TN: Book Publishing Company, 2002.

Kavasch, E. Barrie. *Native Harvests: American Indian Wild Foods and Recipes*. Mineola, NY: Dover Publications, 2005.

Keating, Ann Durkin. *Rising Up from Indian Country: The Battle of Fort Dearborn and the Birth of Chicago*. Chicago: University of Chicago Press, 2012.

Kenney, William Howland. *Chicago Jazz: A Cultural History, 1904–1930*. New York: Oxford University Press, 1993.

Kinietz, W. Vernon, and Antoine Denis Raudot. *The Indians of the Western Great Lakes, 1615–1760*. Ann Arbor, MI: University of Michigan Press, 1991.

Kirkland, E. S. *Six Little Cooks or Aunt Jane's Cooking Class*. Chicago: Jansen, McClurg, 1877.

Kitagawa, Evelyn M., and De Ver Sholes. *Chicagoland's Retail Market*. Chicago: Chicago Association of Commerce and Industry and Chicago Community Inventory of the University of Chicago, 1957.

Knoblauch, Mark. "Chez Paul Still Fancy (But Predictable) After All These Years." *Chicago Tribune*, June 2, 1985. articles.chicagotribune.com/1985-06-02/entertainment/8502040413_1_turbot-sauce-hollandaise. Accessed January 27, 2015.

Knott, Andy. "Eatery Ends Wild, Grizzly Era." *Chicago Tribune*, May 23, 1986. articles.chicagotribune.com/1986-05-23/news/8602070230_1_wild-game-wild-rice-restaurant. Accessed January 27, 2015.

Kott, Robert. *Summit*. Mount Pleasant, SC: Arcadia Publishing, 2009.

"Kraft, Sara Lee Call Truce in Wiener War." *Chicago Tribune*, September 8, 2011. articles.chicagotribune.com/2011-09-08/business/chi-kraft-sara-lee-call-truce-in-wiener-war-2011 0908_1_national-taste-test-sara-lee-pure-beef. Accessed December 20, 2014.

Kraig, Bruce. *Hot Dog: A Global History*. London: Reaktion, 2009.

Kraig, Bruce. "Restaurants." *Encyclopedia of Chicago*, 2005. www.encyclopedia. chicagohistory.org/pages/1066.html. Accessed January 20, 2015.

Kroc, Ray, and Robert Anderson. *Grinding It Out: The Making of McDonald's*. New York: Macmillan, 1992.

Kuehn, Steven R. "New Evidence for Late Paleoindian–Early Archaic Subsistence Behavior in the Western Great Lakes." *American Antiquity* 63, no. 3 (1998): 457.

Lalley, Heather, and Brendan Lekan. *Chicago's Homegrown Cookbook: Local Food, Local Restaurants, Local Recipes*. Minneapolis, MN: MBI Publishing Company and Voyageur Press, 2011.

Lamb, John. "Lockport, IL." In *The Encyclopedia of Chicago*. Edited by James R. Grossman, Ann Durkin Keating, and Janice L. Reiff. Chicago: University of Chicago Press, 2004. www.encyclopedia.chicagohistory.org/pages/760.html. Accessed September 1, 2014.

Lanyon, Richard. *Building the Canal to Save Chicago*. Bloomington, IN: Xlibris Corp., 2012.

Leavitt, Judith Walzer. *The Healthiest City: Milwaukee and the Politics of Health Reform*. Princeton, NJ: Princeton University Press, 1982.

Lee, Guy A. "The Historical Significance of the Chicago Grain Elevator System." *Agricultural History* 11 (1937).

Leech, Harper, and John Charles Carroll. *Armour and His Times*. New York: D. Appleton-Century Company, Incorporated, 1938.

"Lem's Bar-B-Q." Southern Foodways Alliance. www.southernfoodways.org/interview/lems-bar-b-q/. Accessed July 30, 2014.

Lettuce Entertain You Restaurants. "Lettuce Tell You Our History." www.leye.com/about-us/history. Accessed January 27, 2015.

Levinson, Marc. *The Great A&P and the Struggle for Small Business in America.* New York: Hill and Wang, 2012.

Ling, Huping. *Chinese Chicago: Race, Transnational Migration, and Community since 1870.* Redwood City, CA: Stanford University Press, 2012.

Lippincott, Isaac. "The Early Salt Trade of the Ohio Valley." *Journal of Political Economy* (1912): 1029–52.

Lombardo, Robert M. "Chicago's Little Sicily." *Journal of the Illinois State Historical Society* 100 (2007): 41–56.

Lost Recipes Found. "Red Star Inn–Style Sauerbraten Zweibelfleisch." lostrecipesfound.com/recipe/red-star-inn-style-sauerbraten-zwiebelfleisch-onion-beef-roast/.

Mari Gallagher Research and Consulting Group. *Examining the Impact of Food Deserts on Public Health in Chicago,* 2006. www.marigallagher.com.

"Marigold Arena Sold for Use as Church." *Chicago Tribune,* April 4, 1963. www.archives.chicagotribune.com/1963/04/04/page/105/article/marigold-arena-sold-for-use-as-church. Accessed July 30, 2014.

Markman, Charles W. *Chicago Before History: The Prehistoric Archaeology of a Modern Metropolitan Area.* Springfield, IL: Illinois Historic Preservation Agency, 1991.

Marshall, Richard O., and Earl R. Kooi. "Enzymatic Conversion of D-Glucose to D-Fructose." *Science* 125 (1957): 648–49.

Marvin, Garry, and Susan McHugh. *Routledge Handbook of Human-Animal Studies.* New York: Routledge, 2014.

McGowen, Thomas. *Island within a City: A History of the Norridge-Harwood Heights Area.* Harwood Heights: Eisenhower Public Library District, 1989.

McCafferty, Michael. "A Fresh Look at the Place Named Chicago." *Journal of the Illinois State Historical Society* 95 (2003): 117.

"McDonald's History." McDonald's Corporation. www.aboutmcdonalds.com/mcd/our_company/mcdonalds_history_timeline.html. Accessed November 14, 2014.

McNamee, Tom. "Hunt's on Chicken Vesuvio's a Chicago Original, But Who Created It?: A Stack of Menus, Claims of Invention and Missing Peas. Mystery Is Served . . ." *Chicago Sun-Times,* January 12, 2005. www.highbeam.com/doc/1P2-1568669.html Accessed January 22, 2015.

Megan, Graydon. "Sam Ricobene Sr., 1931–2011: Restaurateur Helped Build Ricobene's into Chain." *Chicago Tribune,* October 22, 2011. articles.chicagotribune.com/2011-10-22/news/ct-met-obit-ricobene-1023-20111022_1_gonnella-baking-new-restaurant-twin-brother. Accessed July 30, 2014.

Melendy, Royal L. "The Saloon in Chicago, IL." *American Journal of Sociology,* 6, no.3 (1900): 289–306.

Melendy, Royal L. "The Saloon in Chicago, IL." *American Journal of Sociology* 6, no. 4 (1901): 433–64.

Michigan Historical Commission. "Michigan Pioneer and Historical Society," In *Michigan Historical Collections 21.* Ann Arbor: University of Michigan Library, 2006. quod.lib.umich.edu/cgi/t/text/text-idx?c=moa;idno=0534625.0021.001. Accessed September 1, 2014.

Miller, Donald L. *City of the Century: The Epic of Chicago and the Making of America.* New York: Simon & Schuster, 1996.

Miller, Jay. "Land and Lifeway in the Chicago Area: Chicago and the Illinois-Miami." In *Indians of the Chicago Area,* edited by Terry Strauss. Chicago: NAES College Press, 1990.

Mintz, Sidney Wilfred. *Tasting Food, Tasting Freedom: Excursions into Eating, Culture, and the Past.* Boston: Beacon Press. 1996.

"Mobile Food Vendor Licenses." City of Chicago Department of Business Affairs and Consumer Protection. www.cityofchicago.org/city/en/depts/bacp/supp_info/mobile_food_vendorlicenses.html. Accessed November 14, 2014.

Moore, Christopher R., and Victoria G. Dekle. "Hickory Nuts, Bulk Processing and the Advent of Early Horticultural Economies in Eastern North America." *World Archaeology* 42 (2010): 595–608.

Moy, Susan. "The Chinese in Chicago: The First One Hundred Years." In *Ethnic Chicago: A Multicultural Portrait*, edited by Melvin G. Holli and Peter d'Alroy. Jones, 378–408. Grand Rapids, MI: Wm. B. Eerdmans Publishing Company, 1995.

"The Necessity of a Ship-Canal between the East and the West. Report of the Committee on Statistics, for the City of Chicago." National Ship-Canal Convention, June 2, 1863. Ann Arbor, MI: University of Michigan Library, 2005.

Neill, E. *The Every-Day Cook-Book and Encyclopedia of Practical Recipes*. Chicago: Regan Printing House, 1892.

Newman, Kara. *The Secret Financial Life of Food: From Commodities Markets to Supermarkets*. New York: Columbia University Press, 2013.

"Norton and Co. Go Under." *Chicago Tribune*, December 27, 1896, 5. archives.chicagotribune. com/1896/12/27/page/5/article/norton-co-go-under. Accessed September 1, 2014.

Old Irving Park Association (Chicago, IL). *Old Irving Park Association Cookbook: A Book of Favorite Recipes*. Leawood, KS: Circulation Service, 1990.

Old Town Triangle Association (Chicago, IL). *The Old Town Dawn Until Dusk Cookbook*. Leawood, KS: Circulation Service, 1970.

"Our Story." Eli's Cheesecake Chicago. www.elicheesecake.com/about/our-story/.

Owen, Mary. "Leon Finney Sr.: 1916–2008 Founded Leon's Bar-B-Q." *Chicago Tribune*, April 6, 2008. articles.chicagotribune.com/2008-04-06/news/0804050372_1_mr-finney-restaurants-eldest-son. Accessed July 30, 2014.

Pacyga, Dominic A. *Chicago: A Biography*. Chicago: University of Chicago Press, 2009.

Pacyga, Dominic A. *Polish Immigrants and Industrial Chicago: Workers on the South Side, 1880–1922*. Columbus: Ohio State University Press, 2003.

Parker, Kathryn E. "The Archaeobotany of the Paleo-Indian and Archaic Components at the Christianson Site (11RI42)." *Illinois Archaeology: Journal of the Illinois Archaeology Survey* 18 (2006): 122.

Paull, Irving S., and W. S. Goodnow. *Congress Hotel, Home of a Thousand Homes: Rare and Piquant Dishes of Historic Interest*. Chicago: Sleepick & Hellman, 1914.

"People and Events." *Journal of Dairy Science* 48 (1965): 18. www.journalofdairyscience.org/article/S0022-0302%2865%2988348-5/pdf. Accessed December 1, 2014.

Peterson, Jacqueline. "The Founding Fathers: The Absorption of the French-Indian Chicago, 1816–1837." In *Ethnic Chicago: A Multicultural Portrait*, 4th edition. Edited by Melvin G. Holli and Peter d'A. Jones. Grand Rapids, MI: Wm. B. Eerdmans Publishing Company, 1995.

Pierce, Bessie Louise. *History of Chicago, Volume I: The Beginning of a City, 1673–1848*. Chicago: University of Chicago Press, [1937] 2007.

Pierce, Bessie Louise. *A History of Chicago, Volume II: From Town to City, 1848–1871*. Chicago: University of Chicago Press, [1940], 2007.

Pierce, Bessie Louise. *A History of Chicago, Volume III: The Rise of a Modern City, 1871–1893*. Chicago: University of Chicago Press, [1957], 2007.

Pierce, Bessie Louise, and Joe Lester Norris. *As Others See Chicago: Impressions of Visitors, 1673–1933*. Chicago: University of Chicago Press, 1933.

Piper, Richard Upton. *Diseased Milk and the Flesh of Animals Used for Human Food*. Chicago: Jameson and Morse, 1879.

Podmolik, Mary Ellen. "Garrett's Popcorn Sued over Chicago Mix." *Chicago Tribune*, September 2, 2014. www.chicagotribune.com/business/breaking/chi-garrett-popcorn-chicago-mix-lawsuit-20140902-story.html. Accessed January 27, 2015.

Poe, Tracy. "African-American Meals from Slavery to Soul Food." In *The Meal: Proceedings of the Oxford Symposium on Food and Cookery*. Edited by Harlan Walker. Devon, England: Prospect Books, 2002.

Pointe de Sable, Jean Baptiste, Jean Lalime, and Milo Milton Quaife. "Property of Jean Baptiste Point Sable." *Mississippi Valley Historical Review* 15 (1928): 89–92.

Poor's Manual of Industrials: Manufacturing, Mining and Miscellaneous Companies. New York: Poor's Manual Company, 1916. play.google.com/store/books/details?id= l2U3AQAAMAAJ&rdid=book-l2U3AQAAMAAJ&rdot=1. Accessed December 15, 2014.

Porubcan, Paula J., Peter J. Geraci, and Melissa L. Baltus. "The Bottlemy Site (11MH495): An Emerging and Mature Late Woodland Occupation in Northeastern Illinois." *Illinois Archaeological Survey, Inc., Illinois Archaeology* 22 (2010): 600.

Pratt, Steven. "Hidden Gems Smaller Firms Thrive with Loyalty, Quality Tortillas Became 'a Miracle' for an Immigrant." *Chicago Tribune,* May 6, 1993.

Quaife, Milo Milton. *Chicago and the Old Northwest, 1673–1835: A Study of the Evolution of the Northwestern Frontier, Together with a History of Fort Dearborn.* 1913, reprint, Urbana: University of Illinois Press, 2001.

Quaife, Milo Milton. *Chicago's Highways, Old and New, From Indian Trail to Motor Road.* Chicago: D. F. Keller & Company, 1923.

Quaife, Milo Milton. "Property of Jean Baptiste Point Sable." *Mississippi Valley Historical Review* 15 (1928): 90–91.

Quaker Oats Company, "Factory to Dairy." Chicago: N. P., 1928. Film. www.youtube.com/watch?v=LAupzdTFqyQ. Accessed December 15, 2014.

Rafert, Stewart. *The Miami Indians of Indiana: A Persistent People, 1654–1994.* Indianapolis: Indiana Historical Society, 1996.

Rammohan, Yasmin. "Puppet Opera." *Chicago Tonight: Cultural Connections*, WTTW Chicago Public Television. December 29, 2011. chicagotonight.wttw.com/2011/12/29/puppet-opera. Accessed July 30, 2011.

Reed, Christopher Robert. *Black Chicago's First Century. Volume I.* Columbia, MO: University of Missouri Press, 2005.

Ress, David. *Governor Edward Coles and the Vote to Forbid Slavery in Illinois, 1823–1824.* Jefferson, NC: McFarland & Company, 2006.

"Review of the Markets." *The Chicago Grocer* 4, no. 24 (1878): 10.

Rice, William. "Oh, How Chicago Loved Its Oysters." *Chicago Tribune*, July 16, 1997. articles.chicagotribune.com/1997-07-16/entertainment/9707170332_1_raw-oysters-restaurant-guide-menu. Accessed January 27, 2015.

Riesenberg, Emily. *Original Recipes Compiled for Wm. J. Moxley, Chicago.* Special Collections. University of Illinois-Chicago, ca. 1910.

Riley, Thomas J., Gregory R. Walz, and Charles J. Bareis. Andrew C. Fortier, and Kathryn E. Parker "Accelerator Mass Spectrometry (AMS) Dates Confirm Early Zea Mays in the Mississippi River Valley." *American Antiquity* 59 (1994): 490–98.

Roediger, David R. *Working toward Whiteness: How America's Immigrants Became White, The Strange Journey from Ellis Island to the Suburbs.* New York: Basic Books, 2005.

Rorer, Sarah T. *Recipes Used in Illinois Corn Exhibit Model Kitchen, Women's Building, Columbian Exhibition.* Chicago: University of Illinois-Chicago, Special Collections, 1893.

Rosenau, Milton J. *The Milk Question.* London: Constable, 1913.

Ross, H. A. *The Marketing of Milk in the Chicago Dairy District.* Urbana, IL: University of Illinois Agricultural Experiment Station, 1925. babel.hathitrust.org/cgi/pt?id=mdp. 35128001191129;view=1up;seq=19. Accessed December 1, 2014.

Roy, William G. *Socializing Capital: The Rise of the Large Industrial Corporation in America.* Princeton, NJ: Princeton University Press, 1997.

Royko, Mike. "Erasing Thoughts of Meatless Ribs." *Chicago Tribune*, September 23, 1986. articles.chicagotribune.com/1986-09-23/news/8603110160_1_vegetarians-gluten-sauce. Accessed July 30, 2014.

R. R. Donnelley & Sons Company. *Ways to a Woman's Heart.* Newberry Library, Special Collections. Chicago: R. R. Donnelly Company, 1948.

Ruby, Jeff. "Arun's in Albany Park: The Accidental Masterpiece." *Chicago*, December 20, 2011. www.chicagomag.com/Chicago-Magazine/January-2012/Aruns-in-Albany-Park-The-Accidental-Masterpiece/. Accessed January 27, 2015.

Ruby, Jeff. "Has Spiaggia Sold Out?" *Chicago*, May 22, 2013. www.chicagomag.com/Chicago-Magazine/June-2013/Italian-Gold/. Accessed January 27, 2015.

Ruhlman, Michael. "Toward Creativity." In *Alinea*. Edited by Grant Achatz, 1–6. Berkeley: Ten Speed Press, 2008.

Samors, Neal S., Eric Bronsky, Bob Dauber, and Penny Pollack. *Chicago's Classic Restaurants: Past, Present and Future.* Chicago: Chicago's Books Press, 2011.

Sarah Hackett Stevenson Memorial Lodging House Association, comp. *Stevenson Memorial Cook Book.* Chicago: Stevenson Memorial Lodging House Association, 1919.

Scarpaci, Vincenza. "Chicago's Little Sicily." *Journal of the Illinois State Historical Society* 100 (2007): 41–56.

Scarpaci, Vincenza. *The Journey of the Italians in America.* Gretna, LA: Pelican Publishing Company, 2008. www.gonnella.com.

Schlosser, Eric. *Fast Food Nation: The Dark Side of the All-American Meal.* Boston: Houghton Mifflin, 2001.

Schmeltzer, John. "Butternut Bread-Maker Closing Chicago Bakery." *Chicago Tribune*, September 24, 2004. articles.chicagotribune.com/2004-09-24/business/0409240329_1_inter state-bakeries-hostess-twinkies-wheat-bread. Accessed December 1, 2014.

Schultz, E. J. "The Quaker Man Is Growing a Milk Mustache." *Advertising Age*, September 8, 2014. adage.com/article/cmo-strategy/quaker-man-growing-a-milk-mustache/294857/. Accessed December 1, 2014.

Schulz, Edward C. *A Functional Analysis of Retail Trade in the Maxwell Street Market Area of Chicago.* Master's Thesis, Northwestern University, 1954.

Schwartz, Bob, Joe Mantegna, and Bob Sirott. *Never Put Ketchup on a Hot Dog: Chicago's Hot Dog Passion.* Chicago: Chicago's Books Press, 2008.

Segal, David. "The Gyro's History Unfolds." *New York Times*, July 14, 2009. www.nytimes.com/2009/07/15/dining/15gyro.html?pagewanted=all. Accessed January 27, 2015.

Sengstock, Charles A. *That Toddlin' Town: Chicago White Dance Bands and Orchestras, 1900–1950.* Urbana: University of Illinois Press, 2004.

Sheridan, Margaret. "It's Down Home Goodness at Gladys' Luncheonette." *Chicago Tribune*, May 1, 1987. archives.chicagotribune.com/1987/05/01/page/136/article/restaurants. Accessed January 27, 2015.

Shircliffe, Arnold. *The Edgewater Beach Salad Book.* Evanston, IL: Hotel Monthly Press, 1926, 11th printing, 1951.

Shuck, Edith G., and Herman N. Bundesen. *Chicago Daily News Cookbook.* Chicago: Chicago Daily News, 1930.

Shuman, Carrie V. *Favorite Dishes: A Columbian Autograph Souvenir.* Chicago: R. R. Donnelley & Sons, 1893.

Simmon's Spice Mill: Devoted to the Interests of the Coffee, Tea and Spice Trades. New York: Spice Mill Publishing Company, 1913.

Simmons, James W. *The Changing Pattern of Retail Location.* Chicago: Department of Geography, University of Chicago, 1964.

Simon, Mary L. "A Regional and Chronological Synthesis of Archaic Period Plant Use in the Midcontinent." In *Archaic Societies: Diversity and Complexity across the Midcontinent*, eds. Thomas E. Emerson, Dale L. McElrath, and Andrew C. Fortier, 81–114. Albany, NY: SUNY Press, 2009.

Simon, Mary L. "Regional Variations in Plant Use Strategies in the Midwest during the Late Woodland." In *Late Woodland Societies: Tradition and Transformation Across the Midcontinent*. Edited by Thomas E. Emerson, Dale L. McElrath, and Andrew C. Fortier, 47–59. Lincoln, NE: University of Nebraska Press, 2000.

Sinclair, Upton. *The Jungle.* Mineola, NY: Dover Publications, 2001, original 1906.

Skilnik, Bob. *Beer: A History of Brewing in Chicago.* Fort Lee, NJ: Barricade Books, 2006.

Skilnik, Bob. "Building Chicago Was Thirsty Work: Brewers Rolled in with a Solution." *Chicago Tribune*, July 16, 1997. articles.chicagotribune.com/1997-07-16/entertainment/9707170336_1_beer-chicagoans-first-brew-pub. Accessed January 27, 2015.

Skilnik, Bob. *The History of Beer and Brewing in Chicago, 1833–1978.* West Conshohocken, PA: Infinity Publishing, 2002.

Slaymaker III, Charles M., and Chaires M. Slaymaker Jr. "Au Sagaunashke Village: The Upper Mississippian Occupation of the Knoll Spring Site, Cook County, Illinois." In *Mississippian*

Site Archaeology in Illinois I, Site Reports from the St. Louis and Chicago Areas, Bulletin No. 8. Edited by James A. Brown and Gregory H. Perino, 244–46. Urbana, IL: Illinois Archaeological Survey, Inc., 1971.

Smith, Andrew F. *Eating History: Thirty Turning Points in the Making of American Cuisine.* New York: Columbia University Press, 2009.

Smith, Andrew F. *Popped Culture: A Social History of Popcorn in America.* Columbia, SC: University of South Carolina Press, 1999.

Smith, Andrew F. *Starving the South: How the North Won the Civil War.* New York: St. Martin's Press, 2011.

Smith, Andrew, and Bruce Kraig. *The Oxford Encyclopedia of Food and Drink in America, Volume 1.* New York: Oxford University Press, 2004, 683. *States of America* 106 (2009): 6561–66.

Smith, Bruce D. *Rivers of Change: Essays on Early Agriculture in Eastern North America, America.* Birmingham, AL: University of Alabama Press, 1991.

Smith, Bruce D., and Richard A. Yarnell. "Initial Formation of an Indigenous Crop Complex in Eastern North America at 3800 B.P." *Proceedings of the National Academy of Sciences of the United States of America.*

Smith, Huron. "Ethnobotany of the Forest Potawatomi Indians." *Bulletin of the Public Museum of the City of Milwaukee* 7 (1933): 104.

Snead, Thornton W., Charles F. Allison, and John C. Stetson. *Perspective for Decision Makers: A Study of the Emerging Retail Environment.* Chicago: Super Market Institute, 1963.

Spear, Allan H. *Black Chicago: The Making of a Negro Ghetto, 1820–1920.* Chicago: University of Chicago Press, 1967.

Stafford, C. Russell. "Archaic Period Logistical Foraging Strategies in West-Central Illinois." *Midcontinental Journal of Archaeology* 16 (1991): 212–46.

Star, Leanne. "The Story of Jewel: A Century of Fresh Ideas." *Chicago Tribune*, February 28, 1999.

State Council of Defense of Illinois. *What to Eat. How to Cook It. Official Recipe Book.* Educational Document 5, Chicago: State Council of Defense of Illinois, 1918.

States Federal Trade Commission Report of the Federal Trade Commission on Milk and Milk Products, 1914–1918. Washington, DC, June 6, 1921.

Steele-Wedeles Papers, Chicago History Museum.

Steinberg, Ellen F. S., and Eleanor H. Hanson. *Learning to Cook in 1898: A Chicago Culinary Memoir.* Detroit: Wayne State University Press, 2007.

Stop and Shop 100th Anniversary Scrapbook. Box Lot 1983.549. Chicago: Chicago History Museum.

Strong, William Duncan. *The Indian Tribes of the Chicago Region.* Chicago: Field Museum of Natural History, 1938.

Sula, Mike. "The First Family of Fried Chicken." *Chicago Reader*, April 14, 2006. www.chicagoreader.com/chicago/the-first-family-of-fried-chicken/Content?oid=921815. Accessed January 27, 2015.

Sula, Mike. "Omnivorous: On the Trail of the Delta Tamale." *Chicago Reader*, May 15, 2008. www.chicagoreader.com/chicago/on-the-trail-of-the-delta-tamale/Content?oid=1109785. Accessed January 27, 2015.

"Super-Markets." *Time*, May 24, 1937.

Swenson, John F. "Chicagoua/Chicago: The Origin, Meaning, and Etymology of a Place Name." *Illinois Historical Journal* 84 (1991): 235–48.

Swislow, William. "Neighborhood Flavor Spices Up Restaurants." *Chicago Tribune*, March 17, 1993. articles.chicagotribune.com/1993-03-17/news/9303180061_1_bridgeport-prime-rib-neighborhood. Accessed July 30, 2014.

Szathmáry, Louis. *From Chicago Kitchens: A Checklist of Selected Chicago Cookbooks Collected by Chef Louis Szathmary on Exhibition with Menus and Other Culinary Memorabilia, June 26–September 25, 1982.* Chicago: Chicago Public Library Cultural Center, Special Collections Division, 1982.

Szathmáry, Louis. *The Chef's New Secret Cookbook.* Chicago: Regnery, 1976.

Tanner, Helen Hornbeck. "Tribal Mixtures in Chicago Area Indian Villages." In *Indians of the Chicago Area*. Edited by Terry Strauss, 18–21. Chicago: NAES College Press, 1990.

Tanner, Helen H., and Miklos Pinther. *Atlas of Great Lakes Indian History*. Norman: Published for the Newberry Library by the University of Oklahoma Press, 1987.

The Taste of Chicago Cookbook. Chicago: City of Chicago, Mayor's Office of Special Events, 1990.

"Ten Big Packers Indicted in Chicago: Heads of Swift, Armour, and Morris Concerns Charged with Conspiracy and Monopoly," *New York Times* (1857–1922), September 13, 1910. query.nytimes.com/gst/abstract.html?res=9807E6DE1330E233A25750C1A96F9C946196 D6CF. Accessed September 1, 2013.

United States Bureau of Corporations. *Report of the Commissioner of Corporations on the Beef Industry*. March 3, 1905. play.google.com/books/reader?id=NLpJAAAAMAAJ&printsec= frontcover&output=reader&hl=en. Accessed December 15, 2014.

United States Department of Agriculture, Bureau of Agricultural Economics in Cooperation with the University of Illinois Department of Agricultural Economics. *Traffic Survey in the South Water Market, Chicago*. Washington, DC, 1940.

Valenze, Deborah M. *Milk: A Local and Global History*. New Haven: Yale University Press, 2011.

"Vast Bakery Dedicated by Kitchens of Sara Lee." *Chicago Tribune*, September 2, 1964. archives.chicagotribune.com/1964/09/02/page/43/article/vast-bakery-dedicated-by-kitch ens-of-sara-lee. Accessed December 1, 2014.

Vettel, Phil. "Le Francais Chef Set High Standard for Fine Dining in Chicago." *Chicago Tribune*. Nov. 25, 2013.

Vogel, Virgil. "The Tribes." In *Indians of the Chicago Area*. Edited by Terry Strauss. Chicago: NAES College Press, 1990.

Wade, Louise C. *Chicago's Pride: The Stockyards, Packingtown, and Environs in the Nineteenth Century*. Chicago, IL: University of Illinois Press, 1987.

Wade, Mary L. *The Book of Potato Cookery: More Than One Hundred Recipes Suitable for the Tables of Rich and Poor Alike, Showing How to Prepare Economical and Nutritious Dishes from the "Noble Tuber."* Chicago: A. C. McClurg, 1918.

Wade, Stuart C. *Rand, McNally & Co.'s Handbook of the World's Columbian Exposition*. Chicago: Rand, McNally & Company, 1893.

Ward, Edward G. *Bulletin: Milk Transportation: Freight Rates for the Largest Fifteen Cities in the United States*. Washington, DC: U.S. Department of Agriculture, Division of Statistics, 1890.

Warnes, Andrew. *Savage Barbecue: Race, Culture, and the Invention of America's First Food*. Athens, GA: University of Georgia Press, 2008.

Werner, Charles J. *A History and Description of the Manufacture and Mining of Salt in New York State*. Huntington, NY: Author, 1917. archive.org/details/historydescripti00wern. Accessed December 15, 2014.

Wilson, Mark R. "Corn Products Refining Company." *Encyclopedia of Chicago: Dictionary of Leading Chicago Businesses*, edited by Janet L. Reiff, Anne Durking Keating, and James R. Grossman. www.encyclopedia.chicagohistory.org/pages/2628.html. Accessed January 27, 2015.

Winder, Gordon. *The American Reaper: Harvesting Networks and Technology, 1830–1910*. Burlington, VT: Ashgate Publishing, 2013.

Winslow, Charles S. *Indians of the Chicago Region*. Chicago: Charles S. Winslow, 1946.

Women's Society of Bethany Union Church, comp. *The Bethany Union Cook Book*. Chicago: H. G. Adair Print Company, 1912.

York, Emily Bryson. "Former Dominick's CEO Opening More Grocery Stores Here." *Chicago Tribune*, February 11, 2013. articles.chicagotribune.com/2013-02-11/business/ct-biz-0211-executive-profile-mariano-20130211_1_bob-mariano-grocery-stores-roundy/2. Accessed July 30, 2014.

Yue, Lorene. "Go Gluten-Free? No, Eat More of It." *Crain's Chicago Business*, August 24, 2013. www.chicagobusiness.com/article/20130824/ISSUE01/308249977/go-gluten-free-no-eat-more-of-it. Accessed December 20, 2014.

Zeldes, Leah. *The Unique Chicago Tamale, a Tuneful Mystery.* Dining Chicago. www. diningchicago.com/blog/2009/12/18/the-unique-chicago-tamale-a-tuneful-mystery/. Accessed January 27, 2015.

Zglenicki, Leon T. *Poles of Chicago, 1837–1937: A History of One Century of Polish Contribution to the City of Chicago, Illinois.* Chicago: Polish Pageant, 1937.

Zurawski, Joseph W. *Polish Chicago: Our History, Our Recipes.* St. Louis, MO: G. Bradley Publishing, 2007.

INDEX